Studies in Regional and Local History

General Editor Jane Whittle

Previous titles in this series
Founding Editor Nigel Goose

Peasant Perspectives on the Medieval Landscape

A study of three communities

Susan Kilby

University of Hertfordshire Press
Studies in Regional and Local History

Volume 17

First published in Great Britain in 2020 by
University of Hertfordshire Press
College Lane
Hatfield
Hertfordshire
AL10 9AB
UK

British Library Cataloguing in Publication Data
A catalogue record for this book is available from the British Library

ISBN 978-1-912260-20-1 hardback
ISBN 978-1-912260-21-8 paperback

Design by Arthouse Publishing Solutions
Printed in Great Britain by Charlesworth Press, Wakefield

For Richard

Contents

Figures

Tables

Studies in Regional and Local History

General Editor's preface

Viewing medieval history from the perspective of the majority of the people who lived during the period, 'history from below' to use the term coined by the famous historian of the working class, E.P. Thompson, presents a challenge. Documents and lasting physical remains were very largely created by and for those in power (kings, lords and clergymen) and thus express their views, strategies and ideals. This is the challenge Susan Kilby takes up in *Peasant Perspectives on the Medieval Landscape*, and one that she tackles with extraordinary imagination and effectiveness. Her particular concern is how peasants viewed the world around them: the fields they ploughed, the paths they walked, and the villages they lived in. In reconstructing these attitudes she turns to a wide range of evidence, including material culture and the landscape itself. None of this evidence is straightforward, and its analysis draws on a wide range of disciplines that go well beyond previous work by social and economic historians on the English peasantry, borrowing approaches from anthropology, ethnography, archaeology, geography, and the study of naming practices (onomastics). It is also an approach that recognises the central importance of place, both to the medieval peasantry, but also to the historian of medieval England. As a consequence, this book provides a window into the mindset of medieval peasants, while at the same time offering a highly original approach to local history.

The study focuses on three communities: Elton, Castor and Lakenheath, located in the East Midlands and East Anglia, in the period between Domesday Book (1086) and the Black Death (1348). Previous studies of the peasantry in this period have concentrated on rights to land, inheritance practices and disputes among villagers. In contrast Kilby's study pays particular attention to names – of both people and places – and to the use of resources. For instance, she shows how the subtle differences between some free and unfree peasant surnames held greater meaning than previously thought. Some free peasants mimicked lords by adopting names taken from a wider area (the name of a vill or settlement), such as 'de Elton', while unfree peasants were more likely to be named after the location of their house, such as 'atte Bridge'. The location of houses within communities also demonstrates divisions between social groups. Lords sought to separate their residences from the rest of the community even in this period, long before the development of the country house. Within the village there is interesting evidence that suggests that free tenants separated themselves from unfree tenants. While lords asserted their ownership over peasant property, particularly that of unfree tenants, peasants fenced their houses and gardens, regarding the space inside as unequivocally theirs. Names of fields reveal knowledge of soil quality and embedded agricultural advice into village culture. Kilby argues that it was peasants, not lords or early writers of agricultural advice, who best understood the management of the land needed to make a living. Their constant interaction and careful knowledge of the land gave them a sense of ownership, expressed in the paths they created across the landscape, even in the face of lords' attempts to classify such free movement as trespass.

Attention to the wider landscape of these communities is a reminder that peasants did not live by arable agriculture alone. Other resources – woods, rivers, fens and rough pasture – were of crucial importance. At Lakenheath on the edge of the fens there were numerous 'hythes' or wharfs and extensive fisheries that were leased to peasant fishermen. On land, for many farmers their wealth lay in sheep flocks rather than ploughland. Castor contrasted with nearby communities due to its fragmented ownership structure, multiple manors and relatively plentiful woodland and heath. Even at Elton, which approximated a classic three-field medieval farming system most closely out of the three case studies, riverside location made meadowland particularly important. Nor was landscape simply an arena for production. Some names of fields and landscape features embedded myth and history in peasants' local knowledge. Castor is reputed to be the location of a convent, founded in the seventh century by Cyneburg, daughter of Penda of Mercia. Its early twelfth-century church was dedicated to her. More than this, however, a local story relates how Cyneburg was attacked while walking through Castor, and the name of a village path, Lady Conneyburrow's Way, retained this memory into the modern period. *Peasant Perspectives on the Medieval Landscape* provides not only evocative glimpses into the lived-world of medieval peasants but also a forceful reminder that the landscape itself is a historical document.

Jane Whittle
November 2019

Preface and acknowledgements

'Unremarkable places are made remarkable by the minds that map them.'
Benjamin Myers, *Under the Rock* (London, 2018)

This book had its genesis in a Masters dissertation and ensuing doctoral thesis, both undertaken at the Centre for English Local History at the University of Leicester, and both generously funded by the Economic and Social Research Council. What is presented here is a revised version of the key research themes explored during my time at Leicester. My research has benefited tremendously from the support and encouragement of a number of scholars, to each of whom I owe an enormous debt. At Leicester, I had the great good fortune to number amongst the last cohort taught by Professor Christopher Dyer. Chris has been unstinting in offering his support, guidance and expertise over the last few years as first the thesis, then the book took shape. I was also lucky enough to arrive at Leicester just as Richard Jones took up his post at the Centre. Encountering the medieval landscape through Richard's teaching and supervision opened up a multitude of possible approaches to my research questions, and this volume is in large part testament to his inspirational teaching, insightful observations and unfailing support as I ventured ever farther from more traditional ways of approaching the medieval rural landscape and its inhabitants. This book could not have been written without the support of either scholar, for which I will be eternally grateful.

This interdisciplinary work has been improved markedly due to the support of many scholars from outside my own academic discipline. Mark Gardiner examined my thesis and ever since then he has been immensely helpful and encouraging as this book developed, patiently reading draft chapters and always offering perceptive observations and suggestions. I have been fortunate indeed to receive support from several onomastic scholars, including David Parsons and Paul Cullen, both of whom responded to my queries about particular names within my dataset with patience and good grace. Special thanks must be extended to Peter McClure, Jayne Carroll and Keith Briggs each of whom has read and commented on one of the chapters devoted to names, and answered numerous questions with great forbearance; and to Philip Shaw, who uncomplainingly looked over all of the field-names with me. Over the last ten years, they have all helped to lead me through the minefield of Middle English, and have undoubtedly saved me from many an error. I am of course entirely responsible should any remaining errors have slipped through the net.

Many others have offered support, assistance and encouragement, and I would especially like to thank Joanna Story, Matt Tompkins, Stephen Mileson, Avril Lumley-Prior, Neil Christie, Colin Hyde, Andrew Hopper, Keith Snell, Ray Graves, Stephen Upex and Charles Phythian-Adams. Also, as the book developed, some of its key ideas and arguments were road-tested at various academic seminars, and my thanks are extended to all who attended and asked penetrating questions, which undoubtedly helped to improve aspects of the final book. I have also received a great deal of help from the many archives and other institutions that I have visited during the course of my research, in particular staff at both the Peterborough and the Cambridgeshire HER, the Manuscripts Reading Room at Cambridge University Library, the Society of Antiquaries, Huntingdonshire Archives, Suffolk Archives at Bury St Edmunds, and Northamptonshire Archives. Special thanks are offered to the Cadbury Research Library at the University of Birmingham and to Jean Birrell for providing access to Lakenheath material; Sir Philip Naylor-Leyland Bt. and the Milton (Peterborough) Estates Company who kindly allowed me to reproduce part of the Fitzwilliam Estate tithe map; to Colin Hyde for some of his fantastic images of the Castor capitals; and to Richard Jones for aerial photography and LiDAR wizardry, and for his patience as I learned to fly the ELH drone.

As might be expected for a book focused on the landscape, I spent a great deal of time wandering through the villages and fields of Elton, Castor and Lakenheath. Some ten years ago, Stephen Upex took me on a walk across Elton's surviving ridge and furrow, and he has continued to give generously of his time and support. Local farmer Robert Fray kindly allowed me access to two of Elton's former medieval fields – *molwellehil* and *boterflyemede* – following a chance meeting as I was out walking. Robert Rolph welcomed me to Lakenheath, sharing his local insight and loaning me some of his books. At Castor, special thanks are offered to William Burke, David Ridgeway and Brian Goode for variously guiding my perambulations around the village, providing a stepladder to photograph the beautiful stag hidden behind the organ, and sharing local maps and modern field-names with me.

The team at the University of Hertfordshire Press has been incredibly patient and supportive, and I would like to thank in particular Jane Housham and Sarah Elvins. My editor, Professor Jane Whittle deserves great credit for her perceptive comments on draft chapters, and for helping me to sharpen their focus. I am certain that this is a better book for all their editorial efforts. In addition to the financial support I received from the ESRC, the Aurelius Trust also generously funded the production of illustrative artwork and maps. Finally, I would like to acknowledge the unstinting support of my family, most especially from Richard.

As Benjamin Myers suggests, when we reconsider historical landscapes from the perspective of contemporary local residents, even seemingly ordinary places are often shown to be remarkable. The minds that mapped the medieval landscapes of Elton, Castor and Lakenheath reveal themselves in myriad ways within the sources that recorded aspects of the lives of each respective peasant population. This book attempts to find new ways to reconstruct and reinterpret these remarkable places.

Abbreviations

BARS	Bedfordshire Archives and Records Service
CMR I	W.H. Hart and P.A. Lyons (eds), *Cartularium Monasterii de Rameseia*, Vol. I (London, 1884)
CMR III	W.H. Hart and P.A. Lyons (eds), *Cartularium Monasterii de Rameseia*, Vol. III (London, 1893)
CN	C.N.L. Brooke and M.M. Postan (eds), *Carte Nativorum: a Peterborough Abbey cartulary of the fourteenth century* (Oxford, 1960)
CPR Ed III	*Calendar of the Patent Rolls, Edward III*
CRL	Cadbury Research Library, University of Birmingham
CRSBI	Corpus of Romanesque Sculpture of Britain and Ireland
DB	Domesday Book (Phillimore)
EDD	*English Dialect Dictionary*
EFB	T. Wing and J. Wing, *Elton field book or an accurate survey of the particulars of all the arable, ley and meadow-ground in the manor of Elton* (1747 and 1748)
EMR	S.C. Ratcliff (ed.) and D.M. Gregory (trans.), *Elton Manorial Records, 1279–1351* (Cambridge, 1946)
EPNE	A.H. Smith, *English place-name elements*, 2 vols (Cambridge, 1956)
ME	Middle English
MED	F. McSparran (ed.), *Middle English Dictionary* (University of Michigan, 2013), <https://quod.lib.umich.edu/m/med/>, accessed 13 August 2019
NRO	Northamptonshire Record Office
ODan	Old Danish
OE	Old English
OED	*Oxford English Dictionary*
ON	Old Norse
RH II	*Rotuli Hundredorum temp. Hen. III and Edw. I*, Vol. II (London, 1818)
Soc. Antiq.	The Society of Antiquaries
SRO(B)	Suffolk Record Office, Bury St Edmunds
TNA	The National Archives
WCL	Worcester Cathedral Library
WH	*Walter of Henley and Other Treatises on Estate Management and Accounting,* D. Oschinsky (ed., trans.) (Oxford, 1971)

Chapter 1

Introduction

In 1311, the clerk of the Lakenheath manorial court enrolled a charter detailing a lease between the prior of Ely and Richard, son of Richard in the Lane for all the demesne fisheries of Lakenheath for a ten-year period in return for annual rent of £13 10s. In the agreement, the prior retained his right to half the bitterns and all the pike of a certain size, as was his prerogative as lord of the manor. For his part, Lane acquired access to the appurtenant weirs and fens, alongside the rights to eighteen courses for fishing boats on the water of *wendilse*, and the custody of the lord's swans. During this period, Lakenheath fisheries were interchangeably described as fens, and almost fifty are detailed in the manorial records. The demesne fisheries would have comprised a small proportion of this number, but, nevertheless, the grant clearly gave Lane rights over a significant acreage of demesne resources.[1] Three years later, an inquisition *post mortem* valued Lakenheath's Clare fee fisheries at £1.[2] It is possible to draw from this that in 1311 Richard in the Lane had access to a greater and more valuable expanse of one of Lakenheath's key seigneurial assets than did Gilbert de Clare, earl of Gloucester and one of England's leading magnates. However, in stark contrast to de Clare, Richard in the Lane was a servile peasant, legally bound to the prior's manor of Lakenheath.

Within this one brief example it is possible to find – in concentrated form – all of the elements that form the principal lines of enquiry followed within this volume. Leasing demesne resources to peasants was not, of course, unprecedented, and in some respects this agreement is unremarkable. Given, however, that certain seigneurial assets, including fisheries, parks, gardens, dovecotes and warrens, were strongly associated with lordship – in actuality and within contemporary literature and illuminations – it reveals a dichotomy between the way lords perceived their rural resources and the practical realities of managing the rural environment, as outlined in chapter two.[3] Despite images showing peasants occupying their rightful place in lords' fields, as they do in the *Luttrell Psalter*, while absent from strictly seigneurial spaces, Richard in the Lane junior's lease of the Lakenheath fisheries dispenses with the myth perpetuated by elites that the local environment was characterised by clear divisions between lordly and peasant space. At the same time, Lane cannot be considered an archetypal peasant in this respect: not all Lakenheath peasants had authorised access

---

1   CUL EDC/7/16/2/1/4/3.

2   TNA C 134/42; the value had been decreasing since 1261: TNA C 132/27/5; TNA C 133/129/1.

3   Literary and artistic representations of the deliberate separation of lordly resources from the lower orders were not mere constructs of the seigneurial mind. In 1381 resources of this nature were specifically targeted by peasants because of their overt association with lords; R. Liddiard, *Castles in context: power, symbolism and landscape, 1066–1500* (Macclesfield, 2005), p. 118.

to demesne resources. Nevertheless, as chapter three shows, authorisation was not always sought by peasants traversing their local landscape. Considering the size and value of the fisheries he leased, Lane's status is noteworthy, complementing the analysis of rural social hierarchies that forms the focus of chapter four. The fishery named in the lease – *wendilse* – reminds us that the rural landscape of medieval England was a patchwork of named places, and that these names had been devised by those who knew it best – the resident peasants. The great importance of the named environment to peasant culture is considered in chapter five. As a servile individual, Lane would have been aware that the details relating to his lease would have been documented by the clerk of the manorial court, creating a permanent record of the transaction. Although they were increasingly drawn to written court records in the later medieval period as an aide-mémoire, the written word was generally untypical of the means through which peasants remembered important events, as outlined in chapter six. The Lakenheath fisheries were clearly an important aspect of Lane's economic wellbeing, and the peasant economy forms the focus for chapter seven. Finally, the lease provides an insight into the ways in which both landscape and resources were managed in the rural environment, and this forms the key consideration for chapter eight.

The study of the medieval rural environment and its inhabitants is at an exciting crossroads. In recent years, landscape archaeologists and historical geographers have begun to turn their attention away from a focus on the physical environment in which debates concerning form and function have dominated the scholarly discourse. Similarly, social and economic historians, formerly preoccupied with comparisons between medieval and modern productivity, have started thinking about rural England and its inhabitants from new perspectives. Today, a growing number of scholars from all these disciplines are concentrating on uncovering the experiences of those living in rural settlements, as Sally Smith outlines: 'focus[ing] on the *people* who occupied the landscape ... explor[ing] the complex webs of social relationships in which they operated, and ... try[ing] to ... enquire into the practices of living in the medieval settlement and the meanings thus invoked and revoked'.[4] Increasingly, scholars following this line of enquiry take an interdisciplinary approach to the challenge of revealing the lived experiences of late medieval rural dwellers. As Matthew Johnson has suggested, in order to approach the rural landscape in this way it is necessary to introduce a range of contextual information allowing us to respond to the complexities of elucidating the human experience of past societies.[5] This requires us not only to draw upon a vast array of sources, including documents, material culture, place-names and the landscape itself, but to explore the approaches adopted by a wide

---

4   S.V. Smith, 'Towards a social archaeology of the late medieval English peasantry: power and resistance at Wharram Percy', *Journal of Social Archaeology*, 9/3 (2009), p. 392. Our European colleagues, perhaps benefiting from more profitable source material, have been ahead of us in this endeavour. See, for example: E. Le Roy Ladurie, *Montaillou: Cathars and Catholics in a French village, 1294–1324*, trans. B. Bray (1978; London, 1990); J.-C. Schmitt, *The holy greyhound: Guinefort, healer of children since the thirteenth century*, trans. M. Thom (Cambridge, 1983).

5   M. Johnson, 'Phenomenological approaches in landscape archaeology', *Annual Review of Anthropology*, 41 (2012), p. 279.

variety of academic disciplines, including onomastics, anthropology, ethnography, landscape archaeology, history and historical geography. It was in this spirit that the Medieval Settlement Research Group recently convened a series of workshops resulting in the report 'Perceptions of Medieval Landscape and Settlement'.[6] Other academic networks subsequently established have followed broadly the same intellectual path; particularly noteworthy in this context was the 2009 collaboration between the universities of Leicester, Nottingham and Durham in assembling a group of interdisciplinary scholars to investigate the sense of place in Anglo-Saxon England.[7]

This open approach adopted by many scholars of the rural environment has been marked by a growing body of interdisciplinary work in which the emphasis has shifted away from a narrow focus on the physical environment to a more anthropic view that places human experience at the centre of the equation – in a sense, 'repopulating' the rural landscape. Archaeologists are now concerned to move beyond the materiality of rural settlements to consider the experiences of those residing there. This ranges from how the built environment and its environs were perceived by those encountering it to a more anthropological focus on the human experience of dwelling and working in rural settlements.[8] In many instances, this new focus extends beyond the residential core and out into the surrounding fields and the wider landscape.[9]

---

6   C. Dyer, 'Perceptions of medieval landscape and settlement', *Medieval Settlement Research Group Annual Report*, 22 (2007), pp. 6–31.

7   R. Jones and S. Semple (eds), *Sense of place in Anglo-Saxon England* (Donington, 2012).

8   For the former, see, for example, J. Campbell, 'A house is not just a home. Means of display in English medieval gentry buildings', in M.S. Kristiansen and K. Giles (eds), *Dwellings, identities and homes. European housing culture from the Viking Age to the Renaissance* (Hojbjerg, 2014), p. 183; O. Creighton and T. Barry, 'Seigneurial and elite sites in the medieval landscape', in N. Christie and P. Stamper (eds), *Medieval rural settlement. Britain and Ireland, AD 800–1600* (Oxford, 2012), p. 63; M. Gardiner and S. Kilby, 'Perceptions of medieval settlement', in C.M. Gerrard and A. Gutiérrez (eds), *The Oxford handbook of later medieval archaeology in Britain* (Oxford, 2018), p. 212; and for the latter, see K. Altenberg, *Experiencing landscapes: a study of space and identity in three marginal areas of medieval Britain and Scandinavia* (Stockholm, 2003), p. 154; K. Giles, 'Seeing and believing: visuality and space in pre-modern England', *World Archaeology*, 39/1 (2007), p. 108; S.V. Smith, 'Materializing resistant identities among the medieval peasantry: an examination of dress accessories from English rural settlement sites', *Journal of Material Culture*, 14/3 (2009), p. 327; M.H. Johnson, *English houses 1300–1800: vernacular architecture, social life* (Harlow, 2010), p. 73; K.A. Catlin, 'Re-examining medieval settlement in the Dartmoor landscape', *Medieval Settlement Research*, 31 (2016), pp. 36–7.

9   N. Whyte, *Inhabiting the landscape. Place, custom and memory, 1500–1800* (Oxford, 2009), p. 3; B. Morris, 'Old English place-names – new approaches', in R. Jones and S. Semple (eds), *Sense of place in Anglo-Saxon England* (Donington, 2011), pp. 47–60; R. Gilchrist, *Medieval life: archaeology and the life course* (Woodbridge, 2012); R. Jones, 'Responding to modern flooding: Old English place-names as a repository of traditional ecological knowledge', *Journal of Ecological Anthropology*, 18/1 (2016); L. ten Harkel, T. Franconi and C. Gosden, 'Fields, ritual and religion: holistic approaches to the rural landscape in the long-term perspective (*c.* 1500BC – AD1086)', *Oxford Journal of Archaeology*, 36/4 (2017), pp. 413–37.

Landscape archaeologists are not alone in this endeavour, and researchers from a range of disciplines have contributed to scholarship on this subject, with many taking an interdisciplinary approach. To date, various themes have been investigated, including the medieval economy,[10] ways of living in the rural environment,[11] ways of organising the landscape of the rural settlement,[12] ways of moving through the landscape,[13] and considerations of ritual and religion.[14]

This interdisciplinary study is situated within this emerging scholarly context and assesses a wide range of source material to consider peasant perspectives on the

---

10 R. Jones, 'Elemental theory in everyday practice: food disposal in the later medieval English countryside', in J. Klápště and P. Sommer (eds), *Food in the medieval rural environment: processing, storage, distribution of food*, Ruralia, 8 (2011), pp. 57–75; D. Banham and R. Faith, *Anglo-Saxon farms and farming* (Oxford, 2014); J. Myrdal and A. Sapoznik, 'Technology, labour, and productivity potential in peasant agriculture: England, c. 1000 to 1348', *Agricultural History Review*, 65/2 (2017), pp. 194–212.

11 S. Kilby, 'A different world? Reconstructing the peasant environment in medieval Elton', *Medieval Settlement Research*, 25 (2010b), pp. 72–7; C. Dyer, 'Living in peasant houses in late medieval England', *Vernacular Architecture*, 44 (2013), pp. 19–27; C. Dyer, 'The material world of English peasants, 1200–1540: archaeological perspectives on rural economy and welfare', *Agricultural History Review*, 62/1 (2014), pp. 1–22; S. Mileson, 'The South Oxfordshire project: perceptions of landscape, settlement and society, c.500–1650', *Landscape History*, 33/2 (2012), pp. 83–98; R. Jones *et al.*, 'Living with a trespasser: riparian names and medieval settlement on the River Trent floodplain', *European Journal of Post-Classical Archaeologies*, 7 (2017), pp. 33–64.

12 D. Hooke, *Anglo-Saxon landscapes of the West Midlands* (Oxford, 1981); N. Whyte, 'The after-life of barrows: prehistoric monuments in the Norfolk landscape', *Landscape History*, 25 (2003), pp. 5–16; B. McDonagh, '"Powerhouses" of the Wolds landscape: manor houses and churches in late medieval and early modern England', in M. Gardiner and S. Rippon (eds), *Medieval landscapes* (Macclesfield, 2007), pp. 185–200; M. Gardiner, 'Oral tradition, landscape and the social life of place-names', in R. Jones and S. Semple (eds), *Sense of place in Anglo-Saxon England* (Donington, 2011), pp. 16–30; A. Reynolds and S. Semple, 'Digging for names: archaeology and place-names in the Avebury region', in R. Jones and S. Semple (eds), *Sense of place in Anglo-Saxon England* (Donington, 2011), pp. 76–100; J. Bourne, *The place-name Kingston and royal power in middle Anglo-Saxon England: patterns, possibilities and purpose* (Oxford, 2017); S. Mileson, 'Openness and closure in the later medieval village', *Past and Present*, 234 (2017), pp. 3–37; J. Blair, *Building Anglo-Saxon England* (Princeton, NJ, 2018).

13 S.V. Smith, 'Houses and communities: archaeological evidence for variation in medieval peasant experience', in C. Dyer and R. Jones (eds), *Deserted villages revisited* (Hatfield, 2010), pp. 64–84; S. Kilby, 'Mapping peasant discontent: trespassing on manorial land in fourteenth-century Walsham-le-Willows', *Landscape History*, 36/2 (2015), pp. 69–88; J. Baker and S. Brookes, 'Gateways, gates and gatu: liminal spaces at the centre of things', in S. Semple *et al.* (eds), *Life on the edge: social, religious and political frontiers in early medieval Europe* (Wendeburg, 2017).

14 S. Semple, 'A fear of the past: the place of the prehistoric burial mound in the ideology of middle and later Anglo-Saxon England', *World Archaeology*, 30/1 (1998), pp. 109–26; S. Kilby, 'Fantastic beasts and where to find them: the Romanesque capitals of St Kyneburgha's church, Castor, and the local landscape', *Church Archaeology*, 19 (2019), pp. 53–72.

medieval landscape between *c*.1086 and *c*.1348. Through a detailed evaluation of three rural settlements – Elton in Huntingdonshire, Castor in Northamptonshire and Lakenheath in Suffolk – this study examines the myriad ways in which the lower orders of society regarded the familiar landscapes in which they lived and worked. Beginning with an assessment of seigneurial perspectives on the rural environment, chapter two takes us from the later Anglo-Saxon period into the fourteenth century, evaluating the evolution of elite aspects of settlement and landscape and the establishment and development of a lordly presence there. This not only helps to demonstrate the ways in which lords viewed rural settlement but also provides insights into how they thought about the resident community. Chapter three follows on from this to consider the organisation of the settlement, beginning with an assessment of the placement of each respective manorial *curia* and its proximity to peasant dwellings. Issues of privacy and ownership are considered, leading us to reflect on the regulation of movement through the settlement and its wider landscape through an analysis of how locals chose to navigate their way through their environment. Chapter four continues to explore socially constructed ideas of place through an examination of topographical bynames and family names – such as *atte grene* – that closely linked particular families with their local environment. In particular, it focuses on why these names were most commonly associated with servile individuals and seeks to explain this phenomenon through a more detailed analysis of Huntingdonshire.

Chapter five then turns more fully to the landscape surrounding the settlement, examining the naming practices adopted by medieval communities using microtoponyms – field-names and other minor landscape names. As these names are generally considered to have been coined by peasants, their importance as a key source cannot be underestimated. It is possible to detect differences in the naming strategies selected by different communities, and the conceivable reasons for this are explored in detail. While this chapter focuses largely on the apparent transparency of landscape names, chapter six offers a detailed case study of a small part of Castor's landscape, drawing on field-names, documents and material culture to emphasise the prominent role that the landscape played as a repository for local legend and folklore. Here, field-names with seemingly straightforward meanings are revealed as having had a potentially more important function in preserving local collective memory. Thus, this chapter offers a cautionary note that field-names are not always unambiguous, and that contextual analysis can reveal meaning that has long since been obscured.

Chapter seven turns toward what might be seen as a more traditional focus – especially for social and economic historians – on the agrarian economy. Its position in the volume does not reflect its lack of importance, but simply emphasises that it is one of a range of themes that have equal standing in a study of this nature. Following a brief overview of each respective demesne enterprise, the documentary records are scrutinised for insights into peasant economies. Various means through which the local environment afforded local peasants a livelihood are examined. Naturally, this leads us to consider arable operations, but, in the settlements under review, sheep farming and fishing were also important economically and are also assessed in detail. Finally, chapter eight contemplates the management of the landscape and examines three specific environments that are important in each case study location: arable, meadow and fenland, considering the strategies that peasants adopted to maximise the potential that these resources had to offer.

Overall, this is a book that aspires to demonstrate that the recovery of peasant perspectives on the environments in which they lived and worked is a realistic and attainable goal. Using largely overlooked evidence, such as field-names and family names, and considering familiar sources – like manorial documents – in new ways, this research reveals how far it is possible to uncover peasants' attitudes toward the English rural landscape. This approach – toward a peasant-centric historical enquiry into the rural environment – coupled with an integration between historical methodologies and those adopted within cognate disciplines, has allowed a greater focus on medieval peasant mentalities than has hitherto been attempted. Thus, the themes explored within this book are a first concerted effort to unveil something of the mentalities of a group of people who were fundamental to the economic success of later medieval England.

Geographic scope

At the heart of this volume is a comparative study of three rural medieval settlements: Elton in Huntingdonshire, Castor in Northamptonshire and Lakenheath in Suffolk (Figure 1.1).[15] These places were selected on a range of criteria: they feature varied geographic, economic and social contrasts, and they are each well documented for the period under review, *c.*1086–1348. Castor is additionally noteworthy because its church, constructed between the late eleventh and early twelfth centuries, features contemporary sculpture, and this has been included within the range of source material assessed. Both Elton and Castor are situated within what Brian Roberts and Stuart Wrathmell have characterised as the Central Province: an area of mostly nucleated settlement stretching from the north-east to the south-west of England across the Midland counties. Drawing on the same framework, Lakenheath sits in the South-eastern Province, which broadly represents a more complex region, demonstrating more diverse settlement patterns.[16] More specifically, Lakenheath straddles the boundaries of the sub-provinces of the Wash (west) and Wash (east), which at this point indicate the limits of fenland and breckland respectively (Figure 1.2).

---

15   Since 1974, Castor has been part of modern Cambridgeshire.
16   B.K. Roberts and S. Wrathmell, 'Dispersed settlement in England: a national view', in P. Everson and T. Williamson (eds), *The archaeology of landscape: studies presented to Christopher Taylor* (Manchester, 1998), p. 109.

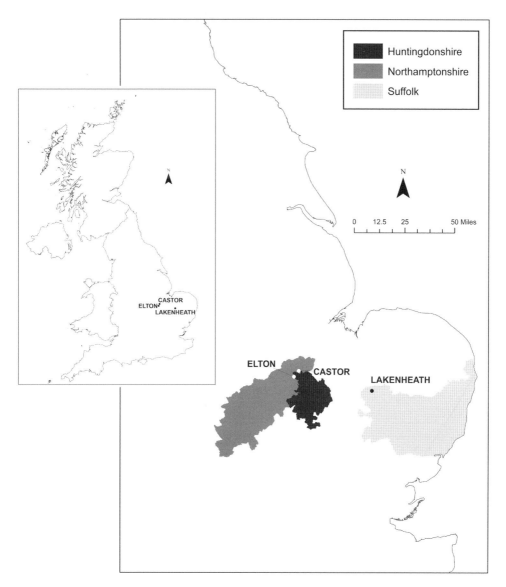

Figure 1.1. Elton, Castor and Lakenheath, based on the Historic Counties, *c*.1888. Source: Historic County Borders Project (2018) <http://www.county-borders.co.uk>

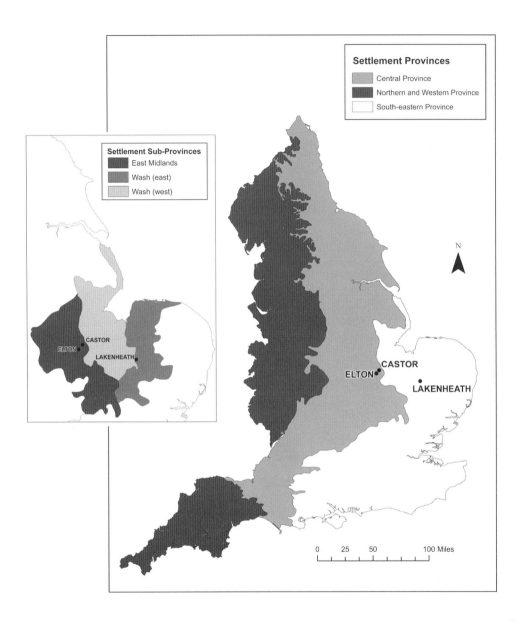

Figure 1.2. Elton (Huntingdonshire), Castor (Northamptonshire) and Lakenheath (Suffolk). Source: A. Lowerre, E. Lyons, B.K. Roberts and S. Wrathmell, *Atlas of rural settlement in England* (York, 2015) <https://doi.org/10.5284/1031493>

Elton, Huntingdonshire

Elton lies in the north-west corner of Huntingdonshire, with the river Nene forming both its westernmost boundary and also the county boundary with Northamptonshire (Figure 1.3). Archaeological surveys have demonstrated sites of occupation in Elton from at least the Roman period onward.[17] The earliest recorded spellings of the settlement name – Æþelingtun and Ælintun – dating from the later tenth century, suggest that it was either 'the prince's settlement' or 'the settlement of a person called Æthel'.[18] *Domesday Book* records three holdings in Elton – two Ramsey Abbey lands and a further one and a half hides belonging to Peterborough Abbey – and the territory recorded in 1086 seems to have extended to 1,872 acres.[19] An extent dated 1218 indicates that the Peterborough lands had been absorbed into the Ramsey holding by this time.[20] Drawn from the Peterborough holding, it is possible to trace the development of a small proto-manor, created between the later twelfth century and 1218, which was held by the de Aylington family.[21]

By this time, Elton was a polyfocal village and parish of 1,896 acres divided into two separate manors: the settlement associated with the main Ramsey manor was at Nether End, close to the river, and the de Aylington manor, alongside its tenant holdings, was situated at Over End.[22] Although there were ostensibly two manors only the documentary records for the Ramsey Abbey holdings survive and if the de Aylington family held a separate manorial court in this period there is now no record of it. In addition to holding a manorial court the abbot of Ramsey also held the franchise for the view of frankpledge in Elton, attended by tenants of both manors. The majority of Elton's resident peasants were servile, and the villein population living on the main manor owed relatively heavy labour services.

The Ramsey manorial records of the thirteenth and fourteenth centuries emphasise that the abbey's agrarian activities were focused on arable production. This was

---

17 S. Carlyle, *Archaeological recording and evaluation in the Old Estate Yard, Over End, Elton, Cambridgeshire* (Northampton, 2006), p. 2.

18 V. Watts (ed.), *The Cambridge dictionary of English place-names* (Cambridge, 2010), p. 215; the earliest spellings date from 972×92 (twelfth-century copy).

19 DB Huntingdonshire, 6,13; DB Northamptonshire, 6,9 and 9,3; this includes both the Ramsey and Peterborough holdings, and estimates the unreported 'ungelded' part of Ramsey Abbey's demesne as 192 acres.

20 *CMR I*, pp. 490–1; it seems likely that the Peterborough fee was considered to be a separate manor in 1086; however, the documentary records only indicate this fully from 1218: *CMR I*, p. 490; two earlier extents exclude this land, and so it seems that the Peterborough fee was transferred sometime between 1160 and 1218: *CMR III*, pp. 257–60; *CMR I*, p. 267. Two virgates of land granted *c.*1160 seem likely to have formed part of the transaction that began the process of creating this small manor: C. Jamison, 'Elton', in Page *et al.*, *VCH Huntingdonshire*, vol. 3 (London, 1932), p. 158.

21 By the early thirteenth century, the settlement name had become shortened to Aylington, and so this family name was effectively 'of Elton'. In 1310 John de Aylington was known as 'John le Lord de Aylyngtone': *CMR III*, pp. 7–8. Note that this small manor was held from Ramsey Abbey: *RH II*, p. 656; by 1451, it had become known as Hall Fee: Jamison, *VCH Huntingdonshire*, p. 158.

22 Over End is marked on the first edition OS map.

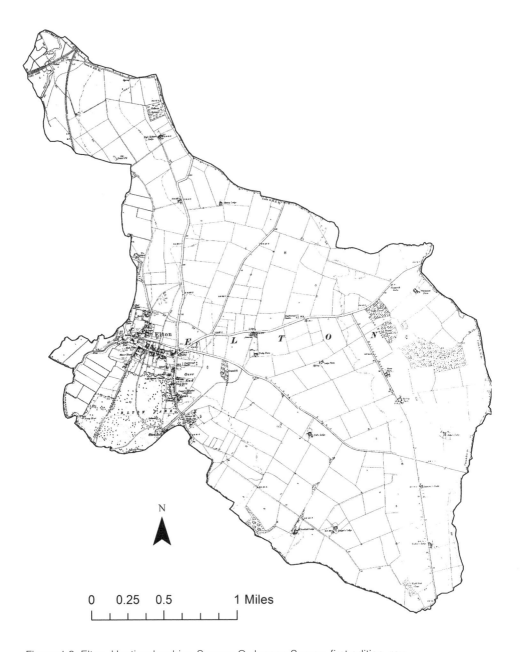

Figure 1.3. Elton, Huntingdonshire. Source: Ordnance Survey, first edition, rev.

typical of many villages in the Central Province and, at this time, Elton's landscape was probably organised in an open-field system consisting of three fields.[23] In 1279 the Ramsey Abbey demesne comprised three hides, a total of 432 acres.[24] The settlement's riverine location also provided plentiful valuable meadowland: in 1086, a total of 184 acres was recorded.[25] An earlier undated survey outlined an agreement between Ramsey Abbey and Thorney Abbey whereby the latter held twenty acres of Elton meadow in exchange for Elton peasants' right to access pasture for their livestock in Farcet Fen (Huntingdonshire), ten miles to the east.[26] The extant surveys make no mention of woodland, and the accounts reveal timber purchased from neighbouring vills.[27] The geology consists of an underlying bedrock largely comprising Jurassic limestone of the Cornbrash and Rutland Formations, alongside Jurassic mudstones of Oxford Clay and Whitby Mudstone Formations. Alluvial and terrace soils border the river, while the remainder of the parish consists of clay or lime-rich soils, of which some of the latter are shallow and largely used for sheep pasture in the modern period.[28]

Castor, Northamptonshire

Castor lies five miles due west of Peterborough in the modern county of Cambridgeshire (Figure 1.4). Between at least 1086 and 1888, however, its territory lay within Northamptonshire. At the time of *Domesday Book* it formed part of the Soke of Peterborough, and was situated within the double hundred of Upton, which later became Nassaburgh hundred.[29] Like Elton, it sits on the river Nene, which forms its southernmost boundary and also the county boundary between what was

---

23 Based on the fact that there were two medieval manors and six open fields by 1605, Stephen Upex suggests that there were six open fields in the later medieval period: S.G. Upex, 'The reconstruction of openfield layout from landscape evidence in Northamptonshire and Cambridgeshire', unpub. PhD thesis (University of Nottingham, 1984), p. 93. The documentary evidence does not bear this out, however, and, additionally, the de Aylington holding was too small to warrant a separate field system: S. Kilby, 'A different world? Reconstructing the peasant environment in medieval Elton', unpubl. MA dissertation (University of Leicester, 2010a), pp. 35–8.

24 *RH II*, p. 656; each hide consisted of six virgates, and each virgate twenty-four acres.

25 DB Huntingdonshire, 6,13; DB Northamptonshire, 6,9 and 9,3; 170 acres held by Ramsey Abbey, and fourteen acres by Peterborough Abbey. In 1218 and 1279, Ramsey held sixteen acres of meadow in demesne: *CMR I*, pp. 490–1; *RH II*, p. 656; note that later documents indicate that not all of Elton's meadow was riverine.

26 *CMR I*, p. 267.

27 See chapter seven, p. 145.

28 British Geological Survey; Cranfield Soil and Agrifood Institute.

29 Nassaburgh's territory differed slightly: J.H. Round, 'Introduction to the Northamptonshire Domesday', in W. Ryland *et al.* (eds), *VCH Northamptonshire*, vol. 1 (London, 1902), p. 296; R.M. Serjeantson and W.R.D. Adkins, 'Soke of Peterborough: Introduction' in R.M. Serjeantson and W.R.D Adkins (eds), *VCH Northamptonshire*, 2, p. 421; between 1888 and 1965 the Soke was separated from Northamptonshire, becoming part of Huntingdonshire. Since 1974 it has been part of Cambridgeshire.

Northamptonshire and Huntingdonshire.[30] The settlement at Castor has Roman origins, as revealed by its name, 'the Roman town', although by the tenth century it was known as *Cyneburge cæstre*, 'Cyneburg's fort', named for Cyneburg, the daughter of Penda of Mercia, who founded a monastery there in the seventh century (see chapter six).[31] Archaeological evidence suggests continued occupation from the fifth century onwards, and the selection of the site as an Anglo-Saxon monastic centre attests to its sustained importance.[32] In the later medieval period the parish of Castor included four hamlets: Ailsworth, Milton, Upton and Sutton.[33] At that time, Castor and Ailsworth formed one vill, with each township consisting of a number of discrete manors.[34]

Domesday Book records Peterborough Abbey as tenant-in-chief, directly holding three hides in Castor and six in Ailsworth. After 1066, in order to provide military support to the crown, the abbey created several knights' fees: three hides in Castor were held by five knights, and an additional three knights held another three hides in Ailsworth. Another two hides were recorded at Milton.[35] While little information survives concerning the original knights' fees, the 1105 *Descriptio Militum de Abbatia de Burgo* lists one Turold of Castor holding two hides, which Edmund King defines as two fees.[36] In *c.*1133 this was reduced to one and a half hides when the church and its advowson was conveyed to Peterborough Abbey by Turold's eldest son Richard, who was its priest and wished to become a monk at the abbey.[37] The remaining lands were retained by the priest's younger brother Geoffrey, who held the fee. The descent

---

30　Castor is downstream of Elton, and approximately eight miles north-east.

31　Watts, *Cambridge dictionary of English place-names*, p. 119; C. Mellows (ed., trans.) and W.T. Mellows (ed.), *The Peterborough chronicle of Hugh Candidus* (Peterborough, 1966), pp. 12 and 27; Castor sits on the opposite bank of the river Nene from the Roman town of *Durobrivae* in modern Chesterton. Two major Roman roads, Ermine Street and King Street, meet in Castor territory, close to the Nene.

32　S. Upex *et al.*, 'The *Praetorium* of Edmund Artis: a summary of excavations and surveys of the palatial Roman structure at Castor, Cambridgeshire 1828–2010', *Britannia*, 42 (2011), p. 25; Blair suggests that neighbouring Chesterton may have been a satellite settlement overlooking a site of administrative or defensive importance, in this case Castor: Blair, *Building Anglo-Saxon England*, p. 201.

33　R.M. Serjeantson and W.R.D. Adkins, 'Castor', in R.M. Serjeantson and W.R.D. Adkins (eds), *VCH Northamptonshire*, 2, p. 472; neither Upton nor Sutton featured in *Domesday Book*. Since they feature in a tenth-century charter they may have formed part of the Castor return. Avril Lumley-Prior suggests that the four townships formed one estate before the end of the ninth century, and were reunited a century later: A. Lumley-Prior, 'The importance of being Ailsworth: its place in the Castor multiple estate', *The Five Parishes Journal*, 2 (2014), p. 13.

34　The nineteenth-century Fitzwilliam estate map shows Castor as a loosely nucleated settlement (see Figure 3.5), which settlement type was noted by Williamson *et al.* in *Champion: the making and unmaking of the English midland landscape* (Liverpool, 2013), p. 77.

35　DB Northamptonshire, 6,4; 6a,1.

36　E. King, 'The Peterborough "*Descriptio Militum*" (Henry I)', *English Historical Review*, 84/330 (1969), p. 99.

37　E. King, *Peterborough Abbey 1086–1310, a study in the land market* (Cambridge, 1973), p. 25.

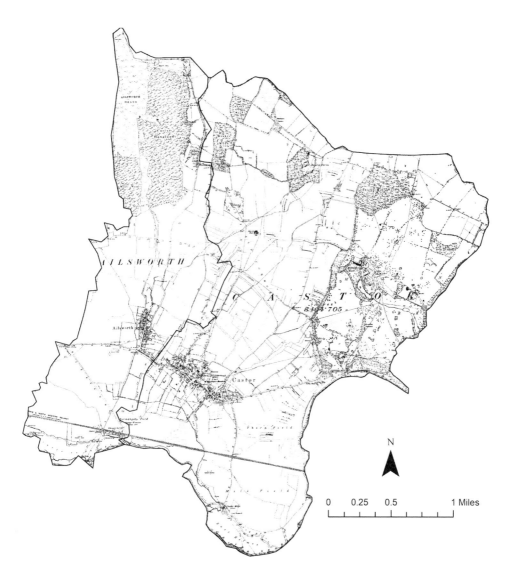

Figure 1.4. Castor, Northamptonshire. Source: Ordnance Survey, first edition, rev.

of the smaller fees is more difficult to determine, but it is possible to detect three small manors in Castor by the thirteenth century. In 1348 the Turold holding remained at one and a half fees.[38] Surveys and charters suggest that the remaining hide of land – consisting of two fees – was held by the Illings and the Cordels, each holding one fee.[39] Despite forming part of the estate of Peterborough Abbey, lordship appears to have been weaker in Castor than it was in Elton under Ramsey Abbey. A survey of 1321 lists just nine villeins and two free tenants, whereas it appears that the majority of the substantial remaining free population were tenants of one of the smaller manors.[40]

The parish contains 7,110 acres, which in the modern period included 750 acres of woodland.[41] By the early fourteenth century the Peterborough Abbey demesne consisted of 195 acres of arable land and thirteen and a half acres of meadow.[42] Although situated in what might appear to be 'classic' champion country – characterised by nucleated villages and regular open-field systems supporting predominantly arable agrarian regimes – Castor seems to have been something of an anomaly. There were five open fields in Castor and four in Ailsworth in the late medieval period.[43] The landscape was also fairly extensively wooded, with over 400 acres recorded in 1215 prior to the onset of extensive assarting, after which reasonably substantial woodland still remained; there was also a large area of heathland. Castor's geology is similar to that at Elton, with Jurassic limestone underlying the higher ground; and in the river valley, sandstone, siltstone and mudstone of the Grantham formations is overlain with river terrace deposits of sand and gravel.[44]

38 CUL PDC/MS 6, The Red Book of John of Achurch, f. ix; by this time, the family name was usually written as Thorold.

39 S. Kilby, 'The late medieval landscape of Castor and Ailsworth', *The Five Parishes Journal*, 2 (2014), pp. 23–4; the survival of a late thirteenth-century charter in which William Cordel lists a tenant's services leaves us in no doubt that he considered himself lord of a small manor in Castor: NRO F(M) Charter 207.

40 J. Sparke (ed.), *Historiæ Anglicanæ Scriptores Varii, e Codicibus Manuscriptis Nunc Prium Editi*, vol. 2 (London, 1723), pp. 175–7; the survey reveals that an additional seven and half virgates of bondland was held by freemen, 'because of the lack of cultivation of the bondmen', reinforcing the sense that the abbey's authority in Castor was relatively weak.

41 Serjeantson and Adkins, *VCH Northamptonshire*, 2, p. 472.

42 Sparke, *Historiæ Anglicanæ*, vol. 2, pp. 175–7.

43 The organisational picture is unclear: Peterborough Abbey documents occasionally refer to Ailsworth fields as part of Castor (e.g., C.N.L. Brooke and M.M. Postan (eds), *Carte Nativorum: a Peterborough Abbey cartulary of the fourteenth century* (Oxford, 1960), p. 210 [1340] lists holdings recorded as Castor, whilst detailing Ailsworth fields); a 1393 survey of Castor also lists Ailsworth fields, and places Wood Field 'between Ailsworth and Castor': BL Cotton MS Nero C. vii/14; Hall outlines five medieval fields in Castor and three in Ailsworth; however, there were four in the latter: Over Field, Doles Field, Nether Field and Wood Field: D. Hall, *The open fields of Northamptonshire* (Northampton, 1995), pp. 229–30.

44 British Geological Survey; Cranfield Soil and Agrifood Institute.

Lakenheath, Suffolk

Lakenheath is a large parish of some 11,000 acres in the north-west corner of Suffolk, close to the boundary between Cambridgeshire and Norfolk (Figure 1.5).[45] The river Little Ouse forms its northernmost boundary, beyond which lies the county of Norfolk. The parish is broadly split between the Fens to the west and the light lands of Breckland to the east. Human activity has been recorded in Lakenheath since the Palaeolithic period, with evidence for settlement continuing from the Iron Age into the Anglo-Saxon period.[46] The earliest extant mention of the settlement name dates from the early eleventh century, when it was recorded in a late Saxon charter as *Lacingahið*, 'the landing place of the people of the stream', or 'called after Laca', the name perhaps indicating the importance of water in the area.[47] This charter outlines a grant of five hides to Thorney Abbey; by 1086, when five carucates were recorded, Ely Abbey held four (including the township of Undley) and Richard de Clare held the remaining one.[48] Following the reorganisation of the abbey's estate in the late twelfth century the former abbatial manor became part of the much smaller Ely Priory estate; and, in 1331, Clare fee was granted to the priory by Elizabeth de Burgh.[49] Unusually, both lords were designated joint chief lords of the vill, with Ely Priory holding the advowson of the church and the Clares – by then earls of Gloucester – the franchise of the leet court and the right to hold a market.[50]

Somewhat unusually for Suffolk, the village, consisting of a long linear settlement close to the fen edge, was nucleated. Lakenheath's topography is diverse: to the west lies approximately 7,000 acres of fenland; 2,000 acres of heathland lie to the east; and the arable portion consisted of 1,500 acres, of which the priory's demesne was *c*.600 acres and the Clare demesne forty acres.[51] Although no survey survives for the conventual manor, the manorial documents for this period record thirty-one

45 M. Bailey, 'The prior and convent of Ely and their management of the manor of Lakenheath in the fourteenth century', in M.J. Franklin and C. Harper-Bill (eds), *Medieval ecclesiastical studies in honour of Dorothy M. Owen* (Woodbridge, 1995), p. 2.

46 M. Adams, *Land north of Broom Road, Lakenheath, Suffolk* (Stowmarket, 2014), pp. 9–14; a substantial Anglo-Saxon cemetery was located on the site of RAF Lakenheath: J. Caruth and S. Anderson, 'RAF Lakenheath Saxon cemetery', *Current Archaeology*, 163 (1999), p. 245.

47 Watts, *Cambridge dictionary of English place-names*, p. 356.

48 DB Suffolk, 21,6–7; 25,36; 28,2; Richard de Clare was more commonly known as Richard Fitz Gilbert. The survey also records the presence of six sokemen who belonged to Ely, alongside four bordars. Undley was assigned to the prior of Ely in the thirteenth century: S. Evans, *The medieval estate of the cathedral priory of Ely: a preliminary survey* (Ely, 1973), p. 10.

49 Bailey, 'The prior and convent of Ely', pp. 2–3; CUL EDC/1/A/1/4; Elizabeth de Burgh was the youngest daughter of Gilbert de Clare, earl of Gloucester.

50 M. Bailey, *A marginal economy? East Anglian Breckland in the later middle ages* (Cambridge, 1989), p. 74; *RH II*, p. 196; TNA C 133/129/1 and C 132/27/5; although court roll transcripts show that the prior's manor also held leet courts before the amalgamation of the two manors: CRL, MS 167.

51 Bailey, 'The prior and convent of Ely', pp. 2–3; TNA C 134/42.

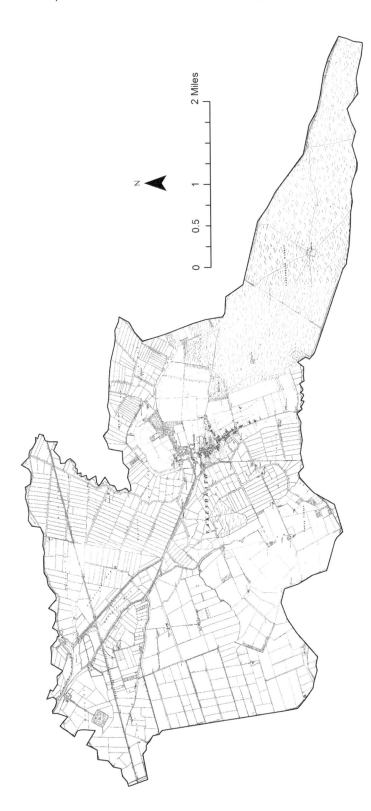

Figure 1.5. Lakenheath, Suffolk. Source: Ordnance Survey, first edition, rev.

villeins holding 465 acres.[52] An inquisition *post mortem* of 1262 indicates that there were 225 acres of villeinage on the Clare fee, although by 1307 this seems likely to have been reduced to 180 acres.[53] The remaining small quantity of arable land must have been divided between molmen, smallholders and free tenants.[54] The fenland supported a large quantity of fisheries, many of which were leased to peasants, as discussed at the beginning of this chapter. In addition, tenants had rights over certain fenland resources, including peat turves and sedge. The heathland provided extensive pasture, but from 1251 it was also licensed by the prior for the hunting of small game, and in 1300 a warren was established.[55] Because of its poor soils Lakenheath's medieval economy was dominated by sheep husbandry, and arable production focused on rye and barley. There were four great fields, which Mark Bailey suggests were probably organised in a shift system, wherein crop rotations were not constrained by fields or furlongs, but ranged more flexibly across the arable land.[56] Lakenheath's bedrock geology predominantly consists of chalk, overlain with sand to the east and peat to the west, with river terrace deposits along the fen edge and alluvium in parts of the fenland.[57]

As outlined above, these three settlements offer a range of contrasts. While Elton and Castor are both situated within the Central Province, amid its predominantly nucleated villages and arable farming, Castor is less typically 'champion' than might be expected, with its appurtenant woodland. Topographically, Lakenheath is again dissimilar, with a greater focus on pastoral husbandry and the exploitation of its fenland resources. Each settlement also has a slightly different social structure. Elton was principally populated by servile individuals, the majority of whom were villeins who

---

52 Bailey suggests that twelve rent-paying villeins also held fifteen acres each; however, intermittent references to molmen (rent-paying tenants of intermediate status) suggest that their holding size varied (for example, the twenty-acre molland tenement recorded in 1299 and 1311). A brief reference to services associated with molland includes the payment of two hens at Christmas, and an entry in the 1307–8 account roll suggests that thirty-two hens were received from rent. It is possible, therefore, that there were sixteen molland tenements, but it is far from certain that all molland rents were uniform: Bailey, 'The prior and convent of Ely', p. 3; TNA CP 25/1/216/44; CUL EDC/7/16/2/1/7; CUL EDC/7/16/1/6. There were, however, twelve villeins on the Clare fee (see footnote below).

53 TNA C 132/27/5; two Clare fee accounts confirm that customary virgates there were fifteen acres: CUL EDC/7/16/1/10–11. Later documents state that there were twelve villeins on the Clare manor, and it is uncertain how the reduced acreage of forty-five acres was reallocated: TNA C 133/129/1; CUL EDC/7/16/1/10–11.

54 Molmen were tenants that paid a cash rent, their customary labour services having been commuted in an earlier period. The conventual account rolls record rents of assize as aggregate sums, with no indication of how much was paid by each sub-group of tenants. The court rolls reveal a number of cottage holders living in Lakenheath and Undley.

55 Bailey, *Marginal economy?*, p. 132; CUL EDC/7/16/1/2.

56 These were North Field, South Field, Middle Field and Windmill Field: CUL EDC/7/16/2/1/6–7; M. Bailey, 'The form, function and evolution of irregular field systems in Suffolk, *c.*1300 to *c.*1550', *Agricultural History Review*, 57/1 (2007), p. 20.

57 British Geological Survey; Cranfield Soil and Agrifood Institute.

owed fairly onerous labour services as part of their rents. Lakenheath was also mainly inhabited by unfree peasants, although the presence of two manors almost certainly meant that the experience of villeins on each manor differed. The records relating to Clare fee do not reveal the extent of peasants' labour services there, but, with a demesne of just forty acres, they were unlikely to have been particularly burdensome. Conversely, the villeins on the conventual manor were obliged to provide extensive labour services, as the works schedules within the surviving account rolls document. Several disagreements recorded in the court rolls there also indicate that the molmen's more intermediate status was not always understood by manorial officials. At Castor, however, the majority of its resident peasants were personally free and lived on one of the smaller fees, whose tenants made up the larger part of the settlement's population, offering an important point of distinction from Elton and Lakenheath – not least because, in studies of English peasant communities, so little is usually known about free tenants.

Sources

The three settlements for this study all have, in addition to the characteristics outlined above, excellent extant documentary material for the period under review. Naturally, there is a wide disparity in survival across the three vills. Whereas there are relatively abundant court and account rolls for both Lakenheath manors and Elton in the period under review, just three account rolls survive for the ecclesiastical manor at Castor.[58] Conversely, there are several manorial surveys for the main manors at Castor and Elton, but none for Lakenheath. Of the peasant records, a large quantity of late medieval charters survives for Castor. Unlike the manorial documents, these charters were largely produced for peasants associated with the small secular manors. In comparison, there are just sixty for Elton – ordinarily, a large collection – and just a handful within monastic cartularies for Lakenheath. The key sources are listed in Table 1.1. Added to this are a number of crown records of varying quality. *Domesday Book* provides the first comprehensive outline of each settlement within our period. The hundred rolls survey of 1279 is exceptionally detailed for Elton, yet provides little additional detail for either Castor or Lakenheath. Inquisitions *post mortem* offer a snapshot into Lakenheath's Clare fee, but none survive for Castor's secular manors. A number of later documents pertaining to the landscape were also used – chiefly maps, field books and later surveys. In addition, where possible, material culture has been introduced either to support a specific argument or as a central form of evidence, as is the case with the twelfth-century church capitals at Castor. Specific peculiarities and cautionary notes pertaining to each source type are considered as required within the text.

The central aim of this book is to establish what it might be possible to determine about peasants' varied relationships with their local environment using the sources that remain to us. As this means drawing upon a wide range of material and interpreting it using methodologies from varied academic disciplines, the results presented focus on a number of inter-related themes, rather than taking the more

---

58   There are a handful of Castor court rolls that post-date this enquiry.

Table 1.1
Principal documentary sources.

Source	Start date	End date	No. of documents	Repository	Notes
Elton					
Account rolls	1286	1346	8	TNA	Non-consecutive dates; translated within *EMR*
Leet court rolls	1279	1342	17	TNA	As above
Charters	13th c.	14th c.	60	TNA	
Castor					
Account rolls	1300	1310	3	NRO	Non-consecutive dates
Charters	13th c.	1348	397	NRO	637 charters in total; final charter dated 1596
Charters	*c.*1272	*c.*1308	27	CUL	Translated in *CN*
Survey	1215	1215	1	CUL	Disafforestation of the Soke of Peterborough, transcribed in King, *Peterborough Abbey*
Survey	1393	1393	1	BL	Field survey of Castor and Ailsworth
Lakenheath					
Account rolls	1283	1348	25	CUL	Non-consecutive dates
Court rolls	1307	1342	433	TNA and CUL	Court rolls include manorial and leet courts; both Lakenheath manors featured. Translated within CRL, MS 167

traditional form of a progressive argument. Care has been taken to concentrate on what the source material selected for this study can reveal, but this necessarily means that some themes – such as religion – remain unexplored. Some material, such as field-names, for example, has to a certain extent been given priority: this is deliberate, as names are one of the very few sources for which a peasant provenance is generally undisputed. If we are to reflect upon the rural environment from the perspective of the later medieval lower orders, then it is vital that – as far as it is possible to do so – we take their worldview into account when we reconsider the sources that reveal something of their lives in rural England. I hope to show that this approach shines a new light on the study of medieval peasant mentalities. Despite the efforts of late medieval elites, peasant experience cannot be diluted to produce a grand narrative that reveals one collective attitude toward the local landscape, even though modern historians frequently treat the peasantry as an aggregated whole. The records of the rural environment reveal – however imperfectly – the multi-faceted relationships between late medieval peasants and the local environments they inhabited and knew intimately.

Chapter 2

Understanding the
seigneurial landscape

Before we attempt to uncover and understand the peasant view of the rural environment, we must first consider the seigneurial perspective. In this endeavour archaeologists have led the way, undertaking work that has helped to establish the evolution of settlement morphology and – most usefully for our purposes – the placement of the lord's hall and the buildings associated with it that later became known collectively as the manorial *curia*. This chapter begins with an overview of these developments, focusing on changes to both the siting and the outward appearance of the elite dwelling house and manorial *curia* across the medieval period. As a more sharply distinguished social hierarchy began to develop from the late Anglo-Saxon period onward, elites adopted various strategies to differentiate and distance themselves from the lower orders, and these are examined in detail. Using documentary sources, lords' relationship with the rural environment is considered, with a particular focus on those at the lower end of the seigneurial scale. Here, in order to help establish how lords perceived the rural environment more generally, it is necessary to look beyond the three vills that form the focus for this book to settlements with surviving evidence that helps to shed further light on seigneurial attitudes. How did lords view the boundaries – real or metaphorical – between elite and peasant space in the rural settlement and its surrounding landscape? Did lords at different levels of the social scale share a common view? And were there differences in the ways in which resident and absent or ecclesiastical and secular lords viewed their place within the rural manor?

From inclusive to exclusive? Seigneurial perceptions of rural settlement in the later Anglo-Saxon period

Middle Saxon settlement seems to have been relatively inclusive and communal. The available evidence suggests that, although the Romano-British and early Anglo-Saxon periods were characterised by dispersed farmsteads, such as that at Mucking (Essex), many middle Saxon communities lived as a collective unit within settlements in which there was no obvious social differentiation.[1] Archaeological surveys of middle Saxon settlement sites encompassing a number of geographically diverse English regions

---

1   M. Farley, 'Middle Saxon occupation at Chicheley, Buckinghamshire', *Records of Buckinghamshire*, 22 (1980), p. 95; H. Hamerow, *Excavations at Mucking, volume 2: the Anglo-Saxon settlement* (London, 1996), pp. 86–9; H. Hamerow, *Early medieval settlements: the archaeology of rural communities in northwest Europe, 400–900* (Oxford, 2002), pp. 91–2.

strongly suggest that, in many places, there was a tradition of community living. At the settlement at Catholme (Staffordshire) there was no dominant building and archaeologists concluded that there were no indications of a hierarchical community.[2] From a socio-cultural perspective, Naomi Sykes argues that the archaeological record emphasises that communal living in this period extended to the sharing of hunting spoils across all social orders.[3]

It is generally accepted by historians and archaeologists that the breakdown of Anglo-Saxon multiple estates into smaller units of territory – often held by men occupying the lower rungs of lordship – took place between the ninth and eleventh centuries and marked the onset of manorialisation, which provided the blueprint for the medieval socio-economic structure beyond the Norman Conquest and into the later Middle Ages. Archaeologists argue that this significant change resulted in the creation of 'a newly emergent social class', suggested by John Blair as sharing similar characteristics to those who would be described as gentry in the later Middle Ages.[4] As these smaller estates became established, many of the associated settlement names were changed to reflect the new regime. Elements of the former place-names were compounded with the personal names of the new lords, and this was instrumental in associating newer landowners more readily with their estates (see chapter five, p. 107).[5] For example, Evesham (Worcestershire) 'Ēof's land hemmed in by water', associated with a person called Ēof, was a replacement for two earlier names: *etham* 'at ham'; and *cronochomme*, 'crane ham'.[6] Lords holding these new territories exhibited clear ideas regarding seigneurial space, which included presenting an assertive seigneurial presence. It is generally accepted that most settlement names were usually bestowed by outsiders; nevertheless, the seigneurial place-names dating from this period must have acted to reinforce both a consciousness of ownership and a clear sense of hierarchy within the rural landscape.[7] In light of this, we should perhaps be unsurprised that, as both Mark Gardiner and John Blair assert, clearly aristocratic spaces within English villages emerge by the tenth and eleventh centuries, and that

---

2 M. Gardiner, 'Manorial farmsteads and the expression of lordship before and after the Norman Conquest', in D.M. Hadley and C. Dyer (eds), *The archaeology of the 11th century: continuities and transformations* (London, 2017), pp. 89–90.

3 N. Sykes, 'Deer, land, knives and halls: social change in early medieval England', *The Antiquaries Journal*, 90 (2010), p. 180.

4 J. Blair, *Anglo-Saxon Oxfordshire* (Stroud, 1994), pp. 133–4; C. Dyer, *Making a living in the middle ages: the people of Britain 850–1520* (London, 2003), pp. 29–30; R. Jones and M. Page, *Medieval villages in an English landscape: beginnings and ends* (Macclesfield, 2006), pp. 70–2.

5 M. Gelling, *Signposts to the past: place-names and the history of England* (London, 1978), pp. 183–4; D. Hall, 'The late Anglo-Saxon countryside: villages and their fields', in D. Hooke (ed.), *Anglo-Saxon settlements* (Oxford, 1988), p. 121, dates this phenomenon from the seventh to the tenth centuries; Blair, *Anglo-Saxon Oxfordshire*, p. 133.

6 D. Hooke, *The landscape of Anglo-Saxon England* (London, 1998), p. 13; Watts, *Cambridge dictionary of English place-names*, p. 220; Evesham was also once recorded as 'æt Ecguines hamme'.

7 R. Coates, 'Place-names and linguistics', in J. Carroll and D.N. Parsons (eds), *Perceptions of place: twenty-first century interpretations of English place-name studies* (Nottingham, 2013), pp. 145–6.

the buildings associated with these spaces were expressly designed to promote the wealth and status of the lords associated with them.[8]

Coincident with this significant change, in the tenth century there was a transformation in the planning and positioning of buildings associated with this nascent seigneurial class that simultaneously detached the elite from the rest of the community. In a departure from the more communal arrangements of the earlier period, in which it appeared that no one structure dominated the settlement, lords designed their hall and associated chamber in a long range, presenting an 'extended façade' devised to stimulate admiration in visitors. These manorial buildings were frequently enclosed within ditches and banks, effectively separating them from the remaining dwellings in the settlement, although Gardiner notes that, in this period, siting was less important than promoting a visual expression of lordship.[9] Nevertheless, in this century the East Anglian ealdorman Æthelwine's manor house at Shillington (Bedfordshire) was constructed 'on the highest site ... in a clearing in the wood ... [and] the village ... and fields could be seen from the gate'. Wareham argues that Æthelwine had no grand lordly residences, but from this description it is clear that the manorial dwelling had been constructed in a setting that not only separated the seigneurial area but elevated it above the rest of the settlement.[10]

From the eleventh century these seigneurial sites underwent further change, with buildings being arranged in a courtyard style. At the beginning of this phase the main lordly dwelling was situated towards the rear of the courtyard, moving towards the front of this configuration from the late eleventh century.[11] In a period in which it could be difficult to distinguish a minor lord from a wealthy peasant, overt displays of lordship – expressed through not only the style of seigneurial buildings but also their distinct separation from the dwellings of the lower orders – were important. The implicit suggestion is that late Anglo-Saxon elites were becoming more aware of a link between status and landscape and, in particular, of the need to differentiate themselves from those lower down the social scale.[12]

---

8   Gardiner, 'Manorial farmsteads', pp. 88–97; Blair, *Anglo-Saxon Oxfordshire*, pp. 133–6; Blair, *Building Anglo-Saxon England*, pp. 282 and 388.

9   Gardiner, 'Manorial farmsteads', pp. 90–1; R. Faith, 'Tidenham, Gloucestershire, and the history of the manor in England', *Landscape History*, 16 (1994), p. 43; M. Gardiner, 'The origins and persistence of manor houses in England', in M. Gardiner and S. Rippon (eds), *Medieval landscapes* (Macclesfield, 2007), p. 180.

10 A.F. Wareham, *Lords and communities in early medieval East Anglia* (Woodbridge, 2005), p. 26.

11 Gardiner, 'Manorial farmsteads', pp. 90–7; Gardiner, 'Origins and persistence of manor houses', p. 172.

12 C. Senecal, 'Keeping up with the Godwinesons: in pursuit of aristocratic status in late Anglo-Saxon England', in J. Gillingham (ed.), *Anglo-Norman studies 23, proceedings of the Battle conference, 2000* (Woodbridge, 2001), p. 261; Sykes, 'Deer, land, knives and halls', p. 175; Gardiner, 'Manorial farmsteads', p. 99; Blair, *Building Anglo-Saxon England*, pp. 356 and 401.

Conspicuous display and veiled privacy: from the Norman Conquest to the Black Death

The period leading up to and beyond the Norman Conquest witnessed a number of changes in the spatial arrangements of manor houses and manorial *curia*. These changes were at one time interpreted by landscape archaeologists and historians as a linear progression of the placement of lordly buildings from an integrated position within the village via a location on the periphery to a final position that was entirely isolated from their associated communities in the early modern period.[13] While this was broadly the case, current scholarship now demonstrates that the reality was much more nuanced, and scholars have sought to understand these changes in more detail. From the end of the eleventh century Gardiner notes a more 'assertive presentation of lordship' in which the site of the hall moved to the front of the courtyard and elaborate gatehouses were constructed.[14] Clearly, in this period it was important to lords that they were actively seen by the wider community and their peers as being in possession of the accoutrements of lordship, and this extended to the range of buildings associated with the manorial complex. Where possible, lords also sought to ensure that both style and setting were impressive and befitting of their social rank. For arrivistes this was perhaps especially important, as demonstrated by Laurence de Ludlow's thirteenth-century fortified manor house at Stokesay (Shropshire), where the external appearance of the building was clearly given great consideration.[15] Appearances were undoubtedly a vital part of the public face that lords presented to the outside world and, even when finances were squeezed, some families considered it essential to maintain outward show – the Mohuns of Dunster in Somerset, for example, kept a poem (preserved in their cartulary) reminding them that this was imperative, even when times were hard.[16]

As part of the process of distinguishing themselves from those lower down the social scale, in some instances there were moves in the twelfth century to separate the manorial site from the rest of the settlement. Moreover, while there was a continuation of the reorganisation of seigneurial spaces witnessed in the eleventh century, lords were also beginning to look beyond the boundary of the manorial *curia* to consider the wider landscape of the village. In this period two dominant morphological forms are apparent in settlements, especially within the Central Province. There was often a spatial connection between manorial sites and churches; in some instances the

13   T. Williamson and L. Bellamy, *Property and landscape: a social history of land ownership and the English countryside* (London, 1987), pp. 60–71.

14   Gardiner, 'Manorial farmsteads', p. 97; O. Creighton and S. Rippon, 'Conquest, colonisation and the countryside: archaeology and the mid-11th- to mid-12th-century rural landscape', in D.M. Hadley and C. Dyer (eds), *The archaeology of the 11th century: continuities and transformations* (London, 2017), p. 69; Gardiner and Kilby, 'Perceptions of medieval settlement', p. 212; Blair, *Building Anglo-Saxon England*, p. 388.

15   Liddiard, *Castles in context*, p. 46.

16   C. Dyer, 'The ineffectiveness of lordship in England, 1200–1400', in C. Dyer *et al.* (eds), *Rodney Hilton's middle ages: an exploration of historical themes* (Past and Present Supplement, 2) (Oxford, 2007), p. 73.

former lay on the periphery of settlements, either in conjunction with the church or at a distance from it.[17] In a wide-ranging survey Jill Campbell notes a shift from the twelfth century whereby manorial sites became much more likely to be built more than half a kilometre from the main settlement, and she attributes this change to lords' greater need for privacy.[18] In the Yorkshire Wolds peripheral sites were numerous, and Briony McDonagh suggests that these also largely dated from the twelfth century.[19] Like Richard Jones and Mark Page, McDonagh argues that lords' decision-making regarding the positioning of their manor sites was largely focused on ensuring separation between the elite complex and the homesteads of the lower orders.[20]

In some places this meant that the peasants' dwellings formerly clustered around the demesne or the manorial *curia* were moved away, rather than the manorial complex resited.[21] In the mid-thirteenth century at Wick Hamon (Northamptonshire) peasant tofts were moved and replaced by a new capital messuage, and *c.*1300 in Northolt (Middlesex) peasant houses were moved a quarter of a mile in order to clear space for a moated manor house.[22] Historians are generally in agreement that at the end of the twelfth century another great reorganisation of the peasantry took place, following which peasant freedom or servitude was more firmly set in place, and peasant holdings became (initially, at least) uniform blocks of land held for rents

---

17　In parts of eleventh-century Lincolnshire, David Stocker and Paul Everson also note spatial connections between churches and topography (such as springs and rivers); and also with large village greens. In more than half of their sample, the churches were subsequently associated with manorial *curia* following settlement reconfiguration: D. Stocker and P. Everson, *Summoning St Michael. Early Romanesque towers in Lincolnshire* (Oxford, 2006), pp. 61 and 65.

18　J. Campbell, 'Understanding the relationship between manor house and settlement in medieval England', in J. Klápště (ed.), *Hierarchies in rural settlements*, Ruralia, 9 (Turnhout, 2013), pp. 279–80; Roberts suggests that lords' increasing wealth lies behind their motivation to move their manor houses: B.K. Roberts, *The making of the English village* (Harlow, 1987), p. 152.

19　McDonagh, '"Powerhouses" of the Wolds', pp. 190–7; in twelfth-century Goltho (Lincolnshire), while the manorial site did not move, it was elevated and separated from the adjacent peasant community, and its entrance faced away from the settlement: Creighton and Rippon, 'Conquest, colonisation and the countryside', p. 69.

20　Jones and Page, *Medieval villages*, p. 198; McDonagh, '"Powerhouses" of the Wolds', p. 198; this is also noted at Weoley (Worcestershire) by Dyer: C. Dyer, 'Households great and small. Aristocratic styles of life across the social spectrum in England, 1200–1500', in C.M. Woolgar (ed.), *The elite household in England, 1100–1550* (Donington, 2018), p. 7; although assessing Cambridgeshire examples of relocated villages separated from non-residential manorial *curia*, Taylor argues that the detachment should be attributed to agricultural changes designed to improve demesne farming: C. Taylor, 'Landscape history, observation and explanation: the missing houses in Cambridgeshire villages', *Proceedings of the Cambridge Antiquarian Society*, 95 (2006), p. 131.

21　R. Faith, *The English peasantry and the growth of lordship* (London, 1997), p. 201; see also Smith, 'Towards a social archaeology', p. 401.

22　Jones and Page, *Medieval villages*, p. 183; J.G. Hurst, 'Rural building in England and Wales', in H.E. Hallam (ed.), *The agrarian history of England and Wales, vol. 2, 1042–1350* (Cambridge, 1988), p. 904.

and customary services.[23] This does not necessarily seem to have strengthened lords' motivation to distance themselves further from peasant dwellings, as this process had already been underway for some decades. However, it may well have encouraged those further down the social order to differentiate themselves – in particular, free peasants from their servile neighbours[24] – and this would naturally have had an impact on the aspirations of lords at the lower end of the seigneurial hierarchy. In vills in which there was a spatial correlation between the church and the manorial complex it has generally been considered that the physical proximity of the two sites demonstrated seigneurial patronage and ownership. Oliver Creighton suggests that a corollary of this is that, in order to access the church, the peasant community was then compelled to enter this more overtly seigneurial space – one of the more public aspects of the lordly sphere. In contrast, Jones and Page continue to favour the idea that lords deliberately wished to segregate themselves from the lower orders, suggesting that in some instances the church could be used by resident lords to screen the manor house from the rest of the settlement.[25]

These arguments sound mutually exclusive, but that need not necessarily be the case. Hitherto, scholars have tended either to posit the idea that, on the one hand, lords sought to manipulate seigneurial space in order to assert their status, or, on the other, they attempted to distance themselves physically from the residential areas associated with their peasants. These ought to be seen, perhaps, not as competing theories but rather as distinct elements forming part of a panorama of seigneurial perspectives on their place – both physically and mentally – within the rural medieval settlement. These differing perspectives, both equally valid in a range of cases, emphasise the tension between the need for both privacy and openness, and between the need to disassociate themselves from the ordinariness of the main settlement and its occupants while simultaneously demonstrating their status to those people. In this respect, achieving a balance would have been far more difficult for lords at the lower end of the seigneurial spectrum.

Contemporary illuminations where peasants are depicted within the manorial environment, of which the early fourteenth-century *Luttrell Psalter* is typical, seem to emphasise the segregation of medieval society's orders (Figure 2.1). While the peasants are depicted labouring in the appropriate setting of the manorial fields, it is difficult to imagine that Geoffrey Luttrell's water-mill would have been entirely devoid of peasants. Nevertheless, there is a subtle message being relayed here: that there were certain manorial spaces considered by the nobility to be suitable only for peasants, while their own domains were private. Within the *Luttrell Psalter*, these aristocratic spaces also included the garden and the warren. In reality, peasants would have

---

23 Faith, *The English peasantry*, pp. 201 and 218–19; C. Dyer, *Standards of living in the middle ages: social change in England c.1200–1520* (1989, Cambridge, 1998), p. 137; S.H. Rigby, *English society in the later middle ages: class, status and gender* (Basingstoke, 1995), pp. 28–9; P.R. Schofield, *Peasant and community in medieval England 1200–1500* (Basingstoke, 2003), p. 36.

24 Mileson, 'Openness and closure', p. 17.

25 McDonagh, '"Powerhouses" of the Wolds', pp. 193–4; O.H. Creighton, *Designs upon the land: elite landscapes of the middle ages* (Woodbridge, 2013), p. 56; Jones and Page, *Medieval villages*, p. 198.

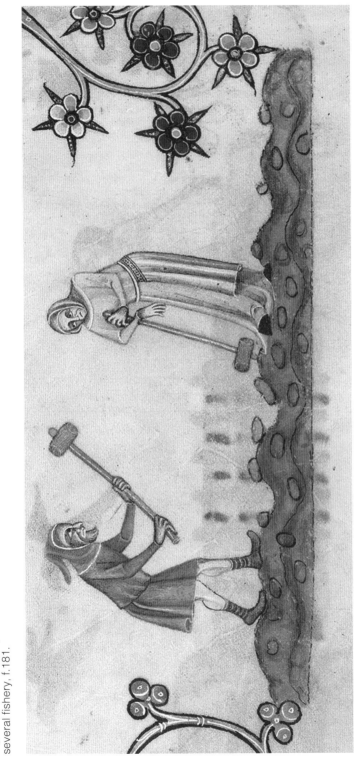

Figure 2.1. Lords and peasants in the manorial landscape. Source: BL Add MS 42130, *The Luttrell Psalter*: breaking up clods, f. 171v, and the lord's several fishery, f.181.

been found working within all these sites, as countless manorial documents testify. However, as Michael Camille attests, the images depict the rural manor as lords wished to visualise it, rather than offering a realistic portrait.[26] A fourteenth-century poem eulogising the landscape of Owain Glyn Dŵr's castle of Sycharth focuses entirely on the seigneurial resources that were emphasised in the *Luttrell Psalter*.

> ... orchard, vineyard and whitefort.
> The famed hero's rabbit park ...
> And in another, even more
> Vivid park, the deer pasture ...
> A stone dovecote on a tower.
> A fishpond, walled and private ... [27]

The most well-known example of artistic seigneurial segregation is the fifteenth-century French *Très Riches Heures*. The images within it, Jonathan Alexander argues, show contempt for the peasants and emphasise the segregated and enclosed landscape dominated by seigneurial power.[28] In this period the peasant was considered to be synonymous with the soil itself, and so it should perhaps come as no surprise to witness this steady seigneurial retreat from a close association with the manorial environment.[29] These texts perhaps offer a means of revealing seigneurial mentalities regarding the rural environment, suggesting that lords were happy to promote indisputably aristocratic spaces but, in so doing, ensuring that peasants remained firmly in their rightful place.

In analysing the landscape of the *Luttrell Psalter* Camille suggests that the images of the fields themselves are understated because they had become less important than the peasants' cash rents and labour services; thus greater prominence was given to these elements.[30] But another reading could be that it was considered inappropriate for any lord to associate himself too closely with his fields, the natural domain of the peasant. In an undated Elton extent (pre-dating 1218) the land is described in terms of its size and all of the tenant holdings are listed.[31] The inclusion of tenants in a document whose purpose was to outline resources is important, placing them as

---

26 For example, in fourteenth-century Lakenheath the court rolls identify the peasant offices of warrener, miller and gardener. M. Camille, *Mirror in parchment. The Luttrell Psalter and the making of medieval England* (London, 1998), p. 192.

27 Quoted in Liddiard, *Castles in context*, pp. 116–17.

28 J. Alexander, '*Labeur* and *paresse*: ideological representations of medieval peasant labor', *The Art Bulletin*, 72/3 (1990), pp. 442 and 450.

29 P. Freedman, *Images of the medieval peasant* (Stanford, 1999), pp. 143–4; O.G. Hill, *The manor, the plowman, and the shepherd: agrarian themes and imagery in late medieval and early Renaissance English literature* (London, 1993), p. 27; *Bracton on the laws and customs of England*, S.E. Thorne (trans.), vol. 3 (London, 1977), p. 132; P.R. Hyams, *King, lords and peasants in medieval England: the common law of villeinage in the twelfth and thirteenth centuries* (Oxford, 1980), p. 26.

30 Camille, *Mirror in parchment*, p. 181.

31 *CMR III*, p. 257.

simply one element in a list of important lordly possessions. To medieval lords, these estates were predominantly resources to which a monetary value could be attached and from which, insofar as their day-to-day running was concerned, a certain personal distance ought to be maintained.

This stands in stark contrast to the more sensitive descriptions of environments that were actively inhabited by elites, particularly their gardens, forests and chases – depictions that might be identified more closely with modern ideas of landscape.[32] There are many references to the landscape in the burgeoning elite literature of the twelfth century onward. The prevailing settings in these texts are gardens and forests, in this context claimed by elites as seigneurial spaces, and these dominate the narrative. In the twelfth century William of Malmesbury wrote extensively on the local environment of many monasteries that he visited, and seems to offer an objective view of what he witnessed. He was clearly unimpressed with Sherborne (Dorset), declaring that it was 'attractive neither for a large population, nor for its setting, and it is surprising, almost shaming, that an Episcopal see lasted there for so long'.[33] In contrast, he clearly considered Thorney (Cambridgeshire) among the finest places he had ever seen:

> … It is the image of paradise, and its loveliness gives an advance idea of heaven itself. For all the swamps surrounding it, it supports an abundance of trees, whose tall smooth trunks strain towards the stars. The flat countryside catches the eye with its green carpet of grass; those who hurry across the plain meet nothing that offends. No part of the land, however tiny, is uncultivated. In one place you come across tall fruit trees, in another, fields bordered with vines, which creep along the earth or climb high … . Nature and art are in competition: what the one forgets the other brings forth … . A vast solitude allows the monks a quiet life: the more limited their glimpses of mortal men, the more tenaciously they cleave to things heavenly. Any woman seen there is regarded as a freak … . It would be fair to say that the island is an abode of chastity, a society of uprightness, a training ground for godly philosophers.[34]

William's description of Thorney includes references to agricultural husbandry and cultivation, but the vital difference is that he clearly saw Thorney as a monastic landscape first and foremost and was undoubtedly writing in the *locus amœnus* tradition.[35] As one of the many fenland islanded communities, Thorney is to a degree isolated and segregated from secular society; the abbey dominated the local landscape, and the village settlement in this period barely registers in the historical record.[36] Could this help explain William's enthusiasm in singling out Thorney for such lavish praise? Here, at last, we have a rural agricultural landscape that could

---

32 Kilby, 'A different world?' (2010a), pp. 20–1.

33 William of Malmesbury, *Gesta pontificum anglorum*, vol. 1, M. Winterbottom and R.M. Thomson (eds, trans.) (Oxford, 2007), p. 277.

34 William of Malmesbury, *Gesta*, pp. 493–5.

35 C.A.M. Clarke, *Literary landscapes and the idea of England, 700–1400* (Cambridge, 2006), p. 83.

36 R.B. Pugh, 'Thorney', in R.B. Pugh (ed.), *VCH Cambridgeshire*, vol. 4, p. 221.

be eulogised because it had no overt association with the peasantry. However, regardless of the fact that the monastic community probably outnumbered the local peasants, there would, of course, still have been a small peasant population labouring in and around the abbey on the monks' behalf.

Despite their apparent and increasing need to separate themselves from the lower orders of society, the aristocracy nevertheless needed to encounter the rural environment at some level, and for at least some of the time. Certainly until well into the fourteenth century, noble households were peripatetic institutions.[37] Even ecclesiastical lords visited their manors, frequently making lengthy visits. Bruce Campbell describes the aristocracy treating their manors as 'refuges to retire to', which gives an impression of their use of the manor as a rural retreat or escape from the pressures of political or ecclesiastical life.[38] He outlines a nine-week visit by the earl and countess of Norfolk to their manor of Forncett (Norfolk) in 1273, while the bishops of Winchester favoured residences in Downton (Wiltshire) and Witney (Oxfordshire), and the abbots of Westminster in La Neyte (Middlesex), Pyrford (Surrey), Denham (Buckinghamshire), Islip (Oxfordshire) and Sutton-under-Brailes (Warwickshire).[39] What links all these manors, with the exception of one – La Neyte, which will be discussed shortly – is an association with hunting. Forncett, while perhaps not as grand as the earl of Norfolk's main seat of Framlingham (Norfolk), nevertheless had a *curia* described as 'palatial' and had access to hunting small game in its warren, as did the abbot of Westminster's manor of Sutton-under-Brailes.[40] Downton, Witney, Pyrford and Denham all had parks, and Islip was situated on the Oxfordshire forest bounds.[41] Could this be a coincidence? Providentially, there is a reasonable quantity of surviving data outlining the movements of Walter de Wenlok, abbot of Westminster (1283–1307) during much of his abbacy. Assessing visits of four nights or more (excluding his stays at Westminster itself), an interesting pattern emerges, outlined in Table 2.1. Despite Westminster Abbey holding more than 150 manors in twenty-two counties, Wenlok stayed at only thirteen places for more than four nights between 1284 and 1307. Of those places, his favourite residence was that at Pyrford, which he visited thirty-six times, frequently staying for long periods, the longest being a seventy-seven-day stretch between 1 December 1286 and 15 February 1287. Denham, another favourite residence, was granted back to Westminster Abbey only in 1292, but he wasted no time in visiting and followed up his initial stay with a twenty-eight-night visit between October and November of that year.[42] Wenlok's other favourite residence,

---

37 C.M. Woolgar, *The great household in late medieval England* (London, 1999), pp. 46–7.

38 B.M.S. Campbell, *English seigniorial agriculture 1250–1450* (Cambridge, 2000), p. 200.

39 Campbell, *English seigniorial agriculture*, p. 200.

40 F.G. Davenport, *The economic development of a Norfolk manor, 1086–1565* (Cambridge, 1906), pp. 20–1 and 75; L.F. Salzman, 'Sutton-under-Brailes', in *VCH Warwickshire*, vol. 5, p. 157.

41 S.A. Mileson, *Parks in medieval England* (Oxford, 2009), pp. 62–4; D.L. Powell, 'Pyrford', in H.E. Malden (ed.), *VCH Surrey*, vol. 3 (London, 1911), pp. 433–4; B. Harvey, 'Islip', in M.D. Lobel (ed.), *VCH Oxfordshire*, vol. 6, p. 212; R.H. Lathbury, *The history of Denham* (Uxbridge, 1904), p. 63.

42 Lathbury, *History of Denham*, pp. 67 and 71; B.F. Harvey (ed.), *Documents illustrating the rule of Walter de Wenlok, abbot of Westminster, 1283–1307* (London, 1965), pp. 34–45.

Table 2.1
The itinerary of Walter de Wenlok, abbot of Westminster, visiting his estates between 1284–1307
(stays of four nights or more).

Manor	Total no. of visits of => four nights	Mean average no. of nights	Standard deviation from mean	Shortest stay (nights)	Longest stay (nights)
Pyrford (Surr.)	36	20	18.7	4	77
Ebury/Eye/La Neyte (Mdx)	15	11	6.9	5	22
Sutton-under-Brailes (Warks.)	12	14	9.8	5	33
Islip (Oxon)	11	6	2.1	4	9
Laleham (Mdx)	6	6	1.5	4	8
Denham (Bucks.)	5	11	11.1	4	28
Morton Foliot[1] (Worcs.)	4	16	9.6	7	26
Battersea (Surr.)	2	6	2.8	4	8
Hampstead (Mdx)	1	6	-	-	-
Paddington (Mdx)	1	6	-	-	-
Todenham (Glos.)	1	6	-	-	-
Wenlock[2] (Shrops.)	1	5	-	-	-
Pershore (Worcs.)	1	4	-	-	-

Source: B.F. Harvey (ed.), *Documents illustrating the rule of Walter de Wenlok, abbot of Westminster, 1283–1307* (London, 1965), pp. 34–45.

Notes:

1. Now Castlemorton.

2. Wenlock was not part of Westminster Abbey's estates, but the birthplace of Walter de Wenlok.

Morton Foliot (Worcestershire), not mentioned by Campbell but frequently visited, was situated within Malvern Forest.[43] It seems clear that each of his favourite residences, except La Neyte and Laleham, had an association with hunting.

Laleham is easily explained. It appears in connection with both Westminster and Pyrford in almost every instance throughout the period within which detailed itineraries survive (1284–92). For example, in December 1288 Wenlok spent fourteen nights in Pyrford and then two nights at Laleham before returning to Westminster. Similarly, he stayed at Pyrford in February and March 1290, and returned to Westminster via Laleham. It seems clear that Laleham was a convenient stopping point en route between these two locations. Depending on travelling conditions, a household could usually cover between ten and twenty-three miles each day; using modern roads, it is twenty-eight miles from Westminster to Pyrford.[44] The explanation for the popularity of La Neyte is quite different. It was an 'islanded estate' that lay approximately one mile from Westminster Abbey, along a stretch of land close to the Thames described by Edward the Confessor's biographer as 'a delightful place, surrounded with fertile

---

43   A. Spilman, 'Castlemorton', in *VCH Worcestershire*, vol. 4, p. 49.

44   Woolgar, *The great household*, p. 187.

lands and green fields, near the main channel of the river'.[45] It was part of the manor collectively known as Eye; from the thirteenth century, one component of the manor became known as Ebury, and La Neyte continued to be used as the abbot's own moated residence.[46] A map of 1614 shows La Neyte as an artificial island surrounded by a moat, close to the Thames and one of its tributaries.[47] Running directly to the manor house was a causeway across marshy ground called the Willow Walk, shown on the 1614 map and again on a map dated 1723. Rutton assumes that this footpath was in situ by the fourteenth century, although there is only speculative evidence for this. He suggests that the abbots of Westminster would probably have followed a route across *abbotesbrege*, a reference to which is found in one of the early fourteenth-century account rolls.[48] At this time, Norwich cathedral priory had a walled pleasure garden with tree-lined walkways, and so this kind of landscaping within a monastic context was not without precedent.[49] What was the purpose of this moated residence? According to Rutton, the moated site contained just two acres; this, and a further three and a half acres nearby, encompassed the abbatial dwelling, 'buildings, yards, gardens, orchards, fishings and other commodities'.[50]

Perhaps the site's proximity to the Thames meant that the moat offered additional drainage facilities. Yet the manorial centre of Eybury lay nearby, further away from the river. It seems not to have been moated, and could have provided a suitable location for a residence if flooding was an issue. The planting of trees along ditches and drains helps to strengthen banks lying adjacent to water, and this may explain the willows along the raised causeway.[51] However, this was a walkway, not a drainage ditch, and it did not run alongside running water, except at the narrow end of its easternmost point, where it began. A willow-lined footpath would have provided a secluded causeway, with the trees effectively veiling the surrounding agricultural landscape. The overall impression is of a landscaped environment deliberately manipulated to provide more aesthetically pleasing surroundings. La Neyte had other aristocratic connections: it was chosen as a temporary dwelling by John of Gaunt, and it was the birthplace of one of the duke of York's sons.[52] Returning to Campbell's suggestion that rural manors could be considered by elites as retreats, it seems clear that very specific rural sites were prized, with hunting a key priority, while La Neyte was favoured partly because

45   B.F. Harvey, *Westminster Abbey and its estates in the middle ages* (Oxford, 1977), p. 414; D. Sullivan, *The Westminster corridor: an explanation of the Anglo-Saxon history of Westminster Abbey and its nearby lands and people* (London, 1994), pp. 136–7.

46   Harvey, *Westminster Abbey*, p. 350.

47   W.L. Rutton, 'The manor of Eia, or Eye next Westminster', *Archaeologia*, 62 (1910), p. 36; its name suggests that it was islanded, or gave the impression of raised ground surrounded by wetter land.

48   Rutton, 'The manor of Eia', pp. 40 and 48.

49   C. Noble *et al.*, (eds, trans), *Farming and gardening in late medieval Norfolk* (Norwich, 1996), p. 10; Noble also notes the prevalence of monastic moated gardens (p. 4).

50   Rutton, 'The manor of Eia', p. 56.

51   H.E. Hallam, 'Drainage techniques', in H.E. Hallam (ed.) *The agrarian history of England and Wales, vol. 2, 1042–1350* (Cambridge, 1988), pp. 498–9.

52   Rutton, 'The manor of Eia', p. 43.

Figure 2.2. Undley Island and Causeway, Lakenheath. Source: © Environment Agency copyright and/or database right 2015. All rights reserved; Ordnance Survey, first edition, rev.

of its proximity to Westminster Abbey and – given the propinquity of Eybury – because of its attractive setting, which was certainly segregated from the rest of the manor.[53] And if the *abbotesbrege* of the early fourteenth century crossed Eye stream at the site of a contemporary walkway beyond the stream, it may also have shielded its residents from having to look upon the fields and tenements occupied by local peasants. It is also worth noting that, in Suffolk, one of the prior of Ely's preferred rural manors was Undley, described by Munday as a 'small isle … too small to support [a] communit[y]' that was accessed by a causeway across the fen, effectively separating it from the peasant population of Lakenheath (Figure 2.2).[54]

The paucity of surviving documentation for lesser secular lords means that it is difficult to say very much about them with any great certainty. At the baronial level there is much evidence to suggest that lordly residences were set apart from the manorial environment. In the fourteenth century the Talbot family, for example, did not

---

53 Although islands were highly prized from an ecclesiastical perspective, because they represented exile, asceticism and hardship; Liddiard, *Castles in context*, pp. 118–19 briefly discusses landscaping used as a means of social exclusion within castle sites.

54 J.T. Munday, *Eriswell-cum-Coclesworth: chronicle of Eriswell, part one – until 1340* (Brandon, 1969), p. 3; although the court rolls show that a small number of cottagers resided there, perhaps serving the abbot.

always live at one of their several castles, but even their smaller houses were overtly seigneurial, such as Blakemere (Shropshire), with its manor house set within parkland and surrounded by a mere.[55] Meanwhile, the household accounts of the knightly de Norwich family in East Anglia show that, of five manors held, during one seven-month period Katherine de Norwich stayed in only two: Mettingham (Suffolk) and Blackworth (Norfolk).[56] The family had been granted a licence in 1342 to crenellate these two manors by Edward III, and both had hunting facilities in the form of warrens.[57] However, small manors, comprising fewer than 500 acres, were more prevalent than their larger counterparts, and so any review of seigneurial attitudes to local landscape must attempt to encompass the lesser nobility.[58] It has been acknowledged that the greater lords, with their vast estates, were much more likely to cultivate a sense of detachment from their manors, but historians commonly agree that this was not the case when considering lesser lords holding fewer manors, where the general consensus is that they adopted a more hands-on approach,[59] evidenced by the much greater emphasis placed on the demesne within the sphere of lower lordship. Campbell and Bartley have assiduously shown that small lay estates accrued their income principally through the profits of the demesne, as opposed to the rents and perquisites available in greater quantity from middling and large manors.[60] Other enduring characteristics of the smaller manor were its weaker lordship and the general predominance of free peasants, making for a demesne that could not rely on a customary workforce and which, it has been assumed, was managed much more closely by the lord. If we are to unpick the seigneurial outlook concerning the local environment, one vital issue is an understanding of what a 'hands-on approach' actually meant in the thirteenth and fourteenth centuries. Naturally, because of the few sources available, a small number of examples have been used time and again to illustrate the attention that lesser lords paid to their estates. It is nevertheless worth reconsidering some of these documents in an attempt to understand what exercised these men concerning their lands.

In the late thirteenth century Adam de Stratton held a chamberlainship of Isabella de Fortibus, countess of Aumale.[61] His estate included manors in Wiltshire, Berkshire and Oxfordshire, all of which were forfeit to the crown in 1289 following his alleged

---

55   B. Ross (trans., ed.), *Accounts of the stewards of the Talbot household at Blakemere 1392–1425* (Keele, 2003), p. vii.

56   C.M. Woolgar, *Household accounts from medieval England, part I* (Oxford, 1992), pp. 177–8.

57   *CPR* Ed III, 6, p. 106; C.R. Manning, *Mettingham Castle and College* (1861), p. 2; Mettingham was moated.

58   E.A. Kosminsky, *Studies in the agrarian history of England in the thirteenth century* (Oxford, 1956), p. 98; Campbell, *English seigniorial agriculture*, p. 62 shows that of 1,511 lay lords studied in his sample, only 20 per cent held more than 500 acres.

59   Campbell, *English seigniorial agriculture*, p. 61; E. Miller and J. Hatcher, *Medieval England: rural society and economic change 1086–1348* (1978, London, 1980), pp. 180–1 and 189; N. Saul, *Scenes from provincial life: knightly families in Sussex 1280–1400* (Oxford, 1986), p. 98.

60   B.M.S. Campbell and K. Bartley, *England on the eve of the Black Death: an atlas of lay lordship, land and wealth, 1300–49* (Manchester, 2006), pp. 76 and 81.

61   M.W. Farr, *Accounts and surveys of the Wiltshire lands of Adam de Stratton* (Devizes, 1959), p. xv.

guilt in forging charters. Assessing the manorial surveys that he commissioned, what is striking is their meticulousness. The *c.*1275 extent of Sevenhampton (Wiltshire), for example, outlines the demesne holdings in great detail. Each demesnal *cultura* is identified by name, size and value under general headings for each discrete field.[62] The extent goes on to record scrupulously the peasant holdings and customary services owed. But not all of de Stratton's surveys mirror this detail. At Upton and Blewbury (Berkshire) in 1271 each demesne is described briefly. These documents simply outline the total demesne acreage in each field and ascribe what must have been an average value per acre for each field.[63] At Stratton (Wiltshire) in 1277 the total demesne acreage is offered and there is no sense of the number of fields in operation there.[64] Of these surveys, all but that of Sevenhampton were overseen by John de Berking, who was probably de Stratton's steward.[65] At Sevenhampton there is no mention of the steward's involvement, although that need not mean that he was not present. John de Berking presided over surveys either side of the Sevenhampton extent, and so it seems that he was still steward in 1275.

The additional detail on the Sevenhampton survey is intriguing. It cannot be simple evolution, as the brief Stratton extent post-dates it. What we appear to be witnessing is the customary apparatus of the lay estate survey. Here, there was no great central management, as there was on the larger lay and ecclesiastical estates, where format and content were to a greater extent determined by administrators. At Sevenhampton the jury was made up of both free and servile peasants, although the customary tenants dominated. This was in effect their own version of the local environment, named and familiar, and they noted what they believed was important. Despite the brevity of the other de Stratton estate surveys, there are clues that they too relied heavily upon local input: all the dated surveys, although produced in different years, share a common bond – they were all conducted directly following rogationtide, when the steward knew that a full inspection of the local landscape had taken place. So, what initially appears to elucidate the thoroughness of a lesser lord, one taking a more direct approach to estate management, could instead be interpreted as a lord who may occasionally have left local officials to conduct enquiries of this nature, simply instructing that economic value ought to be noted. It is noteworthy that John at the Gate, reeve of Sevenhampton in 1275, does not feature on the list of fourteen jurors selected to authenticate the 1275 extent. Could the reeve himself have overseen the production of the survey? There are additional points of interest in considering Adam de Stratton's approach to estate management. In a series of Sevenhampton account rolls between 1275 and 1288 he is never recorded as visiting the manor. No doubt his chamberlainship would have kept him primarily in London. While this does not mean that he never visited his other manors, his failure to visit Sevenhampton is striking. It was his largest manor, with a demesne of over 900 acres, and all his estate income

---

62 Farr, *Adam de Stratton*, pp. 2–3.

63 Farr, *Adam de Stratton*, pp. 17–21.

64 Farr, *Adam de Stratton*, p. 25.

65 Although in these documents the bailiff of Sevenhampton, Henry de Aunewyk, is described once as the steward; Farr, *Adam de Stratton*, p. 223.

was centrally received there by the bailiff, so it was also his most important one. Clearly, despite an estate consisting of a small number of manors, Adam de Stratton does not quite fit the profile of a lesser lord with few estate resources and a small demesne. Nevertheless, the survival of a series of manorial records helps to begin to question the idea that meticulous seigneurial estate management was synonymous with an intimate knowledge and appreciation of the manorial environment on the part of the lord.

Fortunately, part of the estate books of two lesser lords with small manors survive. Firstly, the Hotot family held land in Clopton (Northamptonshire) and Turvey (Bedfordshire). What remains of their estate records is in two parts: MS A, which was collated after 1273, and MS B, which now only survives as a transcript from the antiquarian John Bridges' notes.[66] The records consist of documents ranging from copies of charters through to surveys and rentals. The focus here was nevertheless on the family holdings and their descent, the revenue due from these lands – in cash or labour – and the services owed by the Hotots to others. The manuscript begins with a detailed outline of the history of lordship in Clopton, no doubt included to provide evidence of the legitimacy of the Hotot claim.[67] The manorial documents offer the overwhelming impression of a family keeping a watchful eye on their tenants, in terms both of their holdings and of the associated rents and services that were due. In a rental of Turvey outlining individual tenants and rents annotations were made in the 1250s by Thomas Hotot adding detail on the quantity of land being rented, and occasionally adding the furlong names.[68] All this points overwhelmingly to a family that was personally interested in its estates. But their interest was that of the exchequer: ensuring that they had a clear idea of what they could expect to receive each year from their tenants and noting additional detail to determine whether they were receiving an adequate sum for each holding. Unfortunately, no account rolls survive for the Hotot estate, although it is likely that they would have existed.

Secondly, Henry de Bray, a former steward of the priory of Northampton, held a manor in Harlestone (Northamptonshire). His estate book, begun in 1322, has a focus similar to that seen in the Hotot documents, and Henry himself explained that he had 'arranged this present brief as evidence to his heirs; that is, transcriptions of charters and memoranda arising from [my] time'.[69] This statement is interesting and helps to illuminate the perspective of lesser lords such as de Bray and the Hotots. It suggests that these men were aware that evidence of title might be important in proving tenure and offers a rationale for the production of cartularies and family histories at the lowest level of nobility. Willis' translation of these documents suggests that Henry de Bray copied out his accounts between 1289 and 1309.[70] This is not strictly correct. What de Bray outlines are his expenses for various works, but nevertheless these are informative. The majority of expenses listed relate to various building works undertaken

---

66 E. King (ed.), *A Northamptonshire miscellany* (Northampton, 1983), p. 10.

67 King, *Miscellany*, p. 16.

68 King, *Miscellany*, pp. 24–8.

69 D. Willis (ed., trans.), *The estate book of Henry de Bray c.1289–1340* (London, 1916), pp. ix–x.

70 Willis, *Henry de Bray*, p. 48.

and, while some of these are of an agricultural nature, such as the new grange *c.*1292 and a granary in 1304, most works represent the aggrandisement of the *curia* and capital messuage.[71] These included the construction of several buildings from which de Bray could have earned revenue from his tenants – a water-mill, a lime kiln and an oven – along with other structures directly associated with lordship, such as his new hall in 1289 and the later addition of a new chamber, two dovecotes, a walled *herbarium*, fishponds and his walled garden – *le neweyerd* – which was almost 400 feet in circumference, along with the mending of the gate between his hall and the vill. To create his garden de Bray exchanged ten acres of land for just seven selions with a local gentry family.[72]

Henry de Bray incurred expenses constructing houses for local peasants, but the 18s. he spent building a cottage on *le coterowe* in 1296 is rather dwarfed by the 23s. spent mending his gate in 1294 and 46s. spent constructing a dovecote in 1305.[73] And there is evidence that he knew and favoured certain peasants: he described one unfree tenant as 'industrious and trustworthy', and gave him a messuage and land, albeit in exchange for 20s. annual rent and for providing Henry with free stone for his various building projects.[74] This estate book has been used as evidence that lesser lords adopted a more personal approach to estate management.[75] But is this really what we should deduce from these records? Certainly, Henry spent considerably on ensuring that he had suitable agricultural buildings, such as a pigsty and henhouse in 1298, and a new granary and sheepcote in 1304.[76] These changes suggest that the manorial buildings of Harlestone were in need of modernisation. Countless manorial account rolls attest to renewals of this nature, although perhaps not always on such a comprehensive scale as seen at Harlestone, and yet historians use these examples as indicators not of a closer focus on estate management but simply that vital manorial infrastructure needed refreshing. There is also evidence that Henry was familiar with the local landscape, as several of his records outline Harlestone field-names; but we should expect this, as, after all, he was a Harlestone resident.[77] It cannot be ignored that his estate books emphasise two priorities: first, establishing lineage and tenurial

---

71 Willis, *Henry de Bray*, pp. 48–51.

72 Willis, *Henry de Bray*, p. 57; it is possible that *le neweyerd* was already a garden when de Bray acquired it, although it seems more likely that he created it. Certainly, in 1307 he enclosed it within a wall, costing 48s.

73 Willis, *Henry de Bray*, pp. 48–9.

74 Willis, *Henry de Bray*, p. 56.

75 Miller and Hatcher, *Medieval England*, pp. 181 and 188–91.

76 Willis, *Henry de Bray*, pp. 48–50.

77 Jane Whittle's work on the Hunstanton (Norfolk) manor of the minor Le Strange family emphasised that the manorial accounts named individual harvest and *famuli* workers, although the accounts were produced either by the reeve or, later on, the steward. Nevertheless, as a resident lord, again, it seems likely that the lord might be expected know the names of some of his tenants: J. Whittle, 'The food economy of lords, tenants and workers in a medieval village: Hunstanton, Norfolk, 1328–48', in M. Kowaleski *et al.* (eds), *Peasants and lords in the medieval English economy: essays in honour of Bruce M. S. Campbell* (Turnhout, 2015), p. 28.

title; and, secondly, accentuating his status by building a new hall before turning his attention to landscaping: creating, or possibly updating, his fishponds and altering the corresponding watercourse, and laying out a private garden. There is nothing on the actual management of the de Bray estate within these records, although, again, there probably were account rolls that are no longer extant. It seems likely that estate management was important to Henry de Bray, but we should be clear that this plausibly meant a keen focus on the seigneurial purse-strings.

If men such as de Bray and Hotot concentrated on estate management, they did so without being too overt about it, and compensated by ensuring that certain areas of the manor were distinctly seigneurial and segregated from that of the peasantry. Britnell has suggested that the manorial accounts for four minor lords in Essex demonstrate that careful attention was paid to the running of each of the respective agrarian operations. He established that at least one of these lords maintained a close relationship with manorial officials and took an active part in decision-making.[78] This was undoubtedly the case on many manors held by lower-level lords. On the very small proto-manors of John de Aylington at Elton and Roger Cordel at Castor (see chapter three, pp. 46 and 50) a relatively close association with the tenants would have been unavoidable and these minor lords' dependency on demesne output must have resulted in a greater involvement in demesne management on occasion.

Nevertheless, it seems clear that, for most medieval lords, maintaining a close focus on estate management meant keeping a watchful eye on the seigneurial coffers. One of the main reasons for the production of manorial accounts was to ensure that manorial officers could be trusted, and this would have been especially pertinent at the lowest levels of lordship.[79] It did not mean that any lord should undertake agricultural work himself. The agricultural treatise known as *Walter of Henley* had a wide audience that included ecclesiastical and secular lords, but it was predominantly aimed at lesser lords and their officials.[80] The manuscript was written in the style of a sermon or lecture delivered by a father to his son, enabling the author to emphasise subjects that he clearly felt were contentious. He was aware that many lords were unskilled in husbandry and appointed inexperienced officers, and it was clear to him that many manors made losses.[81] Several times the author exhorts the reader to consider his more contentious arguments, using phrases such as 'wille you see it?', 'wille you see how the horse costeth more then the oxe?' and 'do you want to see this?' Indeed, the phrase 'yowe knowe well that in the yeare theare be 52 weeks' suggests that, for the most part, Walter was presenting something unfamiliar to his readership.[82] The treatise provided the lord with information that would enable him to gain greater

---

78   Although he acknowledges that most of the management was undertaken by manorial officials: R.H. Britnell, 'Minor landlords in England and medieval agrarian capitalism', *Past and Present*, 89 (1980), p. 7.

79   C. Dyer, 'Documentary evidence: problems and enquiries', in G. Astill and A. Grant (eds), *The countryside of medieval England* (Oxford, 1994), pp. 12–13.

80   *WH*, pp. 124 and 155.

81   *WH*, c. 6.

82   *WH*, c. 25, c. 30, c. 38, c. 46, c. 62, c. 90.

control over his resources and officials, and therefore increase profits, while the detail on agronomic practice was aimed at the bailiff or steward.[83] Saul suggests that unravelling seigneurial mentalities regarding their estates is tricky, especially at the lower levels of aristocracy.[84] But it seems likely that their concerns were largely financial: attention needed to be paid to officials to ensure they were honest, and to the reckoning of manorial income and expenditure. The broader history of manorial agriculture suggests much the same thing: lords can be seen alternating between leasing their demesnes and managing them directly, depending upon the prevailing economic returns that could be expected.

It could be difficult to determine the difference between a wealthy free peasant and a lower-level lord in the thirteenth and fourteenth centuries, and so means of displaying status were vitally important to the latter.[85] Henry de Bray's evident focus on outward display and expenditure on the trappings of lordship strongly suggest attempts to highlight his status within a landscape that included other gentry families as well as peasants. Revisiting the *Luttrell Psalter* in light of *Walter of Henley*, the agricultural illuminations seem to represent both control and social segregation. Geoffrey Luttrell, himself a member of the lower nobility and the holder of what Kosminsky would describe as 'small' manors, shows that he is omnipresent and cannot therefore be cheated by the peasants performing their labour services. The clearly delineated peasant and noble spaces within the *Luttrell Psalter* illustrate that Henry de Bray's private spaces, walled, gated and locked, were perhaps less about security and more concerned with emphasising seigneurial power over manorial space.[86] It is especially noteworthy that Suffolk, a county generally dominated by weak lordship, boasted more than 700 moated sites associated with small manors and free tenants, and that more than one study has shown that the size of the 'island' was linked to status, with those of free tenants generally smaller than those of their seigneurial counterparts.[87] In *c.*1210 Raoul de Hodenc suggested that 'a knight … will not rise to great heights if he enquires of the value of corn' and, while Coss argues that this was not always practical for the lord of a small manor, and that a focus on estate management was necessary for the maintenance of a reasonable income,[88] based on the evidence found within both the Hotot and de Bray estate books precedence was given to outlining tenurial rights, family lineage and revenue. In some instances, estate management was treated ambivalently within the records of these minor lords. We can detect glimpses in Henry de Bray's estate book that he was familiar with the

---

83   *WH*, p. 127.

84   Saul, *Provincial life*, p. 106.

85   Kosminsky, *Agrarian history*, p. 261; M. Bailey, *Medieval Suffolk, an economic and social history, 1200–1500* (2007, Woodbridge, 2010), pp. 15–18.

86   Although see C. Platt, 'The homestead moat: security or status?' *Archaeological Journal*, 167 (2010), p. 118, who argues in favour of security as a motivation for moated sites.

87   E. Martin, 'Medieval moats in Suffolk', *Medieval Settlement Research*, 4 (1989), p. 14; M. Fradley, 'Warrenhall and other moated sites in north-east Shropshire', *Medieval Settlement Research*, 20 (2005), pp. 17–18.

88   P. Coss, *The origins of the English gentry* (Cambridge, 2003), pp. 179–80.

workings of his estate, but the overriding impression created within these documents was that it was considered inappropriate for any lesser lord to be seen to be too close to the day-to-day practicalities. Seigneurial engagement with the manorial environment, then, was driven overwhelmingly by financial concern; their relationship with the landscape was, for the most part, not one of intimate association, but rather practical and economic.

Chapter 3

Ordering the landscape

Through an examination of the morphology of the medieval village, and by assessing the ways in which local people moved through their environment, this chapter focuses on how the physical organisation of the medieval village and its wider landscape generated socially constructed perceptions of place in the later Middle Ages. We begin by considering how people were situated within the vill, commencing with the respective manorial *curiae* and their proximity to, or distance from, the peasants' dwellings.[1] This is followed by an evaluation of the arrangement of peasant tofts and messuages, focusing in particular on the zoning of different status groups and on the layout and size of peasant tenements across the social spectrum of the lower orders. This naturally leads us to considerations of ownership and privacy, but also to reflect on the levels of access to different areas that peasants enjoyed within the village and its wider landscape. How was rural space regulated, and what did this mean for those living there? Which areas were ostensibly off-limits to peasants, and what can the surviving records reveal about how these places were negotiated in reality?

Moving beyond the homestead, the rest of the chapter concentrates on the ways in which peasants traversed the wider landscape of the rural manor. It will be shown that, in many cases, people eschewed paths that were sanctioned by the lord and community, instead electing to create alternative routeways. Despite being unauthorised, in many instances these pathways were nevertheless enduring. Through the examination of place in the rural settlement at a number of different levels, this chapter shows that the landscape of the rural village and its surrounding area was made up of places that – as Matthew Johnson suggests – were imbued with power and meaning for different groups within each respective community.[2] Consequently, access to certain places was frequently contested and renegotiated and, as a corollary to this, the socially constructed meanings attached to these places were continually changing.[3]

Organising the landscape of the medieval vill: seigneurial and peasant zones

As outlined in chapter two, from the twelfth century onwards the gradual uncoupling of manorial complexes from the rest of the village was underway in many rural settlements. In some instances this involved the relocation of the manorial *curia* to

---

1   This proceeds from the more general discussion on the location of seigneurial spaces within rural villages in the previous chapter. For an explanation of *curia*, see chapter two, p. 20.

2   M. Johnson, *Ideas of landscape* (Oxford, 2007), p. 166.

3   Whyte, *Inhabiting the landscape*, p. 5.

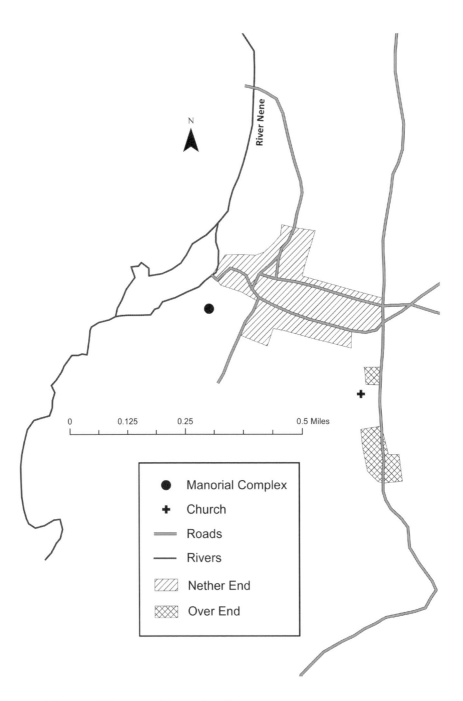

Figure 3.1. Ramsey Abbey manorial complex: Elton.

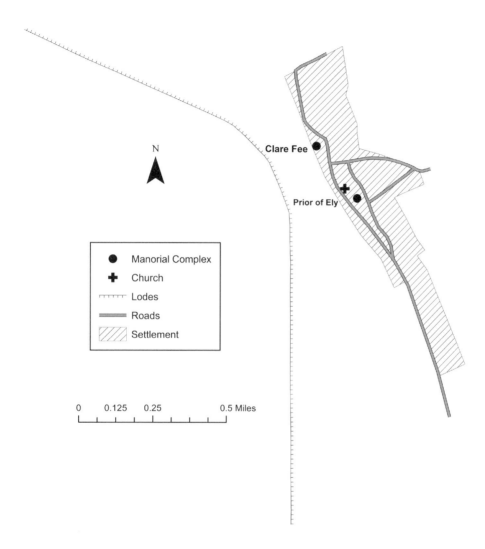

Figure 3.2. Manorial complexes: Lakenheath.

a peripheral site, and in others the deliberate separation of the site using walls and gates. Each of the vills within our case study contained at least two manorial *curiae*.[4] The areas occupied by the principal lords in Elton and Lakenheath can be firmly identified (Figures 3.1–3.2). At Elton, by the thirteenth century the abbot of Ramsey's manorial complex occupied a site of one and a half acres close to the Nene, at some considerable distance from the church. The site was on a raised platform

---

4   In Elton, the de Aylington *curia* dates from *c.*1218.

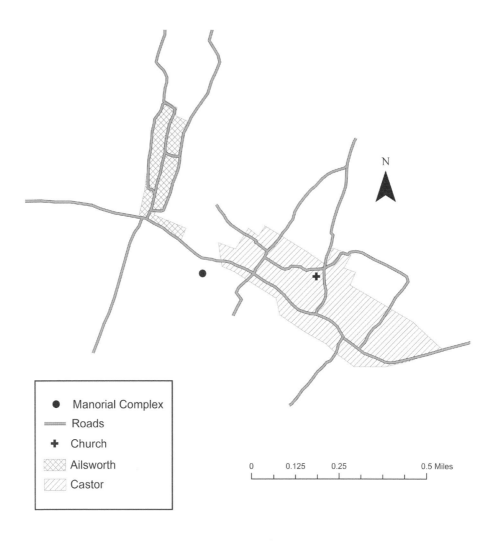

Figure 3.3. Peterborough Abbey manorial complex: Castor.

separated from the rest of the settlement, to which it was linked via a causeway.[5] There are no surviving earthworks indicating the site of the other manorial *curia*, John de Aylington's proto-manor at Over End; these were presumably obscured by the

---

5   *RH II*, p. 656; D.F. Mackreth, 'The abbot of Ramsey's manor, Elton, Huntingdonshire', *Northamptonshire Archaeology*, 26 (1995), p. 134 suggests the complex was thirteenth century. It seems to have been in situ by 1218, as the description in an extent of that date matches that recorded in the 1279 *Rotuli Hundredorum*: *CMR I*, p. 490. The manorial site close to the Nene was evidently carefully selected. A 1950s photograph of the Nene in flood shows the manorial site as one of a few areas of high ground within the surrounding area: A.G. Clark, *A village on the Nene*, vol. 1 (Stamford, 2007), fig. 7.

extensive landscaping prior to the construction of modern Elton Hall, although it is possible to trace the creation of his small fee (see below). At Lakenheath the sites of the manorial complexes of both the prior of Ely and the earl of Gloucester are known. Here, the conventual manor was located near the church. This may reflect the fact that in 1086 Ely priory held the church there, although it was also the case that Ramsey held Elton church at the same date.

At Castor, the most likely site for Peterborough Abbey's manorial *curia* is a moated compound of approximately four and a half acres situated between Castor and Ailsworth (Figure 3.3).[6] Both the location and the moated construction indicate a deliberate separation from the rest of the local population. A tentative location north of the church has been suggested for Turold's manor house in Castor (see below, pp. 46–9), which was known as Uphalle by the thirteenth century. Uphalle indicates an elevated position, and it seems sensible to suggest that the abbot's manorial curia was comparatively lower. Each of the monastic and prioral centres had an absentee lord, and so the continued proximity of the prioral *curia* to the church at Lakenheath is noteworthy. It is possible that the manorial centres at both Castor and Elton had been relocated post-Conquest, and that Lakenheath's unusual topography played a part in the siting of the prior's manorial complex: with fenland due west and heathland to the east, the options for a suitable site may have been more limited. Unusually, at Lakenheath, there was no chief lord of the vill before the conjoining of Clare Fee with the prior's manor, and this may also have been a factor in determining the sites of the respective manorial complexes there.[7]

In almost every case, then, the most important manorial sites in each respective vill lay at some distance from the main settlement core. In Castor, however, the surviving documentary sources also provide sufficient detail to suggest a potential site for the more minor Thorold manorial *curia*.[8] Campbell and Bartley argue that those of knightly rank far outnumbered any other aristocratic group, and therefore a significant proportion of the later medieval population in England lived under the lordship of a lower-ranking lord.[9] This rare opportunity to analyse the location of a small manorial complex allows us to consider something of its spatial relationships at several levels: its physical position within the vill, and its proximity both to the church and to dependent peasant tenements. The Thorold family was known by a number

---

6   *Peterborough New Town: a survey of the antiquities in the areas of development* (London, 1969), p. 26; two additional locations have been posited, currently occupied by Manor Farm and Village Farm respectively, but there is no evidence to support either of these suggestions (pers. comm. S. Upex): C. Collins, *Archaeological test pit excavations in Castor, Cambridgeshire, in 2009, 2010 and 2011* (Cambridge, 2018), p. 20.

7   Bailey, *Marginal economy?* pp. 73–4; The prior of Ely was known to stay at the islanded site of Undley, linked to Lakenheath by a causeway (see chapter two, p. 33), and this may also have had a bearing on the more fixed nature of the Lakenheath manorial *curia*.

8   Known as Turold in the eleventh and twelfth centuries, by the thirteenth century the family name was usually expressed as Thorold. Spellings used throughout reflect those from the period under review in each instance.

9   Campbell and Bartley, *England on the eve of the Black Death*, p. 69.

of bynames at this time. In the late thirteenth century Henry Thorold, the incumbent lord, was variously referred to as Henry de Uphalle, Henry le Lord, Henry Thorold and 'Henry, son of William, called louerd'.[10] In the lay subsidy of 1301 members of prominent free families – Silvester, Cordel, Dionys and Paris – are listed close together alongside Henry, son of William, who paid 7s. 8¾d., and who must have been Henry Thorold (Table 3.1).[11] These families are not recorded in any of the abbey surveys, and were almost certainly tenants of the Thorold fee.[12] This suggests the possibility that the tenants of the Thorold fee occupied one area of Castor and points to the possibility that Henry Thorold's capital messuage lay in the same area of Castor as his tenants' tenements.

The charters that provide evidence for these neighbouring tenements also reveal their proximity to the cemetery of St Andrew the Apostle.[13] The St Andrew's Lane mentioned in a charter of 1330 may be the footpath that still runs due east from the church and skirts land called St Andrew's Piece, which presumably refers to the medieval cemetery.[14] This detail helps to place these peasant tofts within the settlement. Although precisely where they lay is unknown, the documentary evidence suggests that the Thorold tenants' dwellings lay in the area around High Street and east of Stocks Hill, in the vicinity of St Andrew's Lane. Test-pitting undertaken in Castor between 2009 and 2011 suggests that the area south of High Street was less developed than other parts of the village, although an archaeological survey in 1972 noted an eleventh-century peasant dwelling in the north-east angle of High Street.[15] The overriding impression is that the Thorold tenants were clustered in the area below and to the east of the church, and that the seigneurial capital messuage lay close by, near the church and in an elevated position above the main settlement. The surviving documents rarely make reference to servile peasants in Castor, although the clustering of this group of free peasants suggests that different status groups may have occupied different parts of the settlement.

The Fitzwilliam estate version of the tithe map of 1846 shows an enclosed triangular space bounded on two sides by roads, which may be the site of the Thorold manorial complex (Figures 3.4–3.6). In terms of its area, the proposed enclosure is

---

10 NRO F(M) Charters 115, 133, 143, 185 and 399.

11 TNA E 179/155/31/42. Several thirteenth- and fourteenth-century charters confirm this: NRO F(M) Charters 46, 47, 57, 67, 86, 95, 136, 159 and 365.

12 King also suggests this was the case: King, *Peterborough Abbey*, p. 63; it should be noted that by the end of the twelfth century Roger Cordel held a proto-manor in Castor, which a century later consisted of eight messuages, 120 acres of land, thirty-four acres of meadow, nine acres of woodland and 10s. rent. By the thirteenth century the Cordels were styling themselves as lords (see above, p. 14, fn. 39): Kilby, 'The late medieval landscape of Castor', pp. 23–4.

13 NRO F(M) Charter 95.

14 I am grateful to Brian Goode, churchwarden, St Kyneburgha's church for alerting me to the location of St Andrew's Piece.

15 Collins, *Archaeological test pit excavations*, p. 118; D. Mackreth, 'Potter's oven, Castor', *Durobrivae*, 1 (1973), p. 14: Mackreth suggests that this dwelling was slowly developed from 'a peasant's house to something which must have looked like a small manor'.

Table 3.1
Extract from the 1301 lay subsidy, Castor.

Name	Amount paid	Family
Robert Silvester	7s. 7¼d.	Silvester
Roger Cordel	7s. ¾d.	Cordel
Robert Kimborule	2s. 3¾d.	Kimberlee
Henry, son of William	7s. 8¾d.	Thorold
Alice, daughter of Gilbert	16¾d.	Dionys / Paris
Sarah Bertilmeu	9¾d.	Hare
Robert Schardelawe	7s. 4¼d.	
William Parys	3s. 1¼d.	Paris

Source: TNA E 179/155/31/42.

smaller than the site suggested as Peterborough Abbey's manorial complex in Castor, although an adjacent field known today as *Tarrols* may have been part of the complex or demesne several and, with this addition, the size of the site would have been appropriate to its suggested status.[16] A position adjacent to the church would also have been fitting, emphasising the Thorolds' seigneurial status. As resident lords and the holders of the advowson until 1133, it might be expected that the Thorolds would have had a strong association with the church, manifesting itself in close physical proximity between the capital messuage and the church. The aptness of the name Uphalle is evident in the putative site's relief, as it rises almost three metres across a distance of just over 100 metres from the church wall. The development of the site could have followed more than one trajectory. Either a new capital messuage was constructed by the first Turold in *c.*1069, when the knight's fee was created and this part of Castor was under development; or the family acquired an earlier Peterborough Abbey manorial complex.[17] Here, unlike the ecclesiastical manorial *curiae* in Castor and Elton, the Thorold complex lay in an area of the village that seems to have been firmly associated with the knight's fee, creating a distinctive zone within the settlement; yet, despite its undoubted closer proximity to peasant dwellings, both its elevated position and the bifurcating road around two sides of the site would have created a distinct sense of separation from the rest of the village.

However tentative these conclusions, it is important to attempt to locate the seigneurial elements of the Castor villagescape, especially as lords frequently controlled the development of the village core and disassociated themselves physically from the peasant tofts. In Elton there is also evidence to suggest that the residences of peasants of different status groups were grouped together. Surveys suggest that two sets of cotlands were laid out at Elton. The first group, for former demesne workers, was set out sometime before 1154 and by *c.*1161 was reconfigured,

---

16   *Tarrols* is marked on a copy of an Ordnance Survey map seen by the author that was annotated with old field-names by local farmers. I am grateful to Brian Goode for sharing this map with me.

17   I am grateful to Chris Dyer for discussing this with me.

Figure 3.4. The possible site of the Thorold manorial complex. Source: NRO Map 1964 (dated 1846); first edition Ordnance Survey map of Castor.

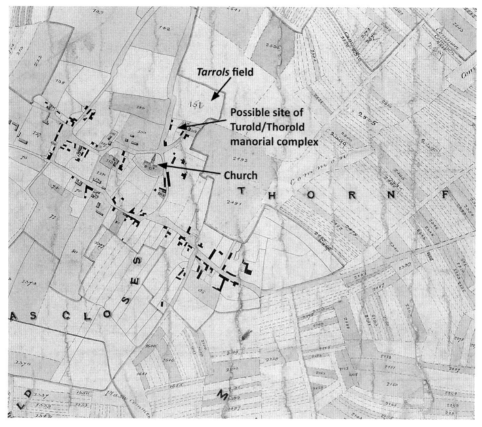

Figure 3.5. An extract from the Fitzwilliam estate map of Castor and Ailsworth, 1846, showing the possible site of the Thorold manorial complex. Source: NRO Map 1964.

Figure 3.6. Aerial photograph showing the possible site of the Thorold manorial complex.
Photo: Richard Jones.

creating fifteen new tofts from demesne land; and the second was laid out *c.*1218, when John de Aylington's new fee was created.[18] The latter group was situated in Over End (see Figure 3.1), close to the church. Although the evidence is incomplete, in both settlement cores there is reason to believe that the homesteads of at least some of the peasant population had been organised by status, and that people from within specific servile categories – such as the de Aylington cottars at Elton – lived in close proximity to one another. This 'zoning' would have created small areas that were recognisably associated with particular peasant groups.

Encountering the built environment: rural peasant dwellings

The previous section highlighted the separation between lordly and peasant spaces within the rural vill, and the documentary evidence suggests that, in Castor, the free tenants on the Thorold fee were clustered together, and that this was also the case with the Elton cottars. This has been noted by other scholars: Paul Harvey suggested that in late medieval Cuxham (Oxfordshire) there were clear indications that peasant tenements were predominantly arranged according to different status groups, with villein tenements to the south and cottagers to the north;[19] while Stephen Mileson noted a similar pattern in parts of south Oxfordshire, with villeins clustering in the centre of settlements and free tenants more likely to occupy peripheral locations.[20] As he notes, this must have had an impact on social relations within the rural village and, with this in mind, this section focuses on peasants' living arrangements at a more micro level, and considers how this contributes toward our understanding of peasant perceptions of their place within the rural settlement.

The documentary sources for Castor and Lakenheath, and to a lesser extent for Elton, reveal some important information regarding peasant messuages, tofts, crofts and cottages within the street plan of each respective vill, although the emerging picture is indistinct and difficult to interpret fully.[21] Peasant dwellings were frequently arranged along one or two main streets, with plot size differing according to personal status. It was commonly the case that cottagers had smaller plots, typically consisting of a dwelling and one or two acres for agricultural use, while customary tenants occupied a toft or messuage, which was usually a uniform size in each manor – albeit varying from place to place – in addition to their standard holding in the open fields.[22] The size of free tenants' messuage plots varied. This was partly because they were

18 *CMR III*, p. 260; Faith, *The English peasantry*, p. 65; *CMR I*, pp. 490–1.

19 P.D.A. Harvey, *A medieval Oxfordshire village: Cuxham, 1240 to 1400* (Oxford, 1965), p. 120.

20 Mileson, 'Openness and closure', pp. 14–16.

21 It should be noted that messuages and tofts were the plots within which peasants constructed their own buildings, including the main dwelling, alongside a range of other buildings, which might include a barn, a byre and a granary; C. Dyer, *Everyday life in medieval England* (1994, London, 2000), pp. 133–65. Dyer suggests that in the Midlands, a toft denotes a plot empty of buildings, and whilst the documentary evidence implies that may have been the case at Lakenheath, it was not the case at Castor: Dyer, *Everyday life*, p. 139.

22 Dyer, *Everyday life*, p. 134; Jones and Page, *Medieval villages*, p. 189.

legally able to alienate their holdings, which provided opportunities to subdivide tenements, whereas lords generally stipulated that the holdings of customary tenants should remain intact.[23]

It is difficult to determine very much regarding peasant dwellings or peasants' attitudes toward them from crown and manorial surveys. This is largely because lords were generally uninterested in them unless they were perceived to have been ruined by those holding them, in which case peasants were considered to be wasting and devaluing seigneurial assets. Thus, it has long been considered that there is more substantial archaeological than documentary evidence for peasant houses. Nevertheless, the archaeological evidence is not without its limitations: much potential archaeology is obscured by modern construction or ground disturbance, and the most useful data often emanate from deserted settlements.[24] Few historians have discussed peasant houses, largely because of the scant nature of the surviving evidence, which generally consists of sporadic references within court rolls.[25] Nevertheless, using data from those court rolls that recorded the size of peasant houses, historians have established that, although dwellings ranged in size from one to three bays, most were of three bays, giving dimensions of 18ft (6m) by 45ft (15m).[26]

In some instances the dimensions of the messuages are known. This does not necessarily mean that it is easy to discern the size of peasant homesteads, which were not always uniform. In 1321 Thomas at the Hithe of Lakenheath inherited a messuage of '*mollond* by rod' at the hithe.[27] In 1329 he confirmed the remaining term of a forty-year lease of a messuage at the hithe to Margaret Hottowe and her son John, following the death of her husband.[28] It was described as 'thirteen perches long (208ft or 63m), [and] 22ft (6.5m) … at the roadway, and 43ft (13m) wide at the other end' – or about one-fifth of an acre.[29] It is unclear if this transfer related to the messuage that Thomas had inherited in 1321, and therefore it is uncertain precisely what type of tenure this messuage was held under. Another messuage of *mollond*, surrendered in court in 1339 by Robert and Agnes Bolt to William Cranewys, was '3½ perches, 1½ft (57½ft or 17.5m) by 2¼ perches, 1½ft (37½ft or 11.5m)', suggesting that the messuage Thomas

---

23 Although this wasn't always the case, especially in eastern England and East Anglia: Dyer, *Everyday life*, p. 140; Schofield, *Peasant and community*, p. 40.

24 Hurst, 'Rural building', p. 898; M. Gardiner, 'Vernacular buildings and the development of the later medieval domestic plan in England', *Medieval Archaeology*, 44 (2000), pp. 159–79.

25 More plentiful data are found after *c.*1380 [C. Dyer, pers. comm.], but see R. Smith, 'Rooms, relatives and residential arrangements: some evidence in manor court rolls 1250–1500', *Medieval Village Research Group Annual Report*, 30 (1982), pp. 34–5; Dyer, *Everyday life*, pp. 133–65; C. Dyer, 'Building in earth in late-medieval England', *Vernacular Architecture*, 39 (2008), pp. 63–70.

26 R.K. Field, 'Worcestershire peasant buildings, household goods and farming equipment in the later Middle Ages', *Medieval Archaeology*, 9 (1965), p. 116; Dyer, 'Living in peasant houses', p. 19.

27 CUL EDC/7/16/2/1/7/ 5. Mollond (or *molland*) was land held by molmen (see above, p. 17), and therefore free from customary labour services.

28 He lived in the neighbouring plot in 1329.

29 CUL EDC/7/16/2/1/8/13; assuming a perch of sixteen feet (see fn. 30, p. 52 below), the messuage was 208 feet in length.

at the Hithe leased to the Hottowes was not *mollond*, or that *mollond* messuages were not a standard size.[30] There is some evidence that there were some standard-sized messuages at Lakenheath, however. In 1308 Ellis Stubbard surrendered 'a moiety of a messuage 24ft (7m) long and 30ft (9m) wide', which was granted to Henry Faukes; and in 1338 Geoffrey Richer transferred a customary messuage of the same dimensions to Gilbert Martin.[31] In 1314 John Aunger transferred a 'messuage *and plot* 60ft (18m) by 24ft (7m)' to Richard and Joan Baker via the manorial court.[32] If the entry relating to the Stubbard moiety gave the full messuage size, then the standard size for a customary messuage was 30ft (9m) by 24ft (7m).

Other messuages held by servile peasants were of differing sizes: Robert Bolt transferred to the Wright family a 'messuage with house thereon … measured by the long hundred … 134½ft by 84ft', suggesting a length of 154½ft (47m) and a plot size of about one-third of an acre; the reeve held a moiety of a messuage 120ft (36.5m) by 33ft (10m); and the Wyles' toft and messuage measured 64ft (19.5m) by 40ft (12m).[33] The regular messuages were all on the prior's manor, whereas those of differing sizes – Bolt, Piper and Wyles – were all originally part of Clare fee, suggesting that there may have been less standardisation there. The messuages at Castor were not of standard sizes, but this is to be expected, as the sample that survives all denote property held by free tenants. Transferring just part of his toft to his daughter, Robert, son of Ranulf recorded that 'it contains in length … 3 perches and 8ft (17m), each perch contains 16 feet'; the measurements for half of the neighbouring toft belonging to Matilda, daughter of Silvester, were 27ft (8.25m) long by 22ft (7m) wide, suggesting that both holdings were almost equal in length if the toft had been halved across its width.[34] William Paris' messuage was 44ft (13.5m) long by 25ft (7.5m) wide; and Roger Dionys' messuage measured 51ft (15.5m) wide as it abutted on the king's way and 50ft (15.25m) wide at its farthest end.[35] The only recorded detail of a peasant toft at Elton is found in an undated charter relating to a family that does not appear elsewhere in the documentary record. The messuage was 58ft (17.5m) by 44ft (13m) and probably related to a free tenement, but little more can be ascertained.[36]

Another important omission in the manorial documents is the configuration of the buildings within the messuage plots. Historians have long known that the detail contained within manorial surveys does not accurately convey peasant living arrangements within each respective messuage.[37] Although little information survives for Elton, one of the undated surveys unwittingly reveals the presence of additional peasant dwellings within the 'official' messuage plots when it confirms that only those living in the main dwelling

30   CUL EDC/7/16/2/1/13/4; this suggests that a Lakenheath perch was sixteen feet (5m). It is also a possibility that *mollond* messuages could be divided up.

31   CUL EDC/7/16/2/1/7/8; EDC/7/16/2/1/7/1.

32   CUL EDC/7/16/2/1/13/2.

33   CUL EDC/7/16/2/1/12/1; EDC/7/16/2/1/7/1; EDC/7/16/2/1/7/4; EDC/7/16/2/2/13/5.

34   NRO F(M) Charters 39 and 157.

35   NRO F(M) Charters 169 and 356.

36   TNA E 40/3286.

37   Dyer, *Everyday life*, p. 140.

owed services: 'each house, having a door open toward the street ... should provide a man for the *loveboon*'.[38] This indicates the presence of other individuals – perhaps extended family – living toward the rear of the messuage plot. It can be difficult to determine the frequency with which this happened, but the Elton survey suggests that it was the norm there. In Castor, while there is evidence that families provided for their relatives within the main messuage, it is important to note that free tenants, as they were elsewhere, were able to transfer divided portions of their homesteads legally. Robert, son of Ranulf, gave to his daughter Mabel 'one part of my toft in the vill of Castor with all buildings', presumably so that she could live separately; and in the late thirteenth century Ralph Brimbel of Castor granted his grandson Ralph, son of Simon de Sutton and Alice Brimbel, 'one part of my capital messuage which contains houses and walls and buildings, in width 20ft (6m) and 24 and 6ft (9m) in length'.[39]

Certainly, these freeholders must have felt more secure in their tenure than the unnamed servile tenants at Elton who occupied dwellings behind the main messuage, out of sight of the street. It also appears from the measurements of the free peasants' subdivided messuages in Castor that they had greater choice in where to situate their main dwelling within the plot. Unlike the many servile individuals hidden from view at Elton, free tenants at Castor could choose to live more publicly if they so desired. For example, although the transferred portion of the Brimbel holding (above) was only 600 square feet (54m²), it nevertheless contained a number of buildings, and Ralph Brimbel's grandson had the choice of either selecting an existing house on the plot or reconfiguring the space. Similarly, when in 1299 John and Matilda at the Cross sold part of their messuage in Castor to Reginald, son of Walter, it was transferred 'just as it lies, in length and breadth near the king's way, between our messuage on one side, and the messuage of Ralph Mason on the other'.[40] In other words, the messuage had been divided along its length, allowing the new owners to decide where they wished to site their house. In 1319 Geoffrey de Pickworth leased to Bernard and Beatrice Paston for their lives:

> his capital messuage in Castor ... surrounded by fences, walls and ditches. The said Geoffrey to have that house situated through the great gate of the said messuage on the east side and near the king's way on the north side occupying at his will while he lives with free ingress and egress ... without obstruction by the said Bernard and Beatrice ... Geoffrey also reserves half of any kind of fruit growing in the garden called *orchard* each year ... with free access to the same ... [Bernard and Beatrice] will keep the house, buildings, walls, hedges and ditches in good repair at their own expense. And they shall pay 32s. annually, and will find for the said Geoffrey every year for one month food and drink, a good chamber with decent furniture and necessaries for his groom and horse as is fitting ... .[41]

---

38 The *loveboon* or *lovebone* denotes additional labour services, usually associated with the harvest, or at peak times in the agricultural calendar. *CMR I*, pp. 487–90.

39 NRO F(M) Charters 31, 32 and 39.

40 NRO F(M) Charter 107.

41 NRO F(M) Charters 254 and 255.

In later documents Bernard Paston is also known as Bernard de Pickworth, and it seems very likely that he was related to Geoffrey. The charter provides a detailed outline of what must have been a sizeable and impressive messuage that was leased, along with substantial lands, in return for an annual payment and a maintenance agreement.[42] Despite relinquishing his capital – or main – messuage to the Paston family, Geoffrey retained the right to occupy a house 'through the great gate … near the king's way', suggesting that the capital messuage was deeper into the plot, and at a distance from the main thoroughfare.[43] It also implies that, as an older resident depending on the maintenance of his family for the rest of his life, some compromise was necessary in terms of his living arrangements: he could no longer occupy the principal house, and may also have had to make concessions regarding the amount of privacy he enjoyed, since his new dwelling was closer to the road.

The maintenance of older people and dependent relatives was also important to peasants in Lakenheath, and formal agreements frequently appear in the court rolls. Henry and Margaret Scarbot granted nineteen acres and one rod of land to their son Richard in return for him keeping them in clothes, food and lodgings for the rest of their lives.[44] In 1314 Laurence and Helewise Bully transferred a messuage and fourteen acres of land to Gilbert Martin, alias Scot. In return he was to provide a house for the Bullys for life within the messuage, and they were to have 'half of all easements and half the courtyard of the house, as far as the pond in the messuage'; Gilbert was to reside in the main dwelling, as was frequently the case in agreements of this nature.[45] It is unclear from the surviving rolls whether the Bullys had any family, but the inference was that they could no longer manage the holding themselves. Earlier, in 1310, Roger Martin leased a plot of his messuage, 28ft (8.5m) by 28ft, for a term of thirty years to his brother Gilbert, with a provision for him to build as he wished and recoup the value of the buildings as ordered by the court at the end of the term.[46] It seems that Gilbert had lived in a number of locations in the manor before he was able to find a permanent holding. Roger Criteman agreed to maintain Richard and Alice Criteman for life upon receiving their messuage in May 1326. Their relationship is uncertain, but it may have been the case that Roger was not due to inherit a substantial holding; throughout the extensive run of court rolls his only other major holding was a cottage acquired in February 1326, which he disposed of in 1334, possibly after the elder Critemans' death.[47] Others continued to relocate

---

42   Maintenance agreements related to the care of individuals (usually family members) who had legally transferred their messuage to someone younger. The maintenance agreements stipulated what, in return, the new tenants were obliged to provide to the grantor, usually for the term of their life.

43   Mileson notes that in south Oxfordshire tenements that did not open directly onto the road were more likely to belong to 'richer freemen (and sometimes villeins)': Mileson, 'Openness and closure', pp. 14 and 17.

44   CUL EDC/7/16/2/1/8/20.

45   CUL EDC/7/16/2/1/6/10; Smith, 'Rooms, relatives and residential arrangements', pp. 34–5.

46   CUL EDC/7/16/2/1/3; EDC/7/16/2/1/7/1.

47   CUL EDC/7/16/2/1/6/45; EDC/7/16/2/1/6/47; EDC/7/16/2/1/9/23.

within the manor as necessary: in 1311 Helewise Snype leased half a messuage and fifteen acres, the latter a standard villein holding, to William Whyt for the duration of her seven-year-old son Simon's minority with the proviso that the 'heir [should] be maintained in as good a state as now'. In 1320, when Simon would have been fifteen, William was granted a cottage and an acre of land; the court rolls record that in 1342 Simon Snype was holding his full fifteen acres.[48] It seems that, although villeins' heirs notionally inherited the main holding, others moved around the manor, building up a holding over a period of time.

The differences in the configuration of peasant messuages, and the ways in which free and servile peasants were able to transfer their messuages, had a major impact on those living in rural settlements. The more uniform villein plots on the prior's fee at Lakenheath reveal the underlying influence of stronger lordship there and give the impression of greater homogeneity and less independence. Conversely, the detailed information on several free tofts in Castor reveals the ease with which the offspring of free peasants there could establish a permanent homestead of their own within the vill, albeit – initially at least – on a smaller scale. This must have had a positive impact on their ability to establish themselves as independent residents. Compared with servile tenants, free peasants also had a greater choice about precisely where within their tofts they wished to situate their main dwelling, allowing them more freedom over how much of their lives were conducted in sight of the public gaze of their neighbours.[49] Conversely, those who were unable to create independent households, such as the children of servile peasants, must have found it more difficult to consolidate their position within the local community and, in early adulthood, were perhaps considered to be lower down the social hierarchy than their more established neighbours.

Delineating peasant space within the medieval manor

The enclosed and segregated seigneurial manorial complexes have already been considered, but how did peasants view their own messuages and extended holdings? In legal terms, the lord had rights over all unfree peasants' holdings, goods and chattels. In practice, many peasants created spaces that could be defined as their own. The limitations of the surviving documents at Elton and Castor mean that we have only fleeting views of peasant messuages there. Archaeological survey in Elton's Nether End outlined ditched medieval property boundaries,[50] which may have been created because of the poorly drained soils in the locality – although, as Astill notes,

---

48 CUL EDC/7/16/2/1/7/8; EDC/7/16/2/1/7/4; EDC/7/16/2/2/13/7.

49 In most instances, villeins needed the lord's permission to make changes to their dwelling. Contemporary court rolls contain many cases of peasants being amerced for dismantling or otherwise 'wasting' their tenements. In Lakenheath in 1337 John Rond was accused of taking away buildings from the tenement of Hugh Wylis, and the messuage was taken into the lord's hands: CUL EDC/7/16/2/1/12/1.

50 Kilby, 'A different world?' (2010a), p. 42; John Samuels Archaeological Consultants, *Proposed development at Duck Street, Elton, Cambridgeshire* (Newark, 1995), pp. 12–18.

bounded peasant tofts were typical in the late medieval period.[51] The ditch made by Ralph Barker 'in the king's highway at *benelondheuden*, 2 perches long (5m) and 2ft wide (0.5m)', was probably made for drainage purposes, as it lay adjacent to the fields.[52] In Castor there is only one mention of a peasant messuage being bounded by a ditch, in Geoffrey de Pickworth's detailed charter (above, p. 53). It is by no means certain whether Geoffrey's main dwelling 'surrounded by fences, walls and ditches' was typical of freeholders, or Castor residents in general, but it does suggest a thorough approach to the creation of a more private environment[53] – an impression strengthened by the fact that the de Pickworth tenement was not accessed directly from the road, but through a 'great gate' at the side of the messuage (above, p. 53).[54] Many of the Castor charters give clear measurements for the messuages and parts thereof, suggesting a desire for precision in the definition of boundaries.

Practical concerns would undoubtedly have played a part in determining arrangements for enclosing peasant messuages. Livestock was often kept within the yard, and it would have been unacceptable for peasants to allow their animals to wander through neighbouring plots, destroying garden produce.[55] The toft that William at the Cross granted to his brother Robert in Lakenheath specified that there was access for draught beasts and carts.[56] At Elton in 1300, the court records noted that Emma Miller 'knocked down a certain wall … by which … the beasts of the neighbours go in and destroy the hay and fodder of Henry Smith'.[57] Since the court convened after the 1299 harvest, the wall in this instance must have been that of a barn in which animal feed had been stored. In Lakenheath in 1328 Margaret Aunger was amerced for failing to repair an enclosure between her messuage and that of Richard Baker, whereby both her and other neighbours' livestock entered Baker's messuage, eating and trampling his vegetables.[58] Enclosing private peasant space beyond the village core was also important for the same reasons. Even in open-field villages there could be many enclosures, and much of the Castor landscape was enclosed, in part because of the greater quantity of free land held there. The abbot of Peterborough had a number of enclosed woods; in 1393 the wood called *estres*, measuring thirty acres, three and a half rods, ten perches and eight feet (12.5ha), was described as several and enclosed.[59] The same survey describes

---

51   G. Astill, 'Rural settlement: the toft and croft', in G. Astill and A. Grant (eds), *The countryside of medieval England* (1988, Oxford, 1994), p. 51.

52   *EMR*, p. 310.

53   Mileson has rightly suggested that the concept of privacy is inaccurate for this period, since there were 'gradation[s] of more and less restricted areas', including within peasant messuages: Mileson, 'Openness and closure', p. 8.

54   Mileson, 'Openness and closure', pp. 14 and 17.

55   W.O. Ault, *Open-field farming in medieval England: a study of village by-laws* (London, 1972), p. 50.

56   CUL EDC/7/16/2/1/8/12.

57   *EMR*, p. 92.

58   CUL EDC/7/16/2/1/8/23.

59   BL Cotton MS Nero C. vii/14. In this context, 'several' is a technical term, meaning private (and usually enclosed).

the wood called *le moore* as several, and in 1308 the accounts confirm that it was enclosed by a hedge of 228 perches (1,146m), alongside the wood of *rowessick*, which extended to 102 perches (513m).[60] A number of peasant woods are listed in the survey of 1215.[61] Although there is no indication of their enclosure, given the quantity of woodland in Castor and its multiple ownership it seems likely that some of these peasant spaces would have been bounded. A copy of an early thirteenth-century charter, in which Thorold granted his thicket to the abbot of Peterborough, describes it as lying 'between the abbot's wood called *w[u]lfhauue*, and the wood of Christiana Parys, and it extends in length as far as the wood of the aforesaid Christiana extends'.[62] The Thorold and Paris woods were of equal length and shared a common boundary, suggesting that some manner of formal boundary would have been necessary to distinguish between the two.

While there are few other references to walls and other physical boundaries, there are several mentions of metes and bounds. In Castor in 1296 Robert, son of Hugh at the Stile, granted to William and Sarah de Pickworth 'one part of my messuage with buildings and appurtenances, which contains in length 48 ft (14.5m) up to the boundary of my aforesaid tenement, just as it is shown by the metes and bounds fixed between us'. In 1331 Agnes le Driver used the same means to demarcate her messuage from that of her neighbour, Ralph Godwyn, 'just as the bounds placed there fully testify'.[63] Several Lakenheath peasants resorted to the manorial court in order to determine and affix bounds between themselves and their neighbours, for which they paid a fine, usually 6d.[64] There is generally little indication within the court rolls that there was any antagonism between neighbours prior to the confirmation and placement of bounds. Richard Scarbote was granted a messuage at the great hithe in June 1333, neighbouring John at the Hithe, and paid to have bounds placed between them in May 1334.[65] If there had been any dispute between the two families it was not recorded by the court. When there were problems, fixed bounds did not necessarily prevent trespassing: despite paying 6d. to have bounds placed in April 1314, Stephen Martin could not prevent John Waryn felling willows in his courtyard the following month.[66] Occasionally, however, conflict was apparent, and some peasants appeared to be more concerned than others over the establishment and maintenance of boundaries. In 1329 Simon Wyles was accused of carrying willows from John Horold's yard; two weeks later Simon suggested that, in fact, John had broken the boundary between them and appropriated part of his land in order to grow the willows. It seems that Simon felt it was his right to enter what was in fact his own land and take what was growing there.[67] In 1331 Horold

60   NRO F(M) Roll 233.

61   King, *Peterborough Abbey*, p. 173.

62   CUL PDC/MS 1, f. 208.

63   NRO F(M) Charters 98 and 331.

64   CUL EDC/7/16/2/1/9/31; EDC/7/16/2/1/8/13; EDC/7/16/2/1/6/6; EDC/7/16/2/1/7/8.

65   CUL EDC/7/16/2/1/9/21; EDC/7/16/2/1/9/31.

66   CUL EDC/7/16/2/1/6/6; EDC/7/16/2/1/7/5.

67   CUL EDC/7/16/2/1/8/15; EDC/7/16/2/1/9/7.

paid to have bounds placed between them. In 1325 he had paid for an inquisition 'to view hedges, ditches and boundaries, and [to] establish bounds' between himself and Richard in the Lane, and so it seems that he was more concerned than most about ensuring that his boundaries were clearly defined.[68] Simon Wyles had encountered previous issues with the borders of his property; in 1326 he presented that John Godhewe, the sergeant, trespassed by placing bounds between his and the prior's land without his consent. Evidently, witnessing the process, particularly the measuring, was essential.[69]

It may have been the case that some of these boundary issues were less about privacy and more about ensuring that neighbours did not encroach on peasant tofts by surreptitiously moving the boundary by a few inches. Nevertheless, there are other indications that peasants sought to create private spaces and that boundaries could occasionally be contentious. Breaching neighbours' boundaries was an offence frequently reported to the courts. Simon Kayston paid a fine of 6d. for breaking a boundary between himself and Reginald de Yarwell in Elton in 1300.[70] In Lakenheath in 1310 John Carpenter was found guilty of entering the property of William Smith and tearing down a palisade, allegedly to William's loss of 80d.; the jurors fined him 12d. and reduced the damages to a more realistic 6d.[71] Perhaps William's memory was long, as sixteen years later he returned the favour, pulling down John's father Hugh's fence, which he was subsequently ordered to raise.[72] In what was clearly a long-running neighbourly dispute, in 1332 Hugh Carpenter was found guilty of 'breaking down [Smith's] gates and entering his close *against his will*'.[73] Cases of trespass on what was ostensibly private property frequently mention loss or damage – fines for fishing in a leased fishery for which rent has been paid or for allowing crops to be destroyed by wandering livestock seem not unreasonable – but here nothing was reported as stolen, but the jurors clearly viewed this intrusion nevertheless as an offence worthy of punishment. Notwithstanding the damaged gates, William Smith evidently saw this as an intrusion into his private space, although if neighbourly relations had broken down perhaps Smith felt this more keenly than he might otherwise have done, particularly as the yard that Carpenter entered must have been seen at best as a transitional zone between public and private space.

There is also evidence of an emerging trend for peasants to associate themselves more keenly with their holdings at Lakenheath. Robert Gopayn's attempt to elicit a strong association between himself and his holding at *gopaynshithe* (see chapter five, p. 114) is mirrored by Thomas Douue's efforts to identify *douuezhithe* with his own family. He described to the court how Walter and Agnes Tailor came armed with sticks

---

68   CUL EDC/7/16/2/1/6/38.

69   CUL EDC/7/16/2/1/6/48.

70   *EMR*, p. 94.

71   CUL EDC/7/16/2/1/6/24.

72   CUL EDC/7/16/2/1/6/41; it is unclear what the palisade had been erected for, but John at the Hithe used one to enclose a garden that he had created by illegally appropriating a piece of common land twenty feet by four feet: CUL EDC/7/16/2/1/8/19.

73   CUL EDC/7/16/2/1/9/13; my emphasis.

to *douuezhithe*, entered the water and trampled the washing being done by Thomas' wife.[74] The use of these names, however narrowly confined that may have been, was undoubtedly designed to emphasise the strong sense of possession these peasants felt regarding their holdings. According to the families that held them, *gopaynshithe* and *douuezhithe* were private, and unsolicited use and entry could be viewed in a very dim light. To name a place is also to exert some form of control over it and, here, family names were used to emphasise control over what were clearly seen as private peasant spaces.[75] Irrespective of their legal rights regarding their holdings, documentary sources accentuate in myriad ways how strongly peasants identified with a sense of their own private space.

Off the beaten track: the hidden morphology of the rural landscape

There are indications that peasants considered their local environment very differently from the ways in which lords viewed the manorial landscape. In Lakenheath, where the lord was absent from his manor, the peasant community's knowledge of the surrounding area would clearly have been superior, and, although the secular lords of Castor and Elton were resident, they would have been unlikely to have involved themselves in the physical toil of agricultural labour, meaning that, again, local peasants would have had a more intimate connection with the local landscape. Much of what has been considered thus far relates to peasants' own homesteads or areas of the demesne leased for their personal use. Nevertheless, as we will see, there are hints that peasants treated what was ostensibly seigneurial space as if it were common land, albeit in a more clandestine manner. In considering subversive acts committed by peasants most historians focus on poaching, but it is possible to develop the idea further by considering other incidences of trespass in which peasants were found in unauthorised places.[76] Generally, trespass considered in this modern sense has been avoided by many historians, largely

---

74 TNA SC 2/203/95; it seems likely that these holdings were wharves; however, as it is clear that some tenants lived 'at the hithe', it is possible that they may have been tenements.

75 It is often considered that names are bestowed upon places by outsiders, but in these instances that is ambiguous at best, and it seems likely that these two families coined the names in question. Taylor suggests that to fully understand a place-name 'it is important to collect as much information as possible from both sides of this interaction', and this is a rare glimpse into medieval naming that offers some context: S. Taylor, 'Methodologies in place-name research', in C. Hough (ed.) with D. Izdebska, *The Oxford handbook of names and naming* (Oxford, 2018), p. 70.

76 See also Smith, 'Towards a social archaeology', p. 407; as a legal term, 'trespass' covered a wide range of wrongdoings (for a full outline see Kilby, 'Mapping peasant discontent', p. 69); here, the focus is on trespassing on 'private' property and, in some instances, behaving inappropriately in 'public' places, such as taking shortcuts or allowing livestock to wander.

because of the difficulty of determining whether it was accidental or deliberate.[77] In an open-field landscape, unintentional damage may frequently have been the norm, especially as many peasants owned livestock that must on occasion have wandered onto neighbouring property or fields, and because peasants themselves frequently needed access to parcels of land that might be at some distance from the settlement.[78] However, the documentary sources suggest that peasants did not always move through the landscape using the roads and paths sanctioned by lords or by the local community. For all the deliberate planning that may have occurred, there are many indications that, once out of sight of the settlement, some people created their own routes through the manorial landscape, and the evidence at Lakenheath suggests attempts by the court to stop this behaviour, rather than licensing it.

While it has been argued that elites regulated peasant movement around the manor[79] it has since been demonstrated that, although lords may have been desirous of this, the reality was somewhat different, and that peasants moved through the rural landscape crossing what were ostensibly both public and private spaces, often transgressively.[80] Archaeologists considering binary oppositions between lords and peasants tend to focus on settlements and the immediately surrounding road network. While these spaces were undoubtedly important, this approach fails to consider more ephemeral paths beyond the built environment that may have been significant to peasants but have left little archaeological trace.[81] Yet again, thorough analysis at Elton and Castor is problematic, thus limiting a truly comparative examination of the three vills. There are, nonetheless, fleeting indications that peasants may have moved through their environment using non-approved routes in both Elton and Castor. In the manorial works accounts of both manors there are references to 'stopping up roads' or paths in the corn. At Elton in 1297 twelve works were dedicated to this task between Michaelmas and Christmas.[82] In Castor in 1301 and 1308 thirty and thirteen works respectively

---

77   Schofield, *Peasant and community*, p. 161; Müller generally considers landed trespass as an act of peasant defiance against the lord: M. Müller, 'Peasant mentalities and cultures in two contrasting communities in the fourteenth century; Brandon in Suffolk and Badbury in Wiltshire', PhD thesis (University of Birmingham, 2001), p. 292; see also Kilby, 'Mapping peasant discontent', pp. 69–88.

78   Kilby, 'Mapping peasant discontent', p. 70.

79   R.A. Dodgshon, *The European past: social evolution and spatial order* (Basingstoke, 1987), pp. 167 and 192; T. Saunders, 'The feudal construction of space: power and domination in the nucleated village', in R. Samson (ed.), *The social archaeology of houses* (Edinburgh, 1990), pp. 183–6 and 193.

80   Müller, 'Peasant mentalities', p. 292; Kilby, 'Mapping peasant discontent', p. 74.

81   Smith, 'Houses and communities', p. 74 considers the more transient nature of paths in dispersed settlements.

82   *EMR*, p. 79.

were aimed at 'blocking up paths with thorns'.[83] It is unclear what these brief and oblique references mean. Might they refer to peasants taking short-cuts or wilfully damaging demesne crops? Or do they indicate that livestock or wild animals such as deer were making their way through demesne corn? Without court records for corresponding dates it is impossible to tell. However, the Lakenheath court rolls reveal that peasants were not averse to creating their own routes, even if that meant traversing demesne land – over both pasture and sown fields. Many Lakenheath peasants committed acts of trespass during the period under review. These ranged from livestock trampling crops and meadow, which may or may not have been accidental, to stealing and poaching under cover of night. Many of these presentments refer to what are described by the clerk of the court as 'illegal' paths that were created by peasants (Table 3.2). Closer examination reveals that such illegal paths were frequently made and used by the same group of peasants, and were often concentrated in specific areas of the manor.

Initial scrutiny of the records suggests only a small number of incidents related to the formation of illegal paths, but in fact many peasants were involved in these activities, several of whom committed a number of similar offences. Of the new paths that were made or reused, 69 per cent were created as cartways, so Table 3.2 also outlines the number of offences presented in court relating to trespass involving damage with carts. It is unclear how cartways were created and regulated, but it seems likely that there must have been peasant input at some level.[84] It would have been in the interests of the whole community to ensure that carts followed designated routes, rather than ranging over the landscape in a haphazard manner. Occasionally, documents shed light on paths that were authorised for use by carts, such as an early fifteenth-century charter relating to land in Hemsworth (Yorkshire) that expressly indicates that there was 'free ingress and egress for carts along a certain path' to and from the close that was being transferred.[85] Nevertheless, locals were perhaps less concerned with damaging demesne land. The details of these incidents make it clear that there were a number of habitual transgressors. Several peasants committed these offences more than once, but a small group repeatedly offended. Sixteen individuals, all but one male, were frequently charged by the court over a lengthy period of time with making or using an illegal path, or with causing damage with a cart (Table 3.3 and Figure 3.7). These individuals, although occasionally acting alone, were invariably amerced within a group.

The court rolls do not record all of the information historians would like to see, and these cases are no exception. Most incidences do not reveal the location of each misdemeanour, merely stating that it took place on demesne pasture, several

---

83 NRO F(M) 2388; NRO F(M) Roll 233; in some places, gaps opened in hedges allowed illicit access into fields – this was especially problematic at harvest time, as it was thought that this allowed thieves unseen access to the cut crop: Ault, *Open-field farming*, p. 37.

84 A dispute at Elton in 1300 between manorial officials and local peasants over the latter's access to a common droveway resulted in customary and free tenants uniting to assert their right of common access: *EMR*, pp. 94 and 98.

85 University of Nottingham Special Collections Ga 9239.

Table 3.2
Illegal paths and damage with carts in Lakenheath, 1310–41.

Illegal paths	
Total unique incidents	32
Total peasants involved	191
Total unique peasants involved	87
Damage with carts	
Total unique incidents	39
Total peasants involved	115
Total unique peasants involved	62

Source: CUL EDC/7/16/2/1.

Table 3.3
Groups of offenders – illegal paths and damage with carts, Lakenheath, 1310–36.

Group One: July 1310–June 1313	
Thomas le Baxtere	Adam Godyng
John Douue	Payn Dikeman
Richard Pistor	
Group Two: June 1321–November 1324	
Thomas le Baxtere	Adam Godyng
John Douue	Payn Dikeman
Group Three: March 1330–March 1331	
Richard Pistor	William at the Cross
John at the Hithe	Thomas Douue
Matthew Outlaw	Robert Pigge
Isabel Douue	William Dikeman
Laurence Criteman	Richard in the Lane
Group Four: May 1332–January 1334	
Richard Pistor	Thomas Douue
John at the Hithe	Robert Pigge
Matthew Outlaw	Isabel Douue
Laurence Criteman	Richard in the Lane
Group Five: October 1334–May 1336	
Richard Pistor	Matthew Outlaw
John at the Hithe	Robert Pigge

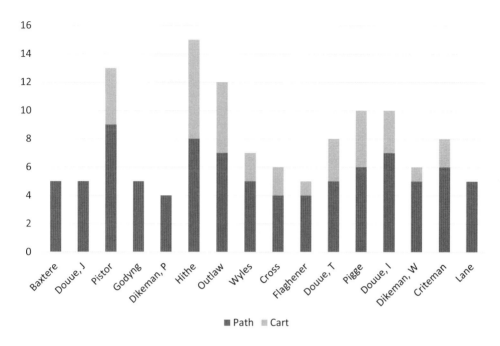

Figure 3.7. Habitual offenders – illegal paths and damage with carts, Lakenheath 1310–36.
Note: I have categorised an habitual offender as someone committing at least four offences, and usually as part of a group.

Table 3.4
Illegal paths at Lakenheath – known locations.

Location	Incidents
Wyteberwe	4
Le Wrongwong	2
Le Wonge	1
The mill	1
Dedchirl	1
Brendhall	1
The warren	1
Below the vill	1

Source: CUL EDC/7/16/2/1.

heath [86], or sown fields. In a small number of incidents, however, we learn the precise location, and these are detailed in Table 3.4. While it is difficult to be conclusive with such a small data set, there appears to be a distinct concentration of activity in *wyteberwe*. In one incident, the location is described as demesne several pasture, and so it is possible that at least some of the non-named locations where illegal paths were used, and which were described in similar terms, may well also have been in *wyteberwe*. Certainly, the new path there was distinct enough that in July 1310 it was used by foreign carters arriving from Ipswich.[87] Despite the imperfections of the data, there is further evidence that the illegal path was employed from this time, as a large group of Lakenheath peasants used it in addition to outsiders, through to October 1330.[88] In 1317 an ambiguous entry in the rolls gave a 'day … to the whole homage under penalty of 80d. to certify to the steward before next court concerning damage done at *whiteberewe* since it has been suggested that the damage amounts to 10 marks', but whether this related to the illegal path is unclear.[89] A similar pattern is apparent in the use of illegal paths at named locations at Walsham-le-Willows (Suffolk): time and again, the paths used were in the same places – usually *angerhalefield* and *oldtoft*. There are also indications that presentments relating to damage with carts in the same places referred to the illegal paths, as suggested within the Lakenheath rolls.[90]

Eleven peasants were involved in the earliest cases at *wyteberwe*, in July 1310. Of these, eight individuals were reported to the court for continuing to use the path. Might the continued use of 'illegal' paths by the same individuals indicate some form of licensing of the use of the new path?[91] Certainly, for incidents before 1324 a standard fine of 3d. was issued. After this point, however, although developments are difficult to pinpoint with precision because of the incomplete nature of the sources, the fines become variable. At around this time the prior appointed a new sergeant, John Godhewe, who replaced the long-serving Ralph de Dereham sometime in or before 1322. Godhewe lived locally and might have had an influence on manorial policy regarding illegal paths. Interestingly, Godhewe numbered among the earliest perpetrators, and was in court three times for using illegal paths, twice at *wyteberwe*: did he have a better

---

86 'Several' in this instance denotes a plot of land that was not part of the open-field system, and in many cases had been enclosed.

87 CUL EDC/7/16/2/1/3.

88 CUL EDC/7/16/2/1/3; EDC/7/16/2/1/6/1; EDC/7/16/2/1/8/5.

89 Here, the whole homage was required to report back to the next court regarding the damage caused at *wyteberwe*, the implication being that those responsible for reporting this offence to the court had in fact concealed it from the manorial officials. CUL EDC/7/16/2/1/6/16.

90 R. Lock, *The court rolls of Walsham le Willows 1303–50* (Woodbridge, 1998), pp. 184, 219, 247, 269, 275, 291 and 294; p. 221 details damage with carts in the lord's several pasture at *angerhale*, and p. 314 at *oldtoft*.

91 Schofield, *Peasant and community*, p. 43.

understanding of the rationale behind the use of the paths than his predecessor?[92] There is certainly no further record of his trespassing activity after his appointment as sergeant – possibly suggesting a form of licensing, and one that need not be paid by officials.

However, further evidence suggests that the peasants were probably not paying a licence fee to use their chosen paths. In 1328 the damage caused by carts in *le wrongwong* by foreign carters from Thetford was brought about 'through the agency of William and Robert at the Cross', the furlong also being damaged by locals: the implication is that either the pair made the Thetford carters aware of an unauthorised shortcut, or they were paid by the carters to allow them access to the shortcut.[93] In 1334 John at the Hithe denied outright that he had committed any offence. One of nine individuals accused, found guilty and amerced, he was one of four fined 6d., all of whom were habitual offenders.[94] If he had simply been paying for a licence there would have been no need to deny the transgression. In any event, on a number of occasions paths were created through sown demesne land and directly through the centre of the lord's fold, 'paths' unlikely in the extreme to have been licensed by manorial officials.[95] The reporting of trespass across *wyteberwe* appears to cease after 1330. Was this the point at which officials decided to sanction the 'new' path, given its frequent use by locals and non-residents alike?

A separate incident in July 1330 reveals how one peasant viewed trespassing on enclosed private land. William Dykeman allegedly seized John de Wangford's horse in *dykemannesdich* and took it to the prior's pound. He claimed that 'the said place is several land where no one should go … and the horse was in the said place to his [Dykeman's] damage'. De Wangford responded that 'in the said place there is a way for conveying with carts, horses and other beasts for the liberty belonging to his [de Wangford's] free tenement … and this can be proved' (in other words, that he had a right to use the path with his horse).[96] The outcome of the dispute is unknown, but it is apparent that these individuals understood the regulations governing movement through the manor using sanctioned routes, but nevertheless each interpreted matters concerning *dykemannesdich* differently. Interestingly, both men used illegal paths, William Dykeman habitually.[97] After 1334 the phrase 'illegal' path or way was no longer used by the scribe of the Lakenheath court. However, the number of incidents involving damage with carts remained high, frequently involving the same habitual offenders, suggesting a permanent change in the wording used to record these incidents ('trespass' being used more generally). A new steward – John

---

92   CUL EDC/7/16/2/1/3; EDC/7/16/2/1/6/1; EDC/7/16/2/1/6/4.

93   CUL EDC/7/16/2/1/8/20.

94   CUL EDC/7/16/2/1/9/23; the others were fined 3d. John at the Hithe was a regular offender.

95   CUL EDC/7/16/2/1/6/14; EDC/7/16/2/1/6/35; EDC/7/16/2/1/8/19; the two incidents involving paths through sown land were both recorded in May courts, suggesting that standing crops were destroyed, rather than stubble.

96   CUL EDC/7/16/2/1/8/9.

97   CUL EDC/7/16/2/1/8/11; EDC/7/16/2/1/8/19; EDC/7/16/2/1/8/20.

Table 3.5
Habitual offenders holding manorial offices in Lakenheath.

Name	Office	Date
Simon Wyles	Sergeant	1310
William at the Cross	Reeve	1312
William Flaghener	Reeve	September 1321 and 1328–9
Thomas le Baxtere	Sergeant	1325
Thomas Douue	Sergeant	1325 and 1328
Laurence Criteman	Sergeant	1325–6 and 1332
William Dykeman	Sergeant	1328
Matthew Outlawe	Reeve	October 1331

Source: CUL EDC/7/16/2/1.

de Aylsham – was appointed around October 1334, coterminous with this apparent change. Before then, it seems likely that at least some transgressions described as 'damage with carts' related to illegal paths, and assessing the habitual offenders bears this out.

Perhaps these frequent users of the paths were simply carters. In 1321 a rod of land had been illegally leased 'to all carters of the vill whereby they may have a path for carts', and the land was ordered to be seized.[98] Those habitually trespassing may have been carters, but they number among almost ninety individuals recorded as owning or having access to a cart in Lakenheath, the majority of whom committed relevant offences either infrequently or never, suggesting that most Lakenheath carters used authorised routeways. No one called Carter was ever linked to incidents relating to illegal cartways or damage with carts. Although these peasants' occupation cannot be categorically determined, half of the frequent trespassers acted intermittently as manorial officials in some capacity, mainly as reeve or sergeant (Table 3.5). Curiously, where data survive, the periods during which these peasants held office coincide precisely with periods when they committed no offences related to illegal paths, much in line with the way in which John Godhewe disappeared from the record concerning similar offences. This suggests that either these men stopped their illegal activity for the duration of their office; that a blind eye was turned; that a notional licence fee was 'allowed' by the lord during the period of their office-holding; or that manorial officials had greater freedom of movement within the manor. Nevertheless, in 1314 the court recorded that the reeve had been fined 15d. because foreign carts had damaged the demesne, suggesting that this was seen as problematic and unlikely to be licensed.[99] Whatever the rationale may have been, it is clear that a small number of Lakenheath peasants were creating their own paths, designed to suit their needs rather than the lord's, and which appear to have been used predominantly by this select group. In fact, if we assess court

---

98   CUL EDC/7/16/2/1/6/27.
99   CUL EDC/7/16/2/1/5.

presentments relating to individuals trespassing on private property in addition to those recording people using unauthorised paths, they reveal that these habitual transgressors were more likely to commit these acts generally, suggesting that they had a different attitude toward moving through the Lakenheath landscape than most. This may also have been connected with the fact that most of them were members of prominent Lakenheath families.

The evidence at Lakenheath seems to link the creation of illegal paths with damage caused by peasant carts. Furthermore, the Lakenheath rolls appear to lean toward attempts by the lord to retain control of routes through the manor, rather than licensing access to those willing to pay. This is further corroborated in the account rolls, which show several peasants paying for licences to create new rights of way for droving their sheep.[100] The reasonable conclusion must be that those creating and using illegal paths did so against the lord's wishes. Some peasants used such paths more routinely than others, suggesting that they may have been less concerned about complying with the lord's wishes than others. Overall, there is overwhelming evidence to suggest that, irrespective of lords' desire to create a regulated environment through which peasants travelled according to strict conventions, they created and used paths that suited them. The sources repeatedly show that peasants wandered, often at will, through private demesne areas and neighbouring peasant properties, regardless of whether they had secured permission. Some went further by committing acts of purpresture – that is, appropriating small areas of land in the fields or adjacent to their tofts and gardens, perhaps hoping that no one would notice. Here, the documentary sources reveal what cannot be discerned by simply assessing plans of reconstructed settlements: that peasants considered their local environment very differently from the way in which lords would like them to have done.

The manner in which the village was organised and regulated reveals peasants' perceptions of their place within rural society, within both the settlement and the wider landscape, in a number of ways. As demonstrated at Castor and Elton, the arrangement of the vill into distinct 'zones' not only effectively separated lords and peasants but also created areas that became associated with specific peasant groups, such as free tenants, villeins and cottars. At Castor, even though the manorial *curia* of the minor knight Thorold lay within the vill, it was in an elevated position and the road layout effectively separated the site from the adjacent peasant messuages. The areas in each village associated with different peasant groups would have been clearly apparent to both residents and visitors, and must have contributed toward peasants' sense of their own place within the settlement – reinforcing some bonds, weakening others. That young adults from free families could establish households more easily meant that they were often at an advantage in being able to attain a more secure position within the village social hierarchy much more rapidly than their servile counterparts and in greater numbers, since unfree peasants in all three vills were not legally permitted to subdivide their holdings. Compared with servile

---

100 CUL EDC/7/16/1/11; EDC/7/16/1/8; in Castor in 1310 John de Cambridge gave a capon for having a right of way across *langgemor* for his draught-beasts: NRO F(M) 2389.

individuals, free peasants also had greater choice in the arrangement of their messuages, and where within their tofts they might place their main dwelling. This also meant that they were better able to control access to the more private areas of their homestead, and to determine the 'façade', or outward show, that they wished to present to the village. There are indications that, across the spectrum, while people understood that some areas of their property – such as the courtyard – could be publicly accessed, when it suited them to think otherwise these notionally public areas could be considered to be private – during neighbourly disputes, for example. Conversely, it also suited some peasants to forget this when accessing the wider rural landscape, and it is clear that many people created and used paths that they knew to be illegal; it is tempting to see this as an expression of control over their course as they journeyed through the familiar terrain of their home landscape.

Chapter 4

The unseen landscape

This chapter continues to draw upon some of the themes explored in chapter three, which focused on socially constructed ideas of place associated with the organisation and arrangement of the rural village. Topographical family names coined by local residents, such as *atte grene* (at the green) or *atte brok* (at the brook), provide, like microtoponyms (see above, chapter one p. 5), a means of visualising aspects of the topography of the medieval settlement and its surrounding landscape.[1] At first glance, these names might be considered as a simple device to identify particular individuals, and perhaps to distinguish them from others by using the location of their dwelling as a referent. Indeed, that was almost certainly the reason behind the initial impetus for the creation of this sub-set of names. The range of peasant bynames within the three case-study settlements suggests, however, that topographical names in the thirteenth and fourteenth centuries were most commonly associated with servile individuals, especially in Elton and Lakenheath. This prompts us to ask about the bestowal of names: how were these names created, and what was the rationale for their selection? Were they passively accepted by those being named? These are not easy questions to answer. As this type of name essentially integrates both 'place' and 'identity', we must also ask why some servile identities were so closely associated with the rural landscape in this way. Issues concerning peasant status in this period have been prevalent in recent scholarship, and so the conclusions drawn here may have implications far beyond the local (see below, p. 202). With this in mind, the findings drawn from the three case-studies were therefore tested further using data from the Huntingdonshire hundred rolls. The results suggest that, in this part of England, topographical naming was a widespread phenomenon, and that settlements in which few free tenants bore topographical names were predominantly associated with highly manorialised areas of strong lordship.

In order to begin to understand why this sub-set of personal names was so closely associated with unfree individuals it is helpful to consider theoretical paradigms of landscape posited by cultural geographers, once again concentrating on socially produced conceptual understandings of landscape as well as the physical landscape itself. Since the later twentieth century cultural geographers have perceived the *idea* of landscape – its symbolic qualities – as 'a sophisticated cultural construction', and argue that any relevant cultural artefact can be examined to uncover the meanings that people

---

1   Name scholars usually use the term 'family name' to denote a second name or surname. The term 'byname' is used to describe a non-hereditary family name, and one individual might be associated with a number of bynames. Although peasant names were stabilising from the thirteenth century onward, the majority were instable until the mid-fourteenth century; therefore, I will use the term byname here throughout.

attach to places.[2] Thus, the landscape is visualised as a text, and the examples chosen by scholars to illustrate this include images, written and – in non-literate societies – oral texts. These texts could, of course, include topographical names – Simon Taylor expressly describes names as 'cultural artefacts'.[3] As Duncan and Duncan suggest, reassessing the landscape in this way allows us to envisage how, from a cultural perspective, landscapes are 'produced' and 'read' by different social groups. They demonstrate that, even in non-literate societies, the landscape, read as a text, can have multiple meanings. In Australian Aboriginal culture, for example, the physical landscape is significant in itself, but its importance is amplified because it is also considered to be the literal embodiment of mythic beings that are spiritually and culturally important.[4] While this dual reading was produced within one culture, it is possible for landscapes to hold multiple meanings, and for social groups to project meaning onto extralocal environments, or onto familiar, known places that they perceive as somehow distinct from the ones that they themselves inhabit. Kay Anderson demonstrates this in a study of early twentieth-century Chinatown in Vancouver, Canada. She describes Chinatown as an area classified by contemporary Westerners in negative terms, but exposes this view as a social construct that serves to highlight the interests and practices of Western society in this period and its means of expressing ideas of belonging and exclusion. Her suggestion that the 'conceptualisation of Chinatown [is] a white European idea' emphasises how one social group might 'read' a landscape; in this instance, a known, shared landscape has been dissected and labelled by one particular group.[5] This theoretical underpinning has interesting implications for the ways in which we might interpret historical landscapes. For John Wylie, these readings are frequently 'expressions of power', in which the narrative of one group dominates; and as Bronach Kane notes, in the medieval period, 'the spatial dynamics of everyday life were far from neutral'.[6] This chapter, then, reassesses topographical bynames from this perspective: as cultural artefacts that may offer us insights into the ways in which medieval peasants 'read' and interpreted the environment of the rural settlement.

---

2   D. Cosgrove and P. Jackson, 'New directions in cultural geography', *Area*, 19/2 (1987), p. 96; anthropologists see landscape in a broadly similar way, in that it is visible at two levels: the landscape as it is observed, and the cultural landscape 'produced through local practice': P.J. Stewart and A. Strathern, 'Introduction', in P.J. Stewart and A. Strathern (eds), *Landscape, memory and history: anthropological perspectives* (London, 2003), pp. 2–3.

3   Taylor, 'Methodologies', p. 70.

4   J. Duncan and N. Duncan, '(Re)reading the landscape', *Environment and Planning D: Society and Space*, 6 (1988), p. 122.

5   K.J. Anderson, 'The idea of Chinatown: the power of place and institutional practice in the making of a racial category', *Annals of the Association of American Geographers*, 77/4 (1987), p. 581.

6   J. Wylie, *Landscape* (Abingdon, 2007), p. 72; B.C. Kane, *Popular memory and gender in medieval England. Men, women and testimony in the church courts, c. 1200–1500* (Woodbridge, 2019), p. 213. Angèle Smith also argues that the ways in which landscape is represented often reinforce social class structure: A. Smith, 'Landscape representation: place and identity in nineteenth-century Ordnance Survey maps of Ireland', in P.J. Stewart and A. Strathern (eds), *Landscape, memory and history: anthropological perspectives* (London, 2003), p. 72.

Understanding topographical bynames

Bynames first appear within the documentary record in the early eleventh century.[7] A byname was a descriptive term that was used in order to distinguish between individuals bearing the same given name (such as Richard or John); this meant that, in the period before names became hereditary, one person might bear a number of bynames. In an evolutionary sense, the earliest peasant bynames tended to be either patronyms or related to occupation. In the mid-twelfth century nicknames began to emerge and, by the end of the century, bynames were a commonplace across all social strata, although they were not necessarily always used. Nevertheless, by the late thirteenth century the application of bynames within written documents had become routine.[8] In terms of heritability, aristocratic bynames became fixed by the early twelfth century, while the peasant equivalent began stabilising in the mid-thirteenth century, but not becoming immutable throughout England for another century.[9] The marked increase in the quantity and survival of written documents from the Conquest onward and the rise in recording peasant bynames supplied historians and linguists with large data sets, the analysis of which resulted in the classification of bynames into four categories – relational, occupational, locative and nicknames – although Cecily Clark warns that it is impossible to select just one category for many names and she criticises scholars who do not always offer a full range of semantic possibilities in defining names.[10] While these groups have remained more or less static, since the late 1960s it has been recognised that, within the locative group of names, toponyms and topographs are markedly different, and were generally

7   C. Clark, 'Onomastics', in N. Blake (ed.), *The Cambridge history of the English language, vol. 2: 1066–1476* (Cambridge, 1992), pp. 552 and 567; C. Clark, 'Socio-economic status and individual identity', in D. Postles (ed.), *Naming, society and regional identity: papers presented at a symposium jointly arranged by the Marc Fitch Fund and the Department of English Local History, University of Leicester* (Oxford, 2002), p. 109; P. Hanks and H. Parkin, 'Family names', in C. Hough (ed.) with D. Izdebska, *The Oxford handbook of names and naming* (Oxford, 2018), p. 216.

8   D. Postles, *Naming the people of England, c. 1100–1350* (Newcastle, 2006), p. 93; C. Clark, 'People and languages in post-Conquest Canterbury', in P. Jackson (ed.), *Words, names and history: selected writings of Cecily Clark* (Cambridge, 1995) p. 179; Clark, 'Onomastics', p. 556.

9   Postles, *Naming the people*, pp. 92 and 107; S. Carlsson, *Studies on Middle English local bynames in East Anglia* (Lund, 1989), p. 11, dates aristocratic hereditary naming to the late twelfth century; Hanks and Parkin, 'Family names', p. 217. Hereditary surnames of this period are known as family names.

10   C. Clark, 'Battle *c.* 1110: an anthroponymist looks at an Anglo-Norman new town', in P. Jackson (ed.), *Words, names and history: selected writings of Cecily Clark* (Cambridge, 1995), pp. 223–5; she is especially critical of P.H. Reaney and R.M. Wilson, *A dictionary of English surnames* (1995, Oxford, 2005). Relational names included patronymics, such as 'son of Richard'; locative names identified a person in relation to a place, such as toponyms, such as 'of Castor', and topographs, such as 'at the Brook'. Peter McClure suggests caution in categorising both toponymic and topographical names, since prepositional phrasing (*atte, de* and so on) were not always recorded by the scribe, especially in southern England: P. McClure, 'The interpretation of Middle English nicknames', *Nomina*, 5 (1981), p. 96; Clark, 'Socio-economic status', p. 102.

associated with people of different status.[11] As this forms an important part of this study, a brief review of the historiography of this particular aspect of the study of bynames is necessary.

In East Anglia Richard McKinley found that better-off peasants bore topographical bynames, but his source material – the subsidy rolls for 1327 and 1329–30 – is especially problematic, given that many people were omitted, including paupers and those with few surplus goods to tax; that tax evasion was a major issue; and that individual status was not recorded within these documents.[12] In a number of later studies it has been identified that servile peasants were much more likely to bear topographical bynames than their free neighbours. Assessing the hundred rolls for Oxfordshire, McKinley noted that the unfree here were twice as likely to be associated with topographs than freemen.[13] He offered little in the way of thorough examination of this trend, despite suggesting that serfdom and topographs were an obvious pairing. Nevertheless, he called for a county-by-county analysis of this phenomenon. The production of a series of county surname histories has stalled, but those that were published considered topographical names. Reviewing the names of Sussex, McKinley noted what he believed to be the highest incidence of medieval topographical bynames that he had then come across and recognised that they were principally connected with the unfree peasantry.[14] A similar phenomenon was observed by David Postles in Leicestershire and Rutland, where, again using lay subsidy rolls (and noting their limitations), he concluded that there was a correlation between topographs and the unfree. He also noted a link between dispersed settlement and a greater incidence of topographical names.[15] Some exceptions should, however, be noted. In northern England topographical names were sometimes associated with peasants from what Postles describes as the 'middling social level', as they were royal jurors of higher peasant status; and, in the urban environment, there was a wider application of topographical names beyond the confines of the extreme lower orders.[16] Nevertheless, in many places in central and southern England the general trend appears to show that topographical bynames were predominantly associated with servile peasants. If, as Taylor asserts (above, p. 70), landscape names are cultural artefacts, then we must consider the possibility that these differences in naming practices may reveal aspects of peasants' cultural 'reading' of the landscape of rural settlements.

---

11   E. Stone (ed.), *Oxfordshire hundred rolls of 1279: the hundred of Bampton* (Oxford 1968), p. 14.

12   R. McKinley, *Norfolk and Suffolk surnames in the middle ages* (London, 1975), pp. 142–3.

13   R. McKinley, *The surnames of Oxfordshire* (Oxford, 1977), p. 43.

14   McKinley, *Surnames of Sussex*, p. 12; Cecily Clark, referring to topographical bynames, also observed that 'Middle English byname styles were to some extent socially stratified': Clark, 'Socio-economic status', p. 101.

15   D. Postles, *The surnames of Leicestershire and Rutland* (Oxford, 1998), pp. 213 and 217–19; see also D. Postles, *The north through its names: phenomenology of medieval and early modern northern England* (Oxford, 2007), p. 183.

16   Postles, *North through its names*, pp. 182–3; although in naming patterns in London Clark notes that topographical names are rare: Clark, 'Socio-economic status', p. 112.

Knowing your place: contrasting peasant landscapes within medieval manors?

The extant manorial documents and charters of Elton, Castor and Lakenheath contain many peasant bynames. In Elton 938 names are recorded in the manorial court and account rolls between 1279 and 1351, representing 324 distinct names; for Castor, there are 705 names in manorial documents and charters between 1215 and 1348, of which 357 are different; and in Lakenheath 1,702 names survive for the period 1273 and 1348, representing 695 distinct names. This corpus of names is undoubtedly statistically significant for this period. The quantity of locative names, with which this chapter is concerned, is outlined in Table 4.1. As already noted, it is not always possible to assign each name to one category, but the proportion of ambiguous names is similar in each manor: 5 per cent in Elton, 7 per cent in Castor and 4 per cent in Lakenheath. The topographical bynames recorded for each of the three settlements are given in Table 4.2. It is extremely likely that there are fewer names of this type in Castor because of the lack of survival of the most useful material for gathering a cross section of names – court rolls and surveys. While Castor's impressive collection of charters contains many names, they are predominantly associated with free peasants, a group that is generally less likely to bear topographical bynames.

Looking through many of the names in Table 4.2, even without the aid of a map, we can quickly begin to build up a mental picture of village topography and, in some instances, the locations of some peasants' messuages.[17] Some of the names are especially useful – it is not difficult to locate where the *atte chirchgate* family lived in Lakenheath, for example. For some names, even where there is a little more ambiguity – as in *atte mere* or *at the wych* – some sensible assumptions can be made. For example, in Lakenheath, which contained at least twelve named meres in the medieval period, it seems likely that the village dwellings either extended as far as one of the meres or that there was a particularly large mere close to the settlement, so that a name that we might perceive as a somewhat vague topographical description was probably very clear to thirteenth- and fourteenth-century locals. Similarly, there may have been few ash and service trees, and so *atte ash* or *atte cirue* might have indicated what were once very specific places. Other names, however, appear to be less useful. At first glance, the various brook topographs in Elton seem appropriate enough, until we discover that there were at least four streams labelled as brooks (as opposed to other types of stream) in Elton in this period.[18] Even if we look for the most obvious brook, the one closest to the settlement, the name would only have been unambiguous either if there were only one dwelling by the brook or, if there were more, the given names of the brook-dwellers were varied.

We have the same issue in Lakenheath with the group of names called *atte hithe* – at the landing place.[19] Again, it might be the case that there was one obvious hithe

---

17   Although, as Clark argues, these names often indicate the location of a dwelling at some point in the recent past, rather than at the point these names were written down, as they may have become heritable and the current name-bearer may live elsewhere: Clark, 'Socio-economic status', p. 116.

18   *lytlebroc, thwertbroke, arnewessebrok, billingbrok*.

19   *EPNE*, vol. 1, p. 278: this name is derived from OE *hȳð*, 'a port, a haven, a landing place on a river-bank'.

Table 4.1
Locative names: toponyms and topographs at Elton, Castor and Lakenheath.

Category	Elton		Castor		Lakenheath	
	Total names	*Distinct names*	*Total names*	*Distinct names*	*Total names*	*Distinct names*
Toponyms	164	84	161	80	273	166
Topographs	98	28	52	26	136	43
Total	262	112	213	106	409	209

Source: Elton: *EMR*, pp. 2–395; *CMR I*, pp. 487–91; various charters, for which see bibliography under TNA; Castor: Soc. Antiq. MS 60/ff. 186–187v.; Soc. Antiq. MS 38; NRO F(M) Charters 1–397; F(M) 2388 and 2389; CUL PDC/MS 1; PDC/MS 6, f. ix; TNA E 179/155/31/m. 42; BL Cotton MS Vespasian E xxii; *CN*; King, *Peterborough Abbey*, pp. 172–4; Lakenheath: CRL MS 67; CUL EDC/7/16/1; EDC/7/16/2; EDR/G3/28/Liber M; TNA E 179/180/12.

Table 4.2
Distinct topographs at Elton, Castor and Lakenheath.

Castor	Elton	Lakenheath
Aboveton	Abovebrook	Ash, at the
Cross, at the	Brook, at the, by the	Boveton, of
Garit, of the	Bury, at the	Church, at the
Hall, of the	Church, at the	Churchgate, at the
Hill, on the	Cross, at the	Cottage, at the
Lane, at the top of the	*Enthebourgh*	Courtyard, at the
Nook, in the	Gate, at the	Cross, at the
Oven, at the	Green, at the	Enclosure, at the
Stile, at the	Hall, at the	Frith, of the
	Lane, in the	Gap, at the
	Nook, in the	Green, at the
	Oven, at the	Hithe, at the
	Pool, at the	Lane, in the
	Riverbank, at the	Mere, at the
	Spring, at	Newhall, at the
	Vill, without the	Path, at the
	Water, at the	Quarry, pit, at the
	Wych, at the	Service tree, at the
	Wynd, at the	Shop, at the
		Slope, at the
		Spring, at the
		Townsend, at the

Notes: Elton and Lakenheath: at the Spring, from atte Well, could be 'by the stream'. Lakenheath: at the Slope, from atte Hilde, could be 'by the elder tree'. Elton: atte Wynd, 'dweller by the winding path or ascent', atte Wych, 'dweller by the wych-elm'. Lakenheath: the original forms of the following names are: at the Cottage – atte Boure; at the Enclosure – atte Hays; at the Quarry or Pit – atte Delf; at the Path – atte Went; at the Service Tree – atte Cirue; at the Shop – atte Choppe.

in Lakenheath or, if that was not the case, that there were dwellings at only one of the hithes. In fact, there were at least seven medieval hithes there, of which at least two were adjacent to peasant homesteads, while a further two – *gopaynshithe* and *douueshithe* – were strongly associated with peasant families.[20] Alongside several other families, the *atte hithe* family lived at the Great Hithe. At *brodehethe* two cottages are recorded in the court roll for 1316, alongside messuages in 1325 and 1336, clearly indicating a place where local peasants lived.[21] Of all Lakenheath's hithes, the Great Hithe – evidently a significant landing place – was perhaps the first to become built up, and early residents were named *atte hithe*.[22] Given the relative fluidity of bynames in this period, as the population at the hithe increased we might expect that *atte hithe* was one of a range of bynames identifying its residents, but the records show that this was not the case. Even after Isabel *atte hithe* married her second husband, John Warin, she was still distinguished by the name *atte hithe*. Here, even after these names had outlived any real utility, they continued to be employed.

A similar argument can be advanced regarding the ubiquitous name *in the lane*, found in each of the three vills here and in widespread use across the country. Attempting to map *lane* names is fraught with difficulty. Again, Lakenheath can be used to demonstrate the problem. Within the thirteenth- and fourteenth-century records there are at least six named lanes, excluding both the king's highway and various named paths.[23] By at least the early fourteenth century all of these lanes were residential.[24] As with the *hithe* names, perhaps the difficulty arises only as a result of the expansion of the settlement – there may have been a time when there was only one lane, or perhaps only one major lane in Lakenheath. Lakenheath's named lanes do not appear in the documentary record until 1320, but this surely provides us with only a *terminus ante quem*. Perhaps at the point at which topographs began to be used there were fewer people living in the lane, or perhaps there was a dominant family with which the name became associated. But again, even if this was the case, as the population expanded up to the end of the thirteenth century the name *in the lane* would have become rapidly less useful in identifying discrete individuals living in more densely inhabited lanes.

Richard Coates thus describes settlement names as 'senseless', as their original meaning becomes obsolete reasonably swiftly, following which they are merely labels.[25] Similarly, Clark suggests that this was the case with family names, especially in instances where the original context of the name had become obsolete. However, we must remember that in this period it was not unusual for peasants to be

---

20 These were *stafishithe, loweheth, kyngeshethe, gopaynshithe, douueshithe, the great hithe* and *brodehethe*.

21 CUL EDC/7/16/2/1/7/2; EDC/7/16/2/1/6/38; EDC/7/16/2/1/7/43.

22 Perhaps this was the hithe from which Lakenheath derived its name.

23 The lanes are *curteslane, gropecunte lane, gygouneslane, maudelines lane, musepese lane* and *pynnerslane*.

24 CUL   EDC/7/16/2/7/4;   EDC/7/16/2/1/9/12;   EDC/7/16/2/1/9/32;   EDC/7/16/2/1/9/39; EDC/7/16/2/1/9/43; EDC/7/16/2/2/13/5.

25 Coates, 'Place-names and linguistics', pp. 148–9.

known by multiple bynames, affording them a range of potential identities.[26] The key point here is that, if bynames were being used as a means of identifying a particular individual, then the obvious solution to the *lane* dilemma would have been for the extended *in the lane* family to adopt (or have been given) an alternative byname, an alias, which might have allowed for more accurate identification given the high number of peasants living in Lakenheath's numerous lanes. However, in Lakenheath this did not happen.

Superficially, there are similar issues with certain peasant toponyms. Prominent (and usually free) individuals tended to be known by local toponyms, such as John de Aylington (the ME form of Elton). While at first sight this may not appear to help in identifying him as an individual, to a certain extent his name makes sense: as a free peasant he had the right to use institutions such as the common law courts, thus creating a dense network of contacts *outside* Elton. Since there were relatively few freemen in Elton, he would have been one of just a handful of men using this name as a form of identification outside the boundaries of Elton parish, and as his network grew beyond Elton this name would have been a sensible and obvious means of recognising him. Nevertheless, he continued to be associated with this name *within* Elton, in the same way as many other leading freemen in other villages, and within a relatively short period toponyms of this type became important as indicators of status. Toponyms used in this context, and applied within the vill to which they related, thus subtly conveyed additional meaning beyond an association with a particular settlement. Naturally, John de Aylington's neighbours knew precisely where he lived, but, more importantly, his name implied an elevated status, and they would undoubtedly have understood the subtext. Very early toponyms were usually associated with elites and their estates, and so it seems reasonable to assume that status-seeking free peasants might also adopt this practice.[27] This is exemplified in Castor and Ailsworth, vills that were principally populated by free peasants, and where numerous individuals were known as 'de Castor' and 'de Ailsworth', alongside others who habitually elected to add the name of the vill as a byname, such as Roger Budde de Castor or Beatrice Butler de Castor. Here, so many individuals were identified in this way that these names cannot realistically have been used solely as a means of recognising particular people, but were used to imply status. It also seems likely that toponyms provided an understated way for free tenants to demonstrate that they were part of an extensive network that extended far beyond the confines of the vill, and that their horizons were far-reaching.

The topographical bynames contained within the documentary sources of Elton and Lakenheath show, much as McKinley and Postles found elsewhere, a strong correlation between this name type and servile status, as outlined in Table 4.3. Despite the difficulties inherent in ascertaining status within manorial and local documents, it

---

26   Clark, 'Socio-economic status', p. 103; one Lakenheath woman, Katherine Gere, was known by at least four bynames.

27   E. Bramwell, 'Names in the United Kingdom', as part of E.D. Lawson, 'Personal naming systems', in C. Hough (ed.) with D. Izdebska, *The Oxford handbook of names and naming* (Oxford, 2018), p. 186.

Table 4.3
Topographical bynames and peasant status – Elton, Castor and Lakenheath.

Elton		Lakenheath	
Name	*Status*	*Name*	*Status*
Robert at the Cross	Villein	Clement at Townsend	Villein
Alexander at the Cross	Villein	William Cote	Neif[1]
John at the Gate	Villein	John at the Cross	Neif
Richard at the Oven	Villein	Robert at the Cross	Neif
John at the Water	Villein	Katherine at the Cross	Neif
Andrew ate Brok	Villein	Thomas at the Hythe	Neif
Philip ate Lane	Villein	Richard (1) in the Lane	Neif
Alexander in the Lane	Villein	Richard (2) in the Lane	Neif
Henry Bovebroc	Villein	John Mor	Neif
John Bovebroc	Villein	Gilbert Mor	Neif
Geoffrey in the Nook	Villein	Agnes at the Cross	Servile[2]
Sarah in the Nook	Cottar	Isabel at the Cross	Servile
Agnes at the Church	Cottar	Ellen at the Cross	Servile
Geoffrey at the Spring	Cottar	John in the Lane	Servile
Alice at the Cross	Cottar	Roger in the Lane	Servile
John at the Green	Cottar	William at the Ash	Servile
Richard at the Water	Cottar	William at the Cross	Servile
Robert at the Water	Cottar	John at the Churchgate	Intermediate
Richard at the Well	Cottar	John at the Hythe	Intermediate
		Isabel at the Hythe	Free
Castor			
Name	*Status*	*Name*	*Status*
Ralph (1) Aboueton	Free	William Aboueton	Free
Ralph (2) Aboueton	Free	Ralph atte Stile[3]	Free

Source: EMR; *RH II*; CUL EDC/7/16/2/1; King, *Peterborough Abbey*, pp. 107–8; NRO F(M) Charter 293.

Notes:

1. 'Neif' was a term used for those born into bondage, a hereditary serf.

2. 'Servile' is indicated where indirect reference to status is noted in the records

3. Either 'stile' or, more probably here, 'steep ascent'.

Table 4.4
Topographical bynames and uncertain status – Castor.

Name	Evidence	Name	Evidence
Reginald de la Garit	Holds by charter	Thomas at the Cross	Holds by charter
Robert Garit	Holds by charter	John ate Style	Holds by charter
John at the Cross	Witness of charters alongside confirmed freemen	Robert atte Stok[1]	Mentioned in charter
Reginald at the Oven	Mentioned in charter	Ascelin at the Stile	Mentioned in charter
Thomas of the Hall	Witness of charter	Ascelin at the Stocks[2]	Mentioned in charter

Notes:

1. Either 'by the stump' or 'by a footbridge'.

2. *ad stipitem*; there is a Stocks Hill in modern Castor.

is clear that in Elton all of the residents bearing topographical bynames – a total of nineteen individuals – were servile.[28] This pattern is repeated in Lakenheath, with only one instance of a known free peasant having a topographical byname. At Castor the opposite is true, with a small group of individuals bearing topographical bynames. Of these, four were unequivocally free.[29] A further group, detailed in Table 4.4, is harder to define. Of these, John at the Cross is very likely to have been personally free; he appears as a witness in a charter in which all of the additional witnesses were freemen.[30] Several other men holding land by charter – legally, a right held only by free individuals – bore topographical bynames. But, given the complexities of Castor landholding, and the fact that *Carte Nativorum* shows that several Peterborough Abbey villein tenants held land by charter, this is an unsafe conclusion to draw from such insubstantial evidence. At Elton Henry Godsweyn, identified as a villein in the hundred rolls, transferred land by charter.[31] Nevertheless, it is clear that, in contrast to Elton and Lakenheath, there was undoubtedly a quantity of freemen who were associated with topographical bynames at Castor. Unlike Castor, Elton and Lakenheath were principally populated by servile peasants and Elton in particular was dominated by strong lordship. The fact that – in contrast to Elton and Lakenheath, both dominated by strong lordship – there were free individuals associated with topographical bynames at Castor – characterised by weaker lordship – is striking.

Given the patterns that emerge in the data from Elton, Lakenheath and Castor, it seemed appropriate to test these data further against a larger dataset. Given the twin problems of survival and the inconsistencies in data recording within medieval documents, this is not easy to find. Nevertheless, surveys – both crown and manorial – are the most appropriate materials to consider, as they generally detail individual tenants alongside their status. The 1279 hundred rolls is a reasonably dependable crown source, although only approximately one-tenth of the original survey survives. Little remains for either Northamptonshire or Suffolk, but fortunately most of Huntingdonshire survives in great detail, wherein attempts at uniformity can be detected and, more importantly, the personal status of each individual recorded was noted. Huntingdonshire is also generally regarded as a county characterised by strong lordship, with high numbers of servile peasants burdened with abundant labour services. Crucially, if status holds the key to understanding the eventual meaning of topographical bynames, we would expect to see fewer free tenant topographs in places exhibiting strong lordship, such as Elton and Lakenheath; and, conversely, topographs distributed more evenly across peasant status groups in places where weaker lordship prevailed, as was the case at Castor. This premise is tested below using Huntingdonshire as a benchmark and beginning with Norman Cross hundred.

---

28   Also noted in Kilby, 'A different world?' (2010b), p. 74.
29   Although the Abouetons were all from the same family.
30   NRO F(M) Charter 87.
31   TNA E 40/1271.

Table 4.5
Free tenants with topographical bynames – Norman Cross hundred.

Free tenant	Vill
Walter at the Fen	Conington
William at the Grange	Conington
Adelina Abouetoun	Glatton
Robert Wythoutetoun	Glatton
Mariota of the Hall	Glatton
Mariota of the Hall	Holme
Hugh at the Top of the Vill	Sibberston
Roger at the River[1]	Stanground and Farcet

Source: RH II

Note:

1. This name is listed as 'ad Gavam'. I am grateful to Dr Jacques Beauroy for advising that this is an Old French word, used in the Béarn vernacular.

Mapping topographical bynames: Norman Cross hundred

Norman Cross consisted of twenty-seven vills within which a total of 1,493 people were listed as landholders in the hundred rolls.[32] Within this dataset there are seventy-two individuals who each bore one of thirty distinct topographs, eight of whom were free tenants (Table 4.5).[33] These names are particularly interesting, as all but two reference the built environment, specifically in the form of the vill itself or buildings closely associated with elites. Walter at the Fen, who held land in Conington, also appears to be listed as a cottar in the same vill.[34] If this is the same individual, which seems likely, then this may help to explain his topographical byname. Since Glatton shares a parish boundary with Holme, it is probable that the Mariotas of the Hall who are listed as a tenant in each manor are one and the same person. The names *of the hall* and *of the grange* are likely to be occupational rather than locative, indicating someone who worked in the hall or the grange. Setting aside those topographical names in Norman Cross that seem likely to denote occupation, all but one of the remaining names reference the vill. These names place their bearers outside the heart of the settlement. They are above the vill, outside it or at its extreme end, engendering

---

32 Luddington and Wansford (Northamptonshire) are included in Norman Cross, suggesting that a small portion of each lay within this hundred. Morborne, which was in Norman Cross, appears not to have been surveyed. The same caveats apply here regarding the possibility of duplicated individuals and those that were omitted because they were landless or held leasehold land.

33 Not all the Elton topographs listed in Table 3.1 feature here, as these data were drawn from a wider range of source material.

34 The byname *ad Moram* could mean moor, marsh or fen. Here, fen is more likely, as the local place-name is Conington Fen; A. Mawer and F.M. Stenton, *The place-names of Bedfordshire and Huntingdonshire* (Cambridge, 1926), p. 183.

a distinct sense of separation from those more closely associated with it and its infrastructure of lanes, bridges, nooks, gardens and so on. Is it a coincidence that this type of topography should be associated with free peasants? Free tenants living in villages frequently lived away from the heart of the settlement, and so perhaps we should not be surprised that they became associated with names that emphasised a certain distance from the settlement core.[35]

Nevertheless, the perceived separation from central village life as articulated through these names is worth considering further, as it suggests that notions of belonging may have been expressed by a small group of free peasants within their local environment. Assessed from the perspective of a cultural geographer, these names have particular significance, because as cultural constructs they offer insights into the socially produced landscape of the medieval village. Even if, as outlined above (p. 69), these names were initially coined specifically to identify an individual by their place of abode, the meanings associated with names are not always static and new social contexts often give rise to new connotations.[36] Returning to the development of toponyms – from originally signifying the place from where someone hailed to eventually also representing a marker of status – the idea that names could be useful as transmitters of cultural concepts such as status must have already been prevalent within rural society in this period.[37] Given that all but one of the topographical names associated with free peasants in the hundred comprised a sub-set that effectively separated them from the servile bearers of other topographical names in Norman Cross, it seems unlikely that the connection between this name type and status would have gone unnoticed. If this reading is correct then, by extension, the places distinguished by these names could no longer have been seen as neutral, especially by free individuals. Kane's assertion that 'spaces and places assumed ideological roles in facilitating social hierachies' supports this view.[38] The idea of socially produced landscape is echoed in the work of sociologists: according to Lefebvre, space seen through this prism is necessarily an instrument of domination and control.[39] This seems especially significant given the apparent tendency for the association of most topographical bynames with servile peasants in the late medieval period on the one hand and the link between free tenants with names that effectively separated them from the settlement on the other.

---

35 Mileson, 'Openness and closure', p. 14; in some deserted medieval settlements this name is associated with elevated terrain (C. Dyer pers. comm.).

36 B. Rymes, 'Naming as social practice: the case of Little Creeper from Diamond Street', *Language in Society*, 25/2 (1996), p. 242.

37 This is also true, of course, of nicknames.

38 Kane, *Popular memory*, p. 213.

39 H. Lefebvre, *The production of space*, trans. D. Nicholson-Smith (1974, Oxford, 1991), p. 26; see also A. Buttimer, 'Social space and the planning of residential areas', in A. Buttimer and D. Seamon (eds), *The human experience of space and place* (London, 1980), p. 27, who suggests that socially produced places are always socially significant.

Aboveton: from indicator of place to socially constructed landscape

In order to establish how useful these names might be in revealing contemporary socio-cultural mentalities, we must examine this name type in the context of personal identity, and how naming practices were formulated in the thirteenth and fourteenth centuries: specifically, how far did individuals identify with the names bestowed upon them? This sub-set of names can be examined more closely using the name Aboveton, which was commonly associated with free individuals in Huntingdonshire, and also in Castor. Several Castor charters feature a family bearing the name Aboveton.[40] Ralph Aboveton is either a grantor or grantee of land in some fourteen charters[41] and a witness in a further thirty-six.[42] He also features in a further two in *Carte Nativorum*. Of the fourteen charters where he features as grantor or grantee, ten were produced by Eustace *scriptor*, and in each of these documents Ralph is described as *Radulphus filius Roberti a Boueton de Castre*.[43] So, perhaps this better reflects Eustace's, rather than Ralph's, perception of Ralph's personal identity. In the four charters not produced by Eustace Ralph is described as *Radulfus de Bowetone de Castre* or *Radulphus aboueton de Castre*; in other words, he is not described in relation to his father.[44]

Significantly, one of the early fourteenth-century charters attributed to Eustace *scriptor* carries a wax seal impression bearing the legend 'the seal of Ralph Buvt[on] of Cast[or]'.[45] The seal matrix seems likely to have been commissioned by Ralph, and it emphasises his strong association with the name Aboveton (and its variant spellings). Two further transactions focused on land associated with this family. One charter describes land that was transferred to lord Geoffrey Russel, knight: 'all of my meadow that is called *Bowetoneholm* that lies between the water that is called Nene, and the land of Henry, son of William Torald'.[46] In another, Andrew Russell of Milton transferred to John le Boteler of Castor the rights of 'my part of *bouetonhay* with appurtenances, namely that part which lies near the vill of Castor, sometime the gift of Ralph Aboveton, and which lies near the enclosure of the said John and near my land'.[47] These field-names, alongside the wax seal impression, emphasise the strength of Ralph Aboveton's association with his surname: his personal identity was clearly strongly connected to this name. They also suggest that the name Aboveton did not emanate from those landholdings unattached to the main dwelling, since the meadow was clearly sited

---

40   Generally written as 'aboueton'.

41   NRO F(M) Charters 105, 133, 135–46; only 105 is dated (1297).

42   In these he is variously described as Ralph *de Boueton, Bouetun, Abovetoun* and *a Bouetoun*; his father Robert witnessed around forty charters.

43   With some slight variation on the spelling of *a Boueton*.

44   NRO F(M) Charter 105, 139–40 and 146; but note the affix 'de Castre'– in one context, a signifier of status.

45   NRO F(M) Charter 145: *S' Radvlfi Buvt[on] D[e] Cast[re]*.

46   NRO F(M) Charter 139. Since this meadow lay below the vill, the name clearly relates to the Aboveton family.

47   NRO F(M) Charter 74; King, *Peterborough Abbey*, p. 63 suggests that *bouetonhay* was a park, but this seems to be a misreading of NRO F(M) Charter 74, which says '*p[ar]tem meam de bouetonhay*'; *parcus* would not decline in this way.

south of the vill, close to the river Nene. Thus, these field-names originate from the family name, and not vice versa. These documents highlight the strong and enduring link between the Aboveton family and their perception of their place within the Castor landscape, expressed over a long period through their continued preference to identify themselves with a name that distanced them from the centre of the vill. Clearly, the way that the tenement associated with this family was depicted was the result of a process of social production – perhaps originating in a previous generation from a need to identify one individual through their connection to a particular place, but nevertheless eventually encapsulating a wider cultural meaning. Through the continued strong expression of this family's place in the Castor landscape, and their ability to control their identity (at least to some extent) through the use of documents predominantly associated with free individuals, we can detect elements of what cultural geographers and sociologists might perceive as being part of one group's dominant narrative in the interpretation of the landscape of the settlement in Castor.

The detail found within this small corpus of documents supports the idea that, for one Castor family, the use of a topographical name helped to set them apart from their neighbours. In this instance, we can establish an affinity with this family name – as it is evident that it had become hereditary at some point during the thirteenth century – but this is not always possible. In Lakenheath four individuals bore the byname *de Boueton* – William, John, Matilda and Amice – although, frustratingly, there is no mention throughout the court rolls of their status. Nevertheless, some surviving prosopographical information helps piece together more detail. An undated copy of a charter in *Liber M*, the Ely Priory cartulary, identifies one 'William Buutun' as a witness.[48] This document lists a transfer of rents from Matthew, son of Hugh de Lakenheath, to Alan of Swaffham, the rector of Lakenheath. Most of the rents outlined are owed by individuals not featured in the court roll series, and so it is likely to predate 1307, the earliest of these. This William acted as witness alongside several aristocratic men and so it seems unlikely that he was of servile status.[49] William de Boueton, possibly the same man, or perhaps a successor of the *Liber M* William, featured in the court rolls in 1326 when he was appointed the attorney of William, son of Geoffrey de Undeley, a holder of free land – suggesting that he had received some level of education.[50] In 1329 he employed several men, including a shepherd, and he held a fen from the prior of Barnwell.[51] He is not listed as holding any offices in Lakenheath, undertook no land transactions in the manorial court there and is unconnected with typical servile fines. In the 1327 lay subsidy he is listed in Eriswell, paying the enormous sum of 10s. 2d. in tax.[52] This does not prove conclusively that he was free and, as it is likely that he resided in Eriswell, perhaps we should not expect to see land transactions in Lakenheath. Nevertheless, only Robert de Tuddenham and

---

48 CUL EDR/G3/28/Liber M, f. 292.

49 Munday notes mention of William *Bovetoun* of Eriswell in a copy of a 1217 charter in the *Cartulary of Colchester Abbey*, and suggests that this William was a freeman: Munday, *Eriswell-cum-Coclesworth*, p. 14.

50 CUL EDC/7/16/2/1/6/42.

51 CUL EDC/7/16/2/1/10/2.

52 S.H.A. Hervey, *Suffolk in 1327, being a subsidy return* (Woodbridge, 1906), p. 198.

John de Boueton paid more tax in 1327.[53] There is less information relating to John de Boueton. He too employed a shepherd, held no offices in Lakenheath, transferred no land through the manorial court there and paid no fines denoting servility.[54] A man of this name is listed as paying tax in 1327 in both Lakenheath (2s. 3d.) and Eriswell (10s. 8d.).[55] None of these incidents are diagnostic of status, but it seems clear that both William and John were men of substance, and that, if they were descendants of the earlier William, they were probably free men. At Lakenheath in a small number of land transactions the land being transferred is described as 'above town', but it cannot be linked with any individuals named Aboveton. One such transaction in 1315, in which William and Katherine Godde transferred half an acre of land to John de Bircham junior, describes the land as lying 'abouetoun, next to the messuage of Adam Outlawe', whose byname may possibly represent his own 'outsider' status.[56]

Mapping topographical bynames: Huntingdonshire – the bigger picture

The pattern outlined within the Norman Cross data – that free peasants tended to be associated with names such as Aboveton that separated them from the settlement – is repeated within two more of the Huntingdonshire hundreds, Leightonstone and Hurstingstone hundreds (Table 4.6). In Leightonstone, the six topographical names associated with free peasants all reference a disconnection from the vill in the manner outlined above.[57] The data for Hurstingstone are incomplete, and were therefore supplemented by surviving surveys from both Ramsey and Ely muniments.[58] The two topographical names associated with freemen in that hundred, both 'William of the Hall', are very likely to be occupational. Toseland hundred, however, appears to differ significantly from the rest of the county, and there are clearly parishes in which large numbers of free tenant topographs are evident, such as Great Staughton, Eynesbury and Godmanchester. This is not the only point of difference. Tom Williamson discusses the characteristics of this area of south Huntingdonshire, which, alongside parts of west Cambridgeshire and east Bedfordshire, contrasts markedly with its neighbouring landscape, which is more typically champion. He suggests that, while its soils are reminiscent of champion country, the characteristics of the landscape are decidedly

---

53   Robert de Tuddenham held two knight's fees in Eriswell: J.T. Munday (ed.), *A feudal aid roll for Suffolk 1302–3* (Lakenheath, 1973), p. 27.

54   CUL EDC/7/16/2/1/6/28.

55   Hervey, *Suffolk in 1327*, p. 198.

56   CUL EDC/7/16/2/1/7/2.

57   Five of these peasants were named Aboueton, and the sixth was called Beyond the Water. In Alconbury, Alconbury Weston and Brampton, twenty villein sokemen bore topographical bynames.

58   The data drawn from these sources differ in date from the hundred rolls by at least one generation. The Ramsey surveys (Abbot's Ripton; St Ives, Woodhurst and Waldehurst; and Wistow) are dated 1251–2; the Ely surveys (Colne, Earith, Fenton, Pidley and Somersham) are dated 1249–50.

Table 4.6

Topographical bynames in Huntingdonshire, 1279.

Hundred	No. of individuals	No. of topographical names	No. of individual name bearers	Topographs – servile	Topographs – free	Topographs – uncertain status
Norman Cross	1,493	30	72	64	8	0
Leightonstone	1,487	15	34	28	6	0
Hurstingstone	Unknown[1]	28	52	48	2	2
Toseland	1,804	21	51	3	44	4

Source: *RH II; CMR I;* F. Willmoth and S. Oosthuizen (eds) and E. Miller (trans.), *The Ely coucher book, 1249–50. The bishop of Ely's manors in the Cambridgeshire fenland* (Cambridge, 2015). The same caveats apply here with regard to the possibility of duplicated individuals and those that were omitted because they were landless or held leasehold land.

Note:

1. Missing manors are Ramsey, Bury, Great Raveley, Hartford and King's Ripton. It is not possible to determine an overall figure for the number of households in Hurstingstone hundred.

more 'woodland'.[59] The region features many dispersed hamlets in addition to some nucleated villages, albeit often poorly nucleated. Similarly, Roberts and Wrathmell describe this area as a 'sub-province' bearing the hallmarks of both woodland and champion landscapes.[60] In addition to these observations it is also apparent that – at least in the three parishes mentioned above, which appear as something of an aberration when set against the rest of the county as a whole – weaker lordship prevailed. Great Staughton was made up of at least nine manors in the late thirteenth century, while Eynesbury contained more than ten. In Godmanchester there was a relatively large population of free tenants bearing topographical bynames. Again, the tenurial structure is interesting. From the Conquest onward, Godmanchester had ancient demesne status and, in the hundred rolls, the inhabitants stated that ' … they are free sokemen, and there is no bondman among them'.[61] This was clearly a place characterised by weaker lordship, and where all the tenants saw themselves as equal in status.

In all three of the Toseland vills reviewed here the range of topographs is much more general, referencing a wide variety of topography within the vill, unlike the 'separated' nature of the more northern Huntingdonshire names. In Huntingdonshire,

---

59 Great Staughton has been described as 'mainly woodland down to the thirteenth century': M.E. Simkins, 'Great Staughton', in W. Page, G. Proby and S. Inskip Ladds (eds), *VCH Huntingdonshire*, vol. 2, p. 354.

60 T. Williamson, *Shaping medieval landscapes: settlement, society, environment* (Oxford, 2010), pp. 72–79; Roberts and Wrathmell, 'Dispersed settlement', pp. 102–3.

61 This was important in the thirteenth century, as unfree tenants on ancient demesne lands were not subject to increased services and rents, unlike servile tenants on other manors: C. Dyer, 'Memories of freedom: attitudes towards serfdom in England, 1200–1350', in M.L. Bush (ed.), *Serfdom and slavery: studies in legal bondage* (London, 1996), p. 278; *RH II*, p. 591.

then, notwithstanding the usual problems in dealing with the source material, the data point to two clear trends. In the majority of the county, which was characterised by strong lordship, there were few free tenants bearing topographical bynames, and the names of those that did appear to have been limited in their scope, referencing a detachment from the centre of the vill. In contrast, in those parts of Toseland hundred where there are places associated with weaker lordship there was a mixture of both free and servile topographical bynames, and these names are much more representative of topographs generally. This perhaps goes some way to explaining Postles' assertion that topographs are more likely to be linked with dispersed settlement, which, in turn, is commonly associated with weaker lordship. According to Postles' analysis, settlements in which topographical bynames proliferated tended to be dispersed rather than nucleated and, of course, in these places a greater proportion of the peasant population was usually personally free. But Postles' hypothesis cannot fully explain the distribution of topographs. If the only determinant were topography then we should expect to see a more even spread of topographical names of all kinds between both servile and free peasants in all types of settlement, albeit in greater numbers in dispersed settlements. If, as seems likely, part of the reason for the observed distributions lies within peasants' attitudes toward their personal status, then in order to begin to resolve this we must turn to ideas relating to peasant freedom in the post-Conquest period. Simply put, did status matter? And if so, why?

Conclusions: personal status and topographical bynames

Personal status and peasant freedom are subjects that have been widely treated, although there is disagreement regarding the effects of servile status on peasants themselves and their attitudes towards it. Historians are broadly in agreement that, before the thirteenth century, the lines between freedom and servility were difficult to define precisely.[62] In the early twelfth century, from a legal perspective, villeins were considered to be free. Several manorial surveys and enquiries from this period outline a process of the commutation of some labour services to cash rents by some peasants and, crucially, neglect any reference to the typical tests of unfreedom that form an inherent part of many late thirteenth-century surveys.[63] Hilton suggests that, at that time, the evidence recorded in the surveys provided the measure of freedom against which tenure was assessed: hence some holdings were more free than others.[64] He argued for a sudden

---

62   R.H. Hilton, 'Freedom and villeinage in England', in R.H. Hilton (ed.), *Peasants, knights and heretics: studies in medieval English social history* (Cambridge, 1976), p. 174, first published in *Past and Present*, 31 (1965), pp. 3–19; Dyer, 'Memories of freedom', p. 278.

63   These tests might include, for example, high levels of labour service; their eligibility to serve as reeve; and requiring the lord's permission for the marriage of daughters, the ordination of sons and to leave the manor. They indicate that a change had taken place sometime after the end of the twelfth century, following which villeins were legally considered to be unfree.

64   Hilton, 'Freedom and villeinage', p. 182; Runciman suggests greater social mobility in Anglo-Saxon society, albeit slowing down toward the eleventh century: W.G. Runciman, 'Accelerating social mobility: the case of Anglo-Saxon England', *Past and Present*, 104 (1984), pp. 21 and 26.

change in the late twelfth century following a tightening of the common law, noting that, from *c*.1200 and continuing until the end of the fourteenth century, a significant number of legal cases were brought by villeins disputing their sudden servility.[65] He suggested that the fundamental issue of freedom was of paramount importance to peasants and was a key element in peasant revolt throughout the period.[66] Although this view has been criticised by those historians who argue that status was not a major issue to peasants, Christopher Dyer and Zvi Razi have demonstrated that, for many servile families, it was a sufficiently important matter to expend considerable resources over several generations in order to campaign for their freedom.[67]

On balance, we can conclude that personal status was important to peasants on both sides of the divide, and that the effects of servility would have been felt much more strongly in highly manorialised areas, largely because of the more onerous labour services associated with servility and because of the larger number of unfree tenants in these manors. The patterns of personal naming apparent in the settlements that have been assessed as part of this analysis strongly suggest that there were subtle differences between the names in circulation in places characterised by strong as opposed to weak lordship. In an archaeological study of three Buckinghamshire settlements, Sally Smith has shown that the lived experience of peasants in more nucleated villages differed markedly from those of peasants in dispersed settlements. She demonstrates that the social interactions between people within each settlement type would have been quite dissimilar, with much more intense contact in nucleated villages and much more limited social exchange in areas characterised by scattered settlement, the morphology of which may have resulted in an 'independence from the forces of community'.[68] This is worth exploring further. In villages with a more coherent settlement core, where residents lived in close contact with one another, it would be reasonable to expect that the dissemination of cultural ideas – such as the way in which one group might 'read' the landscape of the settlement – might happen at a more rapid rate than within scattered communities. This is demonstrated at Castor through the frequency of many free tenants there identifying with the name 'de Castor' or 'de Ailsworth', either as a family name or byname, like Ralph Aboveton de Castor.[69] Within the Castor dataset,

---

65 See also Dyer, *Making a living*, p. 140 and Schofield, *Peasant and community*, p. 13.

66 R.H. Hilton, *Class conflict and the crisis of feudalism: essays in medieval social history* (1985, London, 1990), p. 47.

67 J. Hatcher, 'English serfdom and villeinage: towards a reassessment', *Past and Present*, 90 (1981), pp. 3–39; reproduced in T.H. Aston (ed.), *Landlords, peasants and politics in medieval England* (Cambridge, 2006), pp. 247–83; Dyer, 'Memories of freedom', p. 280; Z. Razi, 'Serfdom and freedom in medieval England: a reply to the revisionists', *Past and Present* (2007), Supplement 2, p. 186; E.B. DeWindt, *Land and people in Holywell-cum-Needingworth* (Toronto, 1972); E. Britton, *The community of the vill: a study in the history of the family and village life in fourteenth-century England* (Toronto, 1977); Z. Razi, 'The Toronto school's reconstitution of medieval peasant society: a critical view', *Past and Present*, 85 (1979), pp. 153–5.

68 Smith, 'Houses and communities', pp. 68–71.

69 Within the Castor dataset, over 100 individuals styled themselves either 'de Castor' or 'de Ailsworth' during this period.

over 100 individuals styled themselves either 'de Castor' or 'de Ailsworth' during this period, and so this must have related not to individual identification but rather to their sense of identity. As outlined above (p. 76), the specific use of 'local' toponyms by resident free peasants was probably related to ideas about status. If we were to read these names from a cultural perspective, we might conclude that the bearers wished to emphasise that they were part of a network of contacts beyond the vill – in short, these names demonstrated free tenants' desire to seem more outward looking. They appear in contrast to the servile peasants bearing more parochial topographical names that bound their bearers more closely to the confines of the settlement. This is not to suggest that servile peasants did not develop relationships outside their home villages – many would have made commercial contacts at local markets, for instance.[70]

Nevertheless, free tenants had more opportunities than their unfree neighbours. They had greater choice when it came to legal redress and need not have favoured the local manorial court; they would usually have been expected to attend the hundred court, and had access to the county court and the general eyre. In highly manorialised places the lord made far fewer demands on their time and they were largely spared the frequent labour services that their servile neighbours were obliged to undertake. In settlements in which the introduction and exchange of cultural ideas was relatively swift, the conscious adoption and retention by free tenants of topographical names that disassociated them from the parochiality linked with servile topographs was unlikely to have been accidental. Returning to the idea – as expressed by Wylie and Lefebvre – that social readings of landscape are grounded in power and control – we should also remember that free peasants had better opportunities to control the narrative of their own identities. In addition to the networks they belonged to, in which they were often identified through the use of status-loaded toponyms, they were legally entitled to use charters (and therefore also wax seals). There is no doubt that they had access to a greater number of contexts in which their names could be used to express their identity. This was in direct contrast to servile peasants, who, locally at least, had much less control over their own identity. Names are usually bestowed by others, and, in addition to this, most servile peasant names would have been documented by a scribe connected with the manor or its court. As we have seen, some servile peasants did use charters, but the cost of their production would have limited their use to a wealthier subset of people. Overall, then, unfree individuals had less control over their own identities than did their free neighbours.

It could be argued that, at least in some places, free peasants' seeming wish to differentiate themselves from their servile neighbours simply demonstrates a desire to appear socially superior. Smith's suggestion that communal bonds were weaker in dispersed settlements also supports the idea that cultural constructs such as status mattered less in places like these. Nevertheless, as Lefebvre suggests, mental representations of space were usually initially constructed by elites, and we know that richer, higher-status and aspirational peasants gradually came to reproduce key aspects

---

70 Dyer suggests that, typically, peasants' commercial hinterland probably extended to between six and eight miles (10–13 km): Dyer, *Everyday life*, p. 270; C. Briggs, 'The availability of credit in the English countryside, 1400–1480', *Agricultural History Review*, 56/1 (2008), p. 7.

of lordly residences, especially those relating to privacy and detachment.[71] Furthermore, if it was important to free tenants to differentiate their homesteads in a clearly discernible manner, then it is not too great a leap to consider that, in highly manorialised places where status mattered more, additional, more subtle means of setting themselves apart might have been employed. This is illustrated very clearly in highly manorialised regions in Huntingdonshire through the association of one type of 'detached' topographical byname with free tenants, and the wholesale connection between rural topographical names and servile peasants. Evidence presented here suggests that topographical names went through an evolutionary process. They were initially useful in identifying an individual based on their place of dwelling, but as cultural ideas concerning status developed they became convenient as a subtle means of expressing socially constructed concepts of belonging and exclusion by free peasants.[72] As cultural artefacts, topographical bynames in the thirteenth and fourteenth centuries enable us to read the landscape of the rural settlement as it was seen by some free peasants.

In October 1330 in Lakenheath, Richard in the Lane described to the court how he was defamed by John Waryn, who assaulted him and called him 'false, and a neif', for which he claimed 40s. in damages.[73] Richard's father, known by the same name, was recorded as holding free land in Lakenheath but was described as a neif in another entry; furthermore, he paid for a marriage licence for his daughter, and for the ordination of a son, firmly establishing his servile status.[74] The results of the inquest have not survived, but this episode emphasises the gravity of the insult. The *lane* family are not expressly identified as villeins in the corpus of Lakenheath documents, but the inference is that this was a family who had lost whatever freedom they perceived they had several generations before. Clearly the issue of personal status was vitally important to the *lane* family, as it was to other servile peasants. That there was a predominant association between servile peasants and topographical bynames and family names in late medieval England is beyond doubt. However, the weight of evidence presented here points toward there being subtly different naming practices within settlements that were distinguished by weaker lordship, as distinct from places in which servile peasants laboured under more onerous conditions of servitude. This analysis is far from comprehensive, and is a first attempt to consider the symbolic nature of topographical bynames, and it is fervently hoped that other scholars will find this phenomenon interesting enough to examine these names in more detail beyond the confines of one county.

---

71 Lefebvre, *The production of space*, p. 116.

72 In a recent study, James Chetwood has argued that, rather than functioning solely as identifiers, the adoption of the earliest bynames helped to create a sense of communal cohesion: J. Chetwood, 'Re-evaluating English personal naming on the eve of the Conquest', *Early Medieval Europe*, 26/4 (2018), p. 546.

73 CUL EDC/7/16/2/1/8/5.

74 CUL EDC/7/16/2/1/7/3; EDC/7/16/2/1/6/27; in 1316, a separate court case outlined that freemen could not hold villein land: EDC/7/16/2/1/6/17.

Chapter 5

Naming the landscape

Reassessing minor medieval landscape names

The field-names and minor landscape names found within late medieval documents offer a wealth of detailed evidence concerning the environment, and yet until recently historians have rarely considered them as an important source for examining attitudes toward local landscape.[1] This is partly because – for non-specialists – there are a number of uncertainties associated with interpreting the meanings of, and the rationale behind, the naming of the local environment; and also because, hitherto, minor names have commonly not been deemed worthy of detailed study in their own right, outside onomastic scholarship.[2] In considering field-names and minor landscape names, it is now generally accepted by scholars that peasants were both the authors and custodians of the named landscape; it can be difficult nevertheless to determine precisely when these names originated. Moreover, although the lexical meaning of minor names can often be asserted with some degree of confidence, the social and cultural connotations frequently remain opaque (although see chapter six). Nonetheless, by taking a multi-disciplinary approach to the study of minor landscape names, it is possible to suggest an outline chronology for the development of these names and to consider why certain name types were prioritised and adopted in specific periods of landscape development and change. The first part of this chapter follows a traditional scholarly course, introducing the minor names associated with the landscape itself and evaluating what they can reveal about the landscape in each of the three settlements. In particular, those aspects of the landscape that are especially noted by local people through the naming process will be examined. Following this, the rest of the chapter focuses on the probable historical sequencing of minor landscape names – looking in particular at topographical names – before considering the dynamics of naming and seeking to understand changing peasant naming strategies. To what extent can we detect the mentalities that lie behind the selection of particular name types, and what are the environmental, cultural and agricultural processes that underpin them?

---

1   See Semple, 'A fear of the past', pp. 109–26; Kilby, 'A different world?', pp. 72–7; Gardiner, 'Oral tradition', pp. 16–30; S. Mileson, 'Beyond the dots: mapping meaning in the later medieval landscape', in M. Hicks (ed.), *The later medieval inquisitions post mortem: mapping the medieval countryside and rural society* (Woodbridge, 2016), pp. 84–99; S. Kilby, 'Divining medieval water: the field-names of Flintham in Nottinghamshire', *Journal of the English Place-Name Society*, 49 (2017), pp. 57–93.

2   Onomasts first noted the importance of field-names to linguistic and historical scholarship in the 1930s: A. Mawer, 'The study of field-names in relation to place-names', in J.G. Edwards, V.H. Galbraith and E.F. Jacob (eds), *Historical Essays in Honour of James Tait* (Manchester, 1933), pp. 189–200.

Table 5.1

Summary of late medieval field-name and minor landscape name data for Elton, Castor and Lakenheath.

Vill	No. of names recovered	Date range	Main sources
Elton	145	13th–14th c.	Charters
Castor	227	c.1222–1479	Charters, cartularies, account rolls, surveys
Lakenheath	229	1305–1348	Court rolls, account rolls

Ordering field and furlong

A large quantity of late-medieval field-name and minor landscape name data has been recovered for each of the three vills (Table 5.1), suggesting that a significant number of names from each corpus has been recovered. Place-name scholars typically dissect names into their constituent parts. Whilst names containing just one main word, such as Castor's *lyngg* 'ling, heather' or *le hay* 'the enclosure' are known as 'simplex' names, compound names comprise both 'specific' and 'generic' elements.[3] It might be expected that the generic minor name elements would provide a pen portrait of each settlement's landscape. Castor and Elton were both on the river Nene and near the fen edge, and Castor featured extensive woodland. Lakenheath lies in the Breckland region of Suffolk, with its attendant poor soils, and more than half of its territory was made up of undrained fenland. A navigable channel connected it to the river Little Ouse, which formed its northernmost boundary.[4] So it would be reasonable to assume that there would be a higher number of arable name elements at both Castor and Elton than at Lakenheath, which may perhaps have had a greater focus on the pastoral. Water names should be prevalent in all of the villages: Castor and Elton lie directly on a major river and Lakenheath, as mentioned, contains a large area of fenland. Names associated with woods and trees might be expected to be more abundant in Castor, with its large area of woodland. Table 5.2 outlines the most frequently used generic elements in all three places.

Some of these initial suppositions are correct. There is a dearth of meadow names in Lakenheath, as *wang* can be taken here as 'field' rather than 'meadow'.[5] There are also fewer of the elements that are more typically associated with arable land, such as *land* 'land' and *furlang* 'furlong', although the inclusion of elements such as *æcer* 'acre' and *wang* 'field, in-field or meadowland' reflect the fact that some arable farming was undertaken here, but not on the same scale as it was in Castor or Elton. Names associated with water are apparent in all three vills, but the focus is clearly different

---

3   For example, in Elton's *peselond*, 'pese' is the specific and 'lond' the generic element. For a detailed overview, see P. Cavill, *A new dictionary of English field-names*, with an introduction by R. Gregory (Nottingham, 2018), pp. vi–vii.

4   Bailey, 'The prior and convent of Ely', pp. 2–3.

5   All of the furlongs featuring the generic element *wang* in Lakenheath, and for which there are data detailing field use, were arable.

Table 5.2
Most frequently used generic elements in field-names at Elton, Castor and Lakenheath.

Generic element	Language	Definition	Castor	Elton	Lakenheath
æcer	OE	A plot of cultivated land, specific measure of ploughland	6	6	6
bæc, bece	OE	(1) A low ridge (2) stream valley	0	0	7
brōc	OE	A brook, stream	4	4	1
croft	OE	A small, enclosed field	8	4	4
crouche	ME	A cross	1	0	5
dīc, dík	OE/ON	(1) An excavated trench, either defensive or for the drainage of water (2) embankment	5	3	6
dole	ME	A share of the common field, frequently referring to meadow	4	1	0
ende	OE	End, the end of something	2	6	6
fen, fenn	OE	A fen, a marsh, marshland	0	0	10
furlang	OE	The length of a furrow, a furlong	29	13	3
gāra	OE	A gore, a triangular plot of ground	0	3	0
(ge)hæg	OE	A fence, enclosure	5	0	0
haga	OE	A hedge, an enclosure	5	0	1
hall	OE	A hall, a large residence, a manor house, a place for legal and other public business	0	0	4
haugr	ON	A natural height, a hill, a heap, an artificial mound, a burial mound	9	1	1
hēafod-land	OE	The head of a strip of land left for turning the plough	1	6	4
hege	OE	A hedge, fence	2	0	0
holmr	ON	An island, inland promontory, raised ground in marsh, river meadow	6	7	1
hyll	OE	A hill, natural eminence or elevated piece of ground	14	9	7
hȳð	OE	A port, a haven, a landing place on a riverbank	0	0	8
lād	OE	A watercourse, a channel, a fenland drainage channel, a dyked watercourse	0	0	17
land, lond	OE	Land, a strip of arable land in a common field	6	10	4
mære, mere	OE	(1) A boundary, a border (2) A pool	2	3	11
mersc, merisc	OE	Watery land, a marsh	0	2	2
mōr, mór	OE/ON	A moor, barren wasteland. In the southern counties and midlands, marshland	6	6	7
*rod, *rodu	OE	A clearing	0	3	1
slæd	OE	A valley	2	4	1
trēow	OE	A tree	2	0	0
*wæsse or (ge)wæsc	OE	(1) A place by a meandering river that floods and drains quickly (2) washing, a flood	1	1	0
wang, vangr	OE/ON	(1) A piece of meadowland, open-field (2) A garden, an infield	11	6	10
wella	OE	A well, spring or stream	8	5	4
wer, wær	OE	A weir, a river dam, a fishing enclosure in a river	0	0	6
wudu	OE	A wood, a grove, woodland, forest	5	0	0

Source: *EPNE*; D. Parsons and T. Styles (eds) with C. Hough, *The vocabulary of English place-names* (*Á-Box*) (Nottingham, 1997); D. Parsons and T. Styles (eds), *The vocabulary of English place-names* (*Brace-Cæster*) (Nottingham, 2000).

at Lakenheath. There is only one medieval *brōc* 'brook, stream', whereas *hȳð* 'landing place on a river-bank', *lād* 'dyked water-course', *mere* 'pool' and *wer* 'weir, river-dam or fishing-enclosure in a river' abound, emphasising both Lakenheath's role as an inland port and the profusion of fisheries in the fenland areas of the parish.[6] There would, of course, have been fisheries on the river Nene at both Castor and Elton, but these do not feature clearly in the minor name record. A 1272 inquisition concerning the abbot of Peterborough's waters details the extent of his Nene fisheries and describes the stretches adjacent to Castor as 'from *neutonemilne* up to *billingbrok* ... from *billingbrok* up to *le eweyedyk* ... from *ingewell* up to *alwaltonedam*'; only *ingewelle*, leased to the abbot of Thorney, features in any other document.[7] It is possible, indeed likely, that some or all of the other Castor fisheries were at farm, but no records survive to confirm this.[8] The names associated with fenland are also illuminating. Only at Lakenheath was the element *fenn* 'fen, marsh' used, as well as *mersc* 'watery land, marsh' and *mōr*/*mór* 'marsh, barren upland, moor', suggesting that inhabitants saw these names as representing distinct features.[9] In Castor and Elton only *mersc* and *mōr*/*mór* are found, implying that here, in these non-fenland vills, they meant 'marsh' and 'moor' respectively. There are ditches/dykes in all three places and, while the Lakenheath ditches probably reference drainage, at Castor some at least refer to the extensive Roman earthworks.

There are several names referring to woodland in Castor, including the elements *wudu* 'wood' and *fyrhth* 'woodland, land overgrown with brushwood'. A further element, *hangende* – 'sloping [place]' – appears in a 1393 reference to 'the wood called *castrehanggand*'.[10] It is possible the wood was a later plantation post-dating the name, but the Anglo-Saxons had a term for a sloping *wood* – *hangra* – suggesting a Scandinavian linguistic influence.[11] Two names – *iungeuuode* 'young wood' and *aleuuode* 'alder wood'– are found only in a survey of 1215 relating to the disafforestation of the Soke of Peterborough, and there is no evidence for the survival of either name beyond this time.[12] There are also five more names that suggest that there may have been woodland for which there was no surviving written record. These were *brodewodegates* 'broad wood ways', *menewodesti* 'the common wood

---

6   M. Gelling and A. Cole, *The landscape of place-names* (Stamford, 2000), p. 20; A. Cole, 'The place-name evidence for water transport in early medieval England', in J. Blair (ed.), *Waterways and canal-building in medieval England* (Oxford, 2007), p. 61. Note that *bæc, bece* can mean either 'low ridge in marshy ground' or 'stream valley', and it is unclear which of these is meant for the Lakenheath names.

7   Soc. Antiq., MS 60, f. 172v, *Black Book of Peterborough*; a 1321 Peterborough Abbey extent mentions Castor fisheries; Sparke, *Historiæ Anglicanæ*, vol. 2, p. 176; the lease is outlined in NRO F(M) 2388.

8   Although in 1309–10, the Castor account roll suggests that 18d. was received 'from the sale of a fishery': NRO F(M) 2389.

9   Gelling and Cole, *Landscape of place-names*, p. 58; *Millemarch* in Lakenheath is probably ME *marche*, 'boundary'; the additional name *millemarchmor* supports this: CUL EDC/7/16/1/14.

10 BL Cotton MS Nero C. vii/14.

11 The name has survived as Castor Hanglands – still a sizable woodland.

12 King, *Peterborough Abbey*, p. 173; *iungeuuode* was on the boundary between Castor and Marholm: CUL PDC/MS 1. It is possible (albeit unlikely) that *aleuuode* could be 'temple wood'.

Table 5.3
Names with *(ge)hæg*, *haga*, *hecge* and *heg* in Castor.

Field-name	Gloss	Location	Use
OE *(ge)hæg*			
biryhay	The enclosure belonging to the manor	Normangate Field	
bouetonhay	The enclosure belonging to a man called Aboueton		Pasture
le cornhay	The enclosure associated with (1) cranes (2) corn		Arable
le hay	The enclosure	Normangate Field	Pasture
westhay	The western enclosure	Normangate Field	Arable
OE *haga*			
abbotishauue	The abbot's enclosure	In the lord abbot's wood	The abbot's woodland
ashauue	The ash tree enclosure		
baketeshauue	Uncertain first element + enclosure		
rohauue	Roe-deer or rough enclosure		The abbot's woodland
wulfhauue	Wolf enclosure		The abbot's woodland
OE *hecge*			
irthonehegg	Earthen hedge	A local name for the Roman road Ermine Street	
OE *heg, hege*			
gatacrehegge	Goat acre (1) hay, mowing grass (2) hedge, fence		
glademannesheg	The (1) hay, mowing grass or (2) hedge, fence associated with a person called Gladman		
langedikheg	The hedge called the long ditch or dike	A local name for the Roman road King Street	

path', *middelwodegate* 'the middle wood way', *mikilwodegate* 'the great wood way' and *wodegate* 'the wood way'.[13] Three names – *brake wode* 'fern or thicket wood', *le bretennes wode* 'wood associated with a person called Breton' and *castre wood* 'Castor wood' – first attested in the late fifteenth century may have been earlier.[14] There are also a number of names that reference the clearance of part of Castor's woodland, including *sartis* 'assart' and *stibbing*, *bilmanstibbyng* and *coltstibbingges* 'place where

---

13 NRO F(M) Charters 32, 357, 404, 406 and 577; *CN*, p. 212; it is also possible that the specifiers in each instance referred to the road, rather than each respective wood.

14 There were tenants called Breton in Castor from at least the thirteenth century.

trees were stubbed, a clearing'.[15] The 1215 survey outlines the wood of *eiuig* 'fenced off piece of ground, enclosure', from which a new open field surely took its name in the later thirteenth century.[16] Nevertheless, Castor maintained enough land associated with hunting to retain the services of a forester in the early fourteenth century.[17]

One of the most prominent of the woodland name elements at Castor is *haga* 'hedge, enclosure', in this case indicating enclosed woodland. Indeed, enclosure – a distinctive feature of Castor – would not have been apparent without the field-names. Three elements feature strongly: *haga* 'hedge, enclosure'; *(ge)hæg* 'fence, enclosure'; and *hege* 'hedge, fence'. It is difficult to tell them apart, especially since *haga* can take one of two modern forms, *-haw* or *-hay*, and *(ge)hæg* usually also takes the form *-hay* (Table 5.3).[18] Hooke suggests that *haga* was associated with hunting[19], and at least two of the Castor examples were hunting enclosures. The 1215 survey states that 'the abbot's *rohauue* and *thinferdesland* and *w[u]lfhauue* contain 78 acres and 3 rods of which half is wood covert [*boscus coopertus*] and the other [half] thicket'.[20] The name *rohauue* could mean either roe-deer or rough enclosure, but the former seems more likely in this context, especially as the reference to 'covert' explicitly suggests hunting, while another piece of land called *kydwelwang* 'field by the spring associated with either roe-deer calf or young goats' lay nearby in the open field called Wode Field.[21]

As late as the fourteenth century there is a mention of enclosed woodland in Castor, amounting to 292 perches of hedging in 1309–10.[22] The very specific use for the *haga* enclosures, alongside the fact that they all end in *-hauue*, suggests that the *(ge)hæg* names refer to a different type of feature.[23] *Birihay*, *les hayes* and *westhay* are all recorded as being located in either Normangate Field in Castor or Nether Field in Ailsworth, both close to the river Nene.[24] By the thirteenth century, these furlongs

---

15 BL Cotton MS Nero C. vii/14; NRO F(M) Charters 194, 264 and 357.

16 King, *Peterborough Abbey*, p. 173. I am grateful to Peter McClure for his help in defining this name.

17 NRO F(M) 2388 and 2389.

18 D. Hooke, 'Pre-Conquest woodland: its distribution and usage', *Agricultural History Review*, 37/2 (1989), p. 123; R. Liddiard, 'The deer parks of Domesday Book', *Landscapes*, 4/1 (2003), pp. 6–7; M. Wiltshire and S. Woore, '"Hays", possible early enclosures, in Derbyshire', *Derbyshire Archaeological Journal*, 131 (2011), p. 197.

19 Although, in a recent reconsideration of 'hays', Sarah Wager notes that this was not always the case: S. Wager, 'The hays of medieval England: a reappraisal', *Agricultural History Review*, 65/2 (2017), pp. 178–9.

20 *Rohauue* is included within a group of names unquestionably associated with Castor woodland in the survey reproduced in King, *Peterborough Abbey*, p. 173.

21 BL Cotton MS Nero C. vii/14.

22 NRO F(M) 2389. The Latin term used is *sepis*, which usually translates as 'fence'; however, Hooke suggests that *haga* was later glossed by *sepes/sepis*: Hooke, 'Pre-Conquest woodland', p. 123. A perch was sixteen and a half feet.

23 Although Smith suggests that the latinised 'haia', in its late form, meaning 'part of a forest fenced off for hunting', is derived from *(ge)hæg* (EPNE, vol. 1, p. 215), Wager argues that hays might not always be associated with hunting or woodland: Wager, 'Hays of medieval England', p. 179.

24 NRO F(M) Charters 100 and 275; BL Cotton MS Nero C. vii/14; CN, p. 211.

(alongside the other names ending in -*hay*) are variously described as arable or pasture, which is strongly suggestive of several enclosures which the incumbent holder could use as he saw fit. It is possible that these enclosures may initially have related to late Anglo-Saxon parks, but it seems unlikely, especially since none of these names feature on the 1215 survey. In contrast with Castor, there are few names referencing woodland in either Elton or Lakenheath. The fact that there are, however, references to individual tree species perhaps suggests that trees were in short supply, and that those noted were conspicuous because of this. The Lakenheath name *le frith* is interesting. It seems unlikely to refer to woodland, but may mean 'fenland overgrown with brushwood'.[25]

Distinguishing field and furlong

Assessing the generic name elements is a useful means of understanding how medieval rural landscapes were ordered. But in order to determine how the fields, meadows, woods and fens were seen by local people, the 'qualifying' or 'specific' elements of the names are required. Thus, *akermanlond* described not simply arable land in Elton but the specific arable land held by the tenants known as acre-men.[26] In onomastic scholarship focusing on minor names, the emphasis has been principally etymological and taxonomic, and while this is inarguably an extremely important element in understanding landscape names, nevertheless, these names require consideration within their culturally specific contexts.[27] A typical approach usually categorises the qualifying name terms in accordance with a modern framework. Beyond the fact that this separates the field-names from their socio-cultural frame of reference, it is extremely unclear whether the categories selected for their classification bear any relevance from the perspective of the worldview of the medieval peasant.[28] While some frame of reference is clearly required, this should be simply the first step toward a more culturally focused analysis.

Recently, Jones has posited a model for early medieval place-names based on the Traditional Ecological Knowledge (TEK) framework that underpins the place-naming systems of indigenous peoples.[29] This is an interesting and considered model that offers a useful and more apposite means of assessing medieval place-names than previous attempts. Nevertheless, the shifting sands of medieval scientific and religious worldviews across our period frequently frustrate our attempts to classify some place-

---

25   CUL EDC/7/16/2/1/13/1; *EPNE*, vol. 1, p. 190: the reference Smith quotes is for Cambridgeshire.

26   TNA E 40/7038.

27   This is acknowledged by Ellen Bramwell in considering personal names: E.S. Bramwell, 'Personal names and anthropology', in C. Hough (ed.) with D. Izdebska, *The Oxford handbook of names and naming* (Oxford, 2018), p. 263; and by David Parsons writing on settlement names: D.N. Parsons, 'Churls and athelings, kings and reeves: some reflections on place-names and early English society', in J. Carroll and D.N. Parsons (eds), *Perceptions of place: twenty-first century interpretations of English place-name studies* (Nottingham, 2013), p.54.

28   Kilby, 'A different world?' (2010b), p. 74.

29   Jones, 'Responding to modern flooding': Jones suggests six naming categories: topographical names, subsistence names, social names, memory names, religio-spiritual names and travel and settlement names, while acknowledging that there are many overlaps.

names with any degree of certainty. In particular, until the twelfth century there was no division between the natural and supernatural. Given that, how should so-called supernatural names be categorised? The consideration of names invoking memory is also problematic. While names such as *oldfeld* 'old field' might be more obvious markers of memory, the recollection of past events can also be concealed within seemingly prosaic medieval landscape names that might not be easily recognised today as having a double meaning (see chapter six). We should, perhaps, accept our modern need for some form of categorisation that allows for a systematic analysis, while acknowledging that some medieval field-names defy simple taxonomy as they operate on a number of levels, not all of which are easily revealed to the modern scholar. The rest of this section will assess those names that reveal something of the medieval natural and supernatural worlds, before turning to the dynamics of place-naming.

The natural environment

As might be expected, many field-names referenced flora (Table 5.4). A wider range of names referencing flora is evident at Lakenheath than at Castor or Elton, reflecting the nature of the local environment, with wetland plants such as sedge (*segfen*) and reeds (*redemere*), and places where a useful supply of staves could be found (*staflode*).[30] There was also an area associated with the cutting of peat (*turvewere*).[31] Lakenheath produced 100,000 turves annually in the early fourteenth century, and this must have been the focal point of much of that activity.[32] Those Lakenheath villagers having rights of common accessed a number of places, including *segfen* 'sedge fen' and *wodefen* 'wood fen', the names indicating the resources available in each.[33] Two names refer to grasses, which would also have been abundant in a wetland environment: *besemer* 'pool associated with bent or rough grass' and *gresacre* 'grass acre'.[34] Flax is noted, alongside the colloquial name for vetches in *musepeselane*, 'mouse-peas lane'.[35]

Wild rose-hips are found at Elton (*hypperode*, 'wild rose-hip clearing'); and reeds (*fleggis*, 'Iris, place where reeds grow') and heather (*lyngg*, 'heather') at Castor, alongside *wealh-wyrt*, usually translated as dwarf-elder or Danewort (see chapter six for a detailed discussion).[36] Castor's *tasilhill* records the presence of teasels, which may have been used in the production of cloth.[37] The great majority of these names clearly reference important local resources used by peasants. These observations are supported in some instances by the manorial records. In an account roll referencing the farm of Lakenheath fisheries John le Hyrde paid 12d. 'for the rushes [*cirpus*] and

---

30   CUL EDC/7/16/2/1/6–7; EDC/7/16/1/13.
31   CUL EDR/G3/28/Liber M; the generic element in this name is certainly *wer, wær* 'weir, river-dam, fishing-enclosure in a river', and not *mere* 'pool'.
32   Bailey, *Medieval Suffolk*, p. 94.
33   TNA SC 2/203/94; note that additional common resources were available.
34   CUL EDR/7/16/2/1/4 and 6.
35   CUL EDR/7/16/2/1/9.
36   TNA E 40/10857; NRO F(M) Charter 92; BL Cotton MS Nero C. vii/14.
37   NRO M(T) 34.

Table 5.4
Field-names in Elton, Castor and Lakenheath: floral specifiers.

Flora	Field-names
Castor	
Ash	Asshecroftwong, Hassehil, Ashauue
Bean	Benelond furlong
Birch	Berch
Blackberries, brambles	Brimbelhilheuydlond
Dwarf elder	Walwortwong
Flag	Fleggis
Ling (heather)	Lyngg
Peas	Pesewong, peysefurlong
Plum	Plumtres
Teasel	Tasilhil
Willow	Wyluwes
Wood	Le Wodegate, Wodecroft, Wodehil, Wodecroftfurlong, Wodecroftheued, Middelwodegate, Wodefeld, Menewodesti
Elton	
Bean	Lytelbenelond, Beneyeston, Benelond Heueden, Benelond
Hips	Hypperode
Kale, cabbage	Calmerz
Oak	Okeyerd
Peas	Peselond
Rye	Riewong
Thatch	Thatchdole
Thorn	Pyttlesthornfurlong, le Thorn
Willow	Wylegeylake
Lakenheath	
Aspen	Aspeye
Barley	Berdekeweye, Berdele
Blackberries, brambles	Brambelheude
Bushes	Le Buskes, Middelbusc, Common Boskys[1]
Cherry	Chericrouch
Flax	Lyndich
Fodder	Fodirfen
Grass	Besemer, Gresacre
Medlar (or orache)[2]	Meldeburn
Peas	Peszierd
Reeds	Redemere, the Reedmarsh
Sedge	Segfen
Shrub, plant	Plantelode
Staves	Staflode, Stafholdeend, Stafishithe
Thorn	Wyttisthornshote
Turves	Turvewere
Vetches	Le Fiches, Musepeselane
Willow	Wilwlade, Welues
Wood	Wodefen

Notes:

1. Common boskys could refer to either bushes or woods.

2. *melde* could refer to either medlars or the plant orache (*Atriplex L. ssp*).

reeds [*flagges*] in *wyndilse*' for a twelve-year period.[38] *Flegge* or *flagge* could refer to any reeds or plants of the *Iris* genus, but most probably *Iris pseudacorus L*, the yellow iris, which is native to and common in Breckland along rivers in low marshes, on ditches and by ponds.[39] It is also possible that the field-name *fleggis* at Castor refers to the same plant, as it lay close to the Nene.

It might be expected that many of these elements would have an agricultural association, and that is the case for a few names. Of the main cereal crops, only rye and barley are explicitly mentioned, in *riewong* 'rye field' at Elton and *berdele* 'barley valley' in Lakenheath.[40] Beans and peas feature in each location: *peysfurlong* and *pesewong* 'furlong; and field where peas are grown' and *benelondfurlong* 'furlong on land where beans are grown' (Castor); *peselond* 'land where peas are grown' and *benelond* (Elton); and *pesȝierd* 'yard where peas are found' (Lakenheath).[41] Legumes were frequently grown for animal feed and were also known to improve soil quality. At Lakenheath we see references to vetches, which would also have been used as a feed, in the minor name record (*musepeselane*) and in the accounts.[42] The Lakenheath name *fodirfen*, containing ME *fodder* 'fodder', implies that this was a place where herbage was cut for winter feeding. In 1331 seven peasants were fined for mowing there 'to the damage of all commoners', suggesting that it was a regulated space. In a seventeenth-century survey it was stated that tenants had the right to mow in various places, including *fodirfen*, for 'sufficient feed for all manner of great cattle *sans* number'.[43] Elton's peasants also had access to fenland pasture for their animals ten miles away, at Farcet, but if this distant fen was named it is not recorded in the Elton records.[44]

Livestock and fowl were noted in all three vills, although to a lesser extent in Elton (Table 5.5). Cattle and sheep are found in each location, goats in Castor, geese in Castor and Elton and cranes in Lakenheath and possibly in Castor. Surprisingly, the only horses that are referred to are found in Castor at *coltstibbingges*, despite the fact that they appear in the manorial records in all three places. Several Lakenheath peasants found themselves in court for damaging demesne crops with horses and, although there are fewer instances, the same is true at Elton.[45] At Castor the field-names suggest not only that certain places were associated with different livestock but that young animals may have been separated, as at *calfcroftwong*, *coltstibbingges* and *kydwelwang*.

What is especially noticeable about the agricultural fauna incorporated into the field-names in all three vills is that it seems to reflect peasant rather than demesne stock. There are no doves, yet there were dovecotes in each location; peacocks are

---

38   CUL EDC/7/16/1/6.

39   P.J.O. Trist, *An ecological flora of Breckland* (Wakefield, 1979), p. 93.

40   TNA E 40/3286; CUL EDC/7/16/2/1/10/1.

41   NRO F(M) Charters 440, 534; BL Cotton MS Nero C. vii; TNA E 40/7038 and 10857; CUL EDC/7/16/1/11.

42   CUL EDC/7/16/1/14.

43   CUL EDC/7/16/1/8/3; SRO(B) HD/1720/1.

44   *CMR I*, p. 267.

45   For example: CUL EDC/7/16/2/8/5; EDC/7/16/2/8/9; EDC/7/16/2/8/27; *EMR*, p. 90.

Table 5.5
Field-name elements: faunal specifiers.

Field-name	Gloss	Vill
Cattle		
bosfourwlang	Furlong near the cowstall	Castor
bosweyn	Uncertain. ?Place where the oxcart was stored	Elton
calfcroftwong	Field by the calf croft	Castor
herdwyckbenelond	Land used for growing beans near the herd farm	Elton
hirdeweye, herdewey	The way or road used for cattle	Lakenheath
oucsshel	Uncertain. ?Hut used for oxen	Lakenheath
Horses		
coltstibbingges	Place where trees have been stubbed or cleared, associated with colts	Castor
Sheep		
scipdich	Ditch or dyke associated with sheep	Castor
rameshil	Hill associated with rams	Elton
schepelode	Either dyked watercourse associated with sheep, or near Shippea	Lakenheath
schepewassh	The place where the sheep are dipped	Lakenheath
Other quadrupeds		
gatacrehegg	Goat acre hedge or fence	Castor
everesholmfeld	Field next to a meadow associated with boars	Elton
foxdolis	Share of common land associated with either a fox's earth, or a place frequented by foxes	Castor
foxholes	Either a fox-hole, a fox's earth or a place where limestone is mined	Elton
haresaker	Either the acre overgrown with grey lichen; or frequented by hares	Castor
kydwelwang	Meadowland or open field by the spring associated with young goats or roe deer	Castor
rohauue	Roe deer or rough enclosure	Castor
wulfhauue	Wolf enclosure	Castor
wolvedale	Dale frequented by wolves	Elton
Fowl		
gosholm	Water-meadow frequented by geese	Castor, Elton
gosfurlong	Furlong frequented by geese	Castor
Other birds		
cornhay	Enclosure for either corn, or cranes	Castor
crakereye	Stream associated with crows	Castor
crowefurlong	Furlong associated with crows	Castor
crowepetwong	Meadow or field by the pit frequented by crows	Lakenheath
cranescroft	Croft associated with either cranes, or a person called Crane	Lakenheath
cranesfen	Fen associated with either cranes, or a person called Crane	Lakenheath
cranehilhord	Uncertain. ?The hoard found on crane hill	Lakenheath
earneshowepath	Either the path near the eagle's mound or associated with a person called Earn	Lakenheath
ernishowelle	Either the spring/stream near the eagle's mound or associated with a person called Earn	Lakenheath
pyttelsthornforlong	Uncertain. Perhaps thorn furlong associated with either hawks/kites, or a person called Pyttel[1]	Elton
Fish		
lochewere	Weir, river-dam or fishing enclosure where loach are found	Lakenheath
lusewer	Weir, river-dam or fishing enclosure where pike are found	Lakenheath
Insects		
boterflyemede	Meadow where butterflies are found	Elton

Note:

1. The personal name *Pyttel* is not recorded after the eighth century. 'Hawk's thorn' is semantically possible, but 'kite's thorn' less so. Overall it would be better to treat this name as of uncertain meaning: P. McClure, pers. comm.

included in the stock accounts at Elton and Castor, swans in the accounts of Elton and Lakenheath and ducks in all three places, and yet none of these birds appear in the field-name record.[46] Similarly, rabbits were an important part of the prior of Ely's Lakenheath demesne economy, but aside from the generic term used for the warren, *coninger*, there are no references to rabbits within the corpus of field-names. Another striking omission given each vill's proximity to water and fisheries is the lack of names referencing fish, with just two possibilities in Lakenheath: *lochewere* (loach) and *lusewer* (pike). Could it be that seigneurial rights over certain fish prompted the peasants to think in topographical and economic terms when naming these places? At Lakenheath, pike were reserved for the lord and, if any were caught, fishermen were obliged to offer him first refusal according to the local bylaw.[47] Given that local topographical features were named by the peasants themselves, this suggests the possibility that only those aspects of the agricultural landscape that the peasants had direct and frequent interaction with and, fundamentally, some element of control over were deemed by them to be significant enough to name with precision. If this was the case, then this has important implications for using minor landscape names to gain a better understanding of the peasant worldview, rather than that of the lord.

A number of other animals and birds that are not directly associated with agriculture are also featured in the field-names. Cranes are found in abundance within field-names at Lakenheath, unsurprisingly, as they formed part of the rent within the Clare manor prior to the fourteenth century.[48] However, the possibility that at least two of these names, *cranescroft* and *cranesfen*, derive from family names must be considered, as there was a tenement and half an acre of land at *cranescroft*, suggesting that the name originally referred to its tenant.[49] Crows are found in Castor and Lakenheath, and foxes in Castor and Elton.[50] Crows could be a nuisance, especially in the sowing season, and so it may have been the case that places that were frequented by birds needed to be especially noted, as this might have an effect on crop yield. Similarly, game animals such as wolves, boar, foxes, deer and hares

---

46 NRO F(M) 2388 and 2389; NRO F(M) Roll 233; CUL EDC/7/16/1; *EMR*, p. 77.

47 Although this did not stop peasants poaching and selling pike illegally on occasion. Given the high financial value of pike, it may have been deemed important to name the spot where they were most likely to be caught. CUL EDC/7/16/1/2, 3, 4, 11 and 13; EDC/7/16/2/1/6/5; EDC/7/16/2/1/1/11.

48 An early fourteenth-century IPM outlines a rent of twelve cranes worth 12s., and a 1334–35 collector's account (at which time Clare fee was in the hands of the prior of Ely) reveals that these were due from twelve customers, the value having increased to 36s.: TNA C 134/42; CUL EDC/7/16/1/10.

49 The tenement was decayed in 1318; TNA SC 2/203/94/3; CUL EDC/7/16/2/9/2; J.T. Munday, *Crane's croft* (Lakenheath, 1970), p. 3.

50 The name *foxholes* can sometimes refer to the holes created when mining for slate limestone, but that is unlikely here. D. Blackburn, 'Foxholes, Pendle and Ryelands', *Journal of the English Place-Name Society*, 41 (2009), pp. 127–9; buzzards may feature at Elton: *pyttlesthornfurlong* could denote birds or an individual.

could have an adverse effect on crops and livestock, although the game field-names at Castor almost certainly reference the hunting landscape there.

Of the remaining names, one mentions an insect: the butterfly, at Elton's *boterflyemede*. This appears odd, when we consider that butterflies must have frequented most of Elton's meadows: what was special about this particular meadow? Unlike the majority of Elton's meadows, *boterflyemede* lies at a distance from the river, near an area that had become a cow pasture by the eighteenth century and very close to some of the parish's poorer soils.[51] In 1747 *Hardy Bellands*, which probably evolved from the medieval furlong *herdwykbenelond*, lay near *Butterfly Meadow*.[52] The first element of this name means 'herd farm', suggesting that it was considered the most appropriate land in the parish for livestock. Unlike *boterflyemede*, the meadows that can be identified alongside the river almost all have adjectival names – long meadow, short hyrst, great meadow and so on – which seems like a practical solution for furlongs with similar terrain lying close together. And yet they would all certainly have attracted insects such as butterflies.

Boterflyemede lay on the edge of an area of lime-rich clayey and loamy soil close to the point at which it intersected with an expanse of shallower lime-rich soil. The soil association for this area is Evesham 1, which comprises calcareous clays on an underlying geology of Jurassic clay and limestone, often with limestone bands, and frequently on high ground adjacent to limestone soils, as is the case here (Figure 5.1).[53] Calcareous grasslands are valued for their biological diversity – a square metre might contain as many as forty different wildflower species – and, because of this, they have been described recently as being 'of principal importance in England', not least because of their depletion in modern times.[54] Almost 50 per cent of European native butterflies have been associated with calcareous grassland in a modern study, more than have been found in alpine meadowland; consequently, the high quantity of butterflies found in this habitat has been linked with the richness of plant species.[55] The soil structure of Elton's *boterflyemede* differed from the alluvial soils and gravel terraces on the river Nene floodplain, where the majority of Elton's meadow was situated, resulting in a markedly different microhabitat. This, alongside *boterflyemede*'s more isolated location, meant that those naming it were not confined by the practical aspects as they were by the river, but could focus on one of its most obvious characteristics – its abundance of butterflies.

---

51 Upex, 'The reconstruction of openfield layout', p. 87 and Appendix 6; although local farmer Robert Fray advised that his belief is that *boterflyemede* lies on the adjacent site of medieval *herdwykbenelond* (pers. comm.). Whichever location is correct, both fields share the same soil type and underlying geology.

52 A 1692 glebe terrier includes 'Boltswell', in the same location: Clark, *A village on the Nene*, p. 320.

53 *The Soils Guide*, <www.landis.org.uk>, accessed June 2017. 0411a Evesham 1 comprises Evesham, Haselor, Sherborne and Moreton.

54 C.A.M. van Swaay, 'The importance of calcareous grasslands for butterflies in Europe', *Biological Conservation*, 104 (2002), p. 315; F. Ashwood, 'Lowland calcareous grassland: creation and management in land regeneration', *Best Practice Guidance for Land Regeneration*, 18 (2014), p. 1; by 1747, *boterflyemede* had become an arable furlong: EFB.

55 van Swaay, 'The importance of calcareous grasslands', p. 317.

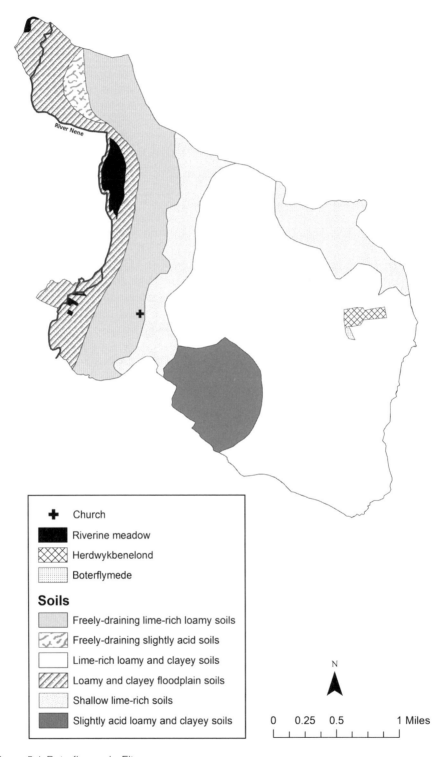

Figure 5.1 *Boterflyemede*, Elton.

It is clear from the natural flora and fauna recorded by the peasants of Castor, Elton and Lakenheath that their world was closely observed, and the attributes they noted largely reflected the individual topography of each place. It is striking that references to fauna exclusively associated with the demesne, and by association with lordship, were excluded. The use of the qualifier *byrig* emphasises this. Neither Castor's *biryhay* nor Elton's *byrilond* reveal anything about the usage, flora or fauna of these lands, simply that it belonged to the demesne. Names such as *les hayes* associated with the Castor demesne also emphasise this. These names appear to lack the attention to detail of names such as *cornhay*, *gosholm* and *coltstibbingges*. In all three vills, servile individuals would have built up an understanding of the qualities of the demesne furlongs through generations supplying labour services. Could it be that, in addition to their reflection of ownership, these less descriptive names signify peasants' lesser interest in these places?[56]

The names referencing topography at Elton, and to a lesser degree at Lakenheath, appear to accentuate the more practical aspects of the landscape. They seem to offer considerations of the type of terrain and, perhaps by implication indicate how it ought to be treated. To make a comparison, the simplex name *stibbing* at Castor tells us that the land has been cleared. But at Lakenheath we learn about places that were excessively wet, such as *seelode* and *stampes*. At Elton a number of qualifying elements reference specific attributes and qualities of the soil, as evidenced in *chalkyhil*, *chiselstonhowe*, *cleyfurlong*, *molwellehyl* and *le sondes*.[57] Some of these name types are apparent in Castor, but in far fewer instances. Greater scrutiny of these more practical names and what they might reveal about aspects of the landscape and the mentalities of those who worked it will be considered in chapter eight.

The supernatural environment

At least one field-name and possibly others have connections with what we might label the supernatural, and this offers another means of exploring local peasant culture.[58] Only one name could be described unequivocally as having a supernatural provenance – *þirspitt*, the 'giants' or demons' pit', located in Ailsworth. In the pre-Christian period certain pits were associated by pagans with the entrance to the underworld, places where communication with supernatural beings might take

---

56 There were undoubtedly fewer servile peasants living in late medieval Castor, and it is possible that these names reflect free peasants' naming practices.

57 The first element in *molwellehyll* could conceivably derive from the personal name Mary (Jayne Carroll, pers. comm.); however, the specific topography of this field strongly suggests that ON *mǫl* 'gravel, gravelly soil' is more likely (see also chapter eight, p. 181).

58 Before the twelfth century medieval society did not formally recognise a distinction between natural and supernatural phenomena. For current scholarly thinking, see C.S. Watkins, *History and the supernatural in medieval England* (Cambridge, 2007), pp. 18–19; A. Hall, *Elves in Anglo-Saxon England* (Woodbridge, 2009), pp. 11–12.

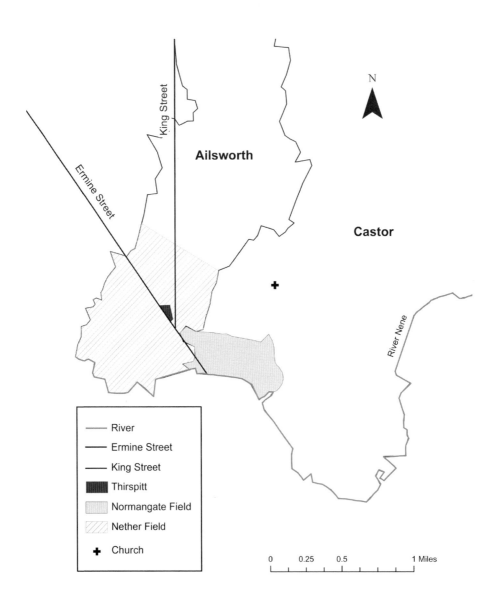

Figure 5.2. The speculative site of the medieval furlong *þirspitt*, Nether Field, Ailsworth. Sources: *Peterborough to Lutton 1050mm gas pipeline: archaeological evaluation, excavation and watching brief, 1998, vol 1: report* (1998); BL Cotton MS Nero C. vii/14; NRO F(M) Charter 534.

place.[59] The furlong *þirspitt* features twice in the medieval documentary record; as *thirspitt* in the 1393 Peterborough Abbey demesnal survey and as both *therspittes* and *thorspittes* in a charter dated 1445.[60] Its etymological root – OE *þyrs* or ON *þurs* – suggests pre-Conquest origins. The survey suggests that it lies in Ailsworth Nether Field, the location of which is known from the tithe map of 1846,[61] although there is nothing further in the documents to pinpoint the exact location of the field. However, a 1998 archaeological report highlights 'an extensive complex of gravel quarry pits, the foundations of a temple-like building with an associated pathway and two stone boundary markers, part of the possible foundations of Ermine Street'.[62] The location of the Roman quarry complex lies within the triangular-shaped piece of land between Ermine Street and King Street (Figure 5.2), significantly perhaps, within the area known as Nether Field by the fourteenth century. *Þirspitt* cannot be firmly connected with the quarry and temple complex excavated in Ailsworth, but the evidence strongly suggests a match, particularly as giants were expected to reside in pits and fissures in the ground in the late Anglo-Saxon period.[63]

Looking backward: naming the landscape

An assessment of each manor's topography through each respective corpus of field-names is illuminating, confirming certain expectations and also raising some noteworthy points for further analysis. The names considered hitherto all emphasise the inspiration provided by a detailed knowledge and understanding of local topography and its flora and fauna. While the evidence has been taken further here than many onomasts have previously permitted, the interpretation nevertheless chimes with modern rationalist thinking. Few would deny that peasants enjoyed a close relationship with their local environment, and that readings such as this do not stray too far from the possibilities. However useful this largely ecological survey may be, though, it offers little in the way of cultural examination and, in the same manner in

---

59 A. Ross, 'Shafts, pits, wells – sanctuaries of the Belgic Britons?' in D.D.A. Simpson and J.M. Coles (eds), *Studies in ancient Europe: essays presented to Stuart Piggott* (Bristol, 1968), pp. 277–8; H.R.E. Davidson, *Myths and symbols in pagan Europe: early Scandinavian and Celtic religions* (Manchester, 1988), p. 26. Lakenheath's *le grynd*, with a possible meaning of 'abyss', might also have supernatural origins, as it is a term associated with the Anglo-Saxon poem *Crist and Satan*: *EPNE*, vol. 1, p. 211; nevertheless, Keith Briggs (pers. comm.) suggests that this name may derive from ODan *grein*, 'fork of a river'.

60 BL Cotton MS Nero C. vii/14; NRO F(M) Charter 534; there is a possible third reference, NRO F(M) Charter 448, dated 1366, mentions *the Pittis* in Ailsworth, but it is unclear whether this is the same place.

61 NRO Map T 236.

62 *Peterborough to Lutton 1050mm gas pipeline: archaeological evaluation, excavation and watching brief, 1998, vol 1: report* (1998), p. 27; figure 12 of this report describes the '?temple' as Romano-British.

63 The reference to the potential later temple is also worth noting. The late tenth-century *Exeter Book* features the poem *The Ruin*, which also associates Roman ruins with giants, and, as Roman architectural remains were plentiful in Castor and Ailsworth, perhaps this is an interesting aside.

which I have criticised purely reconstructionist studies, assessing field-names based solely on environmental factors would be to disregard facets of peasant landscape that until recently have been largely overlooked. Thus far, although a necessary initial exercise has been undertaken, the analysis could be judged one-dimensional. It offers a purely descriptive outline of the terrain, but falls short of a more nuanced understanding of the rationale behind the naming processes. Taking this a stage further, if the naming processes can begin to be understood then it may be possible to identify changes in the patterns of nomenclature and therefore to argue that naming is a dynamic process. This is particularly important in considering why some potentially early field-names endured into the late medieval period.[64] In order to understand what impels people to name places, it is necessary to consider the work of sociologists, anthropologists and those focused on landscape studies, alongside that of onomasts.

Although scholars are increasingly recognising the importance of minor landscape names, little has been written about what drives medieval landscape naming practices in England, and how those naming the landscape made their selection from a potential range of options.[65] This is in part because it is a very difficult question, and a definitive answer seems likely to prove elusive. However, there are several lines of enquiry that may allow us to get closer to understanding something of these complex processes. This sub-section focuses on how minor landscape names may have been created in England, and which name types may have numbered among the earliest. Attempting to identify early name categories is important, as it will aid us in recognising potentially later names, helping to establish a possible chronology which can then be used to assist in our understanding of the dynamics of place-naming. Most medieval field-names began to be documented from the thirteenth century, and if we can determine which groups of names are the earliest, the names recorded from this point onward provide us with a snapshot of a period in which it is possible to witness the dynamics of naming, and thus allow us to assess what drives both the creation of new names and changes to existing name stock – and, perhaps more importantly, to analyse any differences.

Given that we can no longer interrogate those who named medieval fields, a range of evidence will be used to support the argument made here, including British and Old English settlement names and evidence from the naming practices of First Nations people, who, like early medieval rural dwellers, maintained a close relationship with the landscape. Anthropologists and ethnographers have studied the naming practices of indigenous people, who were living in close proximity to an environment

---

64 Recent scholarship suggests that field-names and minor landscape names first recorded in later medieval documents can, in some instances, offer evidence that is applicable to the pre-Conquest landscape: E. Rye, 'Dialect in the Viking-age Scandianivian diaspora: the evidence of medieval minor names', PhD thesis (University of Nottingham, 2016), p. 30 and p. 351; R. Gregory, 'Minor and field-names of Thurgarton Wapentake, Nottinghamshire', PhD thesis (University of Nottingham, 2016), p. 340; Kilby, 'Divining medieval water', pp. 61–2.

65 Although see P. Gammeltoft, 'In search of the motives behind naming: a discussion of a name-semantic model of categorisation', in E. Brylla and M. Wahlberg (eds), *Proceedings of the 21st International Congress of Onomastic Sciences* (Uppsala, 2005), pp. 151–60; Jones, 'Responding to modern flooding'.

that was integral to their worldview. These naming traditions can be usefully compared with medieval practices. The motivation behind early naming practices is difficult to discern, but it has been suggested that a primary stimulus may have been a pressing need to understand the landscape more fully.[66] Kleinschmidt argues that the early medieval landscape lying outside the confines of the settlement was viewed as hostile, and so perhaps naming was a means of neutralising its latent malevolence.[67] This idea suggests labelling was a mechanism designed to demystify the landscape in order to possess and control it more thoroughly. Margaret Gelling argues that some of the earliest settlement names in England were topographical. Assessing the British elements in Romano-British place-names, she found that the overwhelming majority were of this type.[68] She also suggests that some Old English topographical place-names can be dated from the fifth century, and that they chronicle early Anglo-Saxon settlers' perceptions of the English landscape.[69] In several cases the head settlements of Anglo-Saxon estates were topographical, as at Lambourn (Berkshire) 'lamb stream', a phenomenon also associated with Hwiccan minster sites by Hooke.[70] In alignment with Gelling's findings, in detailed studies of Anglo-Saxon boundary clauses Hooke has also noted the marked prominence of physical topography.[71]

In a number of cases topographical settlement names underwent further change, frequently acquiring personal name specifics.[72] As outlined above (chapter two, p. 21), the earliest written forms of Evesham (Worcestershire) were *etham* 'at ham', and *cronochomme* 'crane ham', before finally becoming *Eveshomme*, 'Ēof's land hemmed in by water'.[73] Similarly, Allensmore (Herefordshire), had previously been simplex *mōr* 'marsh, barren upland', while Colne (Gloucestershire), a name

---

66 J. Stuart-Murray, 'Unnameable landscapes', *Landscape Review*, 2 (1995), p. 34.

67 H. Kleinschmidt, *Understanding the middle ages: the transformation of ideas and attitudes in the medieval world* (Woodbridge, 2000), pp. 42–3.

68 Gelling, *Signposts to the past*, p. 50; although Oliver Padel suggests that some settlement names containing Brittonic elements may have been applied later, following migration by Welsh or Cumbric speakers: O. Padel, 'Brittonic place-names in England', in J. Carroll and D.N. Parsons (eds), *Perceptions of place: twenty-first century interpretations of English place-name studies* (Nottingham, 2013), p. 7.

69 Gelling, *Signposts to the past*, pp. 123–6. See also: B. Cox, 'The place-names of the earliest English records', *Journal of the English Place-Name Society*, 8 (1976), p. 56. M. Gelling, *Place-names in the landscape: the geographical roots of England's place-names* (London, 1993), p. 6; Gelling and Cole, *The landscape of place-names*, pp. xix–xxi; D. Hooke 'Place-name hierarchies and interpretations in parts of Mercia', in R. Jones and S. Semple (eds), *Sense of place in Anglo-Saxon England* (Donington, 2012), p. 185; Reynolds and Semple, 'Digging for names', p. 77.

70 Gelling, *Signposts to the past*, p. 123; Hooke, *Landscape of Anglo-Saxon England*, pp. 12–13; Hooke, 'Place-name hierarchies', p. 185; see also Kilby, 'Divining medieval water', pp. 61–3.

71 Hooke, *Anglo-Saxon landscapes*, p. 129.

72 M. Gelling, 'Towards a chronology for English place-names', in D. Hooke (ed.), *Anglo-Saxon settlements* (Oxford, 1988), p. 73.

73 Gelling and Cole, *The landscape of place-names*, p. 53; Hooke, *Landscape of Anglo-Saxon England*, p. 13; E. Ekwall, *The concise dictionary of English place-names* (Oxford, 1960), p. 170.

derived from the river Coln, changed entirely, becoming Bibury 'Bēage's manor house'.[74] There are very few surviving examples of comprehensive name-change in early medieval England, and so it would be inappropriate to suggest that this was a standard trajectory. Nevertheless, it is striking that these names began as purely topographical, before finally becoming immutable as, predominantly, compound names featuring a personal name as the specific element. What this seems to show is that, in some instances, earlier names that described local topography were particularly susceptible to change, especially in the period during which Anglo-Saxon great estates were being broken down into smaller units often held by lesser landowners, between the ninth and eleventh centuries. In contrast, settlement names that changed after this date – usually from the later twelfth century – tended to adopt an affix, frequently associated with the lord's name, such as Stanford Rivers and Stapleford Tawney (Essex).[75]

In a detailed study of Berkshire Gelling argued that early topographical place-names there exhibited a propensity to focus on water in its varied forms – in particular its supply, the control of that supply (Balking 'pool stream'), associated crossing places (Lyford 'flax ford'), and adjacent dry sites for settlement (Goosey 'goose island or raised ground').[76] This mirrors the naming practices of the Kaluli people of Papua New Guinea, where the anthropologist Edward Schieffelin observed that natural environmental features dominated their landscape name vocabulary.[77] In particular, he noted that a key referent was frequently used to name the surrounding landscape, and for the Kaluli this was usually water. He remarked that named streams were often used as the qualifying element for adjacent topography – *stream*-spring, *stream*-slope, etc. A comparable approach to nomenclature has been noted by other anthropologists and ethno-geographers studying the naming practices of native American Indians. For example, the local minor names of the Gitksan Indians of British Columbia, Canada, were principally topographical, as were those of the Apache and Navajo.[78]

---

74 Gelling and Cole, *The landscape of place-names*, p. 59 and p. 61; by 1180, part of Lambourn had become *Esgareston*: G. Fellows-Jensen, 'Grimston and Grimsby: the Danes as re-namers', in R. Jones and S. Semple (eds), *Sense of place in Anglo-Saxon England* (Donington, 2012), p. 352; Gelling, 'Towards a chronology', p. 73; Watts, *English place-names*, p. 54.

75 R. Jones, 'Thinking through the manorial affix', in S. Turner and B. Silvester (eds), *Life in medieval landscapes: people and places in the middle ages, papers in memory of H.S.A. Fox* (Oxford, 2012), p. 254.

76 Gelling and Cole, *The landscape of place-names*, p. xix; Gelling, *Signposts to the past*, pp. 118–19.

77 E.L. Schieffelin, *The sorrow of the lonely and the burning of the dancers* (St. Lucia, Queensland, 1976), p. 30.

78 L.M. Johnson, '"A place that's good", Gitksan landscape perception and ethnoecology', *Human Ecology*, 28/2 (2000), p. 305; K.H. Basso, '"Stalking with stories": names, places and moral narratives among the Western Apache', in E.M. Bruner (ed.), *Text, play, and story: the construction and reconstruction of self and society* (Prospect Heights, IL, 1984), pp. 27–32; S.C. Jett, 'Place-naming, environment, and perception among the Canyon De Chelly Navajo of Arizona', *The Professional Geographer*, 49/4 (1997), p. 486.

One of the knottiest issues in examining field-names and minor landscape names is dating. Documentary evidence provides *terminus ante quem* dating, but determining how far back one can safely extend names is problematic. Nevertheless, it is clear that topography was an important marker in the naming practices of societies living in direct contact with the landscape. In this respect, purely topographical minor names form a significant subset, and may provide a tentative means for assessing the mutability of minor landscape names.[79] It is certainly possible to detect patterns in naming in medieval Castor, Elton and Lakenheath that are similar to those associated with the Kaluli. At Lakenheath, where water abounds, *brademere*, *brademerepettis* and *brademereweye* follow this pattern, as do Elton's *lytlebrok* and *lyttlebrocfurlong*. In Castor, the name *stanewelle* is used in a similar way in *stanewellehil, stanewellebrok and stanuwellefurlong*.[80] In each of these examples, the key referents *brademere*, *lytlebrok* and *stanewelle* must have been named prior to the associated furlongs. A number of potentially chronologically earlier names can be detected in this way; these are outlined in Table 5.6 and expressed diagrammatically in Figure 5.3. In all three places, water appears to be a key referent. This manner of assessing the likely chronology of names produces interesting results, but is unlikely to be complete. As surveys were often selective, only recording names in which the demesne had an interest, it is extremely likely that there are a number of missing names – for example, names such as Elton's *smalewellefurlong* 'furlong associated with a small spring or stream' and *hollewellefurlong* 'furlong associated with a hollow spring or stream' indicate possible 'missing' referents (*smalewelle* and *hollewelle*) that do not appear in the corpus of medieval names.[81] It is also possible that referents with associated cultural specifiers, especially those featuring personal or place-names, such as Elton's *billingbrok* and *hosebernssladewell*, may have undergone a name change similar to that of the settlement name Evesham (above, p. 107).

The dynamics of landscape naming: cultural names

Although the problems with this approach have been highlighted, it is nevertheless useful for drawing broad distinctions between the minor names of each manor. Names with purely topographical elements – especially those indicating water – may represent some of the earliest names. Those exclusively featuring cultural elements, denoting some form of human interaction with the landscape, such as *baillies halfaker*, may signify later names. Field-names with anthroponyms as qualifying elements are especially worthy of further scrutiny as some can be attributed to peasants found within documentary sources, and can therefore be dated more dependably.[82]

---

79 Kilby, 'Divining medieval water', p. 62; whilst in most settlements topography would have been fairly stable, in some places (such as those with a propensity to flood) it is acknowledged that the environment might be more changable.

80 NRO F(M) Charters 63, 68 and 336; *CN*, p. 112; *EMR*, p. 131; TNA E 40/5490; CUL EDC/7/16/2/1/4/3; EDC/7/16/2/1/8/18; EDC/7/16/2/1/8/22.

81 TNA E 40/6856; *EMR*, p. 90.

82 Anthroponyms are personal names (such as Wulfstan), bynames or family names.

Table 5.6
Key minor-name referents: Castor, Elton and Lakenheath.

Referent	Progeny
Castor	
Cuffic	Cufficwelle, Cuffichil, Cuffic lacum, Cuffic milne, Cuffycdam
Carton	Cartonbrok, Cartonwelles, Cartonhowe, the furlong butting on Cartonbrok
Stanewelle	Stanewellebrok, Stanewellebrok furlong, Stanewellehil, Stanewell furlong, Stanewellefeld, Stanewellegate
Norwell	Norwellhill, Norwellwong
Aldwellemor	Aldwellemoresike, Audlemorefurlong
Wridmere	Wridmereslade, Wridemeregate
Langmor	Langmore furlong
Langdyk	Langdykbrok, Langdyke furlong, Langdichgate, Langedikhegg, Overlangdyk, Netherlangdyk
Tasilhil	Tasshelhil furlong
Elton	
Arnewassh	Arnewashbrok
Billingbrok	Billingbrokfurlong
Lytlebrok	Lyttlebrocfurlong
Hollewellmore[1]	Hollewellmorefurlong
Dam, le	Damhalfaker
Clack	Clackuesmor, Clakkisheuden
Longhyl	Longhylslade. Langehilweye
Mersh, le	Merschfurlong
Hosebernsslade	Hosebernssladewell, Hosebernssladeoverende, Hosebernssladenetherende
Lakenheath	
Caldewell	Caldwellwong
Brademere	Brademerepettes, Brademerewong, Brademereweye
Blakemere	Blakemerelond
Fledmere	Fledmerecote, Fledmerefen, Fledmerebeche
Oldlode	Oldlodesende
Mere, le	Merewong
Lochewere	Locheweremor
Millemarch	Millemarchmor
Passeford	Passfordwong
Hellondhel	Hellondhelfurlong, Hellondhelhend
Hereshel	Hereshelwere
Bramhowe	Bramhowemedwe

Note:

1. The survival of *hollewellefurlong* indicates that the referent in this case may have been *hollewelle*. Castor's *aldwellemor* may also have originally derived from a hypothetical *aldwelle*.

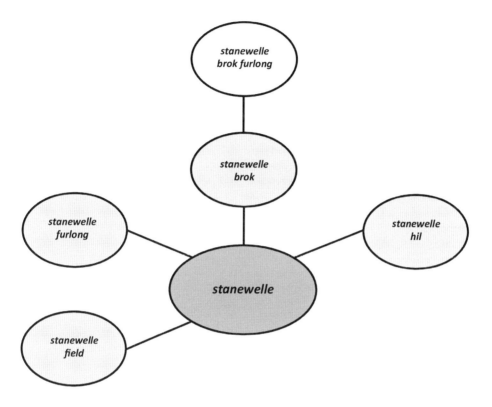

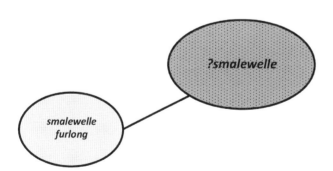

Figure 5.3. A hypothetical model of the chronology of naming at Castor and Elton.

Table 5.7
Field-names and minor landscape names with anthroponymic qualifiers: Elton, Castor and Lakenheath.

Elton	Castor	Lakenheath
Goderichsladesoverende	**Dodesfurlong**	**Stubbardsfen**
Hosebernssladeoverende	**Glademannesheg**	**Woluarderwelle**
Hosebernssladenetherende	**Glademanishirne**	[Bolemanswong]
Hosebernssladewell	**Gunewade**	[Erlespinfold]
?Pyttlesthornfurlong†	**Gunwadewey**	[*Knytesmere*]
?Suonesland	**Thurwardeslond**	[*Kyngeshethe*]
Wul[f]standikes	**Wakerescroft**	[Ladispol]
Wymundeswong	**Wul[f]stansdic**	[*Smetheslond*]≠
[Abbotisholm]	**Wymundfurweyes**	?*Bolesheuedlond*
Athardescroft	[Abbotishauue]	?*Bolewer*
Attirdholm	[Ballies Halfaker]	?*Douesdich*
Saldinescrosfurlong	[Sherrueswong]	*Dykmannesdich*
	Bernardiswro	*Dykmanneswong*
	Bilmanstibbing	*Douuezhithe*
	Bouetonhay	*Flawners*
	Bowetonholm	*Gopayneshithe*
	?*Buddisnabbe*	*Mackesrode*
	Bretteneswode	*Mayhewcruch*
	Butlers	
	Cordelsplace	
	Fremannesacre	
	Illing (the wood)	
	Ingewell	
	Ingewelle medwe	
	Reginald's spring	
	Keten'place	
	Lillefordbalk	
	Lordyslake	
	Lordeston	
	?Maggebuskhert	
	Paris (the wood)	

Notes:

1. [] denotes possible family name.
2. Names in bold are personal names of OE or ON origin.
3. Italicised names denote active bynames found within thirteenth- and fourteenth-century documents.
4. Names prefixed with ? symbolise those that may not relate to personal or family names.
5. ≠ a reference to land associated with customary ironwork was known as *smithsland*, suggesting that this name relates to tenure: CUL EDC/7/16/2/1/8/27.
6. † see also Table 5.5, note 1.

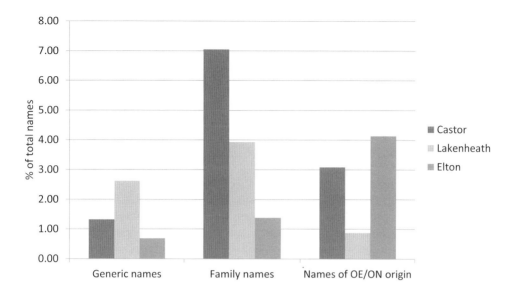

Figure 5.4. The percentage of anthroponyms in field-names: Elton, Castor and Lakenheath.

These names feature in each of the three manors, but they do not all follow a similar pattern (Table 5.7 and Figure 5.4). The names have been divided into three groups: 'generic' names, featuring names that are probably not peasant bynames (such as *sherrueswong*, Castor; *abbotisholm*, Elton; *erlespinfold*, Lakenheath); those having specific family names, or referencing known individuals (such as *lillefordbalk*, Castor; *athardescroft*, Elton; *dykmannesdich*, Lakenheath); and names of OE or ON origin.[83] Associated with the latter group, there is a significantly higher ratio of early personal names connected with field-names at Elton.[84] It seems likely that these names date from the twelfth century or earlier.[85] This, coupled with the fact that there are proportionally fewer known later medieval peasant family names within the field-names, begins to suggest that those at Elton were much more static.

---

83 The generic names are all listed in Table 5.7. It seems unlikely that many of them are peasant bynames (e.g., *erlespinfold*, Lakenheath; *abbotishauue*, Castor and so on). There are peasants named Knight and Kyng at Lakenheath, although they rarely feature in the record, and never in connection with *knytesmere* or *kyngeshethe*, although it is possible that they are associated.

84 Each name has been counted once (e.g., the group of names derived from the name Osbern and Atharde (Elton) count as one individual respectively).

85 Of the names of OE or ON origin, almost all the insular name stock had gone out of use by 1250, suggesting those fossilised in field-names were earlier – perhaps twelfth century or earlier; Hosebern could be either late OE or Continental Germanic, the latter having a greater chance of survival post-1250 (P. McClure, pers. comm.). Nevertheless, these field-names cannot be linked with any of the tenants featured on an Elton extent of 1160x1218: *CMR III*, pp. 257–60.

The two putative later medieval family names referenced at Elton – Athard, and Saldine – appear in the source material.[86] A peasant family named Saladyn appears in records from the late thirteenth century. Philip Saladin was a cottar holding a messuage and half an acre of land, and so hardly a substantial landholder.[87] It is possible that this is not a true reflection of the family's wealth, but nothing in the court rolls suggests that they were a family of substantial means, and they were not taxpayers in 1327 or 1332. Did they take their family name from the field-name, or was there perhaps a long-forgotten story associated with both family and landscape?[88] Similarly, the Athard family appears infrequently in the documentary record. They were villeins, and in 1279 Henry Athard held a virgate of land. Like the Saladyns, they are not recorded taxpayers. Nevertheless, these families are the only contemporary groups that can be associated strongly with the field-names of late medieval Elton.

A greater proportion of individuals can be firmly connected with the local landscape at Lakenheath. While there are no Bolemans in the thirteenth- and fourteenth-century documents at Lakenheath, there are many Douues, Dykemans and Flawners, representatives of whom appear in the 1327 lay subsidy, suggesting that they were from wealthier Lakenheath families. Two tenants called Macke – Gilbert and Richard, deceased by the fourteenth century – both had substantial landholdings including half a sheep-fold, and while *mackesrode* cannot certainly be said to derive from this family it remains a distinct possibility.[89] The only reference to *gopaynshithe* is particularly illuminating. It is mentioned in a dispute between Robert Gopayn and Richard in the Lane in which Lane was alleged to have taken a boat from *gopaynshithe* which subsequently fell into disrepair. In his defence, Lane suggested that it was

> lawful for him to moor his boat … [and that] the place called *gopayneshithe* by Robert Gopayn once belonged to Matthew, son of Seward of Lakenheath who gave it to God and St Edmund … and that never then nor since has Robert Gopayn or his ancestors had any right therein.[90]

The ensuing inquisition found Lane guilty, but the implication was that Gopayn had recently deliberately renamed the landing place to bind his and his family's claim to the land more tightly.[91]

Nevertheless, despite the greater quantity of late medieval family names within field-names in Lakenheath, as compared with Elton, as a proportion of the whole

---

86   References to 'the land of Alotta' have not been interpreted as a field-name: *EMR*, pp. 56–8, 126–8, 158–60 and 204–6.

87   *RH II*, p. 657.

88   The name refers either to 'one who went on the Third Crusade' or to 'someone thought to resemble Saladin in some way': P. Hanks *et al.*, 'Saladine', *The Oxford dictionary of family names in Britain and Ireland* (Oxford, 2016) <http://www.oxfordreference.com/view/10.1093/acref/9780199677764.0001/acref-9780199677764-e-35524>, accessed June 2017.

89   CUL EDC/7/16/2/1/4/3; EDC/7/16/2/1/7/3; EDC/7/16/2/1/7/5.

90   CUL EDC/7/16/2/1/9/7.

91   TNA SC 2/203/95.

corpus Castor family names featured significantly more frequently. Of those that can be identified, the Lords were a knightly family and the Boueton, Cordel, Butler, Illing, Paris and Lilford families were prominent free tenants with considerable landholdings.[92] The single reference to *reginald's spring* comes in a copy of a charter detailing an undated transfer of land between the abbey and William Clerk, son of William, son of Reginald.[93] The name of the spring, given in the document as '*reginald's spring*' [*in iiij acras et dimidiam in motllede iuxta fontem qui vocatur fons reginaldi*], possibly refers to William Clerk's grandfather. *Bernardswro* 'Bernard's nook' is more difficult to assign, but may be associated with Bernard de Pickworth, alias Bernard de Paston, another notable free tenant.[94] There are no recorded field-names featuring the Cordel or Butler families before 1348; however, in fifteenth-century documents their family names are encapsulated within *cordelsplace* and *butlers*.[95] Contemporaneously, the Breton family name is preserved in *brettenneswode*; and it is possible that *buddesnabbe* refers to the Budde family, and may even have replaced the simplex *le nab*.[96] The possibility cannot be ruled out that these names are older than they appear. What seems clear is that, at Castor, unlike at Elton and Lakenheath, none of the personal or family name qualifiers within the field-names can be confidently associated with any servile peasant.

The suggestion that names at Elton were more static is given additional weight once the remaining cultural names are considered. Although the trend is much less marked, the overall proportion of newer names having a cultural influence is fewer at Elton and greatest at Castor, as shown in Figure 5.5. Here, the categories are largely designed to isolate those names where local settlements are used as qualifying elements (place). 'Activity' relates to any reference to an undertaking or to a change of landscape use. These activities are varied and include assarting (such as *sartis*, Castor), meeting places (such as *mutforde*, Lakenheath) and quarrying (such as *lymkilnwong*, Castor). 'Religion' includes all names in *church-*, alongside references to cemeteries and saints.[97] The emerging picture of thirteenth- and fourteenth-century Castor suggests a vill in which naming was a much more dynamic process. Perhaps this should be unsurprising, given the greater relative independence of the resident peasantry – where lordship was weaker, there were perhaps more opportunities for

---

92   The byname Lord was associated with the Thorold family.

93   CUL PDC/MS 1.

94   BL Cotton MS Nero C. vii/14 f. 159d; the potential use of his Christian name is supported by the evidence within the 1301 lay subsidy, where the only tenant of this name is labelled simply *Bernard*, with no cognomen: TNA E 179/155/31/42; there is a reference to an heir of Robert Pickworth transferring a tenement called *bernardisplace* in 1408: NRO F(M) Charter 492.

95   NRO F(M) Charters 496, 515 and 563.

96   NRO F(M) Charters 514, 532 and 533; references to the family names Butler, Bretun, Budde and Cordel are noted from the thirteenth century in Castor. Bretton Woods is still used as a local place-name.

97   The Castor field-name *edmundisleye*, alias *St Edmund's Land* and *St Edmunde's stones furlong*, is counted within 'activity', as it refers to cleared land leased to the abbey of Bury St Edmunds to allow stone quarried in nearby Barnack to reach the Nene across Castor territory.

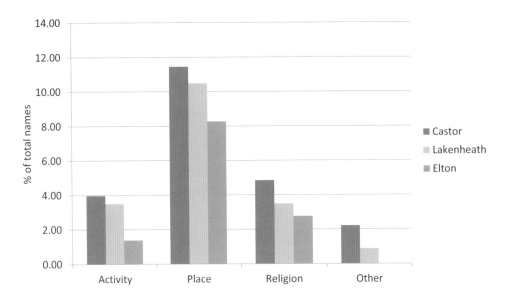

Figure 5.5. 'Cultural' qualifiers in field-names: Elton, Castor and Lakenheath.

reconfiguring the layout of the landscape, here evidenced by plentiful enclosure. It is also possible that this greater independence is manifest in the names of Castor's open fields, where these larger cropping units were given markedly different names to the largely directional appellations apparent in Elton and Lakenheath (Table 5.8). Only once, in a charter dated 1305, is there a reference to a north field; however, the grantor is described as 'Gilbert de Somersham in Upton', suggesting that he was less familiar with the names of the open fields than a Castor resident would have been.[98] In 1354 one charter describes the fields as 'in the east field, 1½ rods together lying in le Thornes … [and] in the field towards the south 1½ rods together lying in Hamfeld', offering their directional positions as well as the open-field names, but this does not imply that the cardinal points were used as alternative names.[99] It is entirely possible that the scribe, more used to detailing directional field names, requested the additional information. The overriding impression remains that the open-field names at Castor are unusual, and that the directional names ascribed to the open fields at Elton and Lakenheath were the result of administrative processes.[100] By the eighteenth century at Elton (and probably a great deal earlier) six fields were in use, most bearing more culturally relevant names: Stockhill Field, Middle Field and Brook Field belonging to

---

98   NRO F(M) Charter 115.

99   NRO F(M) Charter 413.

100 Jones also suggests that directional open-field names were more likely to have been created by distant officials, rather than local peasants: R. Jones, 'Directional names in the early medieval landscape', in R. Jones and S. Semple (eds), *Sense of place in Anglo-Saxon England* (Donington, 2011), p. 198.

Table 5.8
The open fields of Elton, Castor and Lakenheath.

Field-name	Alternative name
Elton	
Great Field	North Field
Middle Field	
Small Field	
Castor[1]	
Eyning[2]	Eiing, Einig, Eying, Eynigge, Heing, Heuyg, Heying
Ham	Hamfeld
Thornes	Le Thornes
Normangate	
Wood Field	
Lakenheath	
North Field	
South Field	
Middle Field	
Windmill Field	

Notes:

1. Ailsworth's fields may have been part of one system: Over Field, Nether Field, Wood Field and Doles.
2. It is unclear whether the name was *Eyning* or *Eyuing*.

Over End; and Arnest Field (probably derived from *arnewassh*), Middle Field and Royston-Hill Field within Nether End.[101]

The overwhelming sense is that the Castor peasants were more actively engaged in renaming their landscape in the thirteenth and fourteenth centuries. This was not done on a wholesale basis, however. The reference to *oldfeld* most clearly indicates change; naturally this piece of land would have had a different earlier name.[102] Some of the names of former wooded areas were incorporated into the newly assarted arable lands, most notably *eyning*, which became an open field, presumably because this was where the majority of assarting was concentrated. Additionally, *estrys*, which, together with *iungeuuode* and *abbotishauue* contained 120 acres, was remembered within the furlong of the same name recorded in the 1393 survey.[103] This latter furlong is mentioned alongside *bilmanstibbyng*, which is undoubtedly a 'new' name, although why some names endured and others were changed is unclear. A tentative answer to the question of Castor's more dynamic nature in terms of the named landscape may lie within the nature of lordship in each of the three vills. Of the three, Castor contained the most manors and Elton the fewest. This suggests that lordship was weaker in Castor, stronger in Lakenheath and at its strongest in Elton. The abbot of

---

101 *EFB*.

102 H.S.A. Fox, 'Approaches to the adoption of the Midland system', in T. Rowley (ed.), *The origins of open-field agriculture* (London, 1981), p. 89.

103 BL Cotton MS Nero C. vii/14 f. 159d.

Peterborough may have been the chief lord of the vill at Castor, but his influence was muted by the presence of other resident lords and an exceptionally high number of free peasants. Given the manifest additional legal freedom afforded to free peasants, it seems that some of the more prominent among them may have been inclined to strengthen their association with their holdings by affixing their names to their land. This is readily apparent through the places associated with the Thorold family at Castor: *lordyslake* is almost certainly a renamed watercourse, and *lordeston* was either thus named since the initial erection of the cross it referenced or a renaming of an existing cross. The Thorolds were minor lords, but they were experiencing declining fortunes by the late thirteenth century.[104] It could be difficult to distinguish minor lords from prominent free peasants and it seems possible that, at Castor, some of the latter were attempting to emulate their social superiors. Perhaps the Bouetons, Cordels, Brettenes, Illings, Lilfords, Pickeworths and Paris' incorporation of their own names into the landscape allowed them in some small way to emulate the Thorolds. Even if the Thorolds were not responsible for affixing their identity to parts of the Castor landscape, the outward impression must have been that this powerfully entrenched affiliation in turn engendered the perception of increased social status, which would have been extremely appealing to this group of important freemen. The contrast in Elton is striking: the several pasture of the prominent free tenant John de Aylington, alias le Lord, was called *hulkecroft*, making no strong association with its owner.[105]

Others have noted changing landscape naming patterns, but these have largely been associated with the period post-1348, in particular the fifteenth century. Kleinschmidt suggests that this was due to a shift in mentality towards more territorialised space at the end of the medieval period, whereas Gardiner suggests that renaming occurred for a variety of reasons: at Romney Marsh (Kent), for example, he argues that the change from arable to pastoral husbandry stimulated a series of changes that renewed the stock of field-names there.[106] Sherri Olson, meanwhile, claims that after the Black Death personal names were used in order to memorialise those lost to the pestilence. However, the evidence from Castor and Lakenheath suggests that the process of embedding personal names within the local landscape in the post-Conquest period was underway well before this time: decades earlier at Lakenheath, and over a century before at Castor.[107] While these watershed moments are undoubtedly noteworthy, the evidence from Elton, Castor and Lakenheath shows that change also occurred during the normal course of events, albeit at different rates in each settlement. The changes outlined here are, to a certain extent at least, fairly transparent and easily identified. However, as anthropologists and ethnographers have long recognised, there is often more to minor names than a cursory glance through a field-book or set of charters might reveal. They acknowledge that many names are

---

104 King, *Peterborough Abbey*, pp. 35–6.

105 TNA E 40/10857.

106 Kleinschmidt, *Understanding the middle ages*, p. 54 and p. 61; Gardiner, 'Oral tradition', p. 23.

107 S. Olson, *A mute gospel: the people and culture of the medieval English common fields* (Toronto, 2009), pp. 191–4, argues that these name types are absent before 1373 at Ellington (Huntingdonshire), but fails to consider that this may be due to the vagaries of the survival of documentation.

not merely descriptive markers for local places or people but are meaningful because they act as the means through which local history and experience is memorialised.[108] These ideas, although a far cry from a purely taxonomic approach, have nevertheless been more widely explored by archaeologists and historians in recent years. Any study of local place-names that fails to engage with this more hidden aspect of the local environment is in danger of missing the very essence of place experienced by its past inhabitants. These aspects will be considered more fully in the next chapter.

Field- and minor-name studies are becoming an increasingly important means of accessing medieval peasant mentalities concerning the rural landscape. Although understanding these names from an etymological perspective remains important, this should be viewed as part of a progression towards a more contextual analysis. While it can be useful to adopt modern classification schemes for analytical purposes, it is also vitally important to consider these names from the contemporary worldview of the peasant if we are to further our attempts to understand what they communicate more fully. Assessing minor names alongside both the chronological development of settlement names and the landscape naming practices of First Nation peoples allows us to see that the labelling of topography was likely to have been important in early medieval landscape naming. This in turn offers a means of determining the stability of the field-name stock from the thirteenth century onwards. It appears that strength of lordship and the balance of different status groups were important factors in determining the permanency of field-names in Castor, Elton and Lakenheath. At Castor, where weaker lordship and higher levels of free individuals prevailed, field-names were subject to earlier and more frequent change than at Lakenheath and Elton.

---

108 S. Feld, 'Waterfalls of song: an acoustemology of place resounding in Bosavi, Papua New Guinea', in K.H. Basso and S. Feld (eds), *Senses of place* (Santa Fe, NM, 1996), p. 102; Stewart and Strathern, 'Introduction', p. 1.

Chapter 6

The remembered landscape

Scholars have recognised for some time now that the landscape of the English manor was intimately known, understood and, ultimately, named by medieval peasants. And yet the potential historical value offered by the rich seam of medieval field-names has hardly begun to be exploited. Modern classification of field-names has almost certainly obscured some elements of their underlying meanings, and re-examining the manorial landscape through the eyes of the peasant community allows us to investigate the rationale behind their naming strategies. Many of the field-names considered thus far have been assessed based on what can be garnered by considering them from a modern, rational perspective that takes the names at face value. They seem to reveal themselves unambiguously: *segfen* indicated an important fenland resource and *riewong* was a good place to grow rye. In this way, onomasts have sought to explain the naming of the landscape, the classic outline being produced by John Field, whose model purports to ensure that almost every English field-name can be codified.[1] This is a useful classification scheme for modern scholars, but it is unlikely that it would be considered entirely valid judged from the perspective and worldview of the medieval peasant, and in some instances it may conceal facets of the original intentions of those naming the fields. For many onomasts, defining names renders them comprehensible. And yet, as Henri Lefebvre suggests, the acquisition of knowledge without consideration of the particular social context renders any understanding partial at best.[2]

Those taking a phenomenological approach have criticised landscape studies for ignoring myth, cosmology and symbolism.[3] Recently, efforts have been made by non-linguistic scholars, particularly in archaeology and history, to reunite medieval furlongs with the people who coined their names and orally conveyed them from generation to generation. A number of these studies concentrate on uncovering local mentalities and tracing changes in outlook across time.[4] Minor names have also begun to be considered by scholars working on memory and the transmission of texts – including

---

1   J. Field, *A history of English field-names* (London, 1993); see also W.E. Cunnington, 'The field-names of Kingsbury (Middlesex)', *Journal of the English Place-Name Society*, 32 (2000), pp. 41–6; H. Daniels and C. Lagrange, 'An analysis of Romsey field-names', *Journal of the English Place-Name Society*, 34 (2002), pp. 29–58.

2   Lefebvre, *The production of space*, p. 81.

3   C. Tilley, *A phenomenology of landscape* (Oxford, 1994), p. 22.

4   For example, Semple, 'A fear of the past', pp. 109–26; Altenberg, *Experiencing landscapes*; Kilby, 'A different world?' (2010b), pp. 72–7; S. Semple, 'In the open air', in M. Carver *et al.* (eds), *Signals of belief in early England: Anglo-Saxon paganism revisited* (Oxford, 2010), pp. 21–48; Gardiner, 'Oral tradition', pp. 16–30; Mileson, 'The South Oxfordshire project', pp. 83–98; Kilby, 'Divining medieval water', pp. 57–93.

landscape – over long time periods. Nevertheless, some historians working on elite notions of memory and memorialisation discount peasant society and its attendant geography. Cubitt suggests that in illiterate societies memory was limited to the span of one lifetime, offering Le Roy Ladurie's *Montaillou* as evidence in support of this. Cubitt accepts Clanchy's view that oral transmission is fundamentally flawed and unlikely to pass between generations intact.[5] However, this simply suggests that Cubitt and Clanchy consider all orally transmitted information as having equal importance, which it cannot have done. Information that was pertinent to local communities as a whole, such as customary law, field-names and other minor landscape names, were fundamentally important in myriad diverse ways. The landscape, as it was perceived, remembered and memorialised by the lower orders, is being increasingly considered by scholars taking a more phenomenological approach.[6]

Social scientists have long considered that a deeper cultural understanding of the rural environment can disclose meanings that are inseparably connected with the local environment and its inhabitants. These meanings are not generally transparent beyond the boundaries of the settlement, and are usually significant only to locals. Naturally, this expresses in a cultural sense the deep and binding ties between local people and the surrounding landscape, but it also articulates ideas of belonging, from both historical and social perspectives. This understanding of the meaning of some minor place-names presents immediate and grave issues with Field's approach. It is a problem already acknowledged by some onomasts focusing on family names, notably Peter McClure: namely that it is unwise to consider the meanings of all names as unambiguous.[7] Names are not mere labels. While some are undoubtedly more topographically descriptive than others, anthropological and ethnographical studies have revealed much deeper levels of significance embedded within the local names coined by people living in close proximity to the natural environment. For Susanne Küchler, the landscape itself is the 'most generally accessible and widely shared aide-mémoire of a culture's knowledge and understanding of its past and future'.[8] Similarly, Stewart and Strathern visualise the landscape as the means through which the history of local places is codified.[9] These views hint that, in some instances, the uncoupling of field-names from the anchorage of their landscape setting renders them unintelligible, reduced to a mere

---

5   G. Cubitt, *History and memory* (Manchester, 2007), pp. 185–9; Gardiner outlines how some local place-names endured solely through oral transmission over 400 years: Gardiner, 'Oral tradition', p. 17.

6   See, for example Tilley, *A phenomenology*, p. 27; J. Fentress and C. Wickham, *Social memory* (1992, Oxford, 1994); S. Küchler, 'Landscape as memory: the mapping of process and its representation in a Melanesian society', in B. Bender (ed.), *Landscape politics and perspectives* (Oxford, 1993), pp. 85–106; P.J. Stewart and A. Strathern (eds), *Landscape, memory and history: anthropological perspectives* (London, 2003); A. Walsham, *The reformation of the landscape: religion, identity, and memory in early modern Britain and Ireland* (Oxford, 2011); Mileson, 'The South Oxfordshire project', p. 89.

7   McClure, 'The interpretation of Middle English nicknames'.

8   Küchler, 'Landscape as memory', p. 85.

9   Stewart and Strathern, 'Introduction', p. 1.

list from which little real meaning can be garnered. In this way, the landscape itself is just as important as its name. As Howard Morphy attests, it is not merely a 'sign system' for past events, or the vehicle through which pertinent information is relayed, but a central component of such information.[10]

Anthropologists and ethnographers in particular have noted the tendency for local stories, myths and legends to become embedded within local landscape. Studying the Western Apache Indians of Cibecue in Arizona, Keith Basso noted that, far from being unassuming reference points, their minor landscape names contained a wealth of information that a simple translation or definition of the name concealed. One of the key drivers in minor place-name creation for the Apache was the need to preserve past events associated with the places in which they occurred, the stories arising from which were then used to provide moral instruction to the wider community.[11] Basso noted that the place-names themselves were integral to the tale that was being conveyed. For the Apache, simply uttering the place-name invoked the associated underlying meaning without the need for the recitation of the story itself. Thus, the history of the Apache was strongly rooted in the local landscape, which was a 'repository of distilled wisdom, a stern but benevolent keeper of tradition'.[12] The Apache place-names appear unremarkable when taken out of context: names like 'big cottonwood trees stand spreading here and there', or 'coarse-textured rocks lie above in a compact cluster' initially seem to describe the topography, enabling the identification of specific places.[13] However, without Basso's interpretations, uncovered through hours of discussion with the Apache people, the deeper, more culturally sensitive meanings are concealed from outsiders, being especially unintelligible from a westernised, rational viewpoint. Similar associations between landscape and story – a form of local folklore – have been noted by others studying local place-names across widespread cultures and time periods, including the Tlingit people of British Columbia, Canada; Melanesian society in Oceania; Australian Aborigine culture; and the Scottish Hebrides.[14] Basso is rightly critical of landscape studies that fail to move beyond more typical socio-economic interests, such as social organisation and economic and subsistence schema, suggesting that to ignore more culturally focused aspects of the landscape is to render any study of attitudes toward local environment incomplete.[15] While this is a criticism that is upheld by several other scholars, most notably Tilley and Gardiner, for scholars of the medieval landscape it can be extremely difficult to venture beyond the mere

---

10   H. Morphy, 'Landscape and the reproduction of the ancestral past', in E. Hirsch and M. O'Hanlon (eds), *The anthropology of landscape: perspectives on place and space* (1995, Oxford, 1997), p. 186.

11   Basso, '"Stalking with stories"', pp. 26 and 30–34.

12   Basso, '"Stalking with stories"', p. 45.

13   Basso, '"Stalking with stories"', pp. 36–7.

14   T.F. Thornton, 'Know your place: the organization of Tlingit geographic knowledge', *Ethnology*, 36/4 (1997), p. 298; Küchler, 'Landscape as memory', p. 85; Morphy, 'Landscape and the reproduction of the ancestral past', p. 186; D. MacAulay, 'De tha ann an ainm … ?', in F. MacLeod (ed.), *Togail Tir, marking time: the map of the Western Isles* (Stornoway, 1989), p. 94.

15   Basso, '"Stalking with stories"', p. 48.

acknowledgement that cultural aspects, such as local folklore, might be integral to contemporary perceptions of the landscape.[16]

The majority of the studies cited here have relied upon direct oral testimony from members of each respective community to reveal stories associated with the landscape and their great importance to each community's cultural identity. The problems faced by medievalists attempting to reconstruct contemporary perceptions of landscape in a more culturally sensitive manner are manifold. In many cases, the only strands of evidence that survive are the late medieval notations of field-names – these sometimes originating in the Anglo-Saxon period – alongside the landscape itself, where it remains reasonably unchanged.[17] Local folklore can be difficult to trace back to the Middle Ages, as much that now remains to us has been orally conveyed, and its origins – both temporal and topographical – are often obscure. It is also far from certain how transparent some field-names really are. There are some within the corpus of names at Elton, Castor and Lakenheath that seem to hint at a more culturally driven provenance, while simultaneously defying any fully meaningful classification. Castor's *maggebuskhert*, Elton's *catfretene* and Lakenheath's *dedcherl* conceal significance long forgotten by each village's respective local inhabitants.[18] Any attempt to offer a more nuanced interpretation of these names is fraught with difficulty, but requires at the very least a detailed knowledge of local topography, alongside contemporary evidence of local history, mythology and folklore. This is a challenging task for the late medieval period generally, but especially so when considering peasant perceptions. Nevertheless, it may be possible to piece together elements of the importance of the historical and mythological landscape to the peasants of one of the more well-documented vills under review here: Castor.

Beyond taxonomy: the secret life of the fields

History is not confined to a discrete number of places. There are stories, myths and folklore associated with places wherever there is, and has been, human habitation. And yet there are undoubtedly some places that have attracted more comment than others. Castor is one such place. Its Roman heritage has fascinated antiquarians since at least the seventeenth century, and the Roman fort of *Durobrivae*, on the opposite bank of the Nene in the parish of Chesterton and often associated with the Roman industrial site in Castor, merited a mention by Henry of Huntingdon in the twelfth

---

16 Tilley, *A phenomenology*, p. 33; Gardiner, 'Oral tradition', p. 22.

17 Kilby, 'Divining medieval water', p. 61.

18 *Maggebuskhert* is difficult to interpret. It either means 'the bush associated with a woman called Margaret or Margery' or 'a bush where magpies perched'. *Catfretene* translates as 'chewed by cats', and perhaps denotes the crumbly nature of the soil in this part of Elton. *Dedcherl* is more straightforward from an etymological perspective – 'dead peasant', but whether it refers to a particular death, or perhaps an execution site, is less certain. I am very grateful to Peter McClure for discussing these names with me.

century.[19] This means that a reasonable quantity of information concerning Castor and Ailsworth's historic and folkloric landscape has survived, predominantly through the work of eighteenth-century antiquarians. Although unconfirmed by archaeological evidence, it is generally considered that Cyneburg (now modern Kyneburgha), daughter of Penda of Mercia, founded a convent there following her widowhood from the Northumbrian, Alhfrith, in the seventh century.[20] The early twelfth-century church is dedicated to her, suggesting that her memory endured for almost 500 years until its construction. Cyneburg is strongly associated with the Castor landscape in the modern period through local folklore. A long surviving story suggests that the saint was attacked while walking through Castor. There are four documented versions of the tale, the earliest version recorded by John Morton in 1712, who recounts that:

> *Kinneburga's* Honour being attempted she fled from the Ruffian thro' those Fields: and ... the Path she took was miraculously mark'd out, as a Trophy of her Purity and Innocence, to be seen in future Ages, and be distinguished by the Name of *Kinneburga's* Way.[21]

In the late nineteenth century Murray suggested that the 'road unrolled itself before her'.[22] And in an unreferenced third version, Cyneburg was chased while walking along *Lady Conneyburrow's Way*, this time by three ruffians; she dropped her basket, which 'sprang up as flowers before her, while a great gulf opened behind and swallowed up her pursuers'.[23] The church guide, again unreferenced, also outlines the miracle of the flowers, but rather than a fissure appearing, it is suggested that thorns sprang up, entrapping her assailants.[24]

In the version recorded by Morton, he also recounted that the path called *Kinneburga's Way* rose up toward Castor from the Nene through Normangate Field. He conjectured that it was once tiled with tesserae, but by the early eighteenth century it was:

> only a narrow tract ... distinguishable from the rest of the Field ... by its being barrener than the Ground on both sides of it ... and when they plow a-cross this Way ... the Plough ... catches ... upon a Stone floor, sometimes [it] throws up wrought stone, as also the above-described little square bricks.[25]

---

19 T. Forester (trans.), *The chronicle of Henry of Huntingdon* (London, 1853), p. 4; historically, *Durobrivae* has been associated with Water Newton (Huntingdonshire), although it lies in Chesterton (Huntingdonshire).

20 A. Morris, 'The Anglian period: the royal ladies of Castor', in *Five parishes: their people and places* (Castor, 2004), p. 48.

21 J. Morton, *The natural history of Northamptonshire* (London, 1712), p. 511.

22 J. Murray, *Handbook for travellers in Northamptonshire and Rutland* (London, 1878), pp. 61–2.

23 Serjeantson and Adkins, *VCH Northamptonshire*, vol. 2, p. 473.

24 H. Tovey (ed.), *St Kyneburga's Church, Castor* (Castor, 2006), p. 9.

25 Morton, *Natural history*, p. 511.

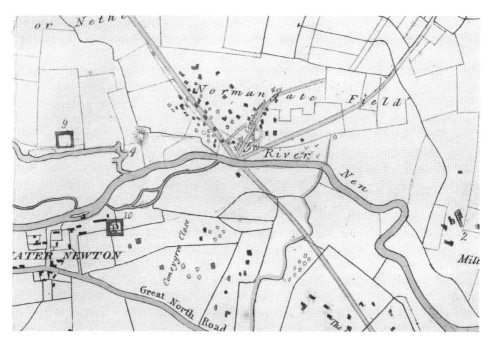

Figure 6.1. Edmund Artis' map of 'Lady Conneyburrow's Way', Normangate Field, Castor, 1828. Source: E.T. Artis, *The Durobrivae of Antoninus* (London, 1828), plate 1. Image kindly supplied by Stephen Upex.

So, the path seems to have been a Roman construction, characterised in the modern period, and possibly earlier, by the lack of vegetation along its length. Morton's reference to it being 'miraculously mark'd out' further supports the idea that in extremely dry periods the path would have been more visible, as aerial photographs of landscape used in archaeological survey attest. Though the phenomenon is due to the shallower root-run over the path resulting in the vegetation becoming parched more quickly than to either side, it may well have seemed incredible to locals in the eighteenth century and earlier, and Morton's specific description of the 'miraculous' nature of the landscape also fits the idea of sanctity associated with saints. Despite the slight variation in the four versions, one element seems to have been consistent: the site of the event in Normangate Field on the path known in the modern period as *Lady Conneyburrow's Way*. The path is marked on a map of Normangate Field produced by the nineteenth-century archaeologist Edmund Artis (Figure 6.1), and its location is consistent with Morton's description of its siting more than 100 years before.[26]

Given the consistency of the application of this legend to the Normangate area of Castor, the link between legend and landscape seems worth examining further. Normangate Field is of particular interest for a number of reasons. It is an exceptionally small field (though undoubtedly considered to be an open field in the late medieval

---

26 Morton, *Natural history*, pp. 510–11.

period) contained within which were a number of furlongs.[27] These were predominantly arable, but there are also references to meadow and pasture. The name *normangate* is derived from OE *norð-mann*, meaning a norseman; and ON *gata*, indicating a road, way or street.[28] It is recorded in almost forty separate documents and, unlike nearby Norman Cross (Huntingdonshire) – frequently written as *norðmannescros*, *normannes cros* – *normangate* was never written in the genitive form, indicating the extreme unlikeliness of its derivation from a personal name.[29] The name almost certainly refers to the Roman road passing through the field, known today as Ermine Street, and indeed Morton confirms that this name continued to reference the Roman road in the early eighteenth century.[30] The road seems a suitable referent for the name of this field, since it must have been a significant feature in the landscape. As Figures 6.2 and 6.4 attest, modern aerial photographs still show Ermine Street very plainly, carving a route north-west from the Nene that is intersected by the putative modern route of *Lady Conneyburrow's Way*. Although Artis' map has no scale, it is clear that he believed the path crossed Ermine Street at the riverbank, a location supported by Morton's written description of the path continuing on to Water Newton (Huntingdonshire) on the opposite bank. Cropmarks shown on Figure 6.3, featuring Castor's Roman industrial site, indicate a path that matches both Artis' map and Morton's description. The putative path is shown more clearly on a second aerial photograph in Figure 6.4.

Ermine Street was not the only Roman road in Castor and Ailsworth. It was joined by King Street, located in Ailsworth's Nether Field, adjacent to Normangate Field (see Figure 6.5), which ran northward towards Lincolnshire. The corpus of Castor and Ailsworth field-names reveals that several names for the Roman roads were in use into the thirteenth and fourteenth centuries. In addition to *normangate* in Castor, the Ailsworth portion of Ermine Street seems to have been known as *irthonehegg*, comprising OE *eorþen* and *hecge* or *hege* – earthen-hedge.[31] The same generic element was also used in the medieval name for King Street – *langgedikheg* – and, although it could denote a hedge in the modern sense, the word was also used to describe earthen banks, suggesting that *irthonehegg* was a suitable description for the Roman agger as it appeared pre-Conquest.[32] Although King Street was known interchangeably as

---

27 By 1597 Normangate Field contained 160 acres, while Ham Field and Thorn Field were just over 400 acres each. Eyning Field contained 780 acres, and was probably extended after the thirteenth-century assarting. Wood Field, which straddled both Castor's and Ailsworth's boundary, was just 132 acres, but was probably newly created from assarted woodland: NRO F(M) Misc. vol. 424.

28 J. Bosworth, *An Anglo-Saxon dictionary online*, T.N. Toller (ed.), S. Christ and O. Tichý (comps), <http://www.bosworthtoller.com/023899>, accessed 14 May 2013; *EPNE*, vol. 1, p. 196.

29 Mawer and Stenton, *The place-names of Bedfordshire and Huntingdonshire*, p. 180; the lack of a genitival -s is not diagnostic; however, since there are over 600 charters detailing the most prominent Castor residents, we might expect to see an individual named Norman if this field-name was derived from a surname. I am grateful to Keith Briggs for discussing this name with me.

30 Morton, *Natural history*, p. 512.

31 BL Cotton MS Nero C. vii/14.

32 NRO F(M) Charter 235; H. Neilson, 'Early English woodland and waste', *Journal of Economic History*, 2/1 (1942), p. 58.

Figure 6.2. Ermine Street from the air, Normangate Field, Castor and Nether Field, Ailsworth. Photo: Richard Jones.

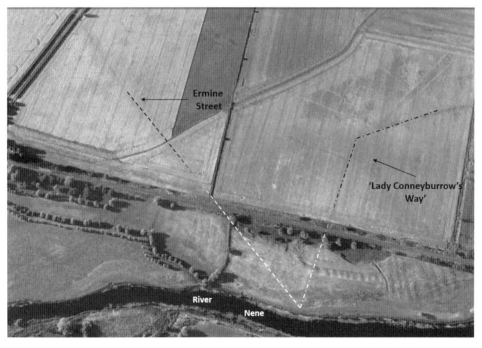

Figure 6.3. 'Lady Conneyburrow's Way', Normangate Field, Castor. Source: Google, 2019 Getmapping plc.

Figure 6.4. Normangate Field, 'Lady Conneyburrow's Way' and Ermine Street, Castor from the air. Photo: Stephen Upex.

langgedikheg, *langediche* or *langedichgate*, it was clearly identified by the same qualifying elements throughout the medieval period.[33] Like Ermine Street, King Street continued beyond the confines of Castor and Ailsworth, and yet, locally at least, it retained the same name regardless. The 1393 demesne survey also records the name in Upton (Northamptonshire), which shared a boundary with Ailsworth.[34]

If it seems obvious that this very imposing landmark should bear a common name beyond parish boundaries, then the use of multiple names for medieval Ermine Street in Castor and Ailsworth requires further consideration. As Figure 6.5 shows, Ermine Street passed through Castor only in a very small section of Normangate Field. Its physical structure seems unlikely to have been any different in this section from that of the sections in Ailsworth and on towards Sutton (Northamptonshire) and Upton, so why did it bear a different name along this extremely small portion of the road? It is possible that a different name was always used in Ailsworth, but the consistency of use of *langedich* in the case of King Street suggests an alternative explanation for the localised naming of the Normangate stretch of Ermine Street. The element *norð-mann* – a late OE term – may also offer a clue.[35] Although it is

---

33   See, for example, NRO F(M) Charters 6, 11 and 172.

34   BL Cotton MS Nero C. vii/14.

35   *EPNE*, vol. 2, p. 52.

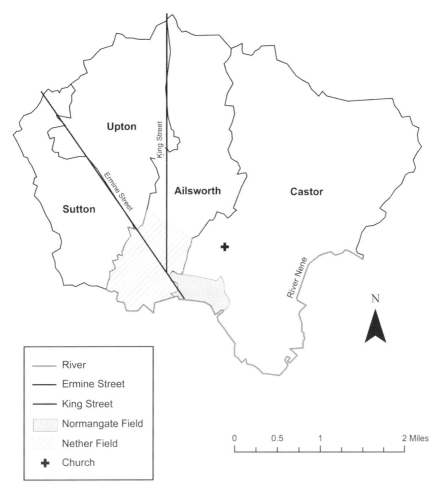

Figure 6.5. Major Roman roads in Castor and Ailsworth.

impossible to date its introduction, given the probably earlier use of *irthonehegg*, it is conceivable that this unique name for Ermine Street in this portion of the vill suggests a late Anglo-Saxon change of name. This being the case, *norð-mann* is especially interesting. The element has been positively endorsed as describing Scandinavians rather than Normans, suggesting that the name had a Viking connection in the minds of those selecting it.[36] In both the late ninth century and the early eleventh century

---

36 'Norman, n.1 and adj.', *OED* online <http://www.oed.com.ezproxy4.lib.le.ac.uk/view/ Entry/128279>, accessed 15 May 2013; Bosworth, *An Anglo-Saxon dictionary* <http://www. bosworthtoller.com/023899>, accessed 22 May 2013; J. Carroll, 'Identifying migrants in medieval England: the possibilities and limitations of place-name evidence', in J. Story *et al.* (eds), *Migrants in medieval England, c. 500–1500* (forthcoming).

Castor was reputed to have been attacked by Vikings, allegedly Danish, who the twelfth-century scribe of the *Peterborough Chronicle*, Hugh Candidus, described as 'servants of the devil'. Candidus mentioned the 'much ruined church at Cyneburch-caster' in the time of Ælfsy, abbot of Peterborough between 963 and 1013, and this has been tentatively associated with the early eleventh-century ravages.[37] Certainly, the eighteenth-century antiquarian William Stukeley suggests that locals believed that Danes destroyed Cyneburg's convent and murdered the nuns.[38] The *Anglo-Saxon Chronicle* documents the later Danish incursions, recording that, by 1011, they had 'overrun' Northamptonshire; and in 1013, alongside other territories, the people of the Five Boroughs, including nearby Stamford (Lincolnshire), had capitulated.[39] Stamford lies directly east of Ermine Street, which connected the town with Castor and Ailsworth, less than ten miles to the south. It seems likely that Ermine Street would have been used as a route by the Danes at this time, and this perhaps explains the putative later change of the field-name: if they entered Castor territory, did the Danes do so via the *normangate*?

In isolation, the name *normangate* hints at some interesting possibilities, but they are little more than conjecture at this point. However, a closer examination of the field-names in this area of the vill reveals some extraordinary evidence that supports the hypothesis that *normangate* might be a medieval reference to cataclysmic local events. The first of these names is *denchemor*, probably derived from OE *denisc* (Danish) and *mōr* (marsh, moor).[40] Based on the detail contained within the main body of the relevant charters, the approximate location of medieval *denchemor* is known: abutting on Normangate Field, and close to the assumed line of the footpath *Lady Conneyburrow's Way* (Figure 6.6). This name is very difficult to explain in isolation, beyond pure definition. However, set in its landscape context alongside *normangate*, perhaps a more culturally relevant picture begins to emerge. The second noteworthy name is *walwortwong*, resulting from Old English *wealh-wyrt* 'dwarf elder', and *wang* 'piece of meadow-land, open field'. Ostensibly, this references flora, and a traditional reading would consider this a place characterised by this plant. *Walwortwong* was situated in the same part of the Castor and Ailsworth landscape as *denchemor*, this time in Nether Field, again close to Ermine Street.[41] Within the corpus of Castor field-

---

37 C.G. Dallas, 'The nunnery of St Kyneburgha at Castor', *Durobrivae*, 1 (1973), p. 17; Morris, 'The Anglian period', p. 51; Mellows and Mellows, *The Peterborough chronicle*, pp. 12 and 27.

38 W. Stukeley, *The family memoirs of the Rev. William Stukeley, and the antiquarian and other correspondence of William Stukeley*, vol. 3 (London, 1887), pp. 56–61.

39 The Abingdon (C) manuscript suggests that Northamptonshire was overrun, but the Peterborough (E) version does not, suggesting that north-east Northamptonshire may have been spared in 1011: M.J. Swanton (ed., trans.), *The Anglo-Saxon chronicle* (London, 1996), pp. 141–4.

40 NRO F(M) Charters 248, 365, 380 and 561; *CN*, p. 116; NRO F(M) Tin Box 1, Castor and Ailsworth, Parcel No. 5 (c) and (d); the variant spellings of *denche* are found in Figure 6.6; it may derive from the personal name Denic, although it is unlikely. Even if that was the case, from at least the late thirteenth century onwards the residents of Castor clearly interpreted the name as 'Danish moor': Peter McClure, pers. comm.

41 BL Cotton MS Nero C. vii/14.

names, and in contemporary English field-names more widely, allusions to flora tend to be confined to the hedgerow, the arboreal and agricultural. In Castor only three additional floral qualifiers are recorded: the simplex names *flegges* (reeds) and *lyngg* (heather); and *tasilhill* (teasels).[42] These plants were useful resources to the medieval peasant as thatching material, fuel, or animal feed, and in cloth production, so it seems plausible that these field-names referred to places where these resources were found.[43] This separates *walwortwong* from these more practically named furlongs. It is possible that dwarf-elder was used for medicinal purposes. However, there were myriad plants with healing properties that might have featured among Castor's field-names but did not. Moreover, *wealh-wyrt* did not appear as frequently as many other common plants in the late Anglo-Saxon collections of herbal remedies: *Lacnunga* lists it only twice and the *Old English Herbarium* once.[44] Furthermore, its precise etymology is problematic. In *Lacnunga* it is spelled *wælwyrt*, which Pettit, following the *Oxford English Dictionary*, translates as '(?) slaughter-wort (?) foreign-wort'.[45] Van Arsdell, who does not offer a transcription, translates the relevant entry as 'the plant called *ebulus* or dwarf elder … [that] some call danewort'.[46] Cockayne's transcription and translation outline both *weal-wyrt* and *wæl-wyrt* in the same document; and Cameron and D'Aronco also transcribe *wæl-wyrt*, which the facsimile copy plainly shows.[47] The late fourteenth-century reference to Ailsworth's *walwortwong* prevents precise etymological definition, as there are no variant spellings to allow discrimination between *wæl* and *wealh*. Modern English folklore associates the plant – in this tradition, usually known by the folk names *daneweed*, *danewort*, or *Dane's blood* – with places in which Danish blood was shed, since its dark reddish-purple berries were reminiscent of blood.[48]

It is often very difficult to determine the origins of local myth, and therefore inadvisable to project folklore recorded in modern documents back into the medieval period without further evidence. While the earliest known written reference to

---

42   NRO F(M) Charters 92, 162, 184 and 357; *CN*, p. 117.

43   J. Grieg, 'Plant resources', in G. Astill and A. Grant (eds), *The countryside of medieval England* (1988, Oxford, 1994), p. 125; Dyer, *Standards of living*, p. 131; Bailey, *Medieval Suffolk*, p. 95.

44   E. Pettit (ed., trans.), *Anglo-Saxon remedies, charms, and prayers from British Library MS Harley 585, The Lacnunga*, vol. 1 (Lampeter, 2001), pp. 58 and 68; A. van Arsdall (ed., trans.), *Medieval herbal remedies: the Old English herbarium and Anglo-Saxon medicine* (London, 2002), p. 129.

45   Pettit, *Lacnunga*, p. 266. *OED* suggests the possibility that forms of the word in *wæl* indicate 'slaughter, the slain in battle'.

46   van Arsdall, *Medieval herbal remedies*, p. 189.

47   T.O. Cockayne, *Leechdoms, wort-cunning and starcraft of early England*, vol. 1 (London, 1961), pp. 38 and 202; M.L. Cameron and M.A. D'Aronco (eds), *The Old English illustrated pharmacopoeia: British Library Cotton Vitellius C iii* (Copenhagen, 1998), p. 54.

48   J. Westwood and J. Simpson, *The lore of the land: a guide to England's legends from Spring-Heeled Jack to the Witches of Warboys* (2005, London, 2006), p. 531; a 1640 herbal suggests that the plant was so-called because it produced 'the "danes", a strong flux or diarrhoea': G. Grigson, *The Englishman's flora* (London, 1958), p. 373, although this term is not referenced in either the *OED* or the *EDD*. I am grateful to Maureen Harris for providing this reference.

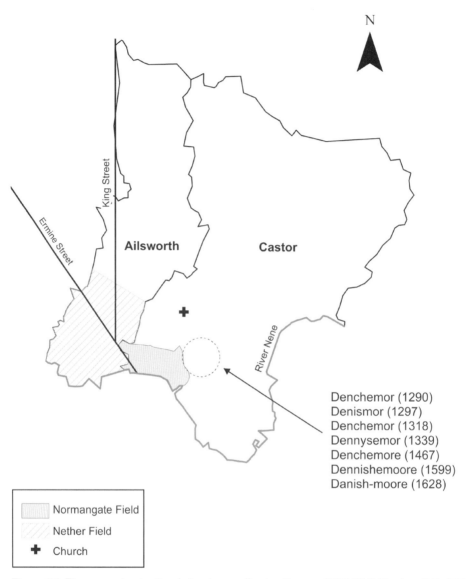

N

Ermine Street

King Street

Ailsworth

Castor

River Nene

✚

Denchemor (1290)
Denismor (1297)
Denchemor (1318)
Dennysemor (1339)
Denchemore (1467)
Dennishemoore (1599)
Danish-moore (1628)

▨ Normangate Field
▨ Nether Field
✚ Church

Figure 6.6. The approximate site of *denchemor*, Castor. Source: NRO F(M) Charters 248, 365, 561; NRO F(M) Tin Box 1, Castor and Ailsworth, Parcel No. 5 c. and d.; *CN*.

'danewort' is Turner's, who writes in 1538 that *ebulus* (dwarf-elder) '*ab Anglis danwort aut walwort vocatur*',[49] it is striking – but cannot be seen as conclusive – that linguists suggest 'slaughter' or 'foreign' as a possible definition of the term, perhaps in this instance offering a tentative link between medieval and modern folklore. When this

---

49   R. Holland and J. Britten (eds), *A dictionary of English plant-names* (London, 1886), p. 143.

name is added to the earlier group of Castor and Ailsworth names in a small area clustered around Ermine Street, the evidence becomes much more compelling. Might it have been the case that an important historic event in late Anglo-Saxon Castor was memorialised within the very landscape in which it occurred, and that over the ensuing centuries the story became conflated with, and finally obscured by, the legend of Cyneburg, reputed to have taken place in the same small area of the vill? While far from diagnostic, it is remarkable that, in over 200 field-names sourced from more than 600 documents, none of the medieval names represent Cyneburg or her footpath, despite the fact that over twenty roads and paths are named within the source material.[50] On visiting Castor in 1737, Stukeley noted that:

> much daneweed still grows upon the Roman Road in Castor Fields. They have still a memorial at Castor of S. Kyniburga ... and of her coming in a coach and six, and riding over the field along the Roman road before Michaelmas. This is the remains of her festival celebrated here, on the day of her obit., 15 Sept., ...[51]

Here, both myth and landscape setting have shifted slightly, and Cyneburg is visualised travelling swiftly along Ermine Street – albeit still in Normangate – rather than walking along a footpath. The timing of Cyneburg's alleged appearance may also be significant. Culpeper advised that 'most ... Elder trees flower in June, and their fruit is ripe ... in August. But the ... Wallwort flowers somewhat later, and its fruit is not ripe until September'.[52] The dwarf-elder's dark berries symbolised the blood associated with the slaughter of the Danes, and its fruit would have been ripe at the same time that, according to local collective memory in the eighteenth century, Cyneburg journeyed along Ermine Street. Assessing the medieval field-name evidence of Normangate Field alongside this 'new' Cyneburg folklore, what Stukeley outlines here appears as a possible mutation of an earlier story, one that fits more readily with the idea of a Danish assault. The field-names, alongside the diminutive size of Normangate Field as an open field and the potential links between medieval and modern folklore, strongly hint at something unusual.

This evidence alone, while incomplete in comparison to the oral testimony gathered by ethnographers, is strikingly reminiscent of the manner in which many non-western societies living in close proximity to the natural world embedded important stories and myths within local landscape. And in fact there is indisputable evidence of this in Castor. In 1330 land known as *St Edmunds' land* was leased by the abbot of Bury St Edmunds to transport Barnack stone across Castor territory to the Nene. By 1597 it was known as *St Edmunds' stones*, referencing the stone markers

---

50 The name *little borugates* may refer to the same path, especially if the qualifier refers to Roman archaeology rather than the town of Peterborough. Margary 250 is modern Lady Conneyburrow's Way, and it is possible that *great borugates* is Margary 25. Charter data show many furlongs lying in Thornes, between these two paths, which would fit topographically: I.D. Margary, *Roman roads in Britain* (London, 1973), p. 198.

51 Stukeley, *The family memoirs*, pp. 56–61.

52 N. Culpeper, *The English physician enlarged* (London, 1698), p. 92.

Figure 6.7. The warrior capital, St Kyneburgha, Castor, *c.*1100–10. Photo: Colin Hyde.

used to identify the riverine landing place. The corresponding colloquial name was recorded as *Robin Hood's stones*, or *Robin Hood and Little John*, and local folklore suggests that the stones mark the point at which arrows fired by Robin Hood from Alwalton (Huntingdonshire) churchyard, on the opposite bank of the river Nene, landed in Castor.[53] It is difficult to determine whether, in the case of Normangate Field and its surrounding landscape, we are witnessing a historical event or local folklore. Nevertheless, the possibility that Normangate Field was a repository of Castor's eleventh-century medieval history is compelling, even though the sources can only hint at the postulated events they perhaps represented. However, there may be further evidence to support this emerging hypothesis.

Within the early twelfth-century church dedicated to Cyneburg there is a magnificent set of Romanesque capitals. While all the capitals are of great interest, one in particular has been unequivocally associated with local folklore and landscape since at least the eighteenth century.[54] This capital depicts two warriors fighting, watched by an alarmed woman (Figure 6.7). This is an intriguing carving that has in

---

53 NRO F(M) Charters 320 and 326; NRO F(M) Misc. vol. 424; NRO F(M) Tin Box 1, Castor and Ailsworth, Parcel No. 5 (c) and (d); Serjeantson and Adkins, *VCH Northamptonshire*, vol. 2, p. 472; J. Bridges, *The history and antiquities of Northamptonshire*, vol. 2 (Oxford, 1791), p. 499; M. Chisholm, 'The medieval network of navigable Fenland waterways II: Barnack stone transport', *Proceedings of the Cambridge Antiquarian Society*, 100 (2011), pp. 172–3.

54 See also Kilby, 'Fantastic beasts', pp. 64–6.

(a)

(b)

(c)

(d)

Figure 6.8. 'Cyneburg' and warriors,
St Kyneburgha, Castor, *c.*1100–10.
Photos: Colin Hyde and Susan Kilby.

modern times generally been understood to be a pictorial rendition of the legend of Cyneburg. The association of the legend with the church capital prior to the modern period is problematic, however. The connection has not been universally accepted, however, and it is easy to see why.[55] The capital shows two warriors fighting each other (Figure 6.8a and b), rather than attacking the woman, who remains motionless to one side (Figure 6.8c). The woman is flanked on an adjacent capital by foliage (Figure 6.8d), which, it has been suggested, might represent the flowers that sprang up to aid Cyneburg's escape. However, the stone foliage is situated behind, rather than in front of, the woman. The two warriors are clearly fighting one another, but close inspection suggests that the warrior (a) defending the woman (c) is fighting a much larger figure (b) with enormous features and a huge head – one that could in fact be interpreted as a giant.[56] The warriors are wielding clubs or maces, the former a weapon associated with giants and peasants.[57] The foliage (d) is also worth closer inspection: it appears to represent a plant crowned with clusters of berries. In comparison, the remaining few foliate capitals in the church are all highly stylised.

Can there be a connection between the iconography within the church and the landscape surrounding it? In light of the earlier evidence, might these capitals represent the putative Danish attack on Castor, alongside the inevitable sprouting of *wælh-wyrt*? Unquestionably, the eleventh-century attack would still have been reasonably vivid in local memory. In order to test this idea further, it is necessary to consider who conceived the decorative scheme and what their purpose was in placing it at the heart of the twelfth-century church. The questions concerning patronage and meaning are especially problematic, and while an interpretation is considered it is acknowledged that this can only ever be speculative. Although the scheme's sponsor will always be difficult to identify conclusively, there are some possibilities that can be explored. The Norman church was constructed in the early twelfth century and dedicated between 1114 and 1124. A dispute in 1133 reveals that the advowson formed part of two knights' fees forming a manor belonging to Turold by *c*.1069, this manor being ultimately held from Peterborough Abbey. By 1133 Turold's younger son held the manor, while the elder son was the local priest, who, deciding to become a monk at Peterborough Abbey, granted the church to the abbey. This was contested by his brother, who asserted that 'the church was part of his fee, and he had the right to service from it', although he later dropped his claim.[58] This suggests that at the time the capitals were carved – *c*.1110 – the advowson was probably held by the original Turold.[59] His youngest son's attitude to the church in 1133 reveals that he considered the church in financial terms, giving up his rights once it was clear that half a fee was to be remitted. Might this also have been the attitude taken by Turold? It is of

---

55   For example, by the CRSBI <https://crsbi.ac.uk/site/371>, accessed 13 August 2019.

56   Kilby, 'Fantastic beasts', p. 64.

57   J.B. Friedman, *The monstrous races in art and thought* (London, 1981), p. 33.

58   King, *Peterborough Abbey*, pp. 28–31.

59   Turold's son did not inherit the fee until 1116–17: King, 'The Peterborough "*Descriptio Militum*"', p. 86; Hugh Candidus describes Abbot Turold and his knights as grasping (*Peterborough Chronicle*, pp. 40 and 44).

course impossible to know; French's conclusion that the local lord wielded influence is pertinent, but Turold was a low-ranking knight holding only two hides, and would have been unlikely to have met the full cost of church construction, especially given the size and magnificence of Castor church.[60]

Might Peterborough Abbey have exercised an influence? The abbey was comprehensively sacked and demolished by the Danes in the ninth century, about which Abbot John de Séez wrote in the early twelfth century:

> The altars all suffered, the monuments all broken, the great library of books of the saints burned, an immense quantity of charters of the monastery were torn, the precious relics of the holy virgins Kyneburga, Kyneswitha and Tibba were trampled underfoot, the walls were overturned, the church itself was burned along with all the other buildings, and throughout the following fortnight it continually burned.[61]

The abbot's description, albeit not a contemporary account, emphasises the gravity of the event and its continued relevance as far as the monastic community of the twelfth century was concerned. Hugh Candidus mentions the arrival of the Danish king Swein in 1070 alongside the alliance between Hereward and the Danes in Ely who sacked Peterborough Abbey in the same year, these events being directly contemporary with the appointment of Turold, the first Norman abbot of Peterborough.[62] It seems extremely unlikely that the capital in Castor's new church memorialised the Norman Conquest, given the pedigree of lord Turold and the new abbot. The most recent common adversaries of the English and the Normans were the Danes, and whatever the full contemporary interpretation of the Castor capital may have been, it seems extremely plausible that the enormous warrior it depicted was Danish. Importantly, this also links the late Anglo-Saxon field-names and the early eleventh-century events with the early twelfth-century capitals, implying a continued local narrative beyond the Conquest.

Castor church's capital scheme as a whole juxtaposes the menacing – including a number of symbols of the devil – and the prosaic (Figure 6.9), and the 'warrior' capital fits into this pattern.[63] The possibility that it has a local landscape context is also strengthened by the inclusion of several images that reflect Castor's hunting landscape – a stag, a wolf and a boar (Figure 6.10). Medieval field-names referencing deer and wolves in a hunting context are found at Castor – *rohauue* and *wulfhauue* – and, alongside the abbot of Peterborough's extensive woodlands at Castor, lord

---

60 K.L. French, *The people of the parish: community life in a late medieval English diocese* (Philadelphia, PA, 2001), p. 28; in Chale (Isle of Wight), the lord was presumed to pay for part of the construction of the church: C.D. Cragoe, 'The custom of the English church: parish church maintenance in England before 1300', *Journal of Medieval History*, 36 (2010), p. 28; see also chapter eight, p. 249.

61 Sparke, *Historiæ Anglicanæ*, vol. 1, p. 18.

62 Candidus, *Peterborough Chronicle*, p. 40.

63 The dragons, wolf and boar all symbolise the devil in later twelfth-century bestiary tradition, and if the giant warrior represented a Dane, this fits Candidus' view of Danes as 'servants of the devil': Kilby, 'Fantastic beasts', pp. 53–72.

Turold also held at least fifty acres of woodland pre-1215.[64] These images were not intended to convey a single message, but taken individually they almost certainly symbolise a range of potential meanings. While acknowledging the likelihood of valid, co-existing alternative narratives, others have interpreted images like this in line with the conclusions drawn here: that they simultaneously represent fauna associated with the local landscape and perhaps reference seigneurial resources and pursuits, such as hunting.[65] Medieval imagery was deliberately designed to be ambiguous, and the generation of multiple meanings would have been seen as a distinct advantage rather than a problem.[66] If these hunting scenes did embody the local landscape, then perhaps the warrior image might also have been seen in the same light. While the warrior capital cannot be linked conclusively with the furlongs of Normangate Field and their conceivable memorialisation of local history, the possibility of a connection cannot be entirely discounted.

Furthermore, if this interpretation is considered to be plausible, it suggests that in order to reveal insights into popular meaning we should move in some instances beyond purely learned and taxonomic considerations. Ultimately, it is unclear whether we are looking at an ordinary landscape in Castor – for which a greater than usual quantity of evidence survives through a number of media and which reveals something of the folkloric qualities of the landscape that are difficult to detect elsewhere – or something more unusual. Was Castor really seen differently by its inhabitants than was Elton, for instance? It is extremely hard to determine this with any precision, largely due to the inconsistent survival of the necessarily wide-ranging evidence needed to test this hypothesis. Little work has been undertaken on the more socio-cultural aspects of the named landscape, although some studies – concentrating on themes such as the supernatural, religion and saints – offer a rare focus on the cultural importance of the rural landscape. Those field-names associated with the supernatural (although few in number), alongside their very obvious association with cosmology, folklore and myth, have ensured that this is one aspect of the named landscape that has been

---

64   King, *Peterborough Abbey*, p. 77; *rohauue* – roe-deer enclosure; *wulfhauue* – wolf enclosure; Kilby, 'Fantastic beasts', p. 58; note that *rohauue* could mean 'rough enclosure'.

65   E. den Hartog, 'All nature speaks of God, all nature teaches man: the iconography of the twelfth-century capitals in the westwork gallery of the church of St Servatius in Maastricht', *Zeitschrift für Kunstgeschichte*, 59 (1996), p. 30; M. Thurlby, *The Herefordshire school of Romanesque sculpture* (Logaston, 2000), p. 51; A. Pluskowski, 'Constructing exotic animals and environments in late medieval Britain', in S. Page (ed.), *The unorthodox imagination in late medieval Britain* (Manchester, 2010), p. 195; Kilby, 'Fantastic beasts', p. 58; Albarella suggests that wild boar were rare in the post-Conquest landscape, and hunting was restricted to elites, further strengthening one interpretation of this group of images as depicting seigneurial resources: U. Albarella, 'The wild boar', in T. O'Connor and N. Sykes (eds), *Extinctions and invasions: a social history of British fauna* (Oxford, 2010), pp. 63–4.

66   For example: E. Mâle, *The gothic image: religious art in France of the thirteenth century,* trans. D. Nussey (London, 1972), pp. 32–3; F. Klingender, *Animals in art and thought to the end of the middle ages* (London, 1971), p. 328; M. Camille, *Image on the edge: the margins of medieval art* (London, 1992), p. 29; Thurlby, *The Herefordshire school*, pp. 45 and 51.

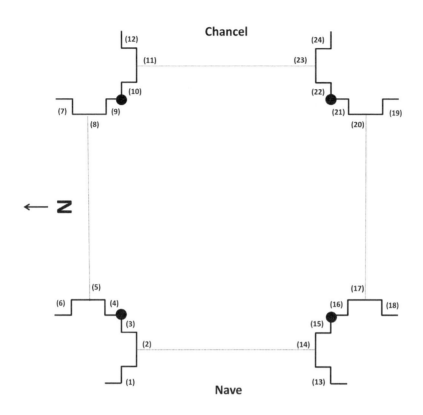

Chancel

Nave

(1) Bird and serpent
(2) Foliage-spewer
(3) Foliage-spewer
(4) Foliage
(5) Foliage
(6) Stag

(13) Birds and tree
(14) Foliage
(15) Foliage
(16) Foliage
(17) Giant, warrior and woman
(18) Foliage

(7) Pruning man
(8) Entwined dragons/basilisks
(9) Man with quadruped and ?iaculus
(10) Bullock
(11) Boar hunt
(12) David and lion

(19) Dragon or salamander
(20) Harvesting vines
(21) Dragon and lion
(22) Dragon and lion
(23) Dragon and lion
(24) Foliage

Figure 6.9. The sculpture of the tower capitals, St Kyneburgha, Castor.

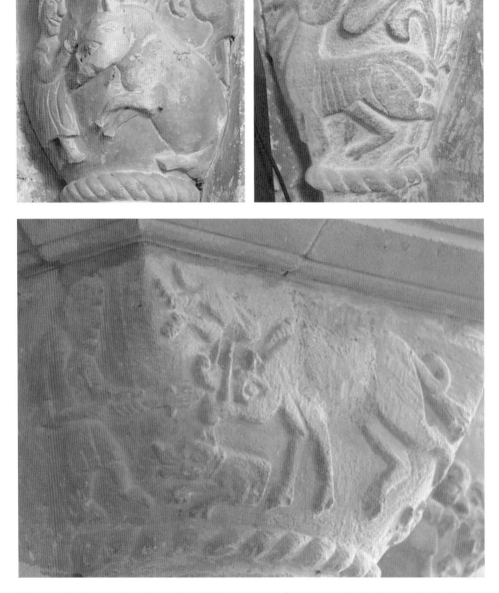

Figure 6.10. Fauna related to hunting, St Kyneburgha, Castor, *c.*1100–10. Photos: Colin Hyde and Susan Kilby.

examined at some length, albeit predominantly within studies that tend to focus on the theme generally rather than offering a thorough examination of particular places.[67] Occasionally, references to stories and folklore associated with the landscape are found within research devoted to other aspects of social history: Whyte records in an early modern context local tradition in modern Weeting (Norfolk) associating Oliver Cromwell with the construction of a barrow and a putative attack on Weeting castle; and Walsham highlights the renaming of the village of Slepe to St Ives (Huntingdonshire) following the discovery by a peasant of the body of St Ives in a field there.[68]

The twelfth-century hagiographer Geoffrey of Burton recalled a supernatural incident that occurred in Drakelowe (Derbyshire), where two headless, revenant peasants persistently wandered through the village and its surrounding landscape, frightening the locals. The story has been rightly highlighted as an example of commonplace supernatural belief during the twelfth century; however, one of the key elements has been overlooked: its landscape setting. Drakelowe would have been the obvious spot for supernatural activity of this nature, since the place-name meant 'dragon burial mound/hill' – a name conjuring up a landscape populated with demons.[69] Similarly, in South Creake (Norfolk), several field-names have definite or possible supernatural associations. The parish has some striking similarities to Castor,[70] the landscape containing significant Iron Age and Roman archaeology: an Iron Age hillfort known in the medieval period as *burghesdykes*, and Roman roads crossing the parish. Its medieval names include *grimeswell* (Devil's well), *elvering* (?elf-ring) and *snakedyke*, alongside later *drakecrundell* (dragon pit) and *pokesty* (goblin path), which may have been coined in the medieval period.[71] At Radley (Berkshire) there were seventeen barrows in two rows, and evidence of Roman archaeology; although an extensive field-name study has not been undertaken, Field noted names including *le buggrove* (grove haunted by a goblin) and *pookes eyett*, which may reference another goblin.[72] Barrowden (Rutland), which itself means 'hill with burial mounds upon it', has the medieval field-names *le berues* (the barrows), *robynilpit* (a reference to the goblin Robin Goodfellow) and *þyrspit*, again focusing on the supernatural by referencing giants or demons.[73]

---

67 Gelling, *Signposts to the past*, pp. 130–61; Semple, 'A fear of the past', pp. 109–26.

68 Whyte, 'The after-life of barrows', p. 7; Walsham, *The reformation of the landscape*, p. 47.

69 Key to English place-names <http://kepn.nottingham.ac.uk/map/place/Derbyshire/Drakelow>, accessed 16 November 2012; J. Harte, 'Hell on earth: encountering devils in the medieval landscape', in B. Bildhauer and R. Mills (eds), *The monstrous middle ages* (Toronto, 2003), p. 180; Watkins, *History and the supernatural*, p. 183.

70 M. Hesse, 'Medieval field systems and land tenure in South Creake, Norfolk', *Norfolk Archaeology*, 43 (1998), pp. 80–4.

71 *Grimeswell* and *pouksty*: Gelling suggests *grim* and *puca* are associated with earthworks, and so these names *may* have medieval origins: Gelling, *Signposts to the past*, p. 150; *Elvering* is more problematic. Although it is at least thirteenth century, it *may* refer to elves or a personal name. If it was coined in the thirteenth century, then it possibly denotes elves (P. McClure and A. Hall, pers. comm.).

72 Field, *History of English field-names*, p. 248.

73 B. Cox, *The place-names of Rutland* (Nottingham, 1994), pp. 232–8.

Given the difficulties associated with the survival of suitable evidence, alongside a relatively recent scholarly focus on interdisciplinary research, it is hardly surprising that detailed studies of the nature undertaken here have not been attempted before. Furthermore, beyond committed interdisciplinarians, the objectives of most researchers have tended to lie elsewhere, either in more socio-economic or purely onomastic fields. However, it is clear that there is at least the potential within both documentary sources and the landscape itself for work similar to that presented here to be attempted elsewhere. More generalised and thematic studies are important, but we should not project their conclusions wholesale over the medieval English rural landscape. As the findings from Castor highlight – much like Gardiner's work on Shetland and Iceland – a tightly confined geographic focus can enrich our understanding of the particular, emphasising the hidden heterogeneity of the local. Whatever the problems that might ensue with these interpretive leaps, the very presence of this group of Castor field-names, alongside the documentary and landscape evidence, demands our attention. Necessarily, this takes us, at times, to the edge of where scholars have previously been prepared to venture. Consequently the interpretations that have been offered above are given in full cognizance of their intrinsic problems, coming with a considerable number of interpretive caveats. They are presented here as a first attempt to take the analysis of these sources in new directions and to encourage others to look at physical, textual and onomastic materials in new ways. As landscape scholars have long been aware, field-names and minor landscape names are sometimes associated with the memories of local events and the stories connected with them. The analysis presented here shows that it is sometimes possible to retrieve at least part of these more complex meanings from the medieval past.

Chapter 7

The economic landscape

The rural environment as an economic resource: the demesne

Historians have acknowledged the difficulties of reconstructing peasant economies. Surviving documents were created for the manorial lord and thus prioritise the demesne economy. While the demesne economy may have relevance for understanding the peasant experience, we should not assume that peasant modes of making a living mirrored those of the lordly demesne. In tracing the economic outlook of one Midland yardlander in Gloucestershire, Christopher Dyer focused on peasant cereal production using records outlining peasant holdings surrendered into the lord's hands alongside tithe receipts.[1] Livestock, garden produce and non-agricultural income sources were also considered. Within his study, peasant success – indicated through probable crop yields and income from additional sources, such as the garden, alongside output in the form of rents, tallages and tolls – was largely dependent upon the size of the holding and the vagaries of the weather.[2] In a pioneering volume on the Breckland area of medieval Suffolk, Mark Bailey emphasised the limitations of historians' understanding of so-called marginal landscapes, highlighting an alternative, thriving economy comprising minimal cereal production.[3] This is of course pertinent when considering the economy of the Lakenheath peasant. Smaller-scale peasant activities such as gardening, fishing and obtaining fuel are traditionally considered fleetingly, in isolation, or not at all.[4] This does not generally reflect an unwillingness among historians to consider such matters, more a recognition of the intrinsic difficulties in gathering valid and sufficient data, although this is not always stated. While it is not feasible to reconstruct a fully comprehensive account of peasant incomes here, it is possible to explore the potential of different sources of income, such as fishing and sheep farming. It is also possible, however briefly, to consider in more detail those aspects of the peasant economy that feature only briefly in manorial documents.

---

1   A yardland was an alternative term for a virgate, which was a standardised plot of villein land, notionally thirty acres. Dyer, *Standards of living*, pp. 111–13. For further scholarship on peasant tithes see B. Dodds, 'Demesne and tithe: peasant agriculture in the late middle ages', *Agricultural History Review*, 56/2 (2008), pp. 123–41.

2   Jane Whittle has also calculated the productivity of a smaller peasant landholding in Hunstanton (Norfolk), and has estimated that, there, just over six acres was required to support a family. She notes the importance of supplementary income to these households: Whittle, 'The food economy', pp. 40–2.

3   Bailey, *Marginal economy?*, p. 18.

4   Bailey, *Marginal economy?*, pp. 161–5; Dyer, *Everyday life*, see also chapter eight, this volume.

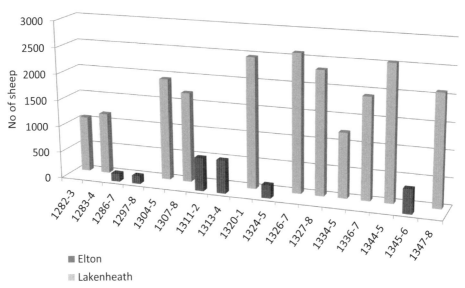

Figure 7.1. Demesne sheep at Elton and Lakenheath, 1282–1348. Source: *EMR*; CUL EDC/7/16/1/2; EDC/7/16/1/3; EDC/7/16/1/4; EDC/7/16/1/6; EDC/7/16/1/7; EDC/7/16/1/9; EDC/7/16/1/11; EDC/7/16/1/13; EDC/7/16/1/14. Note: These figures record Michaelmas flocks.

Nevertheless, it is sensible to begin with a brief overview of the demesne economy, as evidenced within the respective manorial accounts for the main manors in each of the three case-study vills. Elton and Castor were both dominated by arable production, while Lakenheath had a sheep–corn economy. Campbell describes the Castor demesne as marginally dominated by spring-sown cereals, while Lakenheath generally concentrated on rye.[5] While Elton's accounts do not record the area sown with crops, thus denying us the opportunity to calculate crop yields, they do record the issues of corn – the quantity harvested. Spring-sown barley appears to dominate pre-1326 and in most of the years for which accounts survive barley issues constituted more than 50 per cent of the total harvest. In contrast to the arable-dominated demesnes at Castor and Elton, sheep were an important aspect of the Lakenheath demesne economy, where the size of the demesne flock frequently exceeded 2,000 (Figure 7.1).[6] It can be clearly seen that sheep were a less significant element of demesne revenues at Elton, where the flock was frequently smaller than

---

5   Campbell, *English seigniorial agriculture*, pp. 250–1.

6   My dating of the Lakenheath account rolls differs in some respects from the dates used by Mark Bailey in *Marginal economy?* This is due to the (wholly understandable) incorrect dating of the rolls by the CUL archivist, and a full explanation for the rationale behind my revised dates is outlined in S. Kilby, 'Encountering the environment: rural communities in England, 1086–1348', PhD thesis (University of Leicester, 2013), pp. 23–7. This does mean that some of my data may differ from Bailey's. It should also be noted that sheep were often an important part of the economy in manors dominated by cereal production.

some peasant flocks at Lakenheath.[7] Little information on sheep is recorded in the Castor account rolls, although in 1300–1 the total demesne flock numbered 426.[8] On the Peterborough Abbey estate from at least 1307–8 sheep within Nassaburgh hundred, of which Castor was part, were recorded in a separate account and were clearly being managed as a distinct economic unit.[9] The accounts for both Walton (also part of the Soke of Peterborough) and Castor indicate that only wethers were present, suggesting that certain Peterborough demesnes may have specialised in particular types of sheep.

Sheep and cereals were often important aspects of demesne husbandry. However, at Castor and Lakenheath, the economic outlook extended into additional areas of focus, maximising the productive potential of their respective topographies: woodland at Castor, and heath and fenland at Lakenheath. The Elton accounts reveal a range of manorial servants typical of a Midlands champion manor. At Castor, in addition to those working on the arable, a forester was employed.[10] Foresters were evident on a number of Peterborough Abbey manors, although only two manors, Longthorpe (Soke of Peterborough) and Castor, included woodland produce in their respective stock accounts.[11] While at Longthorpe the woodland does not appear to have been commercially managed during the period for which accounts survive, at Castor the few extant accounts detail sales of felled oak.[12] Indeed, plough-beams were 'bought in the wood of Castor' for use at Elton in 1314, alongside timber bought for Elton mill.[13] Since no account survives for this date for Castor, it is impossible to tell whether these sales represented demesne or peasant resources. The 1215 survey of the disafforestation of the Soke of Peterborough reveals extensive woodland in Castor, held by the abbot of Peterborough, the knightly landlords, and some freeholders:

> *einig* of Ralph Munjoye contains 5 acres of thicket. *einig* of the lord abbot contains 5 acres of thicket. *rohauue* and *thinferdesland* and *w[u]lfhauue* of the abbot contain 78 acres and 3 rods, and half is covert and the other half thicket. *frith*, of Torold of Castor contains 25 acres. The wood of Ralph, son of Silvester and the wood of Paris and the wood of Reginald of Ashton contains 25 acres.

---

7   In six sets of accounts between 1286 and 1346 the mean average flock size at Elton was 469 (but a co-efficient of 66.38 emphasizes a high level of dispersion around the mean), *EMR*, pp. 9–337.

8   NRO F(M) 2388.

9   S. Raban (ed., trans.), *The accounts of Godfrey of Crowland, abbot of Peterborough 1299–1321* (Northampton, 2011), p. xxviii; in the 1307–8 and 1309–10 accounts for Castor, only wethers received from customary payments were recorded, whereas the Nassaburgh flock account for 1307–8 indicates that Castor had a stock of 257 wethers that year, and in 1309–10 lambs were transferred to Castor from Eye (Northamptonshire). See also K. Biddick, *The other economy: pastoral husbandry on a medieval estate* (London, 1989), p. 100.

10 NRO F(M) 2388; F(M) Roll 233; (F)M 2389.

11 Longthorpe and Walton were in the Soke of Peterborough in the fourteenth century, now both part of the Peterborough suburbs, in Cambridgeshire.

12 NRO F(M) 2388; F(M) Roll 233; (F)M 2389.

13 *EMR*, pp. 211 and 231.

eylisuuorthemore of the abbot contains 22 acres and 3 rods. The wood of William, son of Gilbert contains 7 acres and 1 rod. *abbotishauue*, *estrys* and *iungeuuode* contain 120 acres. *aleuuode* of the abbot contains 8 acres and of thicket, 1 rod … The wood of William Abuuetun contains 28 acres. The wood of Ralph Cordel contains 6½ acres. The wood of the parson of Castor contains 16 acres. The wood [of] Illing contains 16 acres. *baketeshauue* of the abbot contains 8 acres … *tikkeuuode* of William de Euermue contains 4 acres. *sistremor* of Robert de Meltune contains 25 acres.[14]

Although the Castor woodland listed in 1215 amounted to more than 400 acres, it is difficult to ascertain precisely how much survived after the disafforestation. An undated survey of 1272×1307 indicates that, by that time, woodland six furlongs by four remained, alongside a wood of three furlongs by two in Ailsworth, suggesting that approximately 300 acres of demesne woodland remained.[15] Clearly, this was considered a vital element of the local economy. Conversely, timber was an uncommon resource in Elton and Lakenheath. Woodland is rarely mentioned in the field-name corpora of these two places: *longhyrst* and *schorthyrst* at Elton seem to refer to a wooded hill, but as both places were meadow by the fourteenth century these may represent much earlier names. Other field-names reference either individual trees or small stands of one species (see also chapter five).[16] The account rolls for Elton note purchases of wood and timber being made in Fotheringhay Park (Northamptonshire), Ellington and Weston (Huntingdonshire), in addition to Castor, while Lakenheath was supplied from Wyverstone or Ixworth (Suffolk).[17]

At Lakenheath, although cereals formed an important part of its economy, only a small proportion of the overall parish acreage was dedicated to arable farming. Of its *c*.11,000 acres, 1,500 were dedicated to arable, with 600 acres in demesne. Peat fen covered 7,000 acres and heathland another 2,000 acres, part of which formed the

---

14 King, *Peterborough Abbey*, pp. 172–7; some of these named woods are confirmed as lying in Castor only through other documents: *rohauue* is also referenced within *rohaubroc* (which itself is possibly referenced in the later *le rowessick*) in a Castor charter detailed in a Peterborough cartulary; as is *w[u]lfhauue*, which is later referenced as *wol[f]hauue*; *baketeshauue* later referenced in *basketisuuelle*; *sistremor* also features, and is described as being located in Castor (there is also a *cistermoyr* in Boroughbury, Northamptonshire); CUL PDC/MS 1, The Book of Robert of Swaffham; NRO F(M) Roll 233; Raban, *Godfrey of Crowland*, p. 707; Ralph Munjoye, Geoffrey Illing and William de Euermue were tenants of Peterborough Abbey in *c*.1231: Soc. Antiq., MS 60, ff. 186–187v, *Black Book of Peterborough*.

15 CUL PDC/MS 1, The Book of Robert of Swaffham; based on the measurements provided, and including Ailsworth; naturally, the smaller knights' fees may have increased the total area of Castor woodland; by 1321 a transcript of a survey indicates one common wood, and a small enclosed wood of six acres, suggesting that the assarting process continued into the late thirteenth century: Sparke, *Historiæ Anglicanæ*, vol. 2, pp. 175–7.

16 Gelling and Cole, *The landscape of place-names*, p. 234.

17 *EMR*, pp. 231 and 273; CUL EDC/7/16/1/13–14.

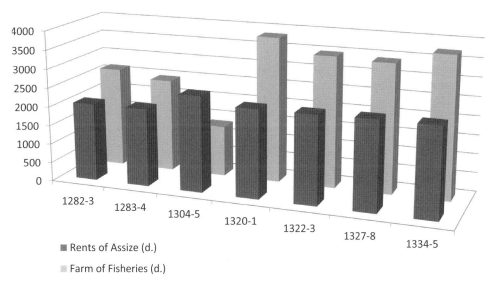

Figure 7.2. Revenues from rents of assize and fisheries at farm, Lakenheath 1282–1335.
Notes: These revenues taken from the prior of Ely's manor; Clare fee had fisheries at farm, but these were much less extensive. Source: CUL EDC/7/16/1/2–4; EDC/7/16/1/7; EDC/7/16/1/9.

warren. In addition, there were extensive fisheries.[18] Peat was an important fenland fuel in the medieval period (see chapter eight). The accounts record enormous quantities of peat turves purchased and transported to Ely, but they are not recorded in the accounts as an economic resource until 1344–5, the same year that sedge is also noted in the stock account.[19] Smaller quantities of rushes feature in the accounts from 1334.[20] Fishing was by far the most lucrative of the non-agricultural activities in terms of revenue; the Lakenheath fisheries were almost continually leased during the period in which accounts survive, and revenues frequently outstripped those received from rents (Figure 7.2), emphasising the importance of this revenue stream to the prior of Ely but also offering an important indicator of the fisheries' significance as a peasant resource, since it was to them that many of the fisheries were leased.

At both Elton and Castor there is little mention of fishing, despite both manors being bounded by the Nene. A survey dated 1218–19 details a demesne several fishery in the Nene at Elton, 'beginning at the head of the mill-pond and extend[ing] to the mill' and a 'common fishery which begins at *derneforde* and extends for a league and a half in length, to *stodholm netherhende*, of which fishery lord John de Baliol by force and power wrongfully withheld for himself from the same Abbot [of

---

18 Bailey, 'The prior and convent of Ely', pp. 2–3.

19 CUL EDC/7/16/1/13; see also chapter seven for analysis of peasant peat and sedge processing. It seems likely that peat was an important Lakenheath resource before this date.

20 CUL EDC/7/16/1/9–11.

Ramsey], and the lady of Baliol still withholds it'.[21] The abbot of Ramsey seems to have finally conceded the larger fishery to the Baliols in return for sole possession of the smaller mill fishery, and fleeting references to that resource appear in the accounts, where it was noted that eel traps were purchased and eels accounted for within the mill account, although the income was negligible.[22] At Castor, nothing is mentioned concerning fisheries until an inquisition dated 17 February 1272, which details all the Peterborough Abbey Nene fisheries and reveals that 'from *ingewell* up to *alwaltonedam* there is a several fishery of the Abbot of Peterborough by right of his demesne of Castor'.[23] In 1308 the watercourse of *iggewelle* was at farm to the abbot of Thorney for half a mark; and in Sparke's transcript of the 1321 survey a several fishery worth two shillings was noted, which was at farm, although it seems unlikely to have been the same resource, the value being far too low.[24]

Demesne records are useful in outlining the general economic outlook of individual manors. Here, they show that each manor had a distinctive land-based economy: Elton had what might be described as a 'classic' Midland open-field structure, largely focused on cereal production, which in this case was based on a three-field system. The resources associated with Castor's large area of woodland formed an important part of its annual revenue generation, and this was also the case at Lakenheath, with extensive fens, fisheries and heathland covering more than half of its territory. In each case we should expect that each of these resources played a considerable part in the economic outlook of local peasants.

The rural environment as an economic resource: peasant arable production

Much of what has been written about the peasant economy is acknowledged as hypothetical and, to a degree, speculative. On establishing the economic situation of his Midland yardlander in Bishop's Cleeve (Gloucestershire), Dyer, although conscious of the many variables arising from differences in manorial custom, social status and landholding, was keen to establish that his model peasant was representative in a wider context.[25] It is likely that the peasant experience at Elton shared similarities with the Bishop's Cleeve model, not least because a three-field system was operated in a landscape dominated by cereal production. Castor is more difficult to pinpoint. First,

---

21 *CMR I*, p. 490; also outlined in 1279: *RH II*, p. 656.

22 *EMR*, pp. 82, 110 and 230–1; *CMR II*, pp. 361–2.

23 Soc. Antiq., MS 60, f. 172v, *Black Book of Peterborough*.

24 Unless it had seriously deteriorated, which was sometimes the case with some of the Lakenheath fisheries; NRO F(M) Roll 233; Sparke, *Historiæ Anglicanæ*, vol. 2, p. 176; *c*.1293, an Ailsworth freeman gave the abbot of Thorney a licence to make and use a wharf on his meadow, opposite Water Newton mill, although it is not specified what it was to be used for: CUL MS Add. 3020, Red Book of Thorney.

25 Dyer's model reconstructed a peasant budget, based on the holding of one Midlands yardlander, including additional income from the garden, and taking into account typical expenditure: Dyer, *Standards of living*, p. 118.

at least five fields are mentioned in the records. Also, in 1321, alongside nine virgates held by villeins, seven and a half virgates of bond land were leased to free tenants 'because of the lack of cultivation of the bondmen', which means that the experience of all virgaters in Castor was unlikely to be uniform.[26] In addition, despite these manors' Midlands location and their focus on arable agriculture, there is very little information pertaining to the peasant economy within surviving records. If there are some similarities at Elton and Castor, the experience of Dyer's Gloucestershire peasant probably differed markedly from that of his contemporaries in Lakenheath, situated on the breck–fen divide and being much less dominated by arable production.

In Elton, no tithe data are recorded in the surviving account rolls for the period, although we know that a virgate was twenty-four acres, suggesting a sown acreage of sixteen acres in its three-field rotation. Some information is forthcoming from additional customary dues. Each customary virgate owed one ring of oats each year for *foddercorn*, a bushel of wheat for *benesad*, and a further quantity of grain for the mill toll.[27] All this reveals is that a quantity of oats and wheat was probably sown each year, but not how much was sown or the quantity kept by the peasants. Technically, the grain for these customary payments could have been purchased, although this seems less likely. If they also sowed legumes, barley and mixed grain, the accounts remain silent. The foldage schedule allowed certain peasants to pay for the right to fold their sheep on their own land, thus increasing soil fertility and probably, therefore, their cereal yield.[28]

At Castor, although there are no tithe data, in the account for 1300–1 the confiscated chattels of a fugitive tenant are recorded (Table 7.1) and, fortunately, these provide a detailed account of the issue of corn from a one-virgate holding. This was no ordinary peasant, however. Robert Lord, alias Robert, son of William Thorold, belonged to a cadet branch of the Thorold family, whose status had diminished by the late thirteenth century (see chapter three).[29] Robert Lord held a messuage with a virgate in 1300, for which he owed annual rent of 24s. and *burwerk*, an obligation to perform customary works in Peterborough. Although no solid yield data can be established from the demesne at Castor, the same account records demesne sowing rates for the cereals also grown by Robert Lord, and so demesne yield can be estimated, as outlined in Table 7.2. Working with these data, it is possible to hypothesise, however tentatively, about the acreage that Robert Lord may have sown (Table 7.3).[30] The

---

26 Sparke, *Historiæ Anglicanæ*, vol. 2, p. 176; might this have related to the Great Famine? In 1231, there were twenty-seven virgates in Castor and Ailsworth (see below, p. 172).

27 *EMR*; a ring is equivalent to half a quarter; *foddercorn* and *benesad* were paid only by customary virgaters, not by those paying cash rents. Note that these dues were not commuted for cash during the period under review.

28 Kilby, 'A different world?' (2010a), p. 73.

29 King, *Peterborough Abbey*, p. 35; NRO F(M) 2388; the knights' fees (reduced to 1½ by 1133) were transferred to successive heirs intact until at least 1348: CUL PDC/MS 6, The Red Book of John of Achurch.

30 It has been assumed here that Robert Lord's confiscated cereals were grown by him and, given his virgate holding, this seems like a reasonable assumption.

Table 7.1
The chattels of Robert Lord of Castor, 1300–1.[1]

Issue of wheat (bsh.)	Issue of rye (bsh.)	Issue of barley (bsh.)	Issue of dredge (bsh.)	Issue of peas (bsh.)	Misc.
38	25	48	98	8	1 old cart
					3s. from the sale of chattels
					Hay, unspecified amount

Source: NRO F(M) 2388.

Note:

1. Note that the quantities were recorded in quarters and skeps. A skep is equivalent to a bushel and, for the sake of uniformity, is used here.

Table 7.2
Estimated demesne yield, Castor, 1300–1.

	Issue (bsh.)	Acres sown	% of sown acreage	Bsh. sown per acre	Mean yield per seed
Wheat	673.5	124	32	2.49	3.2
Rye	393	37	10	2.49	4.2
Barley	366	50	13	4.02	3.3
Dredge	411	42.5	11	4.00	5.3
Oats	1142.5	103	27	4.98	2.4
Peas	120	25	7	2.00	3.0

Source: NRO F(M) 2388; mean yield figures: Campbell, *English seigniorial agriculture*, pp. 316–19; the mean yield for dredge is taken from D. Stone, *Decision-making in medieval agriculture* (Oxford, 2005), p. 38.

Table 7.3
Estimated acreage sown by Robert Lord, Castor, 1300–1.[1]

	Mean yield per seed	Est. bushels sown	Est. acreage sown	% of sown acreage
Wheat	3.2	11.88	4.77	28
Rye	4.2	5.95	2.39	14
Barley	3.3	14.55	3.62	22
Dredge	5.3	16.33	4.62	28
Peas	3.0	2.67	1.33	8
Total			16.73	

Source: NRO F(M) 2388; mean yield figures as above.

Note:

1. Based on demesne sowing rates.

virgate size at Castor is not recorded, but at Upton (Northamptonshire), which borders Ailsworth, and which for a brief period was leased to Peterborough Abbey, it was twenty-four acres.[31] Although it is unclear precisely how cropping operated in Castor, the estimated acreage sown by Robert Lord is convincingly close to what he would have been expected to sow with sixteen acres in production.

Tables 7.2 and 7.3 highlight the different proportions of arable land sown on the Castor demesne and by Robert Lord, based on his estimated sowing schedule. The estimated proportion of land devoted to wheat seems similar, while slightly more land was dedicated to rye on the peasant holding. The significant differences between the demesne and the peasant holding were the higher ratios of barley and dredge sown by Robert Lord.[32] Oats were not part of Lord's confiscated grain stock. The emphasis on demesne oats was probably due to the greater quantities of livestock that required feeding.[33] The quantity of grain taken indicates that it was probably appropriated not long after harvest, and this is supported by the fact that the scribe recorded the confiscated produce as Robert Lord's 'issue', the term used to describe gross cereal output.[34] Nevertheless, we cannot be certain that it constituted a full crop from one year's production, or whether part of the harvest had already been consumed or sold.[35] The significantly higher proportion of land committed to growing dredge is worthy of comment. Robert Lord reserved an estimated 29 per cent of his productive arable land to the crop, compared with just 11 per cent on the demesne.[36] Comparing Robert Lord's output with the confiscated crop of a Warwickshire peasant, Walter Shayll, there are striking similarities in the percentage of land devoted to wheat, rye and, to a lesser extent, dredge, which both Shayll and Lord prioritised.[37]

Only 30 per cent of the demesnes surveyed by Campbell produced dredge in the fourteenth century, the majority located in the east midlands, especially in Bedfordshire, Cambridgeshire and Northamptonshire. It was used predominantly for brewing or pottage, or sold as a cash crop, as on the Wisbech Barton (Cambridgeshire) demesne.[38] The surviving Castor account rolls show that the majority of its issue of dredge was committed to brewing and, once processed, sent to Peterborough Abbey.[39] Since the produce of the Soke manors was generally sent

---

31 R.M. Serjeantson and W.R.D. Adkins, 'Upton' in R.M. Serjeantson and W.R.D. Adkins (eds), *VCH Northamptonshire*, vol. 2, p. 483; S. Raban (ed.), *The white book of Peterborough* (Northampton, 2001), p. 41; at nearby Elton, the virgate was also twenty-four acres.

32 Dredge was a mixed grain comprising barley and oats.

33 Approximately fifty-four quarters of oats were expended in animal feed.

34 For example, '*de exitu t[er]re Roberti Lord*': NRO F(M) 2388.

35 It is also possible that all or part of this stock had been purchased, rather than grown, but since Lord held a virgate of land, this seems unlikely.

36 This assumes that the sowing ratio mirrored that of the demesne, four bushels per acre, and therefore should be treated with caution.

37 R.H. Hilton, *The English peasantry in the later middle ages* (Oxford, 1975), pp. 201–2.

38 Campbell, *English seigniorial agriculture*, pp. 226 and 243–5; D. Stone, *Decision-making in medieval agriculture* (Oxford, 2005), p. 48.

39 NRO F(M) 2388; F(M) Roll 233; F(M) 2389.

to the Abbey rather than entering the local market, it is difficult to deduce Robert Lord's motivation from the demesne strategy. Pretty argued that mixed grains were sown primarily because they were more likely to restrain weeds, but he also showed that on Winchester manors dredge was both productive and cropped consistently, suggesting that it was a pragmatic choice and raising interesting questions about Robert Lord's possible reasons for selecting it as a principal cereal – did he perhaps calculate that sowing dredge might minimise his overall risk?[40] Although these data provide little more than a snapshot of a very brief period for one individual, and we have no means of knowing how productive a farmer Robert Lord was, they nevertheless demonstrate that demesne cropping strategies frequently differed markedly from those of local husbandmen.

At Lakenheath a different set of data offers another snapshot into peasant arable production. There, the account rolls reveal sporadic information concerning peasant tithes.[41] Within most of the extant account rolls data are recorded concerning the issue of lambs, alongside woolfells and fleeces received from peasants. Some of the later account rolls detail grain receipts from the tithe within the stock account, but this process seems to have been developing from the mid-1330s. Crops were not generally recorded until 1334–5, and the following surviving Ely Priory account in 1336–7 sets the tithe out in a supplementary roll, attached to the sergeant's account.[42] The two extant tithe accounts reveal a mixed picture of the peasant arable at Lakenheath, as outlined in Tables 7.4 and 7.5. As in the case of the Castor peasant Robert Lord, the strategy of Lakenheath peasants differed somewhat from that of the demesne, with a greater focus on barley (Figures 7.3 and 7.4).[43]

Nevertheless, when compared with the evidence relating to Robert Lord, some problems are immediately apparent. We know that Lakenheath peasants held *c.*860 acres of arable and, using demesne sowing rates, it is possible to estimate the acreage that may have been sown, as outlined in Table 7.5.[44] Using Lakenheath demesne sowing

---

40 J. Pretty, 'Sustainable agriculture in the Middle Ages: the English manor', *Agricultural History Review*, 38/1 (1990), p. 5. Using tithe data, Alexandra Sapoznik has shown that peasants at Oakington (Cambridgeshire) grew a high proportion of dredge: A. Sapoznik, 'Resource allocation and peasant decision making: Oakington, Cambridgeshire, 1360–99', *Agricultural History Review*, 61/2 (2013), p. 191.

41 Unlike the rich tithe data evaluated by Ben Dodds: B. Dodds, *Peasants and production in the medieval north-east. The evidence from tithes, 1270–1536* (Woodbridge, 2007); Dodds, 'Demesne and tithe', pp. 123–41.

42 For 1336–7 a reeve's account, a sergeant's account and a tithe account survive. In 1347–8 a similar arrangement is apparent, with a sergeant's and a tithe account extant. The remaining account rolls for the post-1336–7 period do not record cereal tithe data, hinting at a series of separate tithe accounts that no longer survive.

43 Dyer argues that on the Worcester cathedral priory estate peasants 'thought independently about their choice of crops': C. Dyer, 'Peasant farming in late medieval England: evidence from the tithe estimations by Worcester Cathedral Priory', in M. Kowaleski *et al.* (eds), *Peasants and lords in the medieval English economy. Essays in honour of Bruce M.S. Campbell* (Turnhout, 2015), p. 95.

44 Bailey, 'The prior and convent of Ely', p. 3.

Table 7.4
Cereal and legume tithe returns, Lakenheath, 1336–7 and 1347–8.

	1336–7			1347–8		
	Quantity (qtr)	*Quantity (bsh.)*	*Total issue (qtr ×10)*	*Quantity (qtr)*	*Quantity (bsh.)*	*Total issue (qtr ×10)*
Wheat	-	-	-	1	3	14
Rye	23	4	235	11	5	116
Barley	74	2	742.5	78	6	787.5
Oats	8.5	-	85	7.5	-	75
Peas	7	4.5	75	1	3	14
Total	112.5	10.5	1,137.5	98.5	17	1,006.5

Source: CUL EDC/7/16/1/11; EDC/7/16/1/14.

Table 7.5
The tithe account: modelling estimated sown acreages using demesne sowing rates
– Lakenheath, 1336–7 and 1347–8.

		1336–7			1347–8		
	Mean yield per seed	*Est. bushels sown*	*Bsh. sown per acre (demesne)*	*Est. acreage sown*	*Est. bushels sown*	*Bsh. sown per acre (demesne)*	*Est. acreage sown*
Wheat	4.6	-	-	-	24.35	2.83	8.60
Rye	3.6	522.22	1.88	277.78	257.78	2.1	122.75
Barley	3.3	1800.00	3.62	497.24	1909.09	4.02	474.90
Oats	2.6	261.54	2.0	130.77	230.77	2.05	112.57
Peas	2.6	230.77	2.0	115.38	43.08	3.33	12.94
Total				1,021.17			731.76

Source: CUL EDC/7/16/1/11; EDC/7/16/1/14; mean average yield figures based on Norfolk pre-1350: Campbell, *English seigniorial agriculture*, pp. 318–19.

rates alongside mean yield data from Campbell's Norfolk database, which includes some Suffolk demesnes, it is clear that these calculations cannot realistically estimate peasant arable production at Lakenheath, as these figures suggest a total sown acreage of over 1,000 acres in 1336–7, considerably more land than was available.[45] Therefore, either the peasants' mean yield per seed was higher, or their sowing rates per acre were greater giving a more densely grown crop. Since Lakenheath's arable land was of extremely poor quality, the latter seems more plausible. While the demesne benefited from folding its own sheep alongside those of the majority of its peasant population on the fallow, very few peasants had a licence to run a foldcourse,

---

45 Campbell, *English seigniorial agriculture*, pp. 318–19; Bailey suggests that on extremely poor soils it was usual to sow much less than the two-thirds that would have been sown on a typical Midlands manor: Bailey, 'The prior and convent of Ely', p. 6; Bailey, 'Form, function and evolution', p. 21.

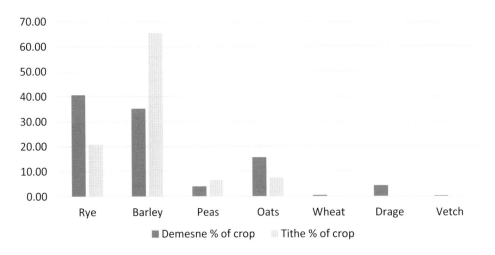

Figure 7.3. Crop percentages (issue) – demesne and tithe returns, Lakenheath, 1336–7.
Source: CUL EDC/7/16/1/11.

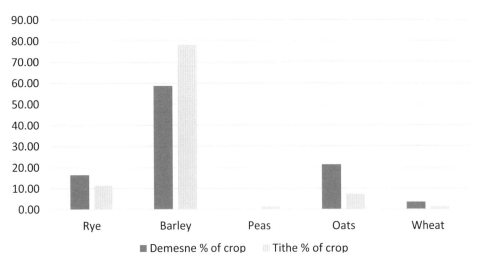

Figure 7.4. Crop percentages (issue) – demesne and tithe returns, Lakenheath, 1347–8.
Source: CUL EDC/7/16/1/14.

suggesting that their ability to manure the land was hampered somewhat, resulting in less fertile soil than that of the demesne, again pointing to higher sowing rates per acre overall. This makes it difficult to determine peasants' agricultural success.

The extent to which peasants had access to manure is crucial to understanding their agricultural production. Bailey argues that peasant lands in Lakenheath were plentifully manured, citing the hiring of the village fold by demesne managers in 1345 to manure four acres and three rods of the lord's land.[46] This is perhaps an optimistic view. It is difficult to determine folding arrangements with precision at Lakenheath; however, Bailey suggests that in this area of Suffolk tenants were generally able to graze their flocks on the stubble after harvest, a period known as 'shack', which was usually between 1 August–2 February. After this period, night-time fallow grazing was restricted to foldcourse owners.[47] Lakenheath's peasants seem to have faced greater restrictions than elsewhere: several incidents were recorded in which residents were amerced for pasturing sheep on stubble 'against the bylaw'.[48] In 1332 a shepherd was amerced because the 'sheep of the common fold lie down outside the demesne fold through his negligence', so it seems that, at night, the village flock, which had a sheep-walk next to that of the rector, was folded with the demesne sheep.[49] Certainly, it was a grave offence if peasants failed to use the demesne fold, and several statements and inquiries confirm this.[50] Furthermore, a village shepherd was paid a stipend alongside other *famuli* every year, albeit at a lower level. It seems unlikely that the lord would pay for work that did not benefit him, and it seems that demesne as well as tenant lands profited from villagers' manure. In 1283 a stipend was paid to a shepherd looking after the parson's fold; again, this arrangement must have benefited demesne lands, otherwise it does not seem sensible.[51] Tenants with fold licences all employed and paid shepherds, and so, for the lord to make these payments, some trade-off seems likely.[52] The accounts for 1326–7 and 1327–8 reveal that 177 acres and 162 acres of demesne lands respectively were manured using the fold.[53] This suggests that if manorial officials felt that supplementary manure was required in 1345 then soil conditions must have been exceptionally poor, especially since the lord felt compelled to compensate the peasants for the loss of what was – for the lord at least – a relatively small quantity of manure.[54]

46   Bailey, *Marginal economy?*, p. 83.
47   Bailey, 'Form, function and evolution', p. 19.
48   Bailey, *Marginal economy?* p. 78; CUL EDC/7/16/2/1/6/40; EDC/7/16/2/1/8/18; EDC/7/16/2/1/9/11.
49   CUL EDC/7/16/2/1/9/11; EDC/7/16/2/1/7/5.
50   CUL   EDC/7/16/2/1/7/2;   EDC/7/16/2/1/9/24;   EDC/7/16/2/1/9/31;   EDC/7/16/2/1/12/2;   EDC/7/16/2/1/13/1.
51   CUL EDC/7/16/1/3.
52   Richard Baker, Robert Bolt, John de Wangford and Isabel and John Douue, all fold owners, all employed shepherds: CUL EDC/7/16/2/1/8/27; EDC/7/16/2/1/8/5; EDC/7/16/2/1/8/12.
53   57 per cent and 50 per cent of demesne land respectively.
54   CUL EDC/1/16/1/6; EDC/7/16/1/7.

Superficially, it seems that a greater proportion of peasant land was dedicated to the production of barley at Lakenheath than at Castor.[55] We might instinctively suppose that Robert Lord benefited from higher grain yields than his Lakenheath counterparts, but we cannot deduce this from the evidence to hand. Although Robert Lord's experience may not be representative of peasant agriculture throughout Castor, it nevertheless offers a rare glimpse into the arable operation of one peasant family at the turn of the fourteenth century, a period that some scholars describe as being characterised by low productivity and deteriorating living conditions.[56] Despite the difficulties inherent in representing the peasant economic outlook satisfactorily, much can be done with fleeting references to peasant production within manorial accounts, even if the picture that emerges is incomplete. Additionally, here, the contrasting geography creates an extra level of complexity that must be taken into consideration. Most obviously, the vastly poorer soil quality clearly impacted peasants at Lakenheath; but it is also possible that different agricultural operations were in force. Although it has been suggested that Suffolk's Breckland area shared similarities with the Midlands system of arable agriculture, two- and three-field systems were unknown there. It seems likely that a shift system was utilised, which means that it is much more difficult to assess the collective size of annual cropping area with any precision.[57] Nevertheless, evaluated singly, both these brief snapshots offer interesting, if incomplete, portraits of part of the peasant economy. Historians have generally preferred to focus their analysis of the peasant economy on arable farming. It is occasionally possible, however, to look beyond the fields to create a more comprehensive representation of the economic life of the medieval peasant.

Hidden peasant economies: fishing

Moving the analysis beyond traditional mixed farming can be problematic: provided peasants paid their rents, tallages, customary dues, tithes and taxes, lords devoted little attention to how they raised the necessary cash. We have already seen that there were fisheries at Castor and Elton, but there are only a few hints within the documentary record that these provided a supplementary source of income or diet for members of the peasant community. At Elton the accounts record a regular payment made each Lady Day of 4d. from every five virgates for 'fishsilver', which represented the commuted service of providing fish for the lord.[58] This suggests that fishing was

---

55 Dyer suggests that barley yielded higher returns than other cereals, and this might explain the emphasis on barley production: Dyer, *Standards of living*, p. 128.

56 Miller and Hatcher, *Medieval England*, p. 59; for a more nuanced view, see C. Dyer, 'The Midland economy and society, 1314–1348: insights from changes in the landscape', *Midland History*, 42/1 (2017), p. 38.

57 Bailey, *Medieval Suffolk*, pp. 104–5; Bailey, 'Marginal economy?', p. 59: here, Bailey highlights a lease of land on which the lessee was granted leave to use the land for '12 crops by reasonable courses': CUL EDC/7/16/2/1/9/4; Bailey, 'Form, function and evolution', p. 20; where full year accounts record sowing rates, between 52 and 76 per cent of demesne land was sown annually.

58 *EMR*, pp. 10–318; presumably this originally provided Ramsey Abbey with supplies of fish during Lent.

probably a frequent peasant activity, as might be expected on a riverine manor. At Castor a reference to peasants poaching in 1363 reveals that peasants occasionally fished there too, but to what extent we cannot know.[59] There is no other mention of local fishing activity throughout the surviving records, although one tantalising reference to a pool once held by a virgater, Geoffrey Illing, in *c.*1231 suggests a potential fishing resource.[60] The poaching incident pinpoints the limitations of the account roll as a source of information for an holistic view of the peasant economy, and hints at the probable presence of more profitable information within the manorial court rolls.

The paucity of information on fishing at Elton and Castor is perhaps surprising, as both vills had river boundaries. However, this anomaly is explained by the lack of relevant surviving documentation. At Castor, the earliest surviving court roll is dated 1363. Three more court rolls from the late fourteenth century provide little further information.[61] At Elton the surviving rolls are for leet courts, limiting the court business somewhat, as the cases that most interest us here were probably recorded in the manorial court. Fortunately, a large number of manorial court rolls survive for Lakenheath, where its fenland geography and the extensive leasing of the demesne fisheries (see above, p. 147) point toward a considerable peasant fishing economy. In the first instance it might be considered relevant to assess the corpus of peasant bynames in all three locations. In all three vills peasants named *Herring* are recorded. This may be a nickname, or refer to fish dealers. At Lakenheath the name *Gudgeon* may refer to the freshwater fish, but might be a nickname for a gullible individual; of greater interest is the Lakenheath name *Wiles*, meaning 'fish-trap', which suggests a topographical byname, or perhaps refers to a skill.[62] Surprisingly, of the two men named *Fisher* or *Fisherman*, neither appears in the documentary record with any connection to fishing. Although they may well have been fishermen, this emphasises the dangers of making assumptions about peasant occupation using bynames alone.[63]

A proportion of the rents from Lakenheath's Clare manor for the Lent period were initially paid in eels. In 1291 '172 sticks of eels for rent' were sold.[64] After the manor was absorbed into the prior's estate in 1331 the early accounts were kept separate and were occasionally very detailed, presumably to assist the prior's officials in familiarising themselves with their employer's new asset. In the 1330s and 1340s 45s. rent was regularly received in Lent from the commutation of 180 sticks of eels

---

59   NRO PDC CR Bundle A3.

60   Soc. Antiq., MS 60, f. 186, *Black Book of Peterborough*; it is not certain that this was a peasant resource. The survey mentions the relaxation of Illing's customary services because of 'the land that he gave for *belasise*, and … the meadow that he gave for the pool of *cufwik*'. *Belsize* was the grange created at Castor in 1214, and following this reading, it may be that he gave meadow in exchange for *cufwik*, or in order for the pool to be created by the abbot.

61   BARS Russell Box 300.

62   P. McClure, pers. comm.

63   Nicholas *Piscator* (alias Fichs, Fyscher) and William le Fischere of Prickwillow (Sfk): CUL EDC/7/16/2/1/6/33; EDC/7/16/2/1/8/3; EDC/7/16/2/1/9/9; in towns, 'Fisher' meant a fishmonger: C. Dyer, pers. comm.

64   Munday, *Crane's croft*, p. 6.

from twelve tenants, each owing fifteen sticks.[65] In 1344–5 a detailed schedule of leased fisheries is recorded. There were three types of tenancy related to fishing at Lakenheath: fisheries were the largest, and commanded high rents, such as the 26s. paid by John Wace and John at the Churchgate for the lease of the fishery of *plantelode*; *botisgongs* offered private access to mooring, allowing fishermen a dedicated place to moor their boats for annual rent of 5s.; and *stikings* were places from which one could fish, rented for 1s. annually.[66] Of the twenty-four individuals listed on the schedule, almost all were men, and several leased more than one resource. Richard Lericok leased three fisheries and a *botisgong* at a total annual rent of 24s., whereas William Sporoun leased two fisheries for 42s., suggesting that they were priced according to their size or the perceived value of their resources.[67]

Payments for leases often went unpaid when the resource became unusable. The earl of Gloucester leased *depemere* for three days each year, but ceased payment when it dried up.[68] Similarly, in 1323, Geoffrey Thury was excused payment for six months' rent on a *botisgong* 'because there was no fishing'.[69] The court rolls occasionally yield information regarding the lease of fisheries. In 1329 Richard, son of Richard in the Lane leased:

> all the demesne fisheries … with weirs, fens [and] courses for 18 boats on *wendilse* with appurtenances for ten years at annual rent of £13 10s. reserving half the bitterns in the fisheries and fens, to be kept at the cost of the lessee until three weeks old; [and] all pike as required price 12d. or above; purchases to be made on the water as before; lessee not to fish with other than customary nets or traps, or to scythe to the injury of swans. He is to take swans for the lord whenever necessary at own cost except for one day marking cygnets at the lord's expense, and is to receive one robe per annum for the custody of swans and nests and to be accountable for those missing.[70]

This entry reveals the complex nature of the resources associated with the fisheries. Here, Lane also took on the role of custodian of the swans, but he also had rights over bitterns and wetland flora, suggesting that lessees of other fisheries may also have had access to these resources.

The evidence from the court rolls shows that some peasants specialised in fishing. Cases involving the Lericok family indicate that fishing and related activities were a major source of income for the family. Little is recorded regarding the Lericok family

---

65   CUL EDC/7/16/1/10–12 and 14; there were twenty-five eels per stick.

66   CUL EDC/7/16/1/13.

67   CUL EDC/7/16/1/13.

68   CUL EDC/7/16/2/1/9/2.

69   CUL EDC/7/16/1/4; fishery rent values on some Devon manors also fluctuated: H.S.A. Fox, *The evolution of the fishing village: landscape and society along the south Devon coast, 1086–1550* (2001, Oxford, 2004), p. 52.

70   CUL EDC/7/16/2/1/4/3; *wendilse* was a large fishery, and both Lakenheath manors had rights over it. In 1290–1 Clare fee leased a fishery there for £2: Munday, *Crane's croft*, p. 6.

landholding, and their status is unclear. Over a period of thirty years Richard Lericok leased several fisheries, often for an extensive term, such as the nine-year lease of *hereshel*, and he features most frequently in the records.[71] Of thirty-one recorded incidents in the court rolls, twenty-three related either directly or indirectly to fishing.[72] In 1327 Richard erected a causeway, causing a nuisance in *wyndilsee*; in 1332 he made a ditch in *le cruchistampe*, which is variously described in the records as a fen and a fishery; and in 1334 he was accused of assaulting Walter White, tellingly while Walter was in his boat.[73] It is possible to trace the development of Richard's occupation as a fisherman. When he first appears in the records in 1315 he reveals himself as an enterprising individual, clearly keen to maximise the potential of his leased assets. He was caught fishing with too many bow-nets 'to the great destruction of the fishery and damage to the lord'.[74] Notwithstanding the melodramatic language employed by the clerk, Richard's behaviour was problematic because he might deplete fish stocks. At the same time he was accused of 'making new *rodes* by *wyndelsee* and elsewhere in the fisheries against the lord's and the bailiff's ban and [against] ancient custom of the manor and fishery, whereby the fisheries are brought to nought'.[75] In May the same year he was accused of selling his fish outside the local market.[76] The impression created by these brief court records is of a man with a resourceful nature, keen to exploit his holdings fully. He is seen periodically reordering Lakenheath's fishing landscape, erecting weirs and creating illegal pools, watercourses, causeways and ditches. In one instance the pool he created prevented fish from reaching the traps set in a weir leased by Stephen Thury.[77] In 1338 he was the lord's buyer of fish, to whom all Lakenheath fishermen had to show their catch, emphasising his perceived skills as a fisherman capable of assessing the merits of local fishermen's hauls.[78]

Other families can also be identified as having more than a passing interest in fishing. The Faukes family were frequently in court for fishing-related incidents. On several occasions John Faukes was presented to the court alongside Richard or John Lericok.[79] The Faukes were villeins, and in 1314 Richard Faukes was the heir to a messuage along with a virgate of land.[80] It seems that the tenure of a fishery came with the responsibility for keeping lades clear, and, that being the case, the court

---

71 CUL EDC/7/16/2/1/6/9; EDC/7/16/1/13.

72 CUL EDC/7/16/2/1/6/12, 14, 22, 27, 37, 42, 44; EDC/7/16/2/1/7/43; EDC/7/16/2/1/8/3, 7, 9, 10, 27; EDC/7/16/2/1/9/12, 15, 17, 18, 33; EDC/7/16/2/1/10/3; EDC/7/16/2/1/12/1; EDC/7/16/2/1/13/2, 5.

73 *Cruchistampe* is described as a fishery in 1313 and 1345: CUL EDC/7/16/1/6; EDC/7/16/1/13.

74 CUL EDC/7/16/2/1/6/14; Bow-net: 'a … trap … [made] of wicker work closed at one end and having a narrow funnel-shaped entrance at the other', *OED*.

75 CUL EDC/7/16/2/1/6/14; *rode* probably meant either 'clearing' or 'path'. As most fish were caught using traps and nets, the sense 'rod' is unlikely here. I am grateful to Keith Briggs for discussions on this point.

76 CUL EDC/7/16/2/1/6/12.

77 CUL EDC/7/16/2/1/13/5.

78 CUL EDC/7/16/2/1/13/2.

79 CUL EDC/7/16/2/1/6/12; EDC/7/16/2/1/6/14; EDC/7/16/2/1/9/43.

80 CUL EDC/7/16/2/1/7/8.

recorded Faukes' implied tenancy of fisheries near *wilwlade* and *morlade*.[81] In 1329 he acknowledged owing Richard in the Lane 13s. 2d., which he promised to pay when he '[could] raise money from his fishery in the summer time', suggesting either that he viewed the fishery as a more useful economic resource than his arable land or that he could convert these resources into cash more easily.[82] While Faukes held fifteen acres, piecing together Richard Lericok's agricultural holdings is more difficult.[83] In 1331 he was amerced for reaping against the bylaw, suggesting that he grew crops on at least a portion of his land. On several occasions he failed to keep his sheep in the lord's fold and, although we cannot know how many sheep he had, it seems unlikely that the majority of his income came from sheep rearing. Although it is difficult to reconstruct a full picture of the economic outlook of a typical peasant, these details, based on what we already know from the tithe receipts, confirm what we might have assumed to have been the case: that additional sources of income and subsistence were a necessity for some in late medieval Lakenheath. It is worth noting that neither man featured in the lay subsidy for 1327, suggesting that neither was considered to be well off.

There is reason to suppose that the Faukes and Lericocks were not the only ones whose economic wellbeing relied heavily on access to Lakenheath waters, although not all peasants were as well documented as these two families. Nevertheless, it is possible to speculate on the number of peasants whose livelihoods were in part reliant on local waters. The Lakenheath court rolls provide much detail concerning distraints.[84] At Elton, where distraints are recorded, the item withheld from the accused party is never revealed; fortunately, at Lakenheath details were often given. Of 114 fully itemised distraints at Lakenheath, boats featured more frequently than any other possession, marginally more than livestock (Figure 7.5).[85] When fishing equipment and fish are included, 38 per cent of all recorded distraints were water-related items. The withheld items were often connected with the owner's occupation, and therefore his or her economic wellbeing. For example, Robert Bolt, a sheep farmer leasing his own fold and employing his own shepherd, was distrained by sixty sheep in 1321.[86] Ralph Dyer was twice distrained by large quantities of cloth.[87] Geoffrey Nethirde was distrained by a cow in 1331; and Thomas Barker had a cow-hide and an ox-hide seized.[88] It seems

---

81 In 1337 John Horold and William Sabyn were joint tenants of a fishery and considered responsible for the condition of the lade: CUL EDC/7/16/2/1/9/43; EDC/7/16/2/1/9/37; EDC/7/16/2/1/7/3.

82 CUL EDC/7/16/2/1/8/16.

83 Only one transaction records Richard Lericok holding land other than fisheries: a small plot of less than an acre in 1319: CUL EDC/7/16/2/1/6/22; a virgate comprised fifteen acres at Lakenheath.

84 Distraints were items temporarily confiscated by the manorial court to guarantee either the attendance of the accused party or the payment of a debt.

85 Although it should be noted that items distrained were not always recorded.

86 CUL EDC/7/16/2/1/6/27; EDC/7/16/2/1/8/27.

87 CUL EDC/7/16/2/1/6/27; EDC/7/16/2/1/6/28; at Walsham-le Willows (Suffolk), John Tailor was distrained by woollen cloth, suggesting a similar policy may have been adopted there: Lock, *Court rolls of Walsham-le-Willows*, p. 234.

88 CUL EDC/7/16/2/1/9/10; EDC/7/16/2/1/6/31.

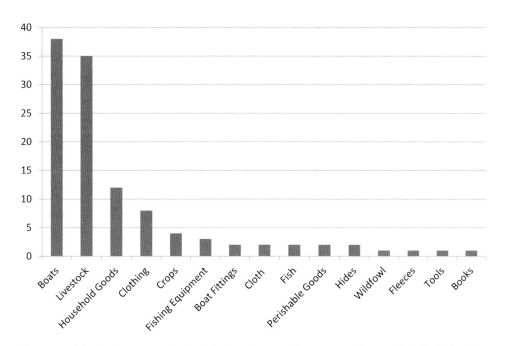

Figure 7.5. Distraint items recorded in Lakenheath court rolls, 1310–40. Source: CUL EDC/7/16/2/1.

that court officials gave careful consideration to the items they detained, attempting to secure the attendance in court of peasants accused of misdemeanours by retaining items that were either valuable or central to peasants' economic success. If this was the case, then the implication must be that access to local waters was of great importance to a significant number of Lakenheath's peasant population. This is underlined by a note on the court roll for 30 May 1325 regarding the detention of John French's boat, where it was ordered to 'answer for its profits at 1d. for every week, since the bailiffs testify it has been let since its attachment'.[89] It had been confiscated for eight weeks, highlighting the pressing need and ready market for river craft.[90]

Unlike that of Dyer's Midland yardlander, it is impossible to reconstruct in detail the economy of any of the Lakenheath fishermen, as there are simply too many unknown variables. The varying rents recorded for different fisheries imply a lack of uniformity. It is probable that, unlike the uniform virgates, the area of each fishery differed, making it hard to establish the real rental value. Additionally, we have no information on the expected yield of fish. It is difficult to determine what proportion of fish were consumed

---

89   CUL EDC/7/16/2/1/6/38.

90   Great quantities of goods transported by water between Lakenheath and Ely further emphasise the revenue potential for those owning boats. Turves, livestock and victuals were frequently shipped by Lakenheath peasants. The economic importance of small craft has been noted by Gardiner: M. Gardiner,'Hythes, small ports, and other landing places in later medieval England', in J. Blair (ed.), *Waterways and canal-building in late medieval England* (Oxford, 2007), p. 106.

by peasant families and how many were sold. There was certainly a market for fish in Lakenheath, but little is known about it. Other than the price of the occasional pike recorded in the account rolls, there is no information on the value of the fish that were caught. Similarly, there is little information on the cost of fishing equipment. In 1332 Richard Lericok was accused of taking fish and nets worth 10s. – an exaggerated sum – from Richard in the Lane's several fishery. He was eventually found guilty of taking four *bowenettes* and the damage was assessed at 8d., suggesting that fishing equipment was relatively inexpensive.[91] The intermittent decay of fisheries mentioned above (p. 158) would also have affected fishing revenues.

Richard in the Lane junior paid the highest recorded rent for a Lakenheath fishery. His annual financial commitment of £13 10s. was significant, and yet in 1327 one Richard in the Lane – either this Richard or possibly his father – was listed as one of the lowest taxpayers in the vill, with a contribution of 12d.[92] Certainly, Lane's original lease of *windelse* had expired by 1327, and the records are silent regarding its further lease. It may be significant that, of the known fishermen, perhaps only Richard in the Lane paid tax in 1327.[93] Given his substantial investment, it seems likely that he was sub-letting part of his fishery, or had perhaps employed local fishermen.[94] Of those taxpayers who appear in the documentary record having chattels distrained, it is striking that those paying a higher rate of tax had livestock – most frequently horses – or clothing confiscated, rather than goods connected with fishing.[95] This adds to the weight of evidence hinting that those making a living principally from fishing did not number among the wealthiest inhabitants of Lakenheath.

Hidden peasant economies: sheep farming

The Lakenheath court rolls are a mine of information on the activities of peasants who focused their attentions on sheep farming. But once again the records of Elton and Castor are less forthcoming. At Elton there are infrequent references to peasant sheep, detailing such incidents as Richard Hubert, John Wrau and Geoffrey Shoemaker failing to fold their sheep with the lord's.[96] In 1345 a peasant flock was noted, when a shepherd was paid for looking after the peasants' sheep. Only once was it mentioned that a peasant had too many sheep, when John Newbond overpastured the common in 1312.[97] At Castor, the account rolls reveal that ten wethers were received each year from customary payments, a custom also recorded in twelfth- and thirteenth-century extents.[98] Unfortunately, this

---

91 CUL EDC/7/16/2/1/9/17.

92 Hervey, *Suffolk in 1327*, p. 198.

93 By 1333 he also held a licence for a sheep-fold.

94 It is possible that Richard Faukes' substantial debt to Richard in the Lane (above, p. 160) related to his use of Lane's fisheries.

95 Miller and Hatcher note that even the cheapest clothing might cost two to four months' wages: Miller and Hatcher, *Medieval England*, p. 163.

96 *EMR*, pp. 117 and 193.

97 *EMR*, pp. 200 and 327.

98 NRO F(M) 2388; F(M) Roll 233; F(M) 2389.

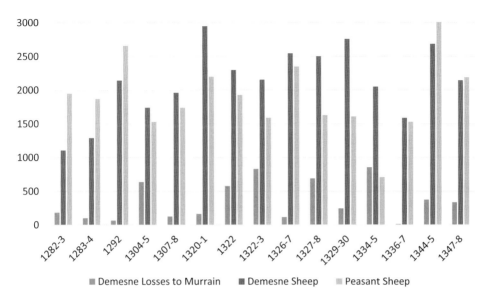

Figure 7.6. Estimated demesne and peasant flock size, Lakenheath, 1282–1348. Source: CUL EDC/7/16/1/1–14. Notes: Losses from murrain have been recorded separately. In 1334–5, 413 hoggets were 'allowed' because they all almost died during the winter, and these have not been deducted from the total here: CUL EDC/7/16/1/9. In 1347–8 there were additional losses to murrain that are now illegible on the account roll: CUL EDC/7/16/1/14.

does not reveal how extensive peasant sheep farming was locally. The 1300–1 accounts record the purchase of reasonably substantial numbers of sheep from two Castor men: 66 wethers and 24 ewes from Roger Paris, a free tenant of one of the minor manors; and 158 wethers and 86 lambs from John de Asfordby, a clerk associated with Castor church.[99] The records reveal nothing further regarding either man's involvement in sheep rearing. Thus, it is to Lakenheath that we must return once again to consider the contribution made by sheep farming to local peasants' economic livelihood.

Mark Bailey calculated that at Lakenheath there were more than 2,000 peasant sheep in the 1340s.[100] Generally, it has been estimated that peasant flocks were twice as large as demesne ones, and Philip Slavin suggests that, in the late thirteenth century, the majority of Breckland sheep belonged to tenants. The Lakenheath tithe data support Slavin's view, but suggest that, unless there was considerable undetected deception, that was not always the case there in the first half of the fourteenth century, as outlined in Figure 7.6.[101] Although the majority of Lakenheath peasants' sheep were part of the village flock and folded with the demesne sheep at

---

99 NRO F(M) 2388.

100 Bailey, *Medieval Suffolk*, p. 40.

101 Bailey, *Marginal economy?*, pp. 120–1; P. Slavin, 'Peasant livestock husbandry in late thirteenth-century Suffolk: economy, environment, and society', in M. Kowaleski *et al.* (eds), *Peasants and lords in the medieval English economy. Essays in honour of Bruce M.S. Campbell* (Turnhout, 2015), p. 10.

Table 7.6
Peasant folds at Lakenheath, 1308–33.

Name	Number of folds	Sheep per fold (where known)	Date	Held from
Legal folds				
Thomas Baker	1		1308	Margaret de Undley
Richard Baker	1		1314	Prior of Ely
Isabel Douue and John Braunch	1	300 + 3 rams	1318	Earl of Gloucester
Robert Bolt	1		1321	Margaret de Undley
William Mayhew	1	300 + 1 ram	1322	Prior of Ely
Isabel and Thomas Douue	1		1327	Prior of Ely
Vicar of Lakenheath	1	180	1327	William de Undley
Simon Wyles and Laurence Criteman			1327	Countess of Gloucester
Simon Wyles and Thomas Douue	1		1327	Countess of Gloucester
Isabel Douue and John Braunch	1	300 + 3 rams	1328	
John de Wangford	1	180 + 2 rams	1333	Sacristan of Ely
Richard in the Lane	1	190	1333	
Illegal folds				
Thomas Douue and Simon Wyles	1		1313	
Adam Strange and John de Beri	1		1327	
Robert Bolt	1		1331	
Isabel Douue	1		1331	
Payn Jakes	1		1332	

Source: CUL EDC/7/16/2/1/1/11; EDC/7/16/2/1/6/4; EDC/7/16/2/1/6/9; EDC/7/16/2/1/6/27; EDC/7/16/2/1/7/1; EDC/7/16/2/1/7/3; EDC/7/16/2/1/7/5; EDC/7/16/2/1/8/2; EDC/7/16/2/1/8/25; EDC/7/16/2/1/9/2; EDC/7/16/2/1/9/3; EDC/7/16/2/1/9/11; EDC/7/16/2/1/9/20; EDC/7/16/2/1/10/1.

night, a number of peasants had rights to their own sheep-fold (Table 7.6, which also details illegal peasant folds). Some folds were clearly inherited, such as that of Isabel Douue, which was jointly held with her brother-in-law John Braunch.[102] Others were authorised by senior officials, such as that of William Mayhew, and Isabel Douue's second fold, held with her son, Thomas, approved by the bailiff in 1327. It is unclear how Richard Baker came by his fold. He may have inherited it from Thomas Baker, but nothing in the records confirms this, and it is only apparent because a number of peasants were amerced for keeping their sheep in his fold illegally.

Clearly, senior manorial officials found it difficult to keep track of such large numbers of sheep, and on several occasions statements were made in court reminding tenants that they should keep their sheep in the demesne fold. There are conflicting statements: in 1316 it was announced that 'it is the custom … that free men as well as neifs should have their ewes … in the demesne fold', but by 1333

---

102 CUL EDC/7/16/2/1/7/3; Braunch transferred his rights in his quarter fold to William, rector of Wangford in 1333: CUL EDC/7/16/2/1/9/23.

only 'neifs and ... tenants in bondage ought to put their sheep in the demesne fold'.[103] Unsurprisingly, several peasants were accused of withholding their sheep from the lord's fold. Some erected their own folds, such as Adam Strange, who was amerced in the prior's court on 26 June 1327 for this offence, and again in the Clare court the following day.[104] John Smith and Payn Jakes habitually kept their sheep from the lord's fold, occasionally folding them in a licensed peasant fold, and on one occasion Jakes was caught with his own illegal fold.[105] Even those having a licence to fold occasionally found themselves requiring more space than they had access to. Sometimes they deliberately overstocked their folds, presumably hoping no one would notice. In 1321 Robert Bolt was caught with sixty sheep above his quota; and in 1331 John de Wangford had forty more sheep than he ought in his fold.[106]

The emerging picture outlines a few peasants actively focused on large-scale sheep farming, with even those having a relatively small flock aiming to capitalise on the manure when they could manage to avoid the notice of the sergeant. Tithe receipts for lambs and fleeces, recorded within most of the surviving account rolls, help to supplement the developing impression. Extrapolating these figures provides an estimate of total peasant sheep, outlined in Table 7.7 and in Figure 7.6, which compares both demesne and peasant flocks. As Ely Priory held the advowson of Lakenheath church, the tithe figures include the sheep raised on Lakenheath's Clare manor.[107]

The accounts for 1327–8 outline a total of 1,630 peasant sheep. Five licensed folds are recorded for this period, and although fold size was not always recorded it seems likely that approximately half of all peasant sheep were part of the village flock during this period. The demesne lost just under 30 per cent of its flock to murrain in 1304–5, 1322–3 and 1334–5. It is clear that in two out of three of these years peasant losses were lower, as fleece tithe receipts were at 81 per cent of the mean average return in 1304–5 and 84 per cent in 1322–3, whereas in 1334–5 this fell to 37 per cent, suggesting a catastrophic year for demesne and tenants alike. It is difficult to determine why peasant flocks fared better in 1304–5 and 1322–3, although we can speculate that the village flock – which was folded with demesne sheep overnight – probably suffered greater losses than sheep kept separately in licensed folds.

It is extremely difficult to calculate the net income likely to have been made by a peasant sheep farmer. Certainly, wool would have provided a steady source of revenue; however, there are few references to the price of fleeces within surviving documents. In 1324 John Joye acknowledged that he owed Richard in the Lane 5d. for a woolfell and John at the Churchgate 18d. for four more.[108] Within the account rolls fleece prices are intermittently recorded, but even where noted they are difficult to interpret, given that the price varied according to the weight of the fleece. In 1283–4 the manor received 2½d. per fleece, whereas in 1304–5 5½d. each was paid. Bailey

103 CUL EDC/7/16/2/1/7/2; EDC/7/16/2/1/9/24.

104 CUL EDC/7/16/2/1/10/1; EDC/7/16/2/1/9/3.

105 CUL EDC/7/16/2/1/9/24.

106 CUL EDC/7/16/2/1/6/27; EDC/7/16/2/1/8/2.

107 The vicar of Lakenheath would not have contributed to the tithe.

108 CUL EDC/7/16/2/1/6/33.

Table 7.7
Estimated total peasant sheep at Lakenheath, 1282–1348.

Date	Lambs (×10)	Fleeces (×10)	Total
1282–3	380	1570	1950
1283–4	400	1470	1870
1292[1]	670	1990	2660
1304–5	250	1280	1530
1307–8	470	1270	1740
1320–1	550	1650	2200
1322[2]	220	1710	1930
1322–3	320	1270	1590
1326–7	580	1770	2350
1327–8	170	1460	1630
1329–30	320	1290	1610
1334–5	50	660	710
1336–7	310	1220	1530
1344–5	640	2370	3010
1347–8	350	1820	2170

Source: CUL EDC/7/16/1.

Notes:

1. Reeve's account April–September 1292.

2. Sergeant's account May–September 1322.

suggests that pre-1348, fleece prices were seldom under 3½d., and this allows us to estimate, very tentatively, what some peasants may have received from wool income.[109] The data in Table 7.7 indicate that lambs made up an average of 19 per cent of peasant flocks each year, suggesting that in 1318 Isabel Douue and John Braunch would have clipped 246 sheep, earning a projected £3 11s. 9d. John de Wangford would have expected to clip 146 sheep, producing approximately £2 2s. 7d. in 1333. More is recorded about his costs. In 1335 he paid a fine of half a mark 'for holding one fold for one year next following, which is called *dalewereslai*'.[110] It is uncertain whether this was an extension of the lease on his existing fold, or a new one that may have allowed him a greater number of sheep, but it is clear from the fine that the lord viewed large-scale sheep farming as a very profitable enterprise.

It is impossible to calculate precisely what de Wangford's costs were, given that it is unclear exactly how many folds he had, but some assumptions can be reasonably confidently made, and are outlined in Table 7.8. It seems likely that the sum paid in 1335 constituted an entry fine, suggesting it was a one-off payment. In 1327 he employed a shepherd, who, based on the earnings of the village shepherd, the lowest paid of the *famuli* shepherds, might have expected to earn 48d. each year.[111] He would have

---

109 Bailey, *Marginal economy?*, p. 245.

110 One mark was 13s. 4d. CUL EDC/7/16/2/1/9/35. This seems to have been the standard fine for a fold.

111 This also suggests that he had a sizeable flock before 1333.

Table 7.8
Estimated income and expenditure on sheep farming, John de Wangford, Lakenheath, *c.*1330s.

	Income	Expenditure/cost	Estimated balance
One-Off			
Entry fine (1335)		6s. 8d.	
Construction of fold		unknown	
Annual			
Rent		6s. 8d.[1]	
Employment costs (1 shepherd)		4s. 0d.	
Upkeep of fold		2s. 6d.	
Veterinary costs (ointment)		5s. – 5s. 7¾d.	
Veterinary costs (shepherd)		1s.0d.	
Branding		negligible	
Washing and shearing		1s. 6½d.	
Tithe – lambs		3s. 0d.	
Tithe – fleeces		4s. 2¾d.	
Stock replenishment		unknown	
Additional feed and hay		unknown	
Total		**£1 8s. 7d.**	
Wool (less tithe)	£2 2s. 7d.		
Ewes milk	4s. 4½d.		
Pelts	unknown		
Total	**£2 6s. 11½d.**		
Balance			**18s. 4½d.**

Source: CUL EDC/7/16/1/9–11.

Note: 1. In 1336–7, income of 6s. 8d. is recorded in the account roll for 'the liberty of a certain fold demised to John de Wangford per annum', suggesting that this was the annual rental value. Fold rents are not recorded separately elsewhere, and a note regarding increment of rent for the Douue/Braunch fold in 1328 indicates that these rents were usually included with Rents of Assize. Since de Wangford's 'rent' was recorded separately, it is possible that it was an entry fine: CUL EDC/7/16/1/7 and 11.

needed to pay for the construction and upkeep of his fold. There is no information on the cost of new folds, and their size must have reflected the quantity of sheep that required penning.[112] It is impossible to know how many sheep his fold may have held, and whether it was built anew or incorporated elements of an earlier structure. The Lakenheath account rolls suggest that hurdles and stakes were used in the construction and repair of folds, and in a few instances the cost was recorded. In 1321 hurdles were purchased at a rate of approximately 0.06 units per sheep, and stakes at a rate

---

112 Entries in 1327–8 suggest that a shepherd was paid 10d. to erect William Mayhew's fold, but this excludes materials: CUL EDC/7/16/1/6–7; on the Winchester manor of Morton (Buckinghamshire) a fold of thirty-six hurdles was erected to house a stranger's sheep for manuring purposes: M. Page (ed.), *The pipe roll of the bishopric of Winchester 1301–2* (Winchester, 1996), p. 170.

of 0.03. Rushes and sedges were used at Lakenheath for wattling folds, and in 1335 these cost 4½d. and 3¼d. per hundred respectively. On the same basis as the hurdles and stakes, approximately 150 sheaves of each would have been required, producing a total estimated cost of 2s. 6d. for the upkeep of the fold. More concrete information is available for the nature and cost of ovine medication. In 1321 sheep were anointed at a rate of 1d. for four, although hoggets cost 1d. each. In 1337 1d. was spent for every three sheep. This suggests that de Wangford would have spent between 5s. and 5s. 7¾d. annually on unguents for treating his sheep. This cost may have been reduced if he produced the ointment himself, and that may have been the case for some of the more typical treatments, including butter and pig fat. He may have chosen to increase his spending on medicaments by including bitumen, verdigris and quicksilver in his regimen, all used on occasion on the demesne sheep.[113] The cost of marking lambs is recorded for demesne livestock in 1321, working out at 0.04d. per lamb.[114] The mean average percentage of peasant and demesne lambs across the period under review was 19 and 20 per cent respectively. If this proportion is valid for de Wangford's 180 sheep, then these costs would have been insignificant. Washing and shearing would have cost slightly more; once again, using the price paid by the lord, de Wangford probably paid less than ¼d. per sheep. Based on the mean number of peasant lambs, an average of 3.4 lambs and 14.5 fleeces would have been handed over for the tithe each year. Demesne lambs were rarely sold in Lakenheath, but in 1334 there is a record of the detinue of a lamb worth 12d. in a court roll. If this can be used as a guide price for lambs, then the loss of de Wangford's tithe lambs cost 3s.[115] His fleeces have already been estimated at 3½d. each, losing him 4s. 2¾d. He may have had additional expenditure. The demesne accounts outline occasional quantities of oats allocated for some of the sheep, but the amount per sheep is not detailed. In Crawley (Hampshire), oats, beans and vetches were invariably given to ewes.[116] There is also the occasional mention of the purchase of hay for feed; again, it is difficult to estimate what this cost.[117]

In terms of income, as already outlined, the largest source of revenue came from wool. Demesne dairy data record that a mean average of 49 per cent of demesne ewes were leased for lactage each year, and in the 1330s this was worth 1½d. per ewe. We cannot know whether peasants leased their ewes and, if they did, what proportion of their flock, but it seems likely that ewes' milk was worth a minimum of what the demesne was prepared to receive for it. If John de Wangford either leased or otherwise used 49 per cent of his ewes' milk in the production of cheese or butter, then it would have been worth at least approximately 4s. 4½d. annually. He would also have derived some income from the skins of animals that died during the year. The

---

113 CUL EDC/7/16/1/3.

114 Sheep were marked with red ochre.

115 CUL EDC/7/16/2/1/9/23; this should only be used as a guide, as lamb prices recorded in the court rolls in other years offer markedly different sums.

116 M. Page, 'The technology of medieval sheep farming: some evidence from Crawley, Hampshire, 1208–1349', *Agricultural History Review*, 51/2 (2003), p. 148; CUL EDC/7/16/1/4; EDC/7/16/1/9; EDC/7/16/1/14.

117 CUL EDC/7/16/1/9.

1335 account details sheepskins sold for 2d. each, but it is impossible to determine how many of his flock were lost each year and, at some point, these would have been replenished, and at a significantly higher cost than the income earned per skin.

So, both the estimated annual gross income and expenditure necessarily have a number of caveats attached. Nevertheless, it can be seen that in a good year, when losses from murrain were low, a profit could be made. Based on these projected figures, John de Wangford probably recouped the cost of his initial entry fine within the first year of operating his fold. It is doubtful, however, that he derived his wealth from sheep farming alone. Between 1319 and 1342 he appears in the court rolls taking possession of small areas of land ultimately comprising almost fifty acres, although we cannot tell how much of this may have been sub-let or worked by family members. In 1337 the account roll enumerates rents alongside 'the farm of … John de Wangford', suggesting a lease of a substantial size.[118] However, from these data it is impossible to construct a more comprehensive picture of his land holdings and so complete a fuller itemisation of his economic outlook following the Dyer model. We know that in 1327 de Wangford paid 10s. 7½d. in tax, the highest rate in Lakenheath and marginally more than Isabel Douue, the second highest taxpayer, who by then ran two folds of 300 sheep each.[119] Was it a coincidence that the three highest contributors to the lay subsidy in Lakenheath in 1327 were tenants running folds – John de Wangford, Isabel Douue and Robert Bolt? In fact, almost all of the principal holders of legal peasant folds listed in Table 7.6 were contributors that year.[120] The fourth highest contributor, Robert de Eriswell, was a wool merchant; and Adam Strange, who erected an illegal fold in 1327, was listed as one of the highest contributors in the neighbouring vill of Eriswell.[121] Sheep farming in Lakenheath, it seems, could be a lucrative enterprise.

Conclusions – hidden peasant economies

Although it can be difficult to determine the extent of peasants' economic success using manorial documents, this chapter has shown that these sources frequently repay efforts to reveal the husbandman's view. In particular, it can be seen that court rolls – which are not traditionally used to elucidate peasant economies – can play a fundamental role in enriching the picture presented by manorial account rolls. This is especially pertinent in places in which peasants' economic perspectives may differ from those generally adopted in the Midlands, as at Lakenheath. One thing seems certain: that we should be thinking in terms of *economies*, rather than *economy*. The documents emphasise peasants' distinctive experiences from both financial and practical perspectives. Although this is most evident in Lakenheath, there are also hints that this was the case at Castor, where Roger Paris appeared as a probable specialist sheep farmer. Peasants' incomes would certainly have been supplemented

---

118 CUL EDC/7/16/1/11.

119 Hervey, *Suffolk*, pp. 197–8.

120 Bailey notes that Breckland's rich peasants owned 73 per cent of the peasant flocks: Bailey, *Marginal economy?*, p. 192.

121 Hervey, *Suffolk*, p. 198.

in alternative or additional ways, but the sources are inadequate or silent on many themes. There are references to the leasing of demesne cows at Lakenheath, for example, and it is clear that several peasants owned cattle. And, despite indications of a small woodland economy at Castor, nothing definite can be said concerning the impact that this had on peasants' livelihoods there, although the woodland supported the pannage of pigs, payment for which is recorded in the account rolls.[122] Allusions to garden crops are noted, as at Elton, where the customary payment of *tollflax* was made in the thirteenth and fourteenth centuries. Wildfowl also must have played a part in the peasant economy: we know that Richard, son of Richard in the Lane of Lakenheath had rights over bitterns. The brief outline offered here is an attempt to uncover peasants' economic experiences, and, as is so often the case, it is imperfect on a number of levels. The case studies cannot elucidate the complete economic position, even if we focus solely on the particular peasants whose lives were briefly illuminated. Nevertheless, by evaluating what can be assessed in detail, it can be seen that, once again, it is incorrect to consider 'the peasant economy' as a standardised entity; rather, it was a series of interlinking economies that were not necessarily aligned with the aims of the demesne. But what this surely does do is re-emphasise the enduring close relationship between peasants and their environment, and its importance to them economically.

---

122 NRO F(M)2388; F(M) Roll 233; F(M) 2389; a coroner's roll dated 1305 also indicates the presence of peasant swine: TNA JUST 2/107.

Chapter 8

Managing the landscape

Waste not, want not: the natural world as a resource

The previous chapter focused on the landscape as an economic resource, considering the predominant agrarian focal points for the late medieval period: cereal production and sheep rearing, alongside the importance of fishing in the fenland landscape of Lakenheath. In this chapter we move away from discussions of sowing rates, yields and returns to evaluate the management of the wider rural environment. The first part of the chapter focuses on the maintenance of soil quality and looks at the strategies employed by peasants to keep the arable land in good condition. Here, we explore the possibility that medieval scientific ideas underpinned the approach to farming that was adopted by rural communities to ensure that their fields were treated in the most effective manner. The second half of the chapter concentrates on peasant involvement with, and responses to, the organisation and governance of the wider rural environment, including meadow, fenland resources and the management of water. Here, it is occasionally possible to detect the contrast between the imposition of lords' – and occasionally prominent peasants' – authority over local husbandmen and those peasants' ensuing reactions and counter-strategies.

Notwithstanding the problems inherent in determining peasants' economic strategies, it is clear that in order to make a living within the three contrasting rural communities explored here it was important to have a comprehensive knowledge of the local environment. To a certain extent, as we have seen, local environmental conditions influenced the decisions that some peasants made about the best way to support themselves from the land. While at Elton and Castor arable farming prevailed, at Lakenheath a greater proportion of peasants derived the bulk of their income from keeping substantial sheep flocks and by fishing. In all three vills there was also a number of smallholders making at least part of their living from artisanal crafts using local resources or their by-products. Traditional scholarship examines occupational bynames to reveal important evidence concerning professions that might otherwise remain unseen (see, for example chapter seven, p. 157). At Elton, Castor and Lakenheath it is possible to supplement these data with information found within the manorial records, but, nevertheless, this often only hints at the use peasants made of the natural resources they found locally. Looking at evidence of this nature frequently reveals something of the range of resources being used, but tells us very little concerning how they were perceived by peasants. By assessing some of the more widely used natural resources in each place in context it is possible to get closer to an understanding of how these important assets were considered.

As common as muck: keeping the land in good heart

In areas where cereal production dominated, the maintenance of soil quality was of paramount importance. It was necessary to keep the land in good condition, which required a thorough knowledge of its composition and qualities, alongside what was required in order to conserve and improve soil nutrients. Account rolls frequently offer detailed information regarding seigneurial soil improvement strategies, which were most often focused on the application of manure. This was certainly the case in all three vills, although the quality of the information differs markedly. In Castor the virgaters owed customary works clearing and spreading dung. The 1231 survey states that: 'each virgater will carry dung every day except Saturday until all the dung from the court-yard is removed, namely, each day six cart-loads'. Twenty-seven virgates in Castor and Ailsworth were listed therein, suggesting that the quantity of demesne dung must have been considerable. The entry follows on from the autumn works, so it seems likely that dung clearing was done after the harvest, in preparation for the new agricultural year.[1] The quantities carted by unfree tenants at Castor declined between 1300 and 1310; however, by then there were few servile tenants on the manor, and it is possible that this activity was undertaken by the *famuli*. In each oat account extra feed was reserved for draught animals carting dung, which were probably led by demesne workers.[2] An Elton works schedule dated 1298 outlines the importance of manuring there. A total of 114 works related to carting and spreading manure and making dungheaps in the fields.[3] As seems to have been the case at Castor, these were all undertaken between Michaelmas and Christmas. A Lakenheath works schedule discloses that twenty-nine customers owed one manuring work each before Christmas, suggesting that this was the standard period in which manuring was concentrated.[4] There, 'each will carry dung with his own horse from sunrise until the ninth hour wherever it is ordered upon the lord's land … each work worth 1d.', although in every year in which manure works are recorded all of them were either commuted for cash or excused.[5] On other manors manure also seems to have been predominantly spread on the fields in winter: this was certainly the case in Culham (Berkshire), where dung was cleared 'in winter, from the *curia* to the fields'. In Cheriton (Hampshire), dung was cleared while summer sowing was underway, but there is no indication that it was spread at that time.[6]

More information on manuring is contained within the Lakenheath records than within those of Elton or Castor, although the data are sporadic and unsystematically

---

1   NRO F(M) 2388; Soc. Antiq., MS 60, *Black Book of Peterborough*. The six daily cart-loads must have been used to clear a substantial accumulation of manure.

2   NRO F(M) 2388–9; F(M) Roll 233.

3   *EMR*, p. 79.

4   Customers were peasants who held their land by customary or villein tenure.

5   Manorial officials were often 'allowed' or excused certain charges or customary dues. CUL EDC/7/16/1/6.

6   Page, *Pipe roll of the bishopric of Winchester*, pp. 183 and 314. Manuring was often associated with cash crops like wheat and rye. These were both sown in winter, and this may also have been a factor when scheduling this activity.

Table 8.1
Lakenheath demesne manuring schedule, 1326–8.

	1326–7				1327–8			
Crop	*Acres sown*	*Manured (fold)*	*Manured (cart)*	*% manured*	*Acres sown*	*Manured (fold)*	*Manured (cart)*	*% manured*
Wheat	-	-	-	-	13	13	0	100
Rye	118	112	0	95	99.5	85	0	85
Barley	115	62	33	83	112.5	64.5	30	84

Source: CUL EDC/7/16/1/6; EDC/7/16/1/7.

recorded. In two years the sergeant recorded the proportion of demesne land that was manured (Table 8.1). Then, only wheat, rye and barley were manured, although a high proportion of the sown acreage of each crop was treated. This may have been because of its predominantly sandy soil – Lakenheath numbered among the least productive of the Breckland vills.[7] The majority was manured using the fold, whereas barley was treated using folded and carted dung, the latter comprising just under 30 per cent. The lower-level manorial officials were of course peasants, but this did not necessarily mean that peasant manuring strategies mirrored those of the demesne. Little is known about the practicalities of peasant manuring, but the surviving records testify to its importance. Countless Lakenheath and Elton residents found themselves in court for causing a nuisance in connection with their dungheaps: they placed them in the road, on the common, even blocking and diverting watercourses through their negligence, and this seems to have been a widespread issue. At Walsham-le-Willows (Suffolk), peasants were fined for placing dung heaps on the common, and in Wakefield (Yorkshire) for siting them on the king's highway.[8] The problem was so acute that in Lakenheath in 1336 the court issued a statement that: 'it is ordained by the whole community of the vill that no one is to make dungheaps in the village and if anyone does so they are to be amerced from court to court.' This clearly had little effect, as just over a year later an inquiry was ordered to determine the names of those still in breach of the bylaw.[9]

It is usually suggested that peasants generated less manure than lords, as they owned fewer animals, although Stone correctly suggested that they needed less.[10]

---

7 Bailey, *Marginal economy?*, p. 31.

8 CUL EDC/7/16/2/1/8/3; EDC/7/16/2/1/9/26; EDC/7/16/1/11; EDC/7/16/2/1/9/37; EDC/7/16/2/1/6/18; *EMR*, p. 197, p. 300; others in Elton paid for a licence to place their dungheaps next to their houses and on the common: pp. 316, 343 and 364; Lock, *Court rolls of Walsham-le-Willows*, pp. 56 and 260; S.S. Walker (ed., trans.), *The court rolls of the manor of Wakefield from October 1331 to September 1333* (Leeds, 1983), p. 127.

9 CUL EDC/7/16/2/1/9/34; EDC/7/16/2/1/13/1.

10 Dyer, *Standards of living*, pp. 128–9; R. Jones, 'Manure and the medieval social order', in M.J. Allen *et al.* (eds), *Land and people: papers in memory of John G. Evans* (Oxford, 2009), p. 215; Stone, *Decision-making*, pp. 263–7.

It is impossible to assess precisely how much manure was produced from peasant livestock in Lakenheath, but some individuals were undoubtedly able to generate a great deal. In 1329, Payn Jakes was amerced for recovering six cartloads of manure from outside his house, but which he had already sold to John de Wangford.[11] If we consider the thirty-three cartloads that were used to treat the demesne barley in 1326, Jakes' manure would have comprised almost one-fifth of the total, and it is far from certain whether this constituted his entire stock. Richard Jones has suggested that lords seemed unlikely to acquire peasant manure.[12] This may have been the case on secular manors, where resident lords were more aware of the content of peasant dungheaps, but at Elton and Lakenheath the demesne officials purchased peasant dung several times.[13] In 1308 the dungheap of the deceased villein Philip Noppe was purchased at Elton, and another was bought in 1325 from a peasant called Shakelock.[14] There are several accounts of dung being purchased at Lakenheath. The majority of these accounts provide little information, but it seems likely that it was locals' manure. The going rate for a cartload of manure at Lakenheath in the 1330s and 1340s was 1d.[15] In 1283–4 8s. was spent on manure for six acres and three rods of land; if at that time the cost was 1d. per load, then ninety-six cartloads were purchased.[16] It is entirely possible that the rate was lower, or that less manure was used in the late thirteenth century, but, irrespective of the quantity purchased, 8s. assuredly bought a large amount and, in most years, the accounts record a substantial purchase (Figure 8.1).

While these figures are informative, they must be treated with caution, as a glance at the data for 1336–7 shows. Here, the very different quantities recorded by the reeve and sergeant reveal that they were each responsible for procuring manure, perhaps from different sources. The reeve's account details the specific quantities, value and former ownership of dung – all local peasants (Table 8.2). The sergeant's account simply notes the aggregate cost of purchased dung, which must have included the 5s. 2d. spent by the reeve. How the decisions were made regarding the quantity of manure required and which official should source it remain uncertain. What seems clear, however, is that in years when only the reeve's accounts survive we are probably seeing only a proportion of the total demesne spend on supplementary manure. The data in the reeve's account for 1336–7 are illuminating. Only in William Cowherd's case is the source of the manure immediately apparent.[17] Of the remaining peasants, only Robert Bole appears in court in connection with livestock, having caused damage to the demesne with his sheep.[18] The

---

11 CUL EDC/7/16/2/1/8/13.

12 Jones, 'Manure and the medieval social order', p. 219.

13 On manors where the lord was absent it is much less likely that the provenance of the manure mattered, and where peasant managers were making day-to-day decisions.

14 *EMR*, pp. 138 and 275.

15 CUL EDC/7/16/1/11; EDC/7/16/1/13.

16 CUL EDC/7/16/1/3; in 1345, 163 cartloads were purchased for 13s. 7d., or 1d. per load: CUL EDC/7/16/1/13.

17 William Cowherd leased the demesne herd, so their dung was effectively his property.

18 CUL EDC/7/16/2/1/9/22.

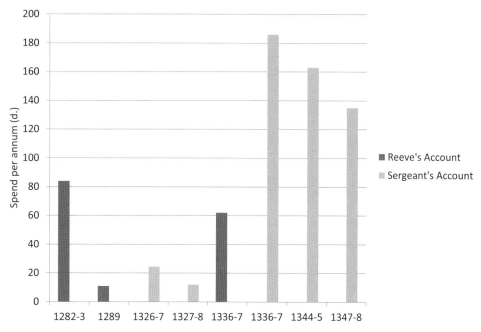

Figure 8.1. Dung purchased by manorial officials, Lakenheath, 1282–1348. Source: CUL EDC/7/16/1. Note: This excludes manure from the demesne and the village fold.

others undoubtedly owned livestock, but they do not feature in the surviving records. The evidence suggests that each of these peasants was poor; the court rolls record that most of them were frequently in court for offences connected with turf digging and sedge mowing, misdemeanours that, as we will see, were more generally associated with the poorer residents (below, p. 194).[19] On the death of John de Bircham senior his heir Thurstan, John junior's younger brother, was due to inherit his father's cottage in Undley; the court records that he paid no heriot, because he was poor, and the land was taken in hand when he failed to present himself.[20] In 1336 Robert Bole claimed to have been dispossessed of a plot of messuage, having tried to retain it by force of arms; he was not associated with any other property transfer, and it seems likely that he was a smallholder.[21] Agnes and William Jakes were amerced several times for debt.[22] The combined evidence for each of the peasant manure sellers seems to imply that they were impoverished. Certainly, as smallholders they needed less manure, but the possibility that some were selling expendable assets cannot be ignored. As Payn Jakes'

---

19 Robert Bole and his father, Hugh were amerced on several occasions for offences associated with turf-cutting and/or sedge mowing, as were John de Bircham and his father; Agnes Jakes' husband William was fined for similar offences.

20 CUL EDC/7/16/2/1/7/5.

21 CUL EDC/7/16/2/1/9/34.

22 CUL EDC/7/16/2/1/6/12; EDC/7/16/2/1/9/22.

Table 8.2
Peasant dung purchased at Lakenheath by the reeve, 1336–7.

Name	Quantity (cartloads)	Price	Price per cartload
Peter Carpenter	24	2s.	1d.
John de Bircham, jnr	[12]	1s.	[1d.]
Agnes Jakes	[6]	6d.	[1d.]
William Cowherd	[13]	13d.	[1d.]
Robert Bole	[7]	7d.	[1d.]
Total	62	5s. 2d.	1d.

Source: CUL EDC/7/16/1/11.

Note:

1. [] denotes assumed quantity/price.

example shows (above, p. 174), it also seems likely that there was an intra-peasant manure market, wherein poorer peasants sold to those with larger holdings. John de Wangford, the buyer of Jakes' six cartloads of dung, was the wealthiest peasant in Lakenheath in 1327. It is worth noting that, following his purchase, the manure remained outside the vendor's house, rather than being moved by the purchaser. In a similar vein, Isabel Douue, the second wealthiest peasant in Lakenheath, was amerced for failing to fill in a 'great cesspit' (*puteum magnum*) containing dung, which therefore cannot have been located on her property. Jones has suggested that, by the end of the Middle Ages, elites avoided a close association with dung and waste material.[23] Were these wealthy peasants attempting to emulate this practice in distancing themselves from compost production processes?[24] Certainly, peasants considered manure to have a commercial value. In Lakenheath in 1333 Ranulf Gardener accused Adam Outlaw of failing to return a cow leased to him for six months, for which he had allegedly agreed to pay 6d. for dung and milk; and Adam Goodhewe held the ignoble position of 'groom of the dungheap', which involved looking after the demesne cow dung, presumably partly because of its perceived value.[25]

Scientific fields: peasants and medieval science

The agricultural treatises of the thirteenth century emphasise medieval farmers' practical concerns regarding attaining a deep understanding of the land and how it should best be worked. Maintaining soil quality was important to manorial officials and peasants alike, peasants' survival being closely linked to their agricultural success. It was necessary to understand the qualities of local soil and know how to treat it in order to get the best return from it. Besides using manure to enhance soil structure,

---

23   R. Jones, 'Understanding medieval manure', in R. Jones (ed.), *Manure matters: historical, archaeological and ethnographic perspectives* (Farnham, 2012), p. 152.

24   CUL EDC/7/16/2/1/10/1; Hervey, *Suffolk*, p. 198; Jones, 'Manure and the medieval social order', p. 217; Jones, 'Elemental theory', p. 62.

25   CUL EDC/7/16/2/1/9/25; EDC/7/16/2/1/9/14.

peasants also dug for chalk, marl and, at Lakenheath, clay in order to aid improvement; rotations also frequently included legumes, which replenished soil nutrients. Peasants understood that the land needed nourishment, but they also had to decide where best to deploy their limited fertiliser stocks, and this required a thorough understanding of the land they worked. Nothing emphasises this more than the field-names, many of which were selected and retained over a long period, and which describe the specific nature of discrete cropping units. This has generally been overlooked by scholars, most of whom seem bound by the confines of modern taxonomic concerns and therefore generally consider medieval field-names anachronistically, through the prism of a nineteenth- and twentieth-century emphasis that privileges classification over contextual analysis.[26] This view fails to take into account the worldview of the late medieval peasant, although scholars are beginning to address this.[27]

By the thirteenth and fourteenth centuries the world had long been understood in elemental terms, and as part of a universal scheme that had been initially transmitted to northern Europe from the Classical world of Plato and Aristotle via scholars such as Isidore of Seville. Everything present in the world, from trees and plants to stones and earth, was essentially considered to be comprised of one of the four elements: air, fire, earth or water. Each element in turn consisted of a combination of two qualities from the four available: hot, cold, moist and dry. The twelfth-century Ramsey Abbey scholar Byrhtferth wrote his manual, *Enchiridion*, to disseminate these ideas concerning the structure of the world – the macrocosm – to novice monks and secular clerics, who were described as 'naive and unlettered'.[28] He referred to the latter group as 'rustic priests' (*uplendiscum preostum*) – and suggested that certain matters were difficult for them to grasp.[29] Nevertheless, he outlined that:

> It is a *commonplace* that there are four elemental bodies, each of which has two qualities, one being intrinsic (confined to itself), the other being shared with another element. Thus, earth possesses coldness and dryness. Dryness is the intrinsic quality of earth; coldness is a quality not peculiar to earth, but to water; and so on.[30]

Although it is impossible to verify conclusively, it is likely that some young Elton men were trained as clerics either at Ramsey or locally by monks who themselves had received their scientific schooling there.

The entire universe was considered in these terms, and in order to ensure harmony it was deemed necessary to attain balance in all things. This indicates that,

---

26 Field, *History of English field-names*; Cunnington, 'The field-names of Kingsbury', pp. 41–6; Daniels and Lagrange, 'An analysis of Romsey field-names', pp. 29–58.

27 Kilby, 'A different world?' (2010b), p. 74; Gardiner, 'Oral tradition', p. 16; Kilby, 'Divining medieval water', p. 58.

28 C. Hart, *Learning and culture in late Anglo-Saxon England and the influence of Ramsey Abbey on the major English monastic schools: a survey of the development of mathematical, medical and scientific studies in England before the Norman Conquest*, vol. 2, book 2 (Lampeter, 2003), p. 434.

29 P.S. Baker and M. Lapidge (eds), *Byrhtferth's enchiridion* (Oxford, 1995), p. 184.

30 Hart, *Learning and culture*, p. 439, my emphasis.

in the medieval worldview, the idea that natural order was maintained through the shifting balance between the four elements and their corresponding qualities was widely understood, even by the uneducated, as Byrhtferth attests. An examination of didactic works from the thirteenth century supports this view. Medieval encyclopaedists emphasise the idea that different types of land require different treatments. Bartholomew the Englishman, writing in the early thirteenth century, was careful to describe the numerous ways in which the land could be worked. For wheat, he suggests that:

> in all corn that is called wheat, generally [I] shall take heed of the ground that it is sown in and of the *quality* of the ground. For some corn thrives in ground and fails in another ... and so it is [for the] understanding of other corn and land.[31]

and he goes on to suggest that other kinds of grain require different treatment again. The characteristics that are being described frequently match the soil types highlighted by Walter of Henley, the author of a thirteenth-century agricultural treatise, as requiring special treatment; and they also match the qualifying elements used in naming this type of field – chalky, clayey, stony and so on. He suggests:

> two sortes of groundes which are for lenton corne see that thow sowe theim tymelye; that is the chalky (white claye) and the Chilterne (stony) lande; and I will telle you whye. If the season be drye in the tyme of Marche then it hardeneth the chalky land verie muche and the stony land dryeth faste, but yet so that it openeth for drynesse ... .[32]

He continues in the same vein, discussing the qualities and respective proposed treatment of chalky, sandy, watery and marshy lands.

Modern field-name taxonomy is a useful classification scheme for modern scholars, but it perhaps conceals facets of the original intentions of those naming the fields. Field suggests, for instance, that 'the impediments to cultivation in Stony Lands ... were as unwelcome in later centuries as they had been in the Middle Ages', but does not elaborate on what he perceived these impediments to be. In the modern era, stony soil can impede mechanical tilling whereupon the stones are frequently removed, so it seems likely that Field considered the stones themselves as problematic; this may have been the case, however, there is no evidence to suggest that this view was widespread in the medieval period.[33] Modern science recognises what medieval farmers knew: that, generally speaking, stony soils frequently number

---

31 M.C. Seymour and G.M. Liegey (eds), *On the properties of things: John Trevisa's translation of Bartholomaeus Anglicus De Proprietatibus Rerum*, vol. 2 (Oxford, 1975), p. 956, my italics.

32 *WH*, p. 323.

33 Field, *English field-names*, pp. 34–5; U.K. Mandal *et al.*, 'Soil infiltration, runoff and sediment yield from a shallow soil with varied stone cover and intensity of rain', *European Journal of Soil Science*, 56 (2005), p. 435.

among the driest soil types.[34] Walter of Henley wrote specifically about maintaining the right elemental balance in the fields. He instructed that in some instances dung ought to be mixed with earth to temper its great heat, and that great care should be taken in considering the qualities of the mixture of fertiliser applied, alongside those of the ground itself. By way of example he suggested using mixed manure on stony or gravelly soil because:

> the time of summer is hot, and the gravel is hot also, and the dung is hot, and when these three heats meet together, by their great heat they vex and burn, after midsummer, the barley that grows in gravel as you may see as you go along by the fields in many places …[35]

Thus, Walter implies that certain soils should be treated rationally from the perspective of medieval science: the specific qualities of stony soil were hot and dry, and adding supplementary heat and dryness during a warm season might be ill-advised. The pragmatic farmer should make careful consideration of both the constituent elements of the material in question – earth and manure – and the right time of year for the most efficacious treatment to increase the chances of a successful harvest. This recognises that, in medieval terms, a field was not just a field: each furlong displayed qualities that must be taken into account when assessing how best to treat it, which, again, Walter of Henley expressly outlines: 'I will tell you what advantage cometh by dung meddled with earth. If the dung were quite by itself, it would endure two or three years *according as the land is cold or hot*, but the dung mingled with [earth] will endure twice so long … .'[36] Jones suggests that these scientific ideas were engaged with at a practical level: medieval elites in some instances may have separated domestic waste according to its particular qualities in order for it to be deployed in the fields as appropriate.[37] The very idea of adding fertiliser to the fields, whether manure, marl, or organic waste, fits with the medieval view that, in order to achieve the perfect conditions, balance must be attained through the careful application of materials containing the right qualities.

Those peasants principally engaged in working the fields were aware of the qualities of the land they tilled. In Lakenheath in 1317 Peter Swift was excused the customary entry fine upon receipt of one acre 'because of the weakness of the land, and the great burden of the customs'; and in 1325 Katherine Faukes surrendered one and a half acres into the lord's hands for the same reason.[38] It is perhaps unsurprising to find that some Lakenheath land was considered inferior by general medieval arable standards, given its Breckland location. However, land described as impoverished

---

34 V. Novák *et al.*, 'Determining the influence of stones on hydraulic conductivity of saturated soils using numerical method', *Geoderma*, 161 (2011), p. 179, demonstrate that as the quantity of stones in soil increases its hydraulic conductivity decreases, particularly in soils featuring smaller stones.

35 *WH*, p. 327; Jones, 'Elemental theory', p. 3.

36 *WH*, p. 329, my emphasis.

37 Jones, 'Elemental theory', p. 8.

38 CUL EDC/7/16/2/1/6/31; EDC/7/16/2/1/7/2.

and too poor to cultivate was surrendered into the lord's hands in Broadwas (Worcestershire); and in a bond agreed at Castor in 1275 Peter Asselin promised to pay John le Butler 3s. 6d. 'for every acre belonging to [John] in the fields of Castor, except one *cultura* which is called *westallewete*'.[39] The name is odd, but may translate either as 'west all wet' or, more probably, 'waste all wet', perhaps indicating its wet nature and lack of worth.[40] It was clearly a matter vitally important to peasants. Might this help to explain obviously descriptive field-names in each of the three vills (Table 8.3)? They reveal, in fact, much more than mere description or close observation: they also succinctly conveyed vital information that assisted peasants' understanding of what might be needed in order to manage them successfully. It is immediately obvious that inferior land might be seen as problematic and worth avoiding from the perspective of a medieval husbandman, whereas *blakemylde*, with its rich dark soil, would be much more appealing.

Looking more closely at some of the furlong names found at Elton, Castor and Lakenheath, alongside Byrhtferth's 'commonplace' ideas, the contemporary scientific understanding of the treatment of land and the agricultural treatises of the period, it is possible that those describing particular characteristics may have had more practical considerations in mind than simply wishing to describe the terrain. A number of the descriptive names reference soil types that Walter of Henley considered especially problematic if treated incorrectly: clayey, chalky, sandy and stony soils.[41] Is it possible that these names survived into the late medieval period specifically because of their mnemonic qualities? One of the most puzzling aspects of the study of field-names is determining what generates change, and conversely, ensures stability. Returning to the consideration that, in their earliest form, field-names most commonly contained a landscape referent (see chapter five, p. 109), clearly some of these survive while other names became obsolete. The names referencing soil type are especially interesting, since they only really make sense when we realise that their environmental context is noteworthy.

At Elton *cleyfurlong*, shown on Figure 8.2, is significant because it lay outside the main band of heavy boulder clay, its name thus acting as a practical reminder of an isolated area of uncharacteristic soil.[42] Figure 8.2 shows that much of Elton's landscape is made up of heavy clay soils, and, within this larger area, the name would have made no sense at all. Similarly, the 'sand' names stand out at Lakenheath, which was in part characterised by its sandy soil. Again, these names initially seem odd, until the location of the medieval furlong *le sondput* is considered (Figure 8.3). It lies in the extreme westernmost portion of the arable, surrounded by fenland. The name suggests that it represents an especially sandy area even by Breckland standards, but also perhaps marks the point at which the peat fen becomes sandy soil. Like Elton's *cleyfurlong*, *le sondput* seems ordinary, but was in fact conspicuous in its contextual difference.

---

39   WCL E 15; NRO F(M) Charter 79.

40   In ME 'waste' was spelled *west, wiste*: *MED*. There is a possibility that the second element was derived from *halh* 'nook, corner of land, low-lying land by a river': J. Carroll, pers. comm.

41   *WH*, p. 323.

42   Kilby, 'A different world?' (2010a), p. 53; Upex, 'Reconstruction of openfield layout', Appendix 3.1.

Table 8.3
Descriptive furlong names at Elton, Castor and Lakenheath.

Furlong	Vill	Definition
Aldwellemor	Castor	Old spring marsh/barren upland
Blakemylde[1]	Castor	Black soil
Blakelonds[1]	Lakenheath	Black lands
Brendlond	Castor	Burned land
Calkeshe	Lakenheath	Chalk
Chalkyhil	Elton	Chalky hill
Chiselstonhowe	Elton	Gravel stone mound or hill
Cley, le	Castor	The clay
Cleyfurlong	Elton	Clay furlong
Caldewell	Elton	Cold spring/stream
Coldfurlong	Castor	Cold furlong
Dedemor	Castor	Dead marsh/barren upland
Kaldewellwong	Lakenheath	Cold spring/stream field
Follewellemor	Elton	Foul spring/stream/marsh/barren upland
Fulond	Castor	Foul land
Folwyndelond	Lakenheath	Very windy land
Molwellehyl	Elton	Gravel spring hill
Sandmere	Lakenheath	Sandy pool
Sondput, le	Lakenheath	Sandy pit
Sondes, le	Elton	The sands
Stanesbeche	Lakenheath	Stony ridge/stream valley
Stanelode	Lakenheath	Stony lode
Stonehylles, Stonihel	Elton, Lakenheath	Stony hill(s)
Stanewelle, Stanewellehil	Castor	Stony spring/stream
Stonywong	Castor	Stony field
Welle	Lakenheath	Spring/stream
Westallewete	Castor	?Waste all wet

Note: 1. Possibly OE *blāc* 'pale', but more likely to be *blæc* 'black'. D. Parsons pers. comm.

These specific field types numbered amongst those highlighted by Walter of Henley as requiring careful treatment. If ideas concerning elemental and humoral theories were commonplace, then perhaps the purpose of these seemingly descriptive field-names was to remind husbandmen to pay greater attention to the balance of the elemental qualities in these fields – in particular how wet/dry, or hot/cold they might be. This might also help to explain the greater longevity of some of the earliest field-names, such as Castor's *aldwellemor* and Elton's *molwellehyl*. In his instructions regarding chalky and sandy soils, Walter reminds the husbandman that they are 'not like to be stirred in great moisture': in other words, they were more likely to be dry: this is a reference to medieval science that would have been obvious to a contemporary readership. Peasants would not have read Walter of Henley, but would certainly have understood the underlying

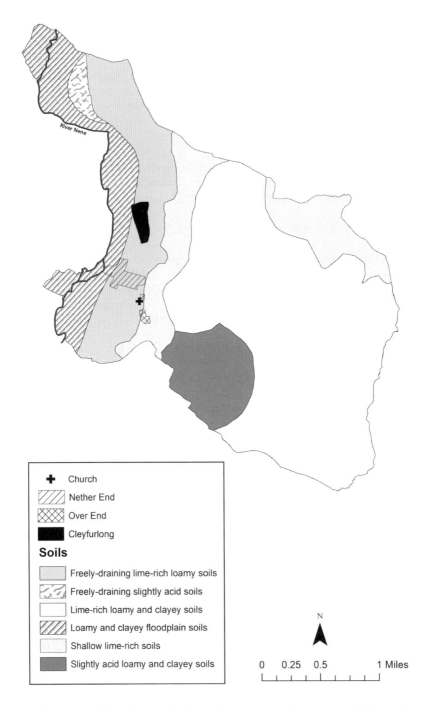

Figure 8.2. *Cleyfurlong*, Elton. Source: S. Upex, 'The reconstruction of openfield layout from landscape evidence in Northamptonshire and Cambridgeshire (unpub. PhD thesis, University of Nottingham, 1984); National Soil Resources Institute, Cranfield University, <http://www.landis.org.uk/development/soilscapes/>

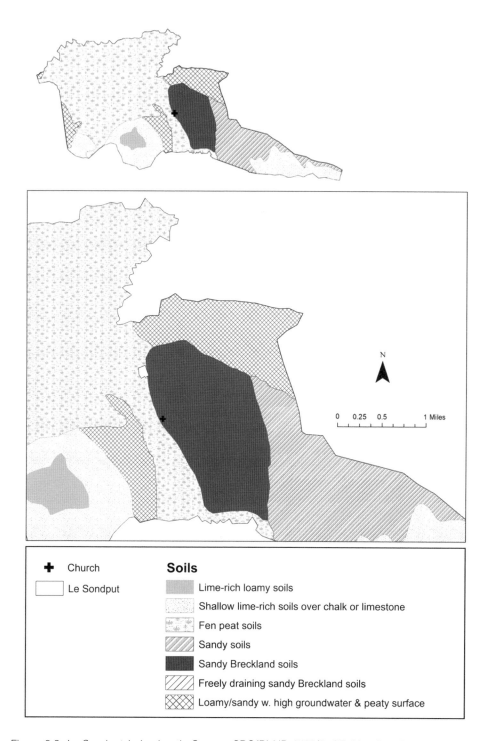

Figure 8.3. *Le Sondput*, Lakenheath. Source: SRO(B) HD 1720/3; J.T. Munday, *Field and furlong* (Lakenheath, 1972); National Soil Resources Institute, Cranfield University, <http://www. landis.org.uk/development/soilscapes/>

Figure 8.4. Modern *molwellehyl*, Elton. Top: modern *molwellehyl* from below. Bottom: limestone brash lying along the ridge of the hill. Photograph: Susan Kilby.

meanings of these commonplace ideas.[43] Conversely, the name *aldwellemor* revealed the land's extreme wetness, since both *welle* and *mor* were wet; and, at *molwellehyl*, in medieval scientific thinking, the wet spring would have been tempered by the dry, hot, gravelly limestone brash that is still a noticeable feature of this part of the landscape today (Figure 8.4).[44] Elton's *chiselstonhowe* contains the elements *cisel* (gravel) and *stān* (stone). If it is accepted that gravel and stones are both separate features, and both are 'dry', then this potentially conveys vital information concerning the more extreme level of dryness in this furlong, and how it might affect treatment of the soil.

The first element of each name is essential to a proper understanding of the environmental context; without it, the 'true' qualities of each furlong are no longer apparent. Notwithstanding the incomplete nature of the corpus of furlong names, there is no other combination of the elements 'well' and 'hill' in Elton, and so, if identification was the sole motivating force behind the creation and retention of the name *molwellehyl*, then 'well-hill' would easily have sufficed. Did the peasant community selectively retain those names that provided the most useful reminder for the treatment of specific and potentially problematic furlongs, creating an orally transmitted mnemonic system? An assessment of late medieval field-names elsewhere reveals an abundance of this type of name. Clayey fields are frequently noted, such as *leirikroft*, 'clayey croft' in Goverton and Bleasby (Nottinghamshire) and *cleyhulle* in Wistow (Huntingdonshire). Sandy fields are also abundant, as at *sandforlonges* in Sevenhampton (Wiltshire), *sondfeld* in Churchdown (Gloucestershire) and *sande fielde* in Walsham-le-Willows (Suffolk); and chalky areas are evidenced in names such as *chalcroft* in Blewbury (Berkshire), *le malmes* in Potterspury (Northamptonshire) and *calcrundell* in South Creake (Norfolk).[45] Stony and gravelly names are particularly widespread, and there are countless examples of this name type in the late medieval period. Additional names with possible 'scientific' references might also include 'wet', 'dry' and 'cold' names. Given the common application of elemental and humoral theories across all levels of medieval society, it is worth considering a more phenomenological rationale for the retention of these names too, rather than considering them as merely descriptive. Archaeological survey confirms that diverse manuring strategies were often adopted within individual manors, and so it follows that it was felt that some furlongs needed particular treatment. Perhaps their names helped to remind peasants how to get the best from them.[46]

---

43 *WH*, p. 323.

44 Kilby, 'A different world?' (2010b), p. 75. It is possible that *mol* could mean 'Mary' (J. Carroll, pers. comm.), however the topography supports the meaning 'gravel, gravelly soil' – see also Figure 8.4.

45 T. Foulds (ed.), *The Thurgarton cartulary* (Stamford, 1994), p. 86; *CMR I*, p. 353; W. Hassall and J. Beauroy (eds), *Lordship and landscape in Norfolk 1250–1350: the early records of Holkham* (Oxford, 1993), pp. 549–50; S.E. West and A. McLaughlin, *Towards a landscape history of Walsham le Willows, Suffolk* (Ipswich, 1998), p. 40; Farr, *Accounts and surveys*, p. 2; Field, *History of English field-names*, pp. 35–6; E. Forward, 'Place-names of the Whittlewood area', PhD thesis (University of Nottingham, 2007), p. 90; Hesse, 'Medieval field systems', p. 92; *malm*, a Middle English term, means 'sandy or chalky soil': *MED*.

46 Jones, 'Manure and the medieval social order', p. 219.

To suggest that peasants understood the fundamental tenets of medieval science might be considered to stretch the boundaries of credibility to their absolute limit. Nevertheless, there is contemporary evidence that supports this view in each of the three vills. Practices that were undoubtedly scientific and grounded in the thinking already outlined were undertaken in both Elton and Castor, the most obvious of which was phlebotomy. Blood-letting was an integral part of the canon of medieval medical treatment, intricately connected to elemental theory through the idea of macrocosm and microcosm: that man mirrored the universe in miniature. Whereas the universe consisted of a combination of four elements, man comprised four humours – blood, phlegm, black bile and yellow bile.[47] Jolly suggests that the basic idea of the microcosm and macrocosm is the 'unstated basis of practices found in both learned … and … *popular* texts' from the early medieval period onward.[48] Man's humoral composition changed at different life stages and when unwell, and it was considered important to try and maintain a balance of all four humours. Blood-letting, alongside purging the body and the application of ointments and plasters, was one of the key means by which it was believed that balance could be restored.[49]

These procedures must have been practised at Castor by William Bloodletter, and this byname certainly related to at least one of William's occupations.[50] Several charters mention the family, who bore three bynames all related to blood-letting: Bloodletter; *fleobo*, which references the instrument William used to extract blood; and *sharp*, a nickname referring to the more wince-inducing elements of his occupation.[51] Even though he was almost certainly a freeman, William was unlikely to have had a university education, and was probably one of a number of common practitioners operating in fourteenth-century England; Voigts argues that the circulation of vernacular treatises on phlebotomy after 1300 reveals an increase in the number of such empiric practitioners.[52] Perhaps even more indicative of the dissemination of these scientific ideas to the lower orders was the porcine blood-letting practised at Elton.[53] Byrhtferth of Ramsey encompassed animals and birds in his writings on humoral theory, as did

---

47   C. Rawcliffe, *Medicine and society in later medieval England* (1995, Stroud, 1997), p. 33.

48   K.L. Jolly, 'Magic, miracle, and popular practice in the early medieval west: Anglo-Saxon England', in E.S. Frerichs *et al.* (eds), *Religion, science, and magic in concert and in conflict* (Oxford, 1989), p. 172, my emphasis.

49   Rawcliffe, *Medicine and society*, p. 61.

50   He is also identified as a tanner: NRO F(M) Charter 368. Curth suggests that animal urine and excrement were often used in medicine, which may help explain William's alternative occupation: L. Curth, *The care of brute beasts: a social and cultural study of veterinary medicine in early modern England* (Boston, MA, 2010), p. 24.

51   NRO F(M) Charters 351, 368, 404, 413 and 462 all refer to William and his wife, Alice.

52   I. Taavitsainen, 'A zodiacal lunary for medical professionals', in L.M. Matheson (ed.), *Popular and practical science of medieval England* (East Lansing, MI, 1994), p. 284; L.E. Voigts, *A Latin technical phlebotomy and its Middle English translation* (Philadelphia, PA, 1984), pp. 6–7.

53   Kilby, 'A different world?' (2010a), pp. 55–8; Kilby, 'A different world?' (2010b), p. 75; these scientific practices were also recorded on other English manors: for example, at Rimpton (Somerset) and East Meon (Hampshire): Page, *Pipe roll of the bishopric of Winchester*, pp. 42 and 286.

the eleventh-century *Lacnunga*, and so it is perhaps unremarkable to discover faunal phlebotomy in Elton.[54]

Of the two mentions of bleeding pigs, the first, in 1298, outlines a payment to 'a certain man for gelding sucking pigs, bleeding pigs and making capons during the year'. The impression given is that these practices were the domain of someone experienced. But in 1308 the account tells a different story. Two *garciones* were sent to Farcet fen, a 'detached attachment' of the manor, to bleed the pigs, 'about the Feast of the Blessed Peter in April' (29 April 1308).[55] Clearly, the task of bleeding the pigs was not considered so specialised that it required a learned practitioner, the implication being that menfolk were taught this practice as part of their education in animal husbandry, most probably learning by observing older kin from a young age. Perhaps more importantly, despite their status they were still expected to know how to perform this scientifically based practice. The tenth-century Bald's *Leechbook* describes in detail the most efficacious times for blood-letting, all of which are closely aligned to the lunar cycle:

> bloodletting is to be abstained from for fifty nights before Lammas and afterwards for thirty-five nights, because then all harmful things are flying and do much injury to people … physicians teach also that no one should let blood when the moon is five nights old and again when it is ten nights and fifteen and twenty and twenty-five and thirty nights old, but between each of the six fives.[56]

The date provided in the account roll is approximate, rather than specific, suggesting that the task could have been undertaken on any of several days. During the period in question the moon was between six and nine days old, which the *Leechbook* suggests was a good phase for blood-letting.[57] The undated folkloric rhyme *The Days of the Mone* specifically suggests that the eighth day was particularly favourable:

Þe viii day, ho so wele,	[The eighth day, who so well,]
Lat hym blod by good skele	[let him blood by good skill]
Whan he seet hys tyme.	[when he set his time.]
But ho so wel schal any dede done,	[But who so well shall any deed done,]
Best hyt ys before þe none,	[best it is before the noon,]
By twyxte underne and pryme.	[between undern and prime.][58]

---

54   Hart, *Learning and culture*, p. 453; Pettit, *Lacnunga*, p. 123.

55   *EMR*, pp. 67 and 142; H.S.A. Fox, 'Exploitation of the landless by lords and tenants in early medieval England', in Z. Razi and R. Smith (eds), *Medieval society and the manor court* (Oxford, 1996), p. 521.

56   M.L. Cameron, *Anglo-Saxon medicine* (Cambridge, 2006), p. 161.

57   F. Espenak, Moon Phases Table, <http://astropixels.com/ephemeris/phasescat/phasescat.html>, accessed 13 August 2019.

58   W. Farnham, 'The days of the mone', *Studies in Philology*, 20 (1923), p. 75; prime was the first hour after sunrise, and undern the third.

The verse singles out blood-letting, but advises that it is best performed before noon, specifically in the three hours following sunrise. The idea that there were good and bad days on which to undertake certain tasks was not limited to medical theory in this period, and the notion that those working the land should have an understanding of the lunar calendar and the moon's effects on husbandry was certainly a commonplace by the sixteenth century. Gervase Markham, editing the sixteenth-century *La Maison Rustique* in the early seventeenth century and applying it to English husbandry, was unequivocal that:

> Notwithstanding that the consideration and observation of the motions ... of the stars ... the sun and the moon ... appertain unto some excellent astrologian than to a simple husbandman ... for as much as the greatest part of matters of husbandry, as beasts, plants, trees and herbs ... take their generation, nourishment [and] growth ... [from] these two organs ... it is very expedient that the farmer ... should have that knowledge ... which teacheth their virtues and powers ... .[59]

Direct evidence from the late medieval period that the lower orders were interested in the lunar calendar is scanty but not completely lacking. Empiric blood-letting practitioners would have been expected to understand the lunar cycle, and the quantity of surviving calendars indicates widespread application. A surviving fourteenth-century hayward's girdlebook also features pictorial information on solar and lunar motions. As, by and large, haywards were selected from the servile manorial population, again this indicates that a certain level of understanding of these scientific ideas was attained at the lowest levels of medieval society.[60]

Sowing seeds and harvesting crops, including the felling of timber, were all rooted in the same scientific belief system. Precise dates for harvesting crops are never offered within manorial accounts, although isolated dates for related matters occasionally feature. An entry in Elton's 1311–12 account roll outlines that 'two carpenters [were] hired during four days ... about mid-Lent for felling, trimming and drying timber', which would mean that the date of their employment was around 6 March 1312.[61] The Roman agronomist Varro, whose works were widely read across the medieval period by encyclopaedists such as Bartholomew the Englishman, suggested that 'some operations should be carried out ... during ... the waning of the moon ... such as the harvest and [the cutting of] wood'.[62] According to Byrhtferth, trees should never be cut in the days following a new moon, but ought to be felled following

---

59   G. Markham (ed.), *La maison rustique or The countrey farme* (1616), p. 22 <http://eebo.chadwyck. com>, accessed August 2019.

60   C.H. Talbot, *Medicine in medieval England* (London, 1967), pp. 125–6; L. Braswell, 'The moon and medicine in Chaucer's time', *Studies in the Age of Chaucer*, 8 (1986), p. 153; J.B. Friedman, 'Harry the Haywarde and Talbat his dog: an illustrated girdlebook from Worcestershire', in C. Fisher and K.L. Scott (eds), *Art into life: collected papers from the Kresge Art Museum medieval symposia* (East Lansing, MI, 1995), p. 115.

61   *EMR*, p. 169.

62   Marcus Porcius Cato, *On agriculture*, and Marcus Terentius Varro, *On agriculture*, W.D. Hooper (trans.) and H.B. Ash (ed.) (1934, London, 1999), p. 261; echoed by Cato, p. 53.

a full moon and its period of waning, as they were 'more resistant to … worms and more durable than those that are cut when the moon is new'.[63] The full moon appeared on 23 February 1312 and waned until the new moon on 9 March. At the time the Elton carpenters were felling trees it would have been in the last quarter of its cycle, and so the trees were felled in accordance with didactic instruction. A fourteenth-century translation of a Roman treatise on horticulture outlines that even wine needed to be handled in accordance with the lunar calendar, lest it be ruined.[64] Moving wine around the full moon would sour it, and the right time for transportation was close to the new moon. Lakenheath carters frequently transported the prior's wine, although the precise date is only given once: on the day of the Holy Innocents [28 December] in 1307 a dole of wine was taken to the prior at Shippea (Cambridgeshire), three days after the new moon.[65] These fleeting glimpses into peasants' scientific worldview are buried deep within the manorial documents. Quantitatively they are insignificant and yet, despite their insufficiency, there is a consistency that suggests we ought not discount the possibilities they present altogether. Having reflected on the ways in which peasants thought about the management of soil, we will now consider how other natural resources were managed.

Ten men went to mow: managing medieval meadowland

Meadow was arguably the most valuable natural resource in the medieval countryside, commonly being worth significantly more per acre than arable land.[66] In the Midlands, especially in the river valleys, it was a relatively plentiful resource, and this was the case in both Elton and Castor. In addition to being an important source of fodder, after mowing had taken place it was usual for all meadow, including the demesne several, to be thrown open for common grazing. It seems likely, however, that this was subject to some restrictions at Elton. An extent – undated, but probably early thirteenth century – outlines the abbot of Ramsey exchanging twenty acres of Elton meadow for an undefined area of fen pasture in Farcet (Huntingdonshire), ten miles east of Elton, 'for the men … with their beasts'. We can be sure that it was the tenants' meadow that the abbot traded, and henceforth these men had limited access to local meadow and a twenty-mile round trip to Farcet with their livestock.[67]

Further constraints are noted. In all but one surviving account roll, the dairy account records the manufacture of rowen cheese, which was produced from a

---

63 Baker and Lapidge, *Byrhtferth's enchiridion*, p. 145; this advice is also offered by Plutarch: Plutarch, *Moralia*, book 8, trans. P.A. Clement and H.B. Hoffleit (London, 1969), p. 277.

64 D.G. Cylkowski, 'A Middle English treatise on horticulture: Godfridus Super Palladium', in L.M. Matheson (ed.), *Popular and practical science of medieval England* (East Lansing, MI, 1994), p. 324.

65 CUL EDC/7/16/1/6.

66 Campbell, *English seigniorial agriculture*, p. 76; in 1321, Castor's arable was worth 4d. per acre, while the meadow was worth 2s. per acre: Sparke, *Historiæ Anglicanæ*, vol. 2, pp. 175–7.

67 *CMR I*, p. 267.

Table 8.4
Cheese production at Elton, 1297–1351.

Accounting year	No. of ordinary cheeses	Production dates	No. of rowen cheeses	Production dates
1297–98	164	19 Apr – 29 Sep	57	29 Sep – 19 Apr
1311–12	158	25 Apr – 29 Sep	21	-
1313–14	157	25 Apr – 29 Sep	36	29 Sep – 25 Dec
1345–46	176	Easter – 29 Sep	57	-
1350–51	161	21 Apr – 29 Sep	29	-

Source: EMR.

second crop of grass (grown after the first cut).[68] This essentially meant that some demesne meadows at least were not thrown open to be grazed after the first mow, which took place at some point between June and the end of July.[69] Rowen grass was not produced on meadow that was grazed immediately after this period, and so we can safely conclude that, at Elton, common grazing on some meadows was forbidden for some time.[70] For those peasants holding a greater share of meadow, perhaps through land transactions, and perhaps for those accessing pasture at Farcet, this might have been less of an issue, as it would for tenants of Over End, whose meadows were situated away from the abbot's Nether End demesne meadow. The meadow commonly allocated to the Nether End tenants, *micheleholm*, would have been enclosed, ensuring that some grazing was available; nevertheless, the manufacture of rowen cheese and butter at Elton must have impacted peasant grazing somewhat and, in some years, delayed access to pasture considerably.[71]

The cheese production schedule, most informative in 1297–8 and 1313–14, shows that rowen cheese was made after Michaelmas, meaning that some Elton meadow was probably out-of-bounds for pasturing across the summer and perhaps into the autumn months; in 1298, rowen cheese was still being made in spring (Table 8.4), from animals fed on rowen hay, indicating an abundant crop. In 1312 thirteen peasants were amerced 3d. each for ruining the meadow of the vill by grazing it with

---

68 *EMR*, pp. 68–384.

69 B.A. Henisch, 'In due season: farm work in the medieval calendar tradition', in D. Sweeney (ed.), *Agriculture in the middle ages: technology, practice, and representation* (Philadelphia, PA, 1995), p. 309; Campbell, *English seigneurial agriculture*, p. 72; Ault suggests that, generally, meadows were thrown open for common grazing three to four weeks after the first mow: Ault, *Open-field farming*, p. 41.

70 G.C. Homans, *English villagers of the thirteenth century* (1941, New York, 1970), p. 60; Hunter suggests that Suffolk meadows reserved for rowen hay would be closed between July and August: A. Hunter, *Georgical essays*, vol. 3 (York, 1773), p. 151.

71 H.S. Bennett, *Life on the English manor: a study of peasant conditions 1150–1400* (Cambridge, 1956), p. 55.

their beasts against the bylaw. Again in 1331, twenty-two peasants were in court for treading down the lord's meadow at *le inmede*, and a further four for mowing the lord's meadow badly at *abbotisholm*. Was this action related to the limiting of access to some of Elton's meadows?[72] This type of common regulation was not unusual, as is shown by a bylaw from late fourteenth-century Great Horwood (Buckinghamshire) that 'ordered that no one … shall have his beasts or cattle in the meadow … unless on his own property between [31 May] and the Nativity of St John the Baptist [24 June]'; but the implied restrictions in certain meadows at Elton were for a much lengthier period, and this seems to have been resented by many residents.[73] In 1345, a year in which a large quantity of rowen cheese was made, the fodder of sixteen demesne plough-oxen was supplemented by hay purchased from the meadows at neighbouring Fotheringhay, suggesting that meadow grass was in short supply locally, and that the rowen hay was reserved for the dairy herd.[74]

Although we cannot know the full reasons behind the local resentment that was expressed through the periodic damaging or indifferent treatment of the lord's meadows, this entry in the account roll indicates that locals perhaps had some justification in responding to the restrictions placed on them regarding the grazing of their own livestock. An undated Elton survey, pre-dating the hundred rolls, hints at additional reasons for peasant discontent. It shows that, at an earlier period, servile tenants owed customary mowing services for just two days each week during haying. By 1279 they were obliged to mow every day of the week until all the demesne meadows were cut. For this, the workers had been able to negotiate a token payment of 8d. for refreshments, recorded in the account rolls as a 'gift', but, as there were so many of them, this can hardly have been considered suitable recompense.[75]

Mires, mores and meres: managing fenland resources

While there was little meadow in Lakenheath, fen plants were an important resource, particularly rushes and sedge, which were used for thatching and bedding – the latter being considered a superior roofing material.[76] Breckland peasants had common rights over certain resources, including mowing rushes and sedge and cutting peat for fuel. These vital resources were managed through a series of bylaws, a great number of which survive within Lakenheath's extensive court rolls, either explicitly or implicitly stated. English bylaws of this period were generated by local peasants as part of the court process and, as such, they are extremely useful for assessing peasant views. Nevertheless, Ault suggests that even where records show that they were introduced 'by the whole homage', or by 'the agreement of the vill', as they were at Lakenheath, in practice they were developed by a select few – the most prominent peasants – which would have meant those who had a strong economic interest, largely excluding

---

72   *EMR*, pp. 200 and 298.

73   Ault, *Open-field farming*, p. 112.

74   *EMR*, pp. 324–5.

75   *RH II*, p. 657; *CMR I*, pp. 487–90.

76   Bailey, *Medieval Suffolk*, p. 95.

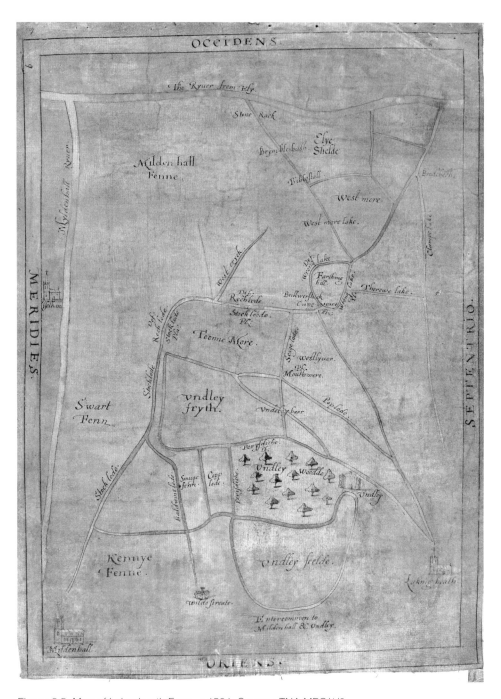

Figure 8.5. Map of Lakenheath Fens, *c.*1581. Source: TNA MPC/1/6.

smallholders and the landless from the process.[77] In order to oversee the fen harvest in Lakenheath two fen-reeves were appointed. In 1321 the clerk of the court recorded that one outgoing fen-reeve, Gilbert Martin, had been selected by the lord and the jurors, suggesting that locals had a stake in the selection process – although, again, this would have been restricted to a privileged few.[78]

The bylaws that survive offer a fascinating insight into the management of the fenland environment. They outline a system whereby the common fens were accessible in rotation, and in strictly delimited time periods. Lakenheath peasants were entitled to cut sedge in the common fens according to a rigid schedule: in 1334 they could mow in *westmor* (shown on Figure 8.5) only before Whitsunday, while mowing in *depfen* was forbidden until 1 August that year. The mowing season continued each year until the end of October, and, after 1 November, any sedge cut and left lying in the fens could be claimed by anyone wishing to gather it.[79] Similar rules governed access to the turbaries. In 1321 digging was forbidden after 24 June and there were stringent regulations indicating where one might dig; in some cases bounds were placed 'by common ordinance' to indicate the limits of a current turbary, as at *le northfen* in 1330.[80] In addition to the restrictions placed on where and when locals might mow or dig, other important constraints dictated that no one should remove any resources from the site until the resources had been seen and accounted for by the officials. This was largely because there were limitations on the amount that each household was entitled to take. Those caught flouting the bylaws were presented in court by the fen-reeve and fined.

It is difficult to ascertain precisely why these bylaws were created. Given the restrictions placed around the harvesting of fen resources, it is tempting to speculate that sustainability was a primary concern for peasants. Determining and marking out bounded territory required consideration and coordinated effort; nevertheless, these restrictions would have also, in theory, given the fen-reeves a smaller area to police, and the sheer size of Lakenheath's fenland territory must have been problematic in this regard. However, it seems likely that there was also a drive to regulate the local market: if peasants were selling resources beyond the control of the vill this would have destabilised the local supply of these products. Was this a concern for those peasants generating and developing the bylaws? It is difficult to be sure; however, there were good reasons to suppose that this may have been the case: the vast majority of those presented to the Lakenheath court who were in breach of these regulations could not be counted among the leading, well-off few. Instead, they were predominantly smallholders, landless individuals and paupers, alongside one or two enterprising fen-reeves making the most of their privileged position.

---

77   W.O. Ault, 'Open-field husbandry and the village community: a study of agrarian by-laws in medieval England', *Transactions of the American Philosophical Society*, 55/7 (1965), pp. 42–3; TNA SC 2/203/94.

78   CUL EDC/7/16/2/1/6/32.

79   CUL   EDC/7/16/2/1/5;   EDC/7/16/2/1/8/9;   EDC/7/16/2/1/9/11;   EDC/7/16/2/1/9/36; EDC/7/16/2/1/6/18.

80   CUL EDC/7/16/2/1/8/10.

Between 1310 and 1342 the majority of those in court accused of bylaw contraventions of the type outlined above, alongside associated cases featuring transactions involving fen resources, were the least prominent residents, including those labelled as paupers. A staggering 54 per cent of those cases involved individuals who did not feature in other records, and would otherwise have been rendered all but invisible in the record.[81] One of the most frequent transgressions involved cutting sedge or digging peat and removing it from the site against the ordinance. Good turves require a drained site and need to be stacked to dry *in situ* before being transported to the peasant's dwelling or to market – clearly a lengthy process.[82] In Lakenheath there are countless references to turves being carried straight from the site, strongly suggesting attempts at clandestine activity; this was often undertaken by individuals or very small groups, presumably in an attempt to avoid detection. In 1331 it was discovered that three men had taken their haul to Thetford, which they had perhaps hoped was at a sufficient distance to evade the authorities.[83] According to a 1336 entry, Gilbert Martin had an annual allowance of 20,000 turves, and so it seems likely that this was considered adequate to provide fuel for a single household for a year.[84] Attempts to conceal activity must have been deemed worth the effort; the price of turves fluctuated wildly, probably because wet, soft, newly cut turves commanded a much lower price than those left to dry in the turbary and accounted for by the fen-reeve.

For poorer residents with limited economic options, the potential to augment their income meant that they might take a philosophical view of getting caught and facing a fine. The 6,000 turves promised by Reginald Bole, a pauper, to one of his neighbours in 1335 for an agreed price of 16d. were almost certainly the inferior 'wet' turves, as opposed to the 10,000 sold for 13s. in 1334 by Simon Wyles.[85] For Nicholas Sabyn, another Lakenheath pauper, it is clear that dealing in fen resources was economically important to him, and he was frequently in court for selling turves and sedge outside the vill. Underlining this, in 1310 he was distrained by a scythe, indicating that this was integral to his livelihood (see chapter seven, p. 161).[86] On occasion it is clear that those engaged in mowing sedge took advance orders for sheaves. In June 1332 Walter Godying brought a case of detinue against William le Redere, having agreed a price of 36d. for 375 sheaves the previous summer, which William had failed to deliver by the agreed deadline.[87] Henry Pyre, a local fisherman, was frequently in court for many similar offences, clearly agreeing terms and promising to cut sedge to order.[88] People also found additional ways to earn money by exploiting Lakenheath's vast

---

81 Out of 577 court cases. It is possible that some of these people were outsiders; however, this was commonly indicated if that was the case.

82 I.D. Rotherham, *Peat and peat cutting* (Oxford, 2011), p. 27.

83 CUL EDC/7/16/2/1/8/4.

84 CUL EDC/7/16/2/1/9/41; although Rotherham suggests that between 8,000 and 12,000 was standard: Rotherham, *Peat*, p. 22.

85 CUL EDC/7/16/2/1/9/30; EDC/7/16/2/1/9/32.

86 CUL EDC/7/16/2/1/3.

87 CUL EDC/7/16/2/1/9/13.

88 See, for example: CUL EDC/7/16/2/1/6/41; EDC/7/16/2/1/8/13; EDC/7/16/2/1/8/12.

Table 8.5
Unlawful turves, 10 March 1329, Lakenheath.

Name	Number of turves cut	Value of turves (d.)	Fine (d.)
John Tunte	1000	10	6
Walter, son of John Tunte	1000	10	6
William Bewys	1000	10	6
Matthew Ketil	900	9	6
Robert Thoury	700	7	12
Robert Gopayn	700	7	6
John Maunsel	700	7	6
John Ponder	500	5	12

Source: CUL EDC/7/16/2/1/9.

fenland. Some peasants generated supplementary income by unlawfully allowing and shielding outsiders' activities. Several poorer residents provided accommodation for 'strangers' cutting sedge and thatch in common fens in 1331, and in 1319 William Jakes and Richard Querour – a man appointed fen-reeve in 1334 – accepted money from Mildenhall men to mow in Lakenheath territory.[89]

It is difficult to establish whether the officials were unable to protect such an extensive territory or whether they simply turned a blind eye: in 1321 the fen-reeve Gilbert Martin was fined for failing to prevent a boatload of turves worth 72d. from leaving the vill.[90] According to local bylaws, these turves ought to have been forfeited. Those managing to get their ill-gotten gains away before being caught must have considered the risk of a fine worthwhile, provided they could evade the manorial officers until the contraband resources were safely off-site. In 1326 Thomas Brid admitted to cutting sedge worth 6s. 8d., which he had clearly already disposed of, and was fined 1s.[91] Matthew Crane was not as fortunate. In 1313 he was caught red-handed and was fined 2s. for threatening and abusing the bailiff and fen-reeves who were busy binding his forfeited rushes.[92] There is only one other reference to confiscated resources in the extant manorial records, when John Wiles reacquired a cartload of sedge that had been commandeered by the bailiff in 1337.[93] Does this help us to determine the nature of the Lakenheath fines, and whether they were in fact a form of licensing of this widespread behaviour? The case is far from clear-cut: setting aside a few years between 1310 and 1315 during which bylaw infringements in the fens were punished by a standard 6d., the fines are varied, and it is often unclear why. In 1328, for example, thirteen peasants were accused of digging and selling turves against the bylaw. These individuals clearly managed to dispose of their turves before the officials

---

89 CUL EDC/7/16/2/1/6/18; EDC/7/16/2/1/9/11.
90 CUL EDC/7/16/2/1/6/32.
91 CUL EDC/7/16/2/1/8/27.
92 CUL EDC/7/16/2/1/6/3.
93 CUL EDC/7/16/2/1/14/2.

caught up with them. Their fines ranged from 2d. to 9d., although no reason is offered for the discrepancy.[94] It might be explained by the quantity of turves dug and sold by each perpetrator: in each instance, as with Thomas Brid, a reasonable profit could still be made despite the fine. This seems to have been the situation in another fenland court, at nearby Downham (Cambridgeshire), where the number of sheaves of sedge were recorded alongside the fines issued. Here, peasants paid 6d. for every additional thousand sheaves of sedge they cut, and Ault's analysis shows that, by 1350, 6d. was a standard fine for a bylaw violation.[95] However, in 1329, in the only case in which detailed data are recorded, the quantities and values of the unlawfully acquired turves of eight men are listed (Table 8.5). Here, John Ponder dug half as many turves as John or Walter Tunte, but was fined double. It is little wonder that he incurred an additional 3d. fine for contempt of court. What did the affeerors take into account in determining the level of the fines levied? Were they perhaps including additional, undeclared resources that they perceived had been concealed? Robert Thoury was a habitual offender, but John Ponder is not recorded elsewhere.

It seems likely that the poorer residents of Lakenheath, who probably needed the additional income they could generate from the fens, were waging a war of attrition against the manorial officers and jurors. Occasionally, there are clear indications that, even if some form of licensing was attempted, it was not always acknowledged by everyone. In 1331 three men brazenly went out to mow in *plantelode* on 'the day after the leet at which the bylaw was made', and there are examples of judicial inquiries being raised to assess whether bylaws had been contravened. Things clearly came to a head in 1335, following what seems to have been a crackdown by the new steward, when the jurors issued a statement outlining that 'whenever anyone does wrong selling sedge outside the vill, they ought by ancient custom to be punished under penalty of 40d.' as indeed eight men were on this particular occasion.[96] While the excessive nature of these fines was rare, it is clear that there was a dichotomy between the ways in which leading peasants and poorer residents thought about and used the fenland resources on their doorstep.

A ditch in time: managing drainage and water resources

In all three vills drainage was a major issue: Lakenheath because of its fenland location, and Elton and Castor since they were both riverine. This is reflected in the works schedules, which reveal the priority given to the maintenance of ditches and drainage dykes. In two out of three years in which accounts survive for Castor, drainage was important: in 1301 and again in 1308 channels were created to allow floodwater to run off, and a runnel was cleared in *penycroft* in neighbouring Sutton 'to protect the corn'.[97] A total of 124 customary works, including 'water-furrowing'

---

94   CUL EDC/7/16/2/1/ 8/16.
95   M. Bailey, *The English manor c.1200–c.1500* (Manchester, 2002), p. 211; Ault, 'Open-field husbandry', p. 47.
96   CUL EDC/7/16/2/1/9/12; EDC/7/16/2/1/13/2; EDC/7/16/2/1/9/36.
97   NRO F(M) 2388; F(M) Roll 233.

and cleaning ditches and fish-ponds, focused on drainage at Elton in 1298.[98] In his diarised account of a farmer's year in 1898, the novelist-turned-farmer Henry Rider Haggard wrote of the importance of maintaining ditches: 'if the ditches are neglected on heavy land, the mouths of the drains get blocked and the soil becomes sour and sodden with water, after which its owner will soon hear that "the mucky old land won't grow northin' at all".'[99] This was a very real issue for riverside and fenland manors, and Elton's court rolls detail a number of longstanding issues with neighbouring manors damming waters on their boundaries, with Yarwell (Northamptonshire), Water Newton, Haddon and Morborne (Huntingdonshire) all persistent offenders.[100] More problematic was the damming of the Great Ouse at Outwell (Norfolk) by the bishop of Lichfield and Coventry, which flooded the Nene at least as far as Elton; that being the case, it must also have impacted Castor and Ailsworth, both closer to the source of the problem.[101]

The upkeep and cleaning of ditches and watercourses was so important that it was one of the specific issues dealt with in the leet court, presentments usually being made by senior manorial officials. This emphasises a more widespread need to manage the environment: concerns with maintaining ditches and watercourses were not confined solely to the officials and residents of fenland and wetland manors.[102] Thirteenth- and fourteenth-century leet court rolls elsewhere record presentments made concerning the condition of ditches and watercourses, including several at Walsham-le-Willows and Wakefield; and, in 1350 at Elmley Castle (Worcestershire), the prior of Worcester was amerced for failing to clean a ditch.[103] The overriding impression is that, while peasants understood the need for maintaining ditches and water resources, their efforts were frequently self-serving. It could prove difficult to rectify the damage caused by obstructing or altering watercourses, especially when the offenders were outsiders. William Miller of Eriswell caused long-standing problems in neighbouring Lakenheath from 1321. In 1326 and 1328 he obstructed *ereswelledam*, causing extensive flooding to meadow and adjacent common land. The court levied a fine of 80d. and also attempted to recover a further 160d. in damages.[104] By 1333 he had still not cleared the impediment, and between 1334 and 1335 he blocked another watercourse at *caldewell*, submerging demesne and common land, and was again fined 80d.[105] In 1333 a group of Mildenhall men erected an embankment in Lakenheath 'one league long and ten feet wide, and diverted a watercourse used beyond memory

---

98 *EMR*, pp. 79–80.

99 H. Rider Haggard, *A farmer's year, being his commonplace book for 1898* (1898–9, London, 1987), p. 11.

100 *EMR*, pp. 4, 34, 151; Kilby, 'A different world?' (2010a), pp. 42–3.

101 Kilby, 'A different world?' (2010a), p. 29; *CMR III*, p. 146.

102 H.G. Richardson and G.O. Sayles (eds, trans), *Fleta*, vol. 2 (London, 1955), p. 176. R. Jones and S. Kilby, 'Mitigating riverine flood risk in medieval England', in C. Gerrard *et al.* (eds), *Waiting for the end of the world. Archaeological perspectives on natural disasters in medieval Europe* (forthcoming).

103 Lock, *Court rolls of Walsham-le-Willows*, p. 123; Walker, *Court rolls of Wakefield*, p. 79; R.K. Field (ed.), *Court Rolls of Elmley Castle, Worcestershire, 1347–1564* (Worcester, 2004), p. 9.

104 CUL EDC/7/16/2/1/9/5; EDC/7/16/2/1/8/19.

105 CUL EDC/7/16/2/1/9/18; EDC/7/16/2/1/9/20; EDC/7/16/2/1/9/26.

of man to the lord's and commoners' damage'.[106] Again, this kind of damage appears in court rolls elsewhere: land at Ingoldmells (Lincolnshire) was flooded as a result of an obstruction in an adjacent manor, and at Wakefield the whole vill of Newton was presented for erecting a bank 'to the damage and hurt of all'.[107]

But these self-interested actions were not uniquely perpetrated by outsiders. At Elton in 1331 John Abovebrook was fined for altering a watercourse.[108] Many Lakenheath peasants were amerced for failing to clean ditches, *broos* and lades, causing damage to fenland and meadow: *toftmedwes* and *holm* were frequently affected. Again, this was not unusual behaviour: at Cressingham (Norfolk) Richard Rysle caused the flooding of an adjacent path through his failure to clean his ditch.[109] Some damage may not have been entirely due to peasant negligence. By 1337 the Lakenheath account records that two new dykes were raised in *toftmedwes* and *holm*, suggesting that, irrespective of peasants' maintenance efforts, these fields were particularly vulnerable to changes in the water level.[110] In 1336 several peasants were amerced for their failure to clean a number of named lades, which allegedly resulted in their drying out.[111] Prompt action could avoid major issues, such as the one caused in 1335 when Richard Faukes failed to clean *wilwlade*, 'whereby Lakenheath fen flooded to the damage of the whole community of the vill'.[112] Even where peasants proactively cleared their own resources, occasionally there was little consideration for others, as when Matthew Faukes 'threw the filth from his cleared pond' into a common watering place; and, again, this was typical of the behaviour of some – John Goldesmith was amerced in Wakefield for throwing tanning effluent into a watercourse and subsequently blocking it.[113]

The account rolls occasionally reveal the problems caused by extensive natural flooding. In Elton in 1351 a severe flood caused the ruination of meadows, the loss of part of the barley crop which was 'rotted by the flood-waters', alongside eight geese and three bee-hives, 'lost in the flood-waters in the summer'.[114] The account records the impact on the demesne, but the plight of many local peasants must have been calamitous. Demesne officials had to be especially vigilant in the fen, which was much more prone to flooding. Livestock were drowned on a number of occasions at Elton's common fen at Farcet in 1314, just prior to the Great Famine of 1315.[115] In Lakenheath

---

106 CUL EDC/7/16/2/1/9/20.

107 W.O. Massingberd (ed., trans.), *Court rolls of the manor of Ingoldmells in the county of Lincoln* (London, 1902), p. 83; Walker, *Court rolls of Wakefield*, p. 79.

108 *EMR*, p. 301.

109 CUL EDC/7/16/2/1/6/11; EDC/7/16/2/1/8/19; EDC/7/16/2/1/9/43: *broo*: the bank of a ditch, *MED*.

110 CUL EDC/7/16/1/11.

111 CUL EDC/7/16/2/1/7/43.

112 CUL EDC/7/16/2/1/9/37.

113 CUL EDC/7/16/2/1/6/18; H.W. Chandler (ed., trans.), *Five court rolls of Great Cressingham in the county of Norfolk* (London, 1885), p. 55; Walker, *Court rolls of Wakefield*, p. 128.

114 *EMR*, pp. 364–85.

115 *EMR*, p. 225; Kershaw suggests the chroniclers were in error when they recorded heavy rainfall in 1314, but it seems the weather must have been wetter than usual that year in Farcet: I. Kershaw, 'The Great Famine and agrarian crisis in England, 1315–1322', *Past and Present*, 59 (1973), p. 6.

in 1283 those responsible for pasturing livestock in the fen at Undley took no chances, returning the demesne stotts to the safety of higher, dryer ground in Lakenheath 'at the time of the great storm'.[116] Occasionally measures were taken to protect demesne resources at Lakenheath, such as the ditch dug and new watercourse created between the garden and the fen at Lakenheath 'for the defence of the garden' in 1345.[117] In 1348 the fens of *saxwarp*, *cranesfen* and *crouchestampe* were newly ditched – the implication being that these replaced older structures. With 126 perches (634 m) at *saxwarp* and 226 perches (1,137 m) for the combined *cranesfen* and *crouchestampe*, this was a major undertaking. Peasants too were alert to the possibility that an inundation of water might cause havoc. Many references to peasant ditches – largely unlicensed – indicate their deep understanding of the fenland landscape and the need to protect their resources. A group of Lakenheath fishermen illegally constructed a series of ditches and ponds near *windelse*; and John Douue enclosed an acre of land with hedges and ditches, which in 1321 was of ten years' standing: he was clearly in no hurry to expose his investment to the fenland elements.[118]

Conclusions – managing the landscape

The maintenance of the agricultural landscape was largely the responsibility of the peasantry. Albeit often under the guidance of an official, the practical day-to-day management of the land fell to those working in the fields. Historians have long been aware that soil quality was of paramount importance to rural husbandmen, but beyond acknowledging that fertilisers of all kinds were vital, there has been little focus on understanding the practicalities of soil management. In open-field country with relatively little enclosure there is evidence to suggest that topographical field-names acted as a mnemonic system, conveying information that was relevant to the conservation of the soil. This might simply indicate soil type, but frequently these names also encapsulated information relating to the elemental qualities of the land, allowing those working the land to consider the best way to treat specific furlongs. Elton, Castor and Lakenheath were all riverine settlements, with fenland also making up a significant proportion of Lakenheath's territory. As such, the management of water and drainage played a key role in agrarian success or failure. Beyond the open fields, the management of pastoral and fenland resources was also vitally important to the peasant economy and, at Lakenheath, it has been shown that turves and sedge were central to the economic prospects of poorer residents. Traditionally, historians examining the medieval documents of rural England – in particular manorial accounts – have focused on production and output. Rereading these documents from a slightly different perspective, focusing on the contemporary worldview of rural husbandmen, can shed new light on the practicalities of peasants' management of the rural environment.

---

116 CUL EDC/7/16/1/3.
117 CUL EDC/7/16/1/13.
118 CUL EDC/7/16/2/1/9/15; EDC/7/16/2/1/6/27.

Chapter 9

Conclusion

Unveiling the peasant environment

This study forms part of the new wave of scholarship on the medieval rural environment in which the lived experience of the lower orders of society is central. If we are to bring peasant perceptions to light, then, as outlined within the preceding chapters, it is necessary to approach familiar forms of evidence from entirely new perspectives. For too long the principal intellectual approach has been to consider both evidence and subject from a modern, rationalist perspective. Even though many historians would generally now eschew this approach, this study signals that scholars can go further in reassessing peasant experience. As demonstrated within this volume, by re-evaluating the source material from the perspective of the peasant worldview it is possible to build a far more detailed representation of rural peasant experience. This approach also requires us to reassess all of the available evidence – including documents, material culture, place- and family names, and the landscape – collectively, rather than continuing to work within discrete academic disciplines. Medieval rural communities did not encounter these aspects of their lives in isolation, but in myriad overlapping and intersecting ways. And so we, as researchers, should also consider these distinct elements synchronously if we are to construct more meaningful accounts of peasants' experience. For some scholars, using elite-sponsored and authored written documentation to consider the mental world of the lower orders of medieval society is problematic. But, here, it has been demonstrated that sensitive assessments of England's abundant documentary sources can offer new insights into rural peasant life. Additionally, peasant names – landscape and family names – provide, if not direct peasant testimony, something very close to that. Rather than assuming peasant perspectives are lost to us, this study emphasises just how much it is possible to recover using the approach outlined here.

Furthermore, in addition to taking a multi-disciplinary approach to the evidence, this study also emphasises the importance of interdisciplinary methodologies. This is a significant change of direction from many contemporary studies of the medieval rural environment and its inhabitants. Again, re-evaluating familiar evidence using non-historical theoretical frameworks can provide new insights into the many ways in which local communities considered the rural environment. For example, cultural geographers' understanding of the ways in which different groups 'read' their local landscape has profound implications for the ways in which we might deconstruct a range of evidence left to us by medieval English peasant communities. Correspondingly, anthropological approaches to place-naming demonstrate the distinct possibility that there were similarities between the naming practices of First Nations people and medieval society – groups of people that enjoyed a similar close connection with their local environment. It can be demonstrated that both groups used key landscape referents, and also used names as a repository for rural culture in the guise of history, folklore and legend. These approaches help to free us from the shackles of rationalist thought and modernistic ways of looking at historical landscapes and communities. Re-evaluating peasant perspectives on the rural environment in three diverse communities using this new methodology also allows us to reconsider some significant and fundamentally important (and frequently interconnecting) historical themes. In addition to enhancing academic understanding of the lived experience, our comprehension of subjects such as social status, peasant agency, peasants' economic experiences and the construction of communal and individual memory can be significantly augmented.

Living in rural communities

It is possible to uncover something of the varied experiences of living within medieval rural English communities. This study emphasises that the common trend from the late Anglo-Saxon period was for lords to distinguish seigneurial spaces from those occupied by the lower orders. Post-Conquest, across all levels of lordship, this tendency generally developed into the construction of walled, gated and moated seigneurial dwellings and *curia* by resident and absentee lords alike by the later medieval period. Additional features such as enclosed parks and gardens were also used in part to aid segregation, and in some instances manorial *curia* were set apart from peasant residences. It seems likely that even in places selected as temporary retreats or retirement residences, such as those favoured by the prior of Ely at Undley and Shippea, the environment had been carefully chosen. Perhaps these locations were preferred for their aesthetic settings, situated as they were in rural isolation on 'islanded' land accessible only by causeway. A more sceptical reading might lead us to imagine that some element of deliberate screening from the rest of the community had been prioritised as part of the process of selecting the most apposite site. At Castor and Elton – and to a certain extent at Lakenheath – documentary evidence suggests that, in the thirteenth century, certain parts of each settlement were made up of specific peasant status-group zones. These included the group of free tenants clustered around the Thorold demesne at Castor and the area occupied by Elton cottars in Over End.

Assessing the organisation of rural villages using a range of sources reveals underlying socially constructed perceptions of place that expose the differing experiences of peasants across the lower social scale, with younger free tenants having more opportunity to establish an independent household at an earlier life-stage than their servile neighbours. While there is much evidence to support the idea that many peasants perceived their own holdings as private spaces – despite often simultaneously infringing the privacy of others – again, free tenants undoubtedly had greater choice over the placement of their main dwelling within the toft, thereby exerting more control over their levels of privacy. Nevertheless, it is possible to detect the sense that peasants across the social spectrum considered their homesteads – to a certain degree – to be private spaces within the bounds of which they clearly believed that they had some autonomy. This notion had filtered down through the social order across the period under review, accelerating in the thirteenth and fourteenth centuries. It is apparent through the naming of peasant holdings – such as *bouetonhay* and *bernardisplace* in Castor and *gopaynshithe* in Lakenheath – and in the importance of establishing and maintaining toft boundaries, both physically and within the documentary record.

Social status reconsidered

A study of this nature allows us to look at old problems in new ways. This approach provides fresh insights into the issue of social status and contributes to the debate about how much personal status actually mattered in later medieval rural communities. There is evidence to suggest that peasants higher up the social scale attempted to emulate some of the ways in which lords set themselves apart from the lower orders within the rural settlement, and lords' desire to promote an outward sense of seclusion seems to have been mirrored in miniature by some of the peasants examined here. This, it is suggested, ultimately had a significant impact on the ways in which some free peasants expressed their sense of identity in the rural settlement in the latter part of this period. This is perhaps most obvious in Bernard de Pickworth's capital messuage in Castor, with its great gate, walls, hedges and ditches, but it is also apparent in the manner in which free peasants in Huntingdonshire generally eschewed topographical bynames and family names that were largely associated with servile individuals. Many free peasants, then, were keen to project an image in which their relationship with the local environment was conducted at a slight distance: behind walls and gates, perhaps deeper within their tofts, and freer from the gaze of their neighbours.

While they may have been somewhat withdrawn from the landscape of the settlement in a physical sense, in bestowing their family names on the landscape Castor's freemen irrefutably associated themselves symbolically with the local environment through overt statements of ownership. Free tenants' perceived unwillingness to be associated with topographical bynames, while simultaneously asserting their attachment to particular places, possibly suggests a desire to be in a position of authority over the environment, akin to elite relationships with the landscape, rather than being more physically associated with it. Similarly, it has been shown that the many free families at Castor and Ailsworth bearing toponymical family names cannot have been using them purely as a means of personal identification; they were also redolent of higher status. Understanding the rationale for these actions and associations is more problematic. We appear to be witnessing a considered initiative on the part of some freemen – especially those living under strong lordship – to distance themselves from their servile neighbours; but whether this sprang from a need to ensure that their legal status was not misunderstood or was more prosaically an attempt at social climbing is unclear. Although this differentiation was clearly apparent in the vills under review here, it seems worthy of wider geographical consideration to assess whether this was a general trend. What is clear, however, is that personal status underlies this trend. Evidently, social status remained important to rural communities into the fourteenth century, irrespective of differing experiences between wealthier and poorer peasants.

Detecting peasant agency

In recent years, typical considerations of peasant agency have tended to focus on themes such as poaching and servile peasants' often indifferent approach to the provision of labour on lords' demesnes. While these are worthwhile avenues for exploration, the approach adopted here has allowed some light to fall on alternative means through which peasants exercised autonomy and made their own decisions. This has already been demonstrated through the high levels of independence enjoyed by Castor free tenants, evidenced by their management of the levels of privacy available to them and by their assertion of a sense of proprietorship over the landscape created by connecting their family names with their enclosed fields. Although in some respects free peasants had greater independence, servile peasants often also found ways to exert free choice. At Castor and Lakenheath, using different datasets, it was possible to support conclusions drawn in recent work by economic historians that peasant agricultural strategies frequently differed from that of the demesne. At Lakenheath, the detail recorded within the manorial court rolls established that – as on many English manors in this period – peasants there frequently disregarded local bylaws and, in order to supplement their income, extracted significantly greater quantities of natural resources, such as sedge and turves, than was customary.

Further examination of the evidence contained within Lakenheath's court rolls revealed behaviour that contradicts the view that lords were always successful in regulating the wider manorial environment. Here, the metanarrative that lords expected the world to accept can be dismantled further as we encounter peasants who moved through the manorial environment with little regard for seigneurial restrictions. These men – for they were predominantly male – created their own paths through the manor, occasionally without regard for standing crops or the lord's livestock. References to these ephemeral tracks are fleeting, but they are vitally important in offering a counterpoint to the impression that peasants' movements were successfully controlled by the upper orders. In short, although these peasants evidently understood what it meant to live in a regulated environment, within which there were many bounded, ostensibly private areas, their recollection of these official and unofficial rules could be conveniently erratic. For many, both overt and covert trespass seems to have been the norm.

The great majority of the field-names and minor landscape names recovered as part of this study were bestowed upon the landscape by resident peasants. They are a vitally important source of evidence in a study of this nature, as they represent rare direct peasant testimony. Many reveal highly nuanced detail regarding the characteristics of the local landscape. Without this corpus, it may have been possible to speculate upon the nature of respective local topographies, such as Lakenheath's vast fens and heathland, but these names not only provide solid evidence of fine distinctions between environmental attributes, such as Castor's *ashauue* or Elton's *arnewassh*, but also offer a partial chronology of change, most obvious within the assarting names recorded in late medieval Castor. Minor landscape names are fundamentally important to a study of this nature, since they offer a tangible link to those naming the landscape. Comprehending the literal meaning of these names is vitally important, but it should be emphasised that for those wishing to uncover peasants' perceptions of the rural landscape, it is but the first element in the process toward understanding their significance more fully.

Memory and history in the rural landscape

As suggested above, when considered in context, field-names and minor landscape names can reveal elements of the landscape as it was visualised by those who named it. As this study emphasises, these field-names were imbued with layers of meaning, elements of which can occasionally be recovered if the names are reconsidered from within their original landscape context. By moving beyond a more traditional approach to field-names, it is possible to re-evaluate them from the varied perspectives of a peasant's worldview. Here, it has been argued that names hitherto categorised as purely descriptive – such as Elton's *cleyfurlong* and *molwellehyl*, and Lakenheath's *le sondput* – were used as part of a mnemonic system, providing an uncomplicated means of encapsulating environmental data that could be transmitted orally and recalled easily by local husbandmen. This system of remembering may also have been used in order to assist in decision-making regarding manuring and fertilising the fields, in accordance with contemporary elemental principles.

It has long been known that the landscape formed an important repository for cultural memory. Extracting meaning in this context from a medieval perspective has generally been confined to the study of particular themes, such as the supernatural, or criminal execution sites, for example.[1] However, through the systematic and holistic analysis of the landscape and material culture of one community – in this case Castor – and where a range of contemporary and later evidence survives to aid in landscape reconstruction, it has been possible to reassess seemingly transparent field-names and to recover something of their importance to local collective memory. Influenced in particular by the work of anthropologists and ethnographers, specific field-names were re-examined from a more phenomenological perspective and considered in combination with contemporary church capitals. Crucially, this approach favours cultural context over pure linguistic definition and taxonomy, attempting to restore later medieval field-names within more temporally appropriate physical and metaphorical frames of reference. This is firmly aligned with emerging scholarship linking cultural memory with the historical landscape and it emphasises that an approach that prioritises landscape and cultural context can yield interesting results. Indeed, this methodology reaffirms the importance of the medieval rural landscape from a socio-cultural perspective.

If the field-names offer us examples of medieval rural communities' great skill in harnessing language to construct powerful aides-mémoire that gave them instant expertise on the attributes of vast tracts of land, then the court rolls provide evidence that peasants' memories were occasionally fallible – often deliberately so. There are numerous accounts of offences against local bylaws. From the Elton men who pastured their sheep illegally to the Lakenheath residents who conveniently forgot that they ought not to mow sedge or cut turves in certain places and at particular times of the year, English court rolls from this period abound with examples of lapsed peasant memory. Although these accounts simply emphasise the means by which peasants attempted to circumvent local ordinances, nevertheless peasant-authored field-names offer an important counterpoint, emphasising the power and substance of rural collective memory.

Making a living in rural England

Turning to the more practical aspects of peasants' relationships with the local environment, it is evident that, while at least some peasants may have shared some common experiences – customary tenants' labour services and *famuli* tasks, for example – it would be incorrect to consider all peasant encounters with the environment in general

---

1   Semple, 'A fear of the past'; R. Gregory, 'Some Nottinghamshire dead men', *Nomina*, 38 (2014), pp. 85–92.

terms. The surviving Lakenheath manorial records emphasise the variety of means by which local peasants made a living. The wealthier residents tended to rear large flocks of sheep, while those less well-off were principally engaged in activities such as fishing and artisanal crafts. Peasants immured in poverty at Lakenheath were also more likely to number among those clandestinely and illegally extracting and selling resources from common reedbeds and turbaries. Despite living in reasonable proximity to one another, the experience and practical knowledge of the environment and its resources accumulated by tenants such as John de Wangford and Richard Lericok must have been markedly different. For some peasants, it was necessary to engage in multiple modes of employment, such as Richard in the Lane's fisheries and sheep-farming in Lakenheath; Castor's William Bloodletter also doubled up as the local tanner.

Other aspects of the use and management of local resources were likely to have been understood more widely, such as the materials used in the construction of local buildings, those used for fuel, and the plants and crops grown for consumption by peasants and livestock, for example. Additionally, it seems likely that most peasants had a reasonably detailed understanding of the physical characteristics of the landscape. This is apparent through the manner in which some furlongs were named and the general adherence toward maintaining the landscape in good order, considering drainage and the communal importance of the production and application of manure to arable land. The evidence from Lakenheath hints that sales of manure may have been associated with poorer peasants, and that, in some instances, better-off peasants may have attempted to disassociate themselves from this kind of refuse. Just as many free peasants avoided associations with topographical family names, perhaps an overt connection with manure – and its strong connotations with foul odours and filth – were deemed undesirable by those aspiring to social elevation.

In order to make a living successfully, husbandmen needed to ensure that both fields and livestock remained in good health. There is undoubted evidence that peasants at even the lowest strata of society had some understanding of medieval science, however loosely that may be defined. References to the medical treatment of swine by agricultural labourers using practices associated with humoral theory confirm that there must have been the medieval equivalent of an apprenticeship in animal husbandry, passed on orally to young men as part of the natural cycle of attaining and disseminating practical information and experience. Additional hints at early veterinary practice are also apparent at Elton, although what this practice actually involved is unclear. Contemporary treatises on husbandry fail to consider disease in livestock adequately, and a tentative conclusion – that treatments practised by peasant husbandmen were conveyed orally and practically between generations, and were the preserve of peasant practitioners – cannot be determined conclusively, but might explain their absence from the treatises. Undoubtedly, assessment of these more practical concerns – whether considering the improvement of the soil through the application of fertiliser or determining the most efficacious time to cut timber – emphasise that the environment influenced peasant decision-making in myriad ways.

Peasant perspectives on the medieval landscape: concluding thoughts

What begins to emerge from these disparate aspects of peasants' experience of their respective local landscapes is that there is no universal narrative that distils peasant perspectives into one all-purpose outlook. Certainly, common threads emerge that suggest some shared principles may have been held across all three vills studied here. This is to some extent apparent when considering personal naming patterns and free tenants' seeming dislike of topographical bynames. While this reveals important evidence regarding free peasants' mentalities, crucially it does not expose the viewpoint of the servile population. Their voice remains largely unheard, and we cannot know whether they tolerated these family names or whether they were content to identify with the local environment in such a manner. The examination of these names appears to provide evidence that supports the idea that, in some ways, attitudes differed between the free and unfree peasant population. This was particularly apparent in Elton and more widely throughout Huntingdonshire. In other respects, however, it did not, particularly when considering how unauthorised pathways through the landscape were considered by free peasants and leading villeins at Lakenheath alike.

There is evidence to suggest that, in some respects, peasants' attitudes toward the local landscape altered between 1086 and 1348. Some changes are hinted at, such as free tenants' disassociation with topographical bynames and family names, but there is too little evidence from before the mid-thirteenth century to be certain that this represented modified attitudes. Transformation is most discernible through changes within the corpus of minor landscape names, especially at Castor and Lakenheath, where family names and cultural elements were more likely to be used as field-name qualifiers in the latter part of this period. There, peasant families strengthened their associations with what they perceived as their exclusive territories by giving these areas their name – there can be no doubting the strength of purpose behind names such as *bouetonhay* and *gopaynshithe*, or that in many instances these names were devised by the tenants associated with these holdings. Others have noted these changes, and although the pace of transition seems to have differed in the three vills assessed here, the general outlook appears to favour a shift toward closer familial associations with aspects of peasant holdings, possibly more so and at a more rapid rate in manors with weaker lordship.[2] This appears to occur across the lines of freedom and servility, and is most notable through the tendency for leading peasant families to forge strong associations with the local landscape using their names.

At the outset it was suggested that one of the principal aims of this study was to uncover – as far is it was possible to do so – peasant perspectives on the rural environment. This was undoubtedly a challenge. For many historians, the primary difficulty is the perceived lack of direct peasant testimony, as the source material was largely elite-sponsored – although this view largely overlooks peasant naming practices. This problem has been outlined by many others venturing into this territory. Gurevich *et al.* argue in response to criticism that there is no other way to approach medieval peasant culture except via sources of this nature, which can be fruitful when treated sensitively.[3]

---

2   Olson, *A mute gospel*, p. 189.

3   J.M. Bak *et al.*, *Medieval popular culture: problems of belief and perception* (Cambridge, 1988), p. 1; A.J. Gurevich, 'Medieval culture and mentality according to the New French Historiography', in S. Clark (ed.), *The Annales School: critical assessments*, vol. 2 (London, 1999), p. 212.

Historians of the Annales School have typically explored material such as penitentials, chronicles, sermons and saints' lives. In England we are fortunate to possess manorial documents and charters, an alternative basis for enquiry. As a body of material these records have proven to be both profitable and problematic. Arguably, the rich seam of evidence provided by the names – minor landscape names and bynames alike – offers an opportunity to assess terms coined by the peasants themselves. Certainly, some had been translated into Latin, but their vernacular equivalents were recorded in sufficient quantity to aid detailed investigation. Where the analysis focused on peasant activities, again, although these were necessarily viewed through the filter of the manorial clerk, much of the data were quantitatively significant, allowing dominant themes, such as the creation of illegal paths, to emerge.

There are, of course, limitations to this approach. Although much has been revealed, the documents themselves restrict our view in important ways. In some instances, especially with regard to the court rolls, we see only those practices deemed subversive by the authorities. As such, the leet court rolls abound with peasant encroachments, but might there have been other issues that did not feature? Undoubtedly, some of these scarcer problems appear periodically, but it is very likely that poorer peasants and women are underrepresented. Moreover, there are aspects of peasants' varied relationships with their environment that remain opaque to us, as – in the case of the three settlements studied here, at least – the texts studied remain silent. Throughout, it has not been the intention to assess cultural ideas that were not expressed – explicitly or indirectly – within the source material. Therefore, some of the most common beliefs frequently associated with the lower orders that were connected with the natural world have not been considered. In particular, the source material reveals little of religious belief, the importance of beating the bounds at rogationtide, or aspects of peasant leisure, for example. These are not insignificant aspects of peasants' lives, and sources – both material and textual – associated with other English rural manors may allow more to be said on some of these themes. Additionally, since documentary records survive in greater quantity from the thirteenth century onward, there is necessarily a greater bias toward the second half of the period under review.

It has proven difficult, too to make more detailed assessments of peasants' knowledge of their local flora and fauna: much that was indisputably familiar either did not feature in the records or did so fleetingly. This undoubtedly means that what is presented here can be only a partial reconstruction of the mental world of the medieval peasant insofar as their relationship with the local environment was concerned. The study of mentalities has been generally concerned with the idea of collective attitudes, and scholars are frequently struck by the difference between elite and popular culture.[4] Again, it has been shown here that a narrative based on an overly simplistic binary opposition between lords and peasants is inappropriate. Collective mentalities were apparent; however, they were apparent within a number of different, fluid groups. We have witnessed freemen operating in apparent concert concerning

---

4   Although this approach has been criticised by some: P. Burke, 'Strengths and weaknesses of the history of mentalities', in S. Clark (ed.), *The Annales School: critical assessments*, vol. 2 (London, 1999), p. 447.

naming practices; groups of leading free and servile peasants acting as one; and, at Elton, the entire peasant community cooperatively disputing the legitimacy of the abbot's actions regarding a common droveway.[5]

Lords and their administrators should not be held to account for these problems and omissions: it was not the purpose of the records reviewed here to preserve the details of the worldview of their tenants. Arguably, the fault lies as much with scholars working in discrete disciplines who have generally failed to consider the local landscape holistically, although, as we have seen, this is now changing. Notwithstanding this, it is fervently hoped that the interdisciplinary approach adopted here will encourage others to follow suit and re-examine the surviving records of additional manors to uncover peasants' views of the rural environment. The analysis presented here focuses on three rural medieval communities; however, many of the conclusions drawn throughout have far wider implications – not just in continuing to develop ways in which we might better understand peasant perspectives on the rural landscape but also in how we might more fruitfully study rural settlements, landscapes and communities. In reuniting all of this illuminating material with its contemporary landscape setting, and seeking to reinterpret it in ways meaningful to the medieval peasant, we may come closer to understanding how the environment was seen by those living and working locally.

Despite the efforts of some to compartmentalise the peasant experience, this study shows that the landscape held myriad meanings for later medieval rural residents. In many respects, the servile peasant we encountered in the opening pages of this book – Richard, son of Richard in the Lane of Lakenheath – exemplifies many of the incongruities exposed within this study. He was derided by one of his neighbours in court as a 'neif' (chapter four, p. 88), and yet leased a greater expanse of demesne fishery than the earl of Gloucester. He was a habitual trespasser – using illegal paths to move through the Lakenheath landscape, and once caught taking a boat from his neighbour's land at *gopayneshithe*; and yet in 1329 he presented three of his neighbours to the manorial court for trespassing on part of his own holding, 'cutting and trampling reeds … [and] fishing' in his several waters without his consent.[6] Economically, he depended on both sheep husbandry and fishing, but also benefited from a small arable holding.[7] What is clear is that the late medieval rural landscape as revealed through the testimony of resident peasants cannot be tightly defined, but formed a series of interlocking places and ideologies – each having greater and lesser validity depending upon social and temporal factors, and the vacillating attitudes of the groups that created them.

---

5   *EMR*, pp. 94 and 98.

6   CUL EDC/7/16/2/1/8/15.

7   CUL EDC/7/16/2/1/6/25.

Bibliography

Manuscript sources

Arranged in alphabetical order by repository

Bedfordshire Archives and Records Service (BARS)

Russell Box 300

The British Library (BL)

Add MS 42130, The Luttrell Psalter
Cotton MS Nero C. vii
Cotton MS Vespasian E. xxii

Cambridge University Library (CUL)

(1) Account Rolls
EDC/7/16/1/1–14
(2) Court Rolls
EDC/7/16/2/1–14
(3) Cartularies
EDC/1/A/1/4 [Ely Priory]
EDR/G3/28/Liber M
MS Add. 3020, Red Book of Thorney
PDC/MS 1, The Book of Robert of Swaffham
PDC/MS 6, The Red Book of John of Achurch
(4) Miscellaneous
PDC/F/MS/55 [Rental]

Elton Hall Library

Wing, T. and Wing, J., *Elton field book or an accurate survey of the particulars of all the arable, ley and meadow-ground in the manor of Elton* (1747 and 1748)

The National Archives (TNA)

(1) Inquisitions *post mortem*
C 132/27/5
C 133/129/1
C 134/42

(2) Court Rolls
SC 2/203/94–95
(3) Ancient Deeds
E 40/1271
E 40/3286
E 40/5490
E 40/6856
E 40/7038
E 40/10857
(4) Lay Subsidies
E 179/155/31/42
E 179/180/12
(5) Coroner's Rolls
JUST 2/107
(6) Feet of Fines
CP 25/1/216/44
(7) Maps
MPC/1/6

Northamptonshire Record Office (NRO)

(1) Court Rolls
PDC CR Bundle A3
(2) Account Rolls
F(M) 2388 and 2389
F(M) Roll 233
(3) Ancient Deeds
F(M) Charters 1–577
(4) Maps
Map 1964
Map T 236
(5) Surveys
F(M) Misc. vol. 424
F(M) Tin Box 1, Castor and Ailsworth, Parcel No. 5
(6) Mellows Transcripts
M(T) 34

The Society of Antiquaries (Soc. Antiq.)

MS 38, *The Great Book of John of Achurch*
MS 60, *The Black Book of Peterborough*

Suffolk Record Office (Bury St Edmunds) (SRO(B))

HD/1720/1, *Terrier of Sir Simeon Styward's Property in Lakenheath* (1533)
HD/1720/3, *Field Survey* (1782 and 1793)

University of Nottingham Special Collections
Ancient Deeds
Ga 9239

Worcester Cathedral Library (WCL)
Court Rolls
E 15

Non-published editions of primary sources

Cadbury Research Library, Special Collections (University of Birmingham) (CRL)
MS 167, Lakenheath court roll translations

Published editions of primary sources

Baker, P.S. and Lapidge, M. (eds), *Byrhtferth's enchiridion* (Oxford, 1995).

Bracton on the laws and customs of England, S.E. Thorne (trans.), vol. 3 (London, 1977).

Brooke, C.N.L. and Postan. M.M. (eds), *Carte Nativorum: a Peterborough Abbey cartulary of the fourteenth century* (Oxford, 1960).

Calendar of the Patent Rolls, Edward III, Vol 6: A.D. 1343–1345 (London, 1902).

Cameron, M.L. and D'Aronco, M.A. (eds), *The Old English illustrated pharmacopoeia: British Library Cotton Vitellius C iii* (Copenhagen, 1998).

Cato, Marcus Porcius, *On agriculture*, and Varro, Marcus Terentius, *On agriculture*, W.D. Hooper (trans.) and H.B. Ash (ed.) (1934, London, 1999).

Chandler, H.W. (ed., trans.), *Five court rolls of Great Cressingham in the county of Norfolk* (London, 1885).

Cockayne, T.O., *Leechdoms, wort-cunning and starcraft of early England*, vol. 1 (London, 1961).

Cylkowski, D.G., 'A Middle English treatise on horticulture: Godfridus Super Palladium', in L.M. Matheson (ed.), *Popular and practical science of medieval England* (East Lansing, MI, 1994), pp. 301–29.

Farnham, W., 'The days of the mone', *Studies in Philology*, 20 (1923), pp. 70–82.

Farr, M.W., *Accounts and surveys of the Wiltshire lands of Adam de Stratton* (Devizes, 1959).

Field, R.K. (ed.), *Court rolls of Elmley Castle, Worcestershire, 1347–1564* (Worcester, 2004).

Forester, T. (trans.), *The chronicle of Henry of Huntingdon* (London, 1853).

Foulds, T. (ed.), *The Thurgarton cartulary* (Stamford, 1994).

Hart, W.H. and Lyons, P.A. (eds), *Cartularium Monasterii de Rameseia*, vol. I (London, 1884).

Hart, W.H. and Lyons, P.A. (eds), *Cartularium Monasterii de Rameseia*, vol. III (London, 1893).

Hassall, W. and Beauroy, J. (eds), *Lordship and landscape in Norfolk 1250–1350: the early records of Holkham* (Oxford, 1993).

Hervey, S.H.A., *Suffolk in 1327, being a subsidy return* (Woodbridge, 1906).

King, E. (ed.), *A Northamptonshire miscellany* (Northampton, 1983).

Lock, R., *The court rolls of Walsham le Willows 1303–50* (Woodbridge, 1998).

Massingberd, W.O. (ed., trans.), *Court rolls of the manor of Ingoldmells in the county of Lincoln* (London, 1902).

Mellows, C. (ed., trans.) and Mellows, W.T. (ed.), *The Peterborough chronicle of Hugh Candidus* (Peterborough, 1966).

Munday, J.T. (ed.), *A feudal aid roll for Suffolk 1302–3* (Lakenheath, 1973).

Oschinsky, D. (ed., trans.) *Walter of Henley and other treatises on estate management and accounting* (Oxford, 1971).

Page, M. (ed.), *The pipe roll of the bishopric of Winchester 1301–2* (Winchester, 1996).

Pettit, E. (ed., trans.), *Anglo-Saxon remedies, charms, and prayers from British Library MS Harley 585, the lacnunga*, vol. 1 (Lampeter, 2001).

Plutarch, *Moralia*, book 8, trans. P.A. Clement and H.B. Hoffleit (London, 1969).

Raban, S. (ed.), *The white book of Peterborough* (Northampton, 2001).

Raban, S. (ed., trans.), *The accounts of Godfrey of Crowland, abbot of Peterborough 1299–1321* (Northampton, 2011).

Richardson, H.G. and Sayles, G.O. (eds, trans), *Fleta*, vol. 2 (London, 1955).

Ross, B. (trans., ed.), *Accounts of the stewards of the Talbot household at Blakemere 1392–1425* (Keele, 2003).

Rotuli Hundredorum temp. Hen. III and Edw. I, vol. II (London, 1818).

Seymour, M.C. and Liegey, G.M. (eds), *On the properties of things: John Trevisa's translation of Bartholomaeus Anglicus de proprietatibus rerum*, vol. 2 (Oxford, 1975).

Sparke, J. (ed.), *Historiæ Anglicanæ Scriptores Varii, e Codicibus Manuscriptis Nunc Primum Editi*, 2 vols (London, 1723).

Stapleton, T. (ed.), *Chronicon Petroburgense* (London, 1869).

Stukeley, W., *The family memoirs of the Rev. William Stukeley, and the antiquarian and other correspondence of William Stukeley*, vol. 3 (London, 1887).

Swanton, M.J. (ed., trans.), *The Anglo-Saxon chronicle* (London, 1996).

Taavitsainen, I., 'A zodiacal lunary for medical professionals', in L.M. Matheson (ed.), *Popular and practical science of medieval England* (East Lansing, MI, 1994), pp. 283–300.

van Arsdall, A. (ed., trans.), *Medieval herbal remedies: the Old English herbarium and Anglo-Saxon medicine* (London, 2002).

Voigts, L.E., *A Latin technical phlebotomy and its Middle English translation* (Philadelphia, PA, 1984).

Walker, S.S. (ed., trans.), *The court rolls of the manor of Wakefield from October 1331 to September 1333* (Leeds, 1983).

William of Malmesbury, *Gesta pontificum anglorum*, vol. 1, M. Winterbottom and R.M. Thomson (eds, trans.) (Oxford, 2007).

Willis, D. (ed., trans.), *The estate book of Henry de Bray c.1289–1340* (London, 1916).

Willmoth, F., Oosthuizen, S. (eds) and Miller, E. (trans.), *The Ely coucher book, 1249–50. The bishop of Ely's manors in the Cambridgeshire fenland* (Cambridge, 2015).

Secondary sources

Adams, M., *Land north of Broom Road, Lakenheath, Suffolk* (Stowmarket, 2014).

Albarella, U., 'The wild boar', in T. O'Connor and N. Sykes (eds), *Extinctions and invasions: a social history of British fauna* (Oxford, 2010), pp. 59–67.

Alexander, J., '*Labeur* and *paresse*: ideological representations of medieval peasant labor', *The Art Bulletin*, 72/3 (1990), pp. 436–52.

Altenberg, K., *Experiencing landscapes: a study of space and identity in three marginal areas of medieval Britain and Scandinavia* (Stockholm, 2003).

Anderson, K.J., 'The idea of Chinatown: the power of place and institutional practice in the making of a racial category', *Annals of the Association of American Geographers*, 77/4 (1987), pp. 580–98.

Artis, E.T., *The Durobrivae of Antoninus* (London, 1828).

Ashwood, F., 'Lowland calcareous grassland: creation and management in land regeneration', *Best Practice Guidance for Land Regeneration*, 18 (2014), pp. 1–7.

Astill, G., 'Rural settlement: the toft and croft', in G. Astill and A. Grant (eds), *The countryside of medieval England* (1988, Oxford, 1994), pp. 36–61.

Aston, T.H. (ed.), *Landlords, peasants and politics in medieval England* (Cambridge, 2006).

Ault, W.O., 'Open-field husbandry and the village community: a study of agrarian by-laws in medieval England', *Transactions of the American Philosophical Society*, 55/7 (1965), pp. 5–102.

Ault, W.O., *Open-field farming in medieval England: a study of village by-laws* (London, 1972).

Bailey, M., *A marginal economy? East Anglian Breckland in the later middle ages* (Cambridge, 1989).

Bailey, M., 'The prior and convent of Ely and their management of the manor of Lakenheath in the fourteenth century', in M.J. Franklin and C. Harper-Bill (eds), *Medieval ecclesiastical studies in honour of Dorothy M. Owen* (Woodbridge, 1995), pp. 1–19.

Bailey, M., *The English manor c.1200–c.1500* (Manchester, 2002).

Bailey, M., 'The form, function and evolution of irregular field systems in Suffolk, *c.* 1300 to *c.* 1550', *Agricultural History Review*, 57/1 (2007), pp. 15–36.

Bailey, M., *Medieval Suffolk, an economic and social history, 1200–1500* (2007, Woodbridge, 2010).

Bak, J.M., Gurevich, A.J. and Hollingsworth, P.A., *Medieval popular culture: problems of belief and perception* (Cambridge, 1988).

Baker, J. and Brookes, S., 'Gateways, gates and gatu: liminal spaces at the centre of things', in S. Semple, C. Orsini and S. Mui (eds), *Life on the edge: social, religious and political frontiers in early medieval Europe* (Wendeburg, 2017), pp. 253–62.

Banham, D. and Faith, R., *Anglo-Saxon farms and farming* (Oxford, 2014).

Basso, K.H., '"Stalking with stories": names, places and moral narratives among the Western Apache', in E.M. Bruner (ed.), *Text, play, and story: the construction and reconstruction of self and society* (Prospect Heights, ILL, 1984), pp. 19–55.

Bennett, H.S., *Life on the English manor: a study of peasant conditions 1150–1400* (Cambridge, 1956).

Biddick, K., *The other economy: pastoral husbandry on a medieval estate* (London, 1989).

Blackburn, D., 'Foxholes, Pendle and Ryelands', *Journal of the English Place-Name Society*, 41 (2009), pp. 127–9.

Blair, J., *Anglo-Saxon Oxfordshire* (Stroud, 1994).

Blair, J., *Building Anglo-Saxon England* (Princeton, NJ, 2018).

Bosworth, J., *An Anglo-Saxon dictionary online*, T.N. Toller (ed.), S. Christ and O. Tichý (comps), <http://www.bosworthtoller.com/023899>, accessed 13 August 2019.

Bourne, J., *The place-name Kingston and royal power in middle Anglo-Saxon England: patterns, possibilities and purpose* (Oxford, 2017).

Bramwell, E.S. 'Names in the United Kingdom', as part of E.D. Lawson, 'Personal naming systems', in C. Hough (ed.) with D. Izdebska, *The Oxford handbook of names and naming* (Oxford, 2018), pp. 186–8.

Bramwell, E.S. 'Personal names and anthropology', in C. Hough (ed.) with D. Izdebska, *The Oxford handbook of names and naming* (Oxford, 2018), pp. 263–78.

Braswell, L., 'The moon and medicine in Chaucer's time', *Studies in the Age of Chaucer*, 8 (1986), pp. 145–56.

Bridges, J., *The history and antiquities of Northamptonshire*, vol. 2 (Oxford, 1791).

Briggs, C., 'The availability of credit in the English countryside, 1400–1480', *Agricultural History Review*, 56/1 (2008), pp. 1–24.

Britnell, R.H., 'Minor landlords in England and medieval agrarian capitalism', *Past and Present*, 89 (1980), pp. 3–22.

Britton, E., *The community of the vill: a study in the history of the family and village life in fourteenth-century England* (Toronto, 1977).

Burke, P., 'Strengths and weaknesses of the history of mentalities', in S. Clark (ed.), *The Annales School: critical assessments*, vol. 2 (London, 1999), pp. 442–56.

Buttimer, A., 'Social space and the planning of residential areas', in A. Buttimer and D. Seamon (eds), *The human experience of space and place* (London, 1980), pp. 21–54.

Cameron, M.L., *Anglo-Saxon medicine* (Cambridge, 2006).

Camille, M., *Image on the edge: the margins of medieval art* (London, 1992).

Camille, M., *Mirror in parchment. The Luttrell Psalter and the making of medieval England* (London, 1998).

Campbell, B.M.S., *English seigniorial agriculture 1250–1450* (Cambridge, 2000).

Campbell, B.M.S. and Bartley, K., *England on the eve of the Black Death: an atlas of lay lordship, land and wealth, 1300–49* (Manchester, 2006).

Campbell, J., 'Understanding the relationship between manor house and settlement in medieval England', in J. Klápště (ed.), *Hierarchies in rural settlements*, Ruralia, 9 (Turnhout, 2013), pp. 274–84.

Campbell, J., 'A house is not just a home. Means of display in English medieval gentry buildings', in M.S. Kristiansen and K. Giles (eds), *Dwellings, identities and homes. European housing culture from the Viking Age to the Renaissance* (Hojbjerg, 2014), pp. 175–84.

Carlsson, S., *Studies on Middle English local bynames in East Anglia* (Lund, 1989).

Carlyle, S., *Archaeological recording and evaluation in the Old Estate Yard, Over End, Elton, Cambridgeshire* (Northampton, 2006).

Carroll, J., 'Identifying migrants in medieval England: the possibilities and limitations of place-name evidence', in J. Story, W.M. Ormrod and E.M. Tyler (eds), *Migrants in medieval England, c. 500–1500* (forthcoming).

Caruth, J. and Anderson, S., 'RAF Lakenheath Saxon cemetery', *Current Archaeology*, 163 (1999), pp. 244–50.

Catlin, K.A., 'Re-examining medieval settlement in the Dartmoor landscape', *Medieval Settlement Research*, 31 (2016), pp. 36–45.

Cavill, P., *A new dictionary of English field-names*, with an introduction by R. Gregory (Nottingham, 2018).

Chetwood, J., 'Re-evaluating English personal naming on the eve of the Conquest', *Early Medieval Europe*, 26/4 (2018), pp. 518–47.

Chisholm, M., 'The medieval network of navigable Fenland waterways II: Barnack stone transport', *Proceedings of the Cambridge Antiquarian Society*, 100 (2011), pp. 171–83.

Clark, A.G., *A village on the Nene*, vol. 1 (Stamford, 2007).

Clark, C., 'Onomastics', in N. Blake (ed.), *The Cambridge history of the English language, vol. 2: 1066–1476* (Cambridge, 1992), pp. 542–606.

Clark, C., 'Battle *c.* 1110: an anthroponymist looks at an Anglo-Norman new town', in p. Jackson (ed.), *Words, names and history: selected writings of Cecily Clark* (Cambridge, 1995), pp. 221–40.

Clark, C., 'People and languages in post-Conquest Canterbury', in p. Jackson (ed.), *Words, names and history: selected writings of Cecily Clark* (Cambridge, 1995), pp. 179–206.

Clark, C., 'Socio-economic status and individual identity', in D. Postles (ed.), *Naming, society and regional identity: papers presented at a symposium jointly arranged by the Marc Fitch Fund and the Department of English Local History, University of Leicester* (Oxford, 2002), pp. 99–122.

Clarke, C.A.M., *Literary landscapes and the idea of England, 700–1400* (Cambridge, 2006).

Coates, R., 'Place-names and linguistics', in J. Carroll and D.N. Parsons (eds), *Perceptions of place: twenty-first century interpretations of English place-name studies* (Nottingham, 2013), pp. 129–60.

Cole, A., 'The place-name evidence for water transport in early medieval England', in J. Blair (ed.), *Waterways and canal-building in medieval England* (Oxford, 2007), pp. 55–84.

Collins, C., *Archaeological test pit excavations in Castor, Cambridgeshire, in 2009, 2010 and 2011* (Cambridge, 2018).

Cosgrove, D. and Jackson, P., 'New directions in cultural geography', *Area*, 19/2 (1987), pp. 95–101.

Coss, P., *The origins of the English gentry* (Cambridge, 2003).

Cox, B., 'The place-names of the earliest English records', *Journal of the English Place-Name Society*, 8 (1976), pp. 12–66.

Cox, B., *The place-names of Rutland* (Nottingham, 1994).

Cragoe, C.D., 'The custom of the English church: parish church maintenance in England before 1300', *Journal of Medieval History*, 36 (2010), pp. 20–38.

Cranfield University, Soil and Agrifood Institute, Soilscapes, <http://www.landis.org.uk/soilscapes/>, accessed 13 August 2019.

Creighton, O.H., *Designs upon the land: elite landscapes of the middle ages* (Woodbridge, 2013).

Creighton, O. and Barry, T., 'Seigneurial and elite sites in the medieval landscape', in N. Christie and P. Stamper (eds), *Medieval rural settlement. Britain and Ireland, AD 800–1600* (Oxford, 2012), pp. 63–80.

Creighton, O. and Rippon, S., 'Conquest, colonisation and the countryside: archaeology and the mid-11th- to mid-12th-century rural landscape', in D.M. Hadley and C. Dyer (eds), *The archaeology of the 11th century: continuities and transformations* (London, 2017), pp. 57–87.

Corpus of Romanesque Sculpture of Britain and Ireland, <https://crsbi.ac.uk/>, accessed 13 August 2019.

Cubitt, G., *History and memory* (Manchester, 2007).

Culpeper, N., *The English physician enlarged* (London, 1698).

Cunnington, W.E., 'The field-names of Kingsbury (Middlesex)', *Journal of the English Place-Name Society*, 32 (2000), pp. 41–6.

Curth, L., *The care of brute beasts: a social and cultural study of veterinary medicine in early modern England* (Boston, MA, 2010).

Dallas, C.G., 'The nunnery of St Kyneburgha at Castor', *Durobrivae*, 1 (1973), p. 17.

Daniels, H. and Lagrange, C., 'An analysis of Romsey field-names', *Journal of the English Place-Name Society*, 34 (2002), pp. 29–58.

Davenport, F.G., *The economic development of a Norfolk manor, 1086–1565* (Cambridge, 1906).

Davidson, H.R.E., *Myths and symbols in pagan Europe: early Scandinavian and Celtic religions* (Manchester, 1988).

den Hartog, E., 'All nature speaks of God, all nature teaches man: the iconography of the twelfth-century capitals in the westwork gallery of the church of St Servatius in Maastricht', *Zeitschrift für kunstgeschichte*, 59 (1996), pp. 29–62.

DeWindt, E.B., *Land and people in Holywell-cum-Needingworth* (Toronto, 1972).

Dodds, B., *Peasants and production in the medieval north-east. The evidence from tithes, 1270–1536* (Woodbridge, 2007).

Dodds, B., 'Demesne and tithe: peasant agriculture in the late middle ages', *Agricultural History Review*, 56/2 (2008), pp. 123–41.

Dodgshon, R.A., *The European past: social evolution and spatial order* (Basingstoke, 1987).

Duncan, J. and Duncan, N., '(Re)reading the landscape', *Environment and Planning D: Society and Space*, 6 (1988), pp. 117–26.

Dyer, C., 'Documentary evidence: problems and enquiries', in G. Astill and A. Grant (eds), *The countryside of medieval England* (Oxford, 1994), pp. 12–35.

Dyer, C., 'Memories of freedom: attitudes towards serfdom in England, 1200–1350', in M.L. Bush (ed.), *Serfdom and slavery: studies in legal bondage* (London, 1996), pp. 277–95.

Dyer, C., *Standards of living in the middle ages: social change in England c.1200–1520* (1989, Cambridge, 1998).

Dyer, C., *Everyday life in medieval England* (1994, London, 2000).

Dyer, C., *Making a living in the middle ages: the people of Britain 850–1520* (London, 2003).

Dyer, C., 'The ineffectiveness of lordship in England, 1200–1400', in C. Dyer, p. Coss and C. Wickham (eds), *Rodney Hilton's middle ages: an exploration of historical themes* (Past and Present Supplement, 2) (Oxford, 2007), pp. 69–86.

Dyer, C., 'Perceptions of medieval landscape and settlement', *Medieval Settlement Research Group Annual Report*, 22 (2007), pp. 6–31.

Dyer, C., 'Building in earth in late-medieval England', *Vernacular Architecture*, 39 (2008), pp. 63–70.

Dyer, C., 'Living in peasant houses in late medieval England', *Vernacular Architecture*, 44 (2013), pp. 19–27.

Dyer, C., 'The material world of English peasants, 1200–1540: archaeological perspectives on rural economy and welfare', *Agricultural History Review*, 62/1 (2014), pp. 1–22.

Dyer, C., 'Peasant farming in late medieval England: evidence from the tithe estimations by Worcester Cathedral Priory', in M. Kowaleski, J. Langdon and P.R. Schofield (eds), *Peasants and lords in the medieval English economy. Essays in honour of Bruce M.S. Campbell* (Turnhout, 2015), pp. 83–112.

Dyer, C., 'The Midland economy and society, 1314–1348: insights from changes in the landscape', *Midland History*, 42/1 (2017), pp. 36–57.

Dyer, C., 'Households great and small. Aristocratic styles of life across the social spectrum in England, 1200–1500', in C.M. Woolgar (ed.), *The elite household in England, 1100–1550* (Donington, 2018), pp. 5–28.

Ekwall, E., *The concise dictionary of English place-names* (Oxford, 1960).

Espenak, F., Moon Phases Table, <http://astropixels.com/ephemeris/phasescat/phasescat.html>, accessed 13 August 2019.

Evans, S., *The medieval estate of the cathedral priory of Ely: a preliminary survey* (Ely, 1973).

Faith, R., 'Tidenham, Gloucestershire, and the history of the manor in England', *Landscape History*, 16 (1994), pp. 39–51.

Faith, R., *The English peasantry and the growth of lordship* (London, 1997).

Farley, M., 'Middle Saxon occupation at Chicheley, Buckinghamshire', *Records of Buckinghamshire*, 22 (1980), pp. 92–104.

Feld, S., 'Waterfalls of song: an acoustemology of place resounding in Bosavi, Papua New Guinea', in K.H. Basso and S. Feld (eds), *Senses of place* (Santa Fe, NM, 1996), pp. 91–135.

Fellows-Jensen, G., 'Grimston and Grimsby: the Danes as re-namers', in R. Jones and S. Semple (eds), *Sense of place in Anglo-Saxon England* (Donington, 2012), pp. 352–63.

Fentress, J. and Wickham, C., *Social memory* (1992, Oxford, 1994).

Field, J. *English field-names: a dictionary* (Newton Abbot, 1972).

Field, J., *A history of English field-names* (London, 1993).

Field, R.K., 'Worcestershire peasant buildings, household goods and farming equipment in the later Middle Ages', *Medieval Archaeology*, 9 (1965), pp. 105–45.

Forward, E., 'Place-names of the Whittlewood area', PhD thesis (University of Nottingham, 2007).

Fox, H.S.A., 'Approaches to the adoption of the Midland system', in T. Rowley (ed.), *The origins of open-field agriculture* (London, 1981), pp. 64–111.

Fox, H.S.A., 'Exploitation of the landless by lords and tenants in early medieval England', in Z. Razi and R. Smith (eds), *Medieval society and the manor court* (Oxford, 1996), pp. 518–68.

Fox, H.S.A., *The evolution of the fishing village: landscape and society along the south Devon coast,*

1086–1550 (2001, Oxford, 2004).

Fradley, M., 'Warrenhall and other moated sites in north-east Shropshire', *Medieval Settlement Research*, 20 (2005), pp. 17–18.

Freedman, P., *Images of the medieval peasant* (Stanford, 1999).

French, K.L., *The people of the parish: community life in a late medieval English diocese* (Philadelphia, PA, 2001).

Friedman, J.B., *The monstrous races in art and thought* (London, 1981).

Friedman, J.B., 'Harry the Haywarde and Talbat his dog: an illustrated girdlebook from Worcestershire', in C. Fisher and K.L. Scott (eds), *Art into life: collected papers from the Kresge Art Museum medieval symposia* (East Lansing, MI, 1995), pp. 115–54.

Gammeltoft, P., 'In search of the motives behind naming: a discussion of a name-semantic model of categorisation', in E. Brylla and M. Wahlberg (eds), *Proceedings of the 21st International Congress of Onomastic Sciences* (Uppsala, 2005), pp. 151–60.

Gardiner, M., 'Vernacular buildings and the development of the later medieval domestic plan in England', *Medieval Archaeology*, 44 (2000), pp. 159–79.

Gardiner, M., 'Hythes, small ports, and other landing places in later medieval England', in J. Blair (ed.), *Waterways and canal-building in late medieval England* (Oxford, 2007), pp. 85–110.

Gardiner, M., 'The origins and persistence of manor houses in England', in M. Gardiner and S. Rippon (eds), *Medieval landscapes* (Macclesfield, 2007), pp. 170–82.

Gardiner, M., 'Oral tradition, landscape and the social life of place-names', in R. Jones and S. Semple (eds), *Sense of place in Anglo-Saxon England* (Donington, 2011), pp. 16–30.

Gardiner, M., 'Manorial farmsteads and the expression of lordship before and after the Norman Conquest', in D.M. Hadley and C. Dyer (eds), *The archaeology of the 11th century: continuities and transformations* (London, 2017), pp. 88–103

Gardiner, M. and Kilby, S., 'Perceptions of medieval settlement', in C.M. Gerrard and A. Gutiérrez (eds), *The Oxford handbook of later medieval archaeology in Britain* (Oxford, 2018), pp. 210–25.

Gelling, M., *Signposts to the past: place-names and the history of England* (London, 1978).

Gelling, M., *Place-names in the landscape: the geographical roots of England's place-names* (London, 1993).

Gelling, M. and Cole, A., *The landscape of place-names* (Stamford, 2000).

Gilchrist, R., *Medieval life: archaeology and the life course* (Woodbridge, 2012).

Giles, K., 'Seeing and believing: visuality and space in pre-modern England', *World Archaeology*, 39/1 (2007), pp. 105–21.

Gregory, R., 'Some Nottinghamshire dead men', *Nomina*, 38 (2014), pp. 85–92.

Gregory, R., 'Minor and field-names of Thurgarton Wapentake, Nottinghamshire', PhD thesis (University of Nottingham, 2016).

Grieg, J., 'Plant resources', in G. Astill and A. Grant (eds), *The countryside of medieval England* (1988, Oxford, 1994), pp. 108–27.

Grigson, G., *The Englishman's flora* (London, 1958).

Gurevich, A.J., 'Medieval culture and mentality according to the New French historiography', in S. Clark (ed.), *The Annales School: critical assessments*, vol. 2 (London, 1999), pp. 197–225.

Hall, A., *Elves in Anglo-Saxon England* (Woodbridge, 2009).

Hall, D., 'The late Anglo-Saxon countryside: villages and their fields', in D. Hooke (ed.), *Anglo-Saxon settlements* (Oxford, 1988), pp. 99–122.

Hall, D., *The open fields of Northamptonshire* (Northampton, 1995).

Hallam, H.E., 'Drainage techniques', in H.E. Hallam (ed.), *The agrarian history of England and Wales, vol. 2, 1042–1350* (Cambridge, 1988), pp. 497–507.

Hamerow, H., *Excavations at Mucking, volume 2: the Anglo-Saxon settlement* (London, 1996).

Hamerow, H., *Early medieval settlements: the archaeology of rural communities in northwest Europe, 400–900* (Oxford, 2002).

Hanks, p. and Parkin, H., 'Family names', in C. Hough (ed.) with D. Izdebska, *The Oxford handbook of names and naming* (Oxford, 2018), pp. 214–36

Hanks, P., Coates, R. and McClure, P., 'Saladine', *The Oxford dictionary of family names in Britain and Ireland* (Oxford, 2016), <http://www.oxfordreference.com/view/10.1093/acref/9780199677764.0001/acref-9780199677764-e-35524>, accessed June 2017.

Hart, C., *Learning and culture in late Anglo-Saxon England and the influence of Ramsey Abbey on the major English monastic schools: a survey of the development of mathematical, medical and scientific studies in England before the Norman Conquest*, vol. 2, book 2 (Lampeter, 2003).

Harte, J., 'Hell on earth: encountering devils in the medieval landscape', in B. Bildhauer and R. Mills (eds), *The monstrous middle ages* (Toronto, 2003), pp. 177–95.

Harvey, B.F. (ed.), *Documents illustrating the rule of Walter de Wenlok, abbot of Westminster, 1283–1307* (London, 1965).

Harvey, B., 'Islip', in M.D. Lobel (ed.), *VCH Oxfordshire*, vol. 6 (London, 1959), pp. 205–18.

Harvey, B.F., *Westminster Abbey and its estates in the middle ages* (Oxford, 1977).

Harvey, P.D.A., *A medieval Oxfordshire village: Cuxham, 1240 to 1400* (Oxford, 1965).

Hatcher, J., 'English serfdom and villeinage: towards a reassessment', *Past and Present*, 90 (1981), pp. 3–39.

Henisch, B.A., 'In due season: farm work in the medieval calendar tradition', in D. Sweeney (ed.), *Agriculture in the middle ages: technology, practice, and representation* (Philadelphia, PA, 1995), pp. 309–36.

Hesse, M., 'Medieval field systems and land tenure in South Creake, Norfolk', *Norfolk Archaeology*, 43 (1998), pp. 79–97.

Hill, O.G., *The manor, the plowman, and the shepherd: agrarian themes and imagery in late medieval and early Renaissance English literature* (London, 1993).

Hilton, R.H., *The English peasantry in the later middle ages* (Oxford, 1975).

Hilton, R.H., 'Freedom and villeinage in England', in R.H. Hilton (ed.), *Peasants, knights and heretics: studies in medieval English social history* (Cambridge, 1976), pp. 174–91.

Hilton, R.H., *Class conflict and the crisis of feudalism: essays in medieval social history* (1985, London, 1990).

Holland, R. and Britten, J. (eds), *A dictionary of English plant-names* (London, 1886).

Homans, G.C., *English villagers of the thirteenth century* (1941, New York, 1970).

Hooke, D., *Anglo-Saxon landscapes of the West Midlands* (Oxford, 1981).

Hooke, D., 'Pre-Conquest woodland: its distribution and usage', *Agricultural History Review*, 37/2 (1989), pp. 113–29.

Hooke, D., *The landscape of Anglo-Saxon England* (London, 1998).

Hooke, D., 'Place-name hierarchies and interpretations in parts of Mercia', in R. Jones and S. Semple (eds), *Sense of place in Anglo-Saxon England* (Donington, 2012), pp. 180–95.

Hunter, A., *Georgical essays*, vol. 3 (York, 1773).

Hurst, J.G., 'Rural building in England and Wales', in H.E. Hallam (ed.) *The agrarian history of England and Wales, vol. 2, 1042–1350* (Cambridge, 1988), pp. 854–930.

Hyams, P.R., *King, lords and peasants in medieval England: the common law of villeinage in the twelfth and thirteenth centuries* (Oxford, 1980).

Jamison, C., 'Elton', in Page, W., Proby, G. and Inskip-Ladds, S., *VCH Huntingdonshire*, vol. 3 (London, 1932).

Jett, S.C., 'Place-naming, environment, and perception among the Canyon De Chelly Navajo of Arizona', *The Professional Geographer*, 49/4 (1997), pp. 481–93.

John Samuels Archaeological Consultants, *Proposed development at Duck Street, Elton, Cambridgeshire* (Newark, 1995).

Johnson, L.M., '"A place that's good", Gitksan landscape perception and ethnoecology', *Human Ecology*, 28/2 (2000), pp. 301–25.

Johnson, M., *Ideas of landscape* (Oxford, 2007).

Johnson, M., *English houses 1300–1800: vernacular architecture, social life* (Harlow, 2010).

Johnson, M., 'Phenomenological approaches in landscape archaeology', *Annual Review of Anthropology*, 41 (2012), pp. 269–84.

Jolly, K.L., 'Magic, miracle, and popular practice in the early medieval west: Anglo-Saxon England', in E.S. Frerichs, P.V.M. Flesher and J. Neusner (eds), *Religion, science, and magic in concert and in conflict* (Oxford, 1989), pp. 166–82.

Jones, R., 'Manure and the medieval social order', in M.J. Allen, N. Sharples and T. O'Connor (eds), *Land and people: papers in memory of John G. Evans* (Oxford, 2009), pp. 215–25.

Jones, R., 'Directional names in the early medieval landscape', in R. Jones and S. Semple (eds), *Sense of place in Anglo-Saxon England* (Donington, 2011), pp. 196–210.

Jones, R., 'Elemental theory in everyday practice: food disposal in the later medieval English countryside', in J. Klápště and p. Sommer (eds), *Food in the medieval rural environment: processing, storage, distribution of food*, Ruralia, 8 (2011), pp. 57–75.

Jones, R., 'Thinking through the manorial affix', in S. Turner and B. Silvester (eds), *Life in medieval landscapes: people and places in the middle ages, papers in memory of H.S.A. Fox* (Oxford, 2012), pp. 251–67.

Jones, R., 'Understanding medieval manure', in R. Jones (ed.), *Manure matters: historical, archaeological and ethnographic perspectives* (Farnham, 2012), pp. 145–58.

Jones, R., 'Responding to modern flooding: Old English place-names as a repository of traditional ecological knowledge', *Journal of Ecological Anthropology*, 18/1 (2016), <http://dx.doi.org/10.5038/2162–4593.18.1.9>, accessed 13 August 2019.

Jones, R. and Kilby, S., 'Mitigating riverine flood risk in medieval England', in C. Gerrard, p. Brown and p. Forlin (eds), *Waiting for the end of the world. Archaeological perspectives on natural disasters in medieval Europe* (forthcoming).

Jones, R. and Page, M., *Medieval villages in an English landscape: beginnings and ends* (Macclesfield, 2006).

Jones, R. and Semple, S. (eds), *Sense of place in Anglo-Saxon England* (Donington, 2012).

Jones, R., Gregory, R., Kilby, S. and Pears, B., 'Living with a trespasser: riparian names and medieval settlement on the River Trent floodplain', *European Journal of Post-Classical Archaeologies*, 7 (2017), pp. 33–64.

Kane, B.C., *Popular memory and gender in medieval England. Men, women and testimony in the church courts, c. 1200–1500* (Woodbridge, 2019).

Kershaw, I., 'The Great Famine and agrarian crisis in England, 1315–1322', *Past and Present*, 59 (1973), pp. 3–50.

Key to English Place-Names <http://kepn.nottingham.ac.uk/>, accessed 13 August 2019.

Kilby, S., 'A different world? Reconstructing the peasant environment in medieval Elton', unpubl. MA dissertation (University of Leicester, 2010a).

Kilby, S., 'A different world? Reconstructing the peasant environment in medieval Elton', *Medieval Settlement Research*, 25 (2010b), pp. 72–7.

Kilby, S., 'Encountering the environment: rural communities in England, 1086–1348', PhD thesis (University of Leicester, 2013).

Kilby, S., 'The late medieval landscape of Castor and Ailsworth', *The Five Parishes Journal*, 2 (2014), pp. 23–39.

Kilby, S., 'Mapping peasant discontent: trespassing on manorial land in fourteenth-century Walsham-le-Willows', *Landscape History*, 36/2 (2015), pp. 69–88.

Kilby, S., 'Divining medieval water: the field-names of Flintham in Nottinghamshire', *Journal of the English Place-Name Society*, 49 (2017), pp. 57–93.

Kilby, S., 'Fantastic beasts and where to find them: the Romanesque capitals of St Kyneburgha's church, Castor, and the local landscape', *Church Archaeology*, 19 (2019), pp. 53–72.

King, E., 'The Peterborough "*Descriptio Militum*" (Henry I)', *English Historical Review*, 84/330 (1969), pp. 84–101.

King, E., *Peterborough Abbey 1086–1310, a study in the land market* (Cambridge, 1973).

Kleinschmidt, H., *Understanding the middle ages: the transformation of ideas and attitudes in the medieval world* (Woodbridge, 2000).

Klingender, F., *Animals in art and thought to the end of the middle ages* (London, 1971).

Kosminsky, E.A., *Studies in the agrarian history of England in the thirteenth century* (Oxford, 1956).

Küchler, S., 'Landscape as memory: the mapping of process and its representation in a Melanesian society', in B. Bender (ed.), *Landscape politics and perspectives* (Oxford, 1993), pp. 85–106.

Lathbury, R.H., *The history of Denham* (Uxbridge, 1904).

Le Roy Ladurie, E., *Montaillou: Cathars and Catholics in a French village, 1294–1324*, trans. B. Bray (1978; London, 1990).

Lefebvre, H., *The production of space*, trans. D. Nicholson-Smith (1974; Oxford, 1991).

Liddiard, R., 'The deer parks of Domesday Book', *Landscapes*, 4/1 (2003), pp. 4–23.

Liddiard, R., *Castles in context: power, symbolism and landscape, 1066–1500* (Macclesfield, 2005).

Lumley-Prior, A., 'The importance of being Ailsworth: its place in the Castor multiple estate', *The Five Parishes Journal*, 2 (2014), pp. 13–21.

MacAulay, D., 'De tha ann an ainm…?', in F. MacLeod (ed.), *Togail tir, marking time: the map of the Western Isles* (Stornoway, 1989), pp. 89–95.

McClure, P., 'The interpretation of Middle English nicknames', *Nomina*, 5 (1981), pp. 95–104.

McDonagh, B., '"Powerhouses" of the Wolds landscape: manor houses and churches in late medieval and early modern England', in M. Gardiner and S. Rippon (eds), *Medieval landscapes* (Macclesfield, 2007), pp. 185–200.

McKinley, R., *Norfolk and Suffolk surnames in the middle ages* (London, 1975).

McKinley, R., *The surnames of Oxfordshire* (Oxford, 1977).

Mackreth, D., 'Potter's oven, Castor', *Durobrivae*, 1 (1973), pp. 14–16.

Mackreth, D.F., 'The abbot of Ramsey's manor, Elton, Huntingdonshire', *Northamptonshire Archaeology*, 26 (1995), pp. 123–40.

McSparran, F. (ed.), *Middle English Dictionary* (University of Michigan, 2013), <https://quod.lib.umich.edu/m/middle-english-dictionary>, accessed 24 September 2019.

Mâle, E., *The gothic image: religious art in France of the thirteenth century*, trans. D. Nussey (London, 1972).

Mandal, U.K., Rao, K.V, Mishra, P.K, Vittal, K.P.R., Sharma, K.L, Narsimlu, B. and Venkanna, K., 'Soil infiltration, runoff and sediment yield from a shallow soil with varied stone cover and intensity of rain', *European Journal of Soil Science*, 56 (2005), pp. 435–43.

Manning, C.R., *Mettingham Castle and College* (1861).

Margary, I.D., *Roman roads in Britain* (London, 1973).

Markham, G. (ed.), *La maison rustique or the countrey farme* (1616).

Martin, E., 'Medieval moats in Suffolk', *Medieval Settlement Research*, 4 (1989), p. 14.

Mawer, A., 'The study of field-names in relation to place-names', in J.G. Edwards, V.H. Galbraith and E.F. Jacob (eds), *Historical essays in honour of James Tait* (Manchester, 1933), pp. 189–200.

Mawer, A. and Stenton, F.M., *The place-names of Bedfordshire and Huntingdonshire* (Cambridge, 1926).

Mileson, S., *Parks in medieval England* (Oxford, 2009).

Mileson, S., 'The South Oxfordshire project: perceptions of landscape, settlement and society, *c*.500–1650', *Landscape History*, 33/2 (2012), pp. 83–98.

Mileson, S., 'Beyond the dots: mapping meaning in the later medieval landscape', in M. Hicks (ed.), *The later medieval inquisitions post mortem: mapping the medieval countryside and rural society* (Woodbridge, 2016), pp. 84–99.

Mileson, S., 'Openness and closure in the later medieval village', *Past and Present*, 234 (2017), pp. 3–37.

Miller, E., and Hatcher, J., *Medieval England: rural society and economic change 1086–1348* (1978, London, 1980).

Morphy, H., 'Landscape and the reproduction of the ancestral past', in E. Hirsch and M. O'Hanlon (eds), *The anthropology of landscape: perspectives on place and space* (1995, Oxford, 1997).

Morris, A., 'The Anglian period: the royal ladies of Castor', in *Five parishes: their people and places* (Castor, 2004), pp. 45–56.

Morris, B., 'Old English place-names – new approaches', in R. Jones and S. Semple (eds), *Sense of place in Anglo-Saxon England* (Donington, 2011), pp. 47–60.

Morton, J., *The natural history of Northamptonshire* (London, 1712).

Müller, M., 'Peasant mentalities and cultures in two contrasting communities in the fourteenth century; Brandon in Suffolk and Badbury in Wiltshire', PhD thesis (University of Birmingham, 2001).

Munday, J.T., *Eriswell-cum-Coclesworth: chronicle of Eriswell, part one – until 1340* (Brandon, 1969).

Munday, J.T., *Crane's croft* (Lakenheath, 1970).

Munday, J.T., *Field and furlong* (Lakenheath, 1972).

Murray, J., *Handbook for travellers in Northamptonshire and Rutland* (London, 1878).

Myrdal, J. and Sapoznik, A., 'Technology, labour, and productivity potential in peasant agriculture: England, *c*. 1000 to 1348', *Agricultural History Review*, 65/2 (2017), pp. 194–212.

Neilson, H., 'Early English woodland and waste', *Journal of Economic History*, 2/1 (1942), pp. 54–62.

Noble, C., Moreton, C. and Rutledge, p. (eds, trans), *Farming and gardening in late medieval Norfolk* (Norwich, 1996).

Novák, V., Kňava, K. and Šimůnek, J., 'Determining the influence of stones on hydraulic conductivity of saturated soils using numerical method', *Geoderma*, 161 (2011), pp. 177–81.

Olson, S., *A mute gospel: the people and culture of the medieval English common fields* (Toronto, 2009).

Padel, O., 'Brittonic place-names in England', in J. Carroll and D.N. Parsons (eds), *Perceptions of place: twenty-first century interpretations of English place-name studies* (Nottingham, 2013), pp. 1–42.

Page, M., 'The technology of medieval sheep farming: some evidence from Crawley, Hampshire, 1208–1349', *Agricultural History Review*, 51/2 (2003), pp. 137–54.

Parsons, D.N. 'Churls and athelings, kings and reeves: some reflections on place-names and early English society', in J. Carroll and D.N. Parsons (eds), *Perceptions of place: twenty-first century interpretations of English place-name studies* (Nottingham, 2013), pp. 43–74.

Parsons, D. and Styles, T. (eds) with Hough, C., *The vocabulary of English place-names (Á-Box)* (Nottingham, 1997).

Parsons, D.N. and Styles, T. (eds), *The vocabulary of English place-names (Brace-Cæster)* (Nottingham, 2000).

Peterborough New Town: a survey of the antiquities in the areas of development (London, 1969).

Peterborough to Lutton 1050mm gas pipeline: archaeological evaluation, excavation and watching brief, 1998, vol 1: report (1998).

Platt, C., 'The homestead moat: security or status?' *Archaeological Journal*, 167 (2010), pp. 115–33.

Pluskowski, A., 'Constructing exotic animals and environments in late medieval Britain', in S. Page (ed.), *The unorthodox imagination in late medieval Britain* (Manchester, 2010), pp. 193–217.

Postles, D., *The surnames of Leicestershire and Rutland* (Oxford, 1998).

Postles, D., *Naming the people of England, c. 1100–1350* (Newcastle, 2006).

Postles, D., *The north through its names: phenomenology of medieval and early modern northern England* (Oxford, 2007).

Powell, D.L., 'Pyrford', in H.E. Malden (ed.), *VCH Surrey*, vol. 3 (London, 1911), pp. 431–7.

Pretty, J., 'Sustainable agriculture in the Middle Ages: the English manor', *Agricultural History Review*, 38/1 (1990), pp. 1–19.

Pugh, R.B., 'Thorney', in R.B. Pugh (ed.), *VCH Cambridgeshire*, vol. 4 (London, 1967).

Rawcliffe, C., *Medicine and society in later medieval England* (1995, Stroud, 1997).

Razi, Z., 'The Toronto school's reconstitution of medieval peasant society: a critical view', *Past and Present*, 85 (1979), pp. 141–7.

Razi, Z., 'Serfdom and freedom in medieval England: a reply to the revisionists', *Past and Present* (2007), Supplement 2, pp. 182–57.

Reaney, P.H. and Wilson, R.M., *A dictionary of English surnames* (1995, Oxford, 2005).

Reynolds, A. and Semple, S., 'Digging for names: archaeology and place-names in the Avebury region', in R. Jones and S. Semple (eds), *Sense of place in Anglo-Saxon England* (Donington, 2011), pp. 76–100.

Rider Haggard, H., *A farmer's year, being his commonplace book for 1898* (1898–9, London, 1987).

Rigby, S.H., *English society in the later middle ages: class, status and gender* (Basingstoke, 1995).

Roberts, B.K., *The making of the English village* (Harlow, 1987).

Roberts, B.K. and Wrathmell, S., 'Dispersed settlement in England: a national view', in p. Everson and T. Williamson (eds), *The archaeology of landscape: studies presented to Christopher Taylor* (Manchester, 1998), pp. 95–116.

Ross, A., 'Shafts, pits, wells – sanctuaries of the Belgic Britons?' in D.D.A. Simpson and J.M. Coles (eds), *Studies in ancient Europe: essays presented to Stuart Piggott* (Bristol, 1968), pp. 255–85.

Rotherham, I.D., *Peat and peat cutting* (Oxford, 2011).

Round, J.H., 'Introduction to the Northamptonshire Domesday', in W. Ryland, D. Adkins and R.M. Serjeantson (eds), *VCH Northamptonshire*, vol. 1 (London, 1902), pp. 257–300.

Runciman, W.G., 'Accelerating social mobility: the case of Anglo-Saxon England', *Past and Present*, 104 (1984), pp. 3–30.

Rutton, W.L., 'The manor of Eia, or Eye next Westminster', *Archaeologia*, 62 (1910), pp. 31–58.

Rye, E.,'Dialect in the Viking-age Scandanivian diaspora: the evidence of medieval minor names', PhD thesis (University of Nottingham, 2016).

Ryland, W., Adkins, D. and Serjeantson, R.M. (eds), *VCH Northamptonshire*, vol. 1 (London, 1902).

Rymes, B., 'Naming as social practice: the case of Little Creeper from Diamond Street', *Language in Society*, 25/2 (1996), pp. 237–60.

Salzman, L.F., 'Sutton-under-Brailes', in *VCH Warwickshire*, vol. 5 (London, 1965), pp. 157–9.

Sapoznik, A., 'Resource allocation and peasant decision making: Oakington, Cambridgeshire, 1360–99', *Agricultural History Review*, 61/2 (2013), pp. 187–205.

Saul, N., *Scenes from provincial life: knightly families in Sussex 1280–1400* (Oxford, 1986).

Saunders, T., 'The feudal construction of space: power and domination in the nucleated village', in R. Samson (ed.), *The social archaeology of houses* (Edinburgh, 1990), pp. 181–95.

Schieffelin, E.L., *The sorrow of the lonely and the burning of the dancers* (St. Lucia, Queensland, 1976).

Schmitt, J.-C., *The holy greyhound: Guinefort, healer of children since the thirteenth century*, trans. M. Thom (Cambridge, 1983).

Schofield, P.R., *Peasant and community in medieval England 1200–1500* (Basingstoke, 2003).

Semple, S., 'A fear of the past: the place of the prehistoric burial mound in the ideology of middle and later Anglo-Saxon England', *World Archaeology*, 30/1 (1998), pp. 109–26.

Semple, S., 'In the open air', in M. Carver, A. Sanmark and S. Semple (eds), *Signals of belief in early England: Anglo-Saxon paganism revisited* (Oxford, 2010), pp. 21–48.

Senecal, C., 'Keeping up with the Godwinesons: in pursuit of aristocratic status in late Anglo-Saxon England', in J. Gillingham (ed.), *Anglo-Norman studies 23, proceedings of the Battle conference, 2000* (Woodbridge, 2001), pp. 251–66.

Serjeantson, R.M. and Adkins, W.R.D., 'The Soke of Peterborough: Introduction', in R.M Serjeantson and W.R.D. Adkins (eds), *VCH Northamptonshire*, vol. 2 (London, 1906), pp. 421–3.

Serjeantson, R.M. and Adkins, W.R.D., 'Castor', in R.M Serjeantson and W.R.D. Adkins (eds), *VCH Northamptonshire*, vol. 2 (London, 1906), pp. 472–80.

Serjeantson, R.M. and Adkins, W.R.D., 'Upton', in R.M Serjeantson and W.R.D. Adkins (eds), *VCH Northamptonshire*, vol. 2 (London, 1906), pp. 483–5.

Simkins, M.E., 'Great Staughton', in W. Page, G. Proby and S. Inskip Ladds (eds), *VCH Huntingdonshire*, vol. 2 (London, 1932), pp. 354–69.

Slavin, P., 'Peasant livestock husbandry in late thirteenth-century Suffolk: economy, environment, and society', in M. Kowaleski, J. Langdon and P.R. Schofield (eds), *Peasants and lords in the medieval English economy. Essays in honour of Bruce M.S. Campbell* (Turnhout, 2015), pp. 3–26.

Smith, A., 'Landscape representation: place and identity in nineteenth-century Ordnance Survey maps of Ireland', in P.J. Stewart and A. Strathern (eds), *Landscape, memory and history: anthropological perspectives* (London, 2003), pp. 71–88.

Smith, A.H., *English place-name elements, 1* (Cambridge, 1956).

Smith, A.H., *English place-name elements, 2* (Cambridge, 1956).

Smith, R., 'Rooms, relatives and residential arrangements: some evidence in manor court rolls 1250–1500', *Medieval Village Research Group Annual Report*, 30 (1982), pp. 34–5.

Smith, S.V., 'Materializing resistant identities among the medieval peasantry: an examination of dress accessories from English rural settlement sites', *Journal of Material Culture*, 14/3 (2009), pp. 309–32.

Smith, S.V., 'Towards a social archaeology of the late medieval English peasantry: power and resistance at Wharram Percy', *Journal of Social Archaeology*, 9/3 (2009), pp. 391–416.

Smith, S.V., 'Houses and communities: archaeological evidence for variation in medieval peasant experience', in C. Dyer and R. Jones (eds), *Deserted villages revisited* (Hatfield, 2010), pp. 64–84.

Spilman, A., 'Castlemorton' in J.W. Willis-Bund (ed.), *VCH Worcestershire*, vol. 4 (London, 1971), pp. 49–52.

Stewart, P.J. and Strathern, A., 'Introduction', in P.J. Stewart and A. Strathern (eds), *Landscape, memory and history: anthropological perspectives* (London, 2003), pp. 1–15.

Stewart, P.J. and Strathern, A. (eds), *Landscape, memory and history: anthropological perspectives* (London, 2003).

Stocker, D. and Everson, P., *Summoning St Michael. Early Romanesque towers in Lincolnshire* (Oxford, 2006).

Stone, D., *Decision-making in medieval agriculture* (Oxford, 2005).

Stone, E. (ed.), *Oxfordshire hundred rolls of 1279: the hundred of Bampton* (Oxford, 1968).

Stuart-Murray, J., 'Unnameable landscapes', *Landscape Review*, 2 (1995), pp. 30–41.

Sullivan, D., *The Westminster corridor: an explanation of the Anglo-Saxon history of Westminster Abbey and its nearby lands and people* (London, 1994).

Sykes, N., 'Deer, land, knives and halls: social change in early medieval England', *The Antiquaries Journal*, 90 (2010), pp. 175–93.

Talbot, C.H., *Medicine in medieval England* (London, 1967).

Taylor, C., 'Landscape history, observation and explanation: the missing houses in Cambridgeshire villages', *Proceedings of the Cambridge Antiquarian Society*, 95 (2006), pp. 121–32.

Taylor, S., 'Methodologies in place-name research', in C. Hough (ed.) with D. Izdebska, *The Oxford handbook of names and naming* (Oxford, 2018), pp. 69–86.

ten Harkel, L., Franconi, T. and Gosden, C., 'Fields, ritual and religion: holistic approaches to the rural landscape in the long-term perspective (*c.* 1500BC – AD1086)', *Oxford Journal of Archaeology*, 36/4 (2017), pp. 413–37.

Thornton, T.F., 'Know your place: the organization of Tlingit geographic knowledge', *Ethnology*, 36/4 (1997), pp. 295–307.

Thurlby, M., *The Herefordshire school of Romanesque sculpture* (Logaston, 2000).

Tilley, C., *A phenomenology of landscape* (Oxford, 1994).

Tovey, H. (ed.), *St Kyneburga's church, Castor* (Castor, 2006).

Trist, P.J.O., *An ecological flora of Breckland* (Wakefield, 1979).

Upex, S.G., 'The reconstruction of openfield layout from landscape evidence in Northamptonshire and Cambridgeshire', PhD thesis (University of Nottingham, 1984).

Upex, S.G. with contributions by A. Challands, J. Hall, R. Jackson, D. Peacock and F.C. Wild, 'The *praetorium* of Edmund Artis: a summary of excavations and surveys of the palatial Roman structure at Castor, Cambridgeshire 1828–2010', *Britannia*, 42 (2011), pp. 23–112.

van Swaay, C.A.M., 'The importance of calcareous grasslands for butterflies in Europe', *Biological Conservation*, 104 (2002), pp. 315–18.

Wager, S.J., 'The hays of medieval England: a reappraisal', *Agricultural History Review*, 65/2 (2017), pp. 167–93.

Walsham, A., *The reformation of the landscape: religion, identity, and memory in early modern Britain and Ireland* (Oxford, 2011).

Wareham, A.F., *Lords and communities in early medieval East Anglia* (Woodbridge, 2005).

Watkins, C.S., *History and the supernatural in medieval England* (Cambridge, 2007).

Watts, V. (ed.), *The Cambridge dictionary of English place-names* (Cambridge, 2010).

West, S.E. and McLaughlin, A., *Towards a landscape history of Walsham le Willows, Suffolk* (Ipswich, 1998).

Westwood, J. and Simpson, J., *The lore of the land: a guide to England's legends from spring-heeled Jack to the witches of Warboys* (2005, London, 2006).

Whittle, J., 'The food economy of lords, tenants and workers in a medieval village: Hunstanton, Norfolk, 1328–48', in M. Kowaleski, J. Langdon and p. Schofield (eds), *Peasants and lords in the medieval English economy: essays in honour of Bruce M.S. Campbell* (Turnhout, 2015), pp. 27–58.

Whyte, N., 'The after-life of barrows: prehistoric monuments in the Norfolk landscape', *Landscape History*, 25 (2003), pp. 5–16.

Whyte, N., *Inhabiting the landscape. Place, custom and memory, 1500–1800* (Oxford, 2009).

Williamson, T., *Shaping medieval landscapes: settlement, society, environment* (Oxford, 2010).

Williamson, T. and Bellamy, L., *Property and landscape: a social history of land ownership and the English countryside* (London, 1987).

Williamson, T., Liddiard, R. and Partida, T., *Champion: the making and unmaking of the English midland landscape* (Liverpool, 2013).

Wiltshire, M. and Woore, S., '"Hays", possible early enclosures, in Derbyshire', *Derbyshire Archaeological Journal*, 131 (2011), pp. 195–215.

Woolgar, C.M., *Household accounts from medieval England, part 1* (Oxford, 1992).

Woolgar, C.M., *The great household in late medieval England* (London, 1999).

Wylie, J., *Landscape* (Abingdon, 2007).

Index